I0029034

Securing Healthcare: Leveraging Blockchain for Data Integrity in Healthcare Services

Edited by

Mohit Angurala

Department of Computer Science
Guru Nanak Dev University College
Pathankot District - Pathankot
Punjab, India

Preet Kamal

Apex Institute of Technology-CSE, Chandigarh University
Mohali, Punjab, India

Aryan Chaudhary

Biotech Sphere Research, Ghaziabad, Uttar Pradesh, India

Rasmeet Singh Bali

Apex Institute of Technology-CSE, Chandigarh University
Mohali, Punjab, India

&

Vijay Bhardwaj

Apex Institute of Technology-CSE, Chandigarh University
Mohali, Punjab, India

Securing Healthcare: Leveraging Blockchain for Data Integrity in Healthcare Services

Editors: Mohit Angurala, Preet Kamal, Aryan Chaudhary, Rasmeet Singh Bali & Vijay Bhardwaj

ISBN (Online): 979-8-89881-063-4

ISBN (Print): 979-8-89881-064-1

ISBN (Paperback): 979-8-89881-065-8

© 2025, Bentham Books imprint.

Published by Bentham Science Publishers Pte. Ltd. Singapore, in collaboration with Eureka Conferences, USA. All Rights Reserved.

First published in 2025.

BENTHAM SCIENCE PUBLISHERS LTD.
End User License Agreement (for non-institutional, personal use)

This is an agreement between you and Bentham Science Publishers Ltd. Please read this License Agreement carefully before using the book/echapter/ejournal (**"Work"**). Your use of the Work constitutes your agreement to the terms and conditions set forth in this License Agreement. If you do not agree to these terms and conditions then you should not use the Work.

Bentham Science Publishers agrees to grant you a non-exclusive, non-transferable limited license to use the Work subject to and in accordance with the following terms and conditions. This License Agreement is for non-library, personal use only. For a library / institutional / multi user license in respect of the Work, please contact: permission@benthamscience.net.

Usage Rules

1. All rights reserved: The Work is the subject of copyright and Bentham Science Publishers either owns the Work (and the copyright in it) or is licensed to distribute the Work. You shall not copy, reproduce, modify, remove, delete, augment, add to, publish, transmit, sell, resell, create derivative works from, or in any way exploit the Work or make the Work available for others to do any of the same, in any form or by any means, in whole or in part, in each case without the prior written permission of Bentham Science Publishers, unless stated otherwise in this License Agreement.
2. You may download a copy of the Work on one occasion to one personal computer (including tablet, laptop, desktop, or other such devices). You may make one back-up copy of the Work to avoid losing it.
3. The unauthorised use or distribution of copyrighted or other proprietary content is illegal and could subject you to liability for substantial money damages. You will be liable for any damage resulting from your misuse of the Work or any violation of this License Agreement, including any infringement by you of copyrights or proprietary rights.

Disclaimer

Bentham Science Publishers does not guarantee that the information in the Work is error-free, or warrant that it will meet your requirements or that access to the Work will be uninterrupted or error-free. The Work is provided "as is" without warranty of any kind, either express or implied or statutory, including, without limitation, implied warranties of merchantability and fitness for a particular purpose. The entire risk as to the results and performance of the Work is assumed by you. No responsibility is assumed by Bentham Science Publishers, its staff, editors and/or authors for any injury and/or damage to persons or property as a matter of products liability, negligence or otherwise, or from any use or operation of any methods, products instruction, advertisements or ideas contained in the Work.

Limitation of Liability

In no event will Bentham Science Publishers, its staff, editors and/or authors, be liable for any damages, including, without limitation, special, incidental and/or consequential damages and/or damages for lost data and/or profits arising out of (whether directly or indirectly) the use or inability to use the Work. The entire liability of Bentham Science Publishers shall be limited to the amount actually paid by you for the Work.

General

1. Any dispute or claim arising out of or in connection with this License Agreement or the Work (including non-contractual disputes or claims) will be governed by and construed in accordance with the laws of Singapore. Each party agrees that the courts of the state of Singapore shall have exclusive jurisdiction to settle any dispute or claim arising out of or in connection with this License Agreement or the Work (including non-contractual disputes or claims).
2. Your rights under this License Agreement will automatically terminate without notice and without the

need for a court order if at any point you breach any terms of this License Agreement. In no event will any delay or failure by Bentham Science Publishers in enforcing your compliance with this License Agreement constitute a waiver of any of its rights.

3. You acknowledge that you have read this License Agreement, and agree to be bound by its terms and conditions. To the extent that any other terms and conditions presented on any website of Bentham Science Publishers conflict with, or are inconsistent with, the terms and conditions set out in this License Agreement, you acknowledge that the terms and conditions set out in this License Agreement shall prevail.

Bentham Science Publishers Pte. Ltd.
No. 9 Raffles Place
Office No. 26-01
Singapore 048619
Singapore
Email: subscriptions@benthamscience.net

BENTHAM SCIENCE

CONTENTS

PREFACE

We now find ourselves at the crossroads of two powerful forces: Blockchain technology, in a never-ending Renaissance landscape of the technology and healthcare industries, and the strong demand for increased integrity, security, and compliance in data stored in health systems. The idea of this book is to venture through this intersection, where immutability and decentralization provided by the blockchain will pave new ways to reshape our strategies to manage, secure, and interact with healthcare data. With greater detail, the content of this book begins with an introduction to blockchain and how it may revolutionize healthcare, followed by an in-depth discussion of its applications across a host of domains. The following chapters provide the entire discussion about the role of blockchain in data integrity and increased compliance with regulatory standards while at the same time protecting sensitive health information. The book itself goes into detail about how blockchain is reframing the healthcare industry through documented case studies, theoretical explorations, and implementation in real-life situations. For sure, the first few chapters make a good point in building a base for discussion on the basics of blockchain technology and its potential to provide solutions for some of the most important problems concerning data transparency, traceability, and security. This is also a way to show how interoperability for health information exchange can be safely achieved by using the blockchain, which drastically changes the way patient data is shared and consumed between different providers and various healthcare institutions.

In the following sections, we detail specific applications of blockchain technology in improving smart contracts' functionality within the healthcare compliance framework, building patient-centric data management systems, and detecting fraud in clinical trials. In each one of these cases, extensive case studies and real-life examples explain to the readers practical insights into the challenges and successes faced in the journey of adopting blockchain in healthcare. Later in this book, blockchain is woven with other emerging technologies, such as the IoT and AI, to illustrate the broad set of applied solutions that will take this a step beyond in upgrading security and efficiency within connected healthcare systems. The chapters also indicate that it will have the potential to enable an advanced data analytics capability ranging from monitoring patients outside the hospital to securely sharing health data across complex networks.

The last two are more future-facing, an indication of what could be the future of blockchain in healthcare. We then discuss the regulations that are in a state of flux, potential issues around scalability and interoperability, and blockchain as an enabler of novel business models and healthcare solutions. In view of these future trends, the book will lead the reader on a knowledgeable and foreseeing journey of the ongoing transformation in the healthcare industry.

While discussed from a more technical perspective in this book, it is an appeal to all healthcare professionals, technologists, policymakers, and researchers to recognize the potential of blockchain and work together to make the future healthcare ecosystem more secure, transparent, and efficient.

Mohit Angurala
Department of Computer Science
Guru Nanak Dev University College
Pathankot District - Pathankot
Punjab, India

Preet Kamal
Apex Institute of Technology-CSE
Chandigarh University, Mohali
Punjab, India

Aryan Chaudhary
Biotech Sphere Research
India

Rasmeet Singh Bali
Apex Institute of Technology-CSE
Chandigarh University, Mohali
Punjab, India

&

Vijay Bhardwaj
Apex Institute of Technology-CSE
Chandigarh University, Mohali
Punjab, India

List of Contributors

Anita Tanwar	Chitkara Business School, Chitkara University, Rajpura, Punjab, India
Ankita Gupta	Department of Computer Science and Engineering, C.T. Institute of Engineering, Management and Technology, Lambri, Punjab, India
Ambika Prakash Mani	Department of Commerce, Graphic Era Deemed to be University, Dehradun, Uttarakhand, India
Deep Mann	Department of Computer Science and Engineering, Thapar Institute of Engineering & Technology, Patiala, Punjab, India
Garima Sharma	Department of Computer Science and Engineering, Graphic Era Deemed to be University, Dehradun, Uttarakhand, India
Gurpreet Singh Panesar	Department of Computer Science and Engineering, Chandigarh University, Mohali, Punjab, India
Kiran Deep Singh	Department of Computer Science and Engineering, Chitkara University Institute of Engineering and Technology, Rajpura, Punjab, India
Keesara Sravanthi	Department of Information Technology, VNRVJIET University, Hyderabad, Telangana, India
Kamlesh Gautam	Department of Advance Computing, Poornima College of Engineering, Jaipur, India
Mandeep Kaur Sandhu	Department of Computer Science, Guru Nanak Dev University College, Pathankot, Punjab, India
Mohit Angurala	Department of Computer Science, Guru Nanak Dev University College, Pathankot, Punjab, India
Mushtaq Ahmad Rather	Department of CSE-IoT, Noida Institute of Engineering and Technology, Greater Noida, India
Meenakshi Mandola	Department of Computer Science and Engineering, Graphic Era Deemed to be University, Dehradun, Uttarakhand, India
Navneet Kumar Rajpoot	Department of Computer Science & Engineering, Graphic Era (Deemed to be University), Dehradun, India
Prabh Deep Singh	Department of Computer Science and Engineering, Graphic Era Deemed to be University, Dehradun, Uttarakhand, India
Pardeep Kumar Jindal	Department of Electronics and Communication, Chandigarh Engineering College, Mohali, Chandigarh, India
P. Prasant	Department of Computer Science, AIPH University, Bhubaneswar, Odisha, India
Riya Sharma	Department of Commerce, Graphic Era Deemed to be University, Dehradun, Uttarakhand, India
Rajbir Kaur	Department of Electronics and Communication Engineering, Punjabi University, Patiala, Punjab, India
Rajeev Kumar Bedi	Department of Computer Science and Engineering, I. K. Gujral Punjab Technical University, Jalandhar, India

Rohan Verma — Department of Computer Science and Engineering, Graphic Era Deemed to be University, Dehradun, Uttarakhand, India

Raminder Kaur Khattri — Department of Commerce, Graphic Era Deemed to be University, Dehradun, Uttarakhand, India

Saptadeepa Kalita — Department of Computer Science and Engineering, Sharda University, Greater Noida, India

Sharon Christa — Department of Computer Science and Engineering, MIT Art Design and Technology University, Pune, Maharashtra, India

Sandeep Singh — Department of Computer Science Engineering, SGT University, Gurugram, Haryana, India

Sonal Rattan — Department of UCRD and Apex Institute of Technology, Chandigarh University, Mohali, Punjab, India

Vikas Kumar — Department of AI & DS, Poornima Institute of Engineering & Technology, Jaipur, Rajasthan, India

Varinder Pabbi — Department of Computer Application, I. K. Gujral Punjab Technical University, Phagwara, Punjab, India

CHAPTER 1

Introduction to Blockchain Technology in Healthcare

Mandeep Kaur Sandhu[1,*] and **Mohit Angurala**[1]

[1] Department of Computer Science, Guru Nanak Dev University College, Pathankot, Punjab, India

Abstract: Blockchain technology is rapidly gaining traction across various sectors, including healthcare, where it is revolutionizing how patient data is managed and shared among hospitals, diagnostic laboratories, pharmacies, and healthcare providers. By leveraging Blockchain networks, healthcare systems can ensure the secure and transparent exchange of medical data, enhancing performance and eliminating errors that could be potentially harmful. This technology empowers medical institutions by providing deeper insights and improving the analysis of medical records, thereby bolstering overall efficiency and security. In this chapter, we explore the transformative potential of Blockchain in healthcare, illustrating its key capabilities, facilitators, and the unified workflow processes it supports through diagrams. We highlight fourteen significant applications of Blockchain in healthcare, emphasizing its pivotal role in combatting fraud in clinical trials and enhancing data efficiency. The presented work ensures secure storage along with the seamless data verification of patients through distinct clinical stages, which further assures legitimacy and accessibility. It also empowers investigators to examine treatment outcomes in real time for large patient populations, thereby improving treatment precision and innovation in the medical field. We also discuss how Blockchain transparently secures and achieves sensitive genetic evidence, addressing issues of data ownership, privacy, and control. Blockchain ensures data integrity and security through its decentralized data storage model, offering versatility, interconnectivity, accountability, and robust authentication mechanisms for data access. This ensures that health records remain confidential and protected from specific threats, addressing concerns about data manipulation in healthcare settings effectively.

Keywords: Blockchain technology, Consent management system, Clinical trials, Electronic health records (EHRs), Healthcare data security, Interoperable healthcare systems.

** **Corresponding author Mandeep Kaur Sandhu:** Department of Computer Science, Guru Nanak Dev University College, Pathankot, Punjab, India; E-mail: gimeti4@gmail.com*

Mohit Angurala, Preet Kamal, Aryan Chaudhary, Rasmeet Singh Bali & Vijay Bhardwaj (Eds.)
All rights reserved-© 2025 Bentham Science Publishers

INTRODUCTION

Blockchain technology forms an immutable chain of records by recording transactions across numerous computers in a way that prevents retroactive manipulation without affecting the following blocks. Blockchain technology is a decentralized and public digital ledger. It is an anonymous and distributed electronic record. The integrity and credibility of the data obtained are maintained and ensured by this feature due to its guarantee of high levels of responsibility. To reduce the risk of exposing the patient to the wrong medications and fight against counterfeit products, Blockchain provides end-to-end tracking that will track the source of the fake products. This is very significant in the health sector and the manufacture of drugs [1]. This architecture amplifies security against cyber-attacks as compared to the traditional centralized databases in an attempt to safeguard patient records and retain their unalterable medical history in a secure domain. It can be noted that with the help of Blockchain, the problem of data handling and its protection is solved, at the same time making the data of all participants in the network to be open and available. Patient engagement is achieved in a separate process – patients learn who has access to their information and for what purpose and make choices concerning their records themselves [2]. Precision medicine applies Blockchain to analyze large-scale modality of anonymized data for enhancing healthcare services. By combining Blockchain IoT and wearable devices, healthcare practitioners are able to monitor real-time parameters such as glucose levels and blood pressure and consequently manage high-risk patients and provide early responses to emergencies [3].

It makes sense to use blockchain in the protection of personal information and to provide the capabilities of fast sharing and pooling of data in a single secure place because blockchain works on the basis of a P2P network of nodes that stores and exchanges information safely [4]. It enhances teamwork because patients' information is stored in a central database, which will enable easy identification of practitioners for the study with specific characteristics. Blockchain is a distributed P2P system characterized by blocks, nodes, and miners that ensures the reliability of records of patients' transactions in distributed systems. This design distributes data across several computers so as to be relatively more immune to manipulation and illegal access than the conventional centralized systems [5]. With the help of different models, such as public, private, hybrid, and consortium Blockchain networks, it enables customers/users to exchange value directly and with or without the help of an intermediary. These networks are made to be applied in specific industries such as logistics, medicine, and finance, where communication is strictly required to be First in, First out, open, and most importantly, secure.

A Blockchain maintains a distributed digital ledger *via* a chain of blocks. Each block contains:

- Data (the type depends on the blockchain's purpose).
- Hash (a unique digital fingerprint).
- Previous hash (linking the current block to the previous one).

This structure ensures data integrity, as tampering with one block would make all following blocks invalid (Fig. **1**).

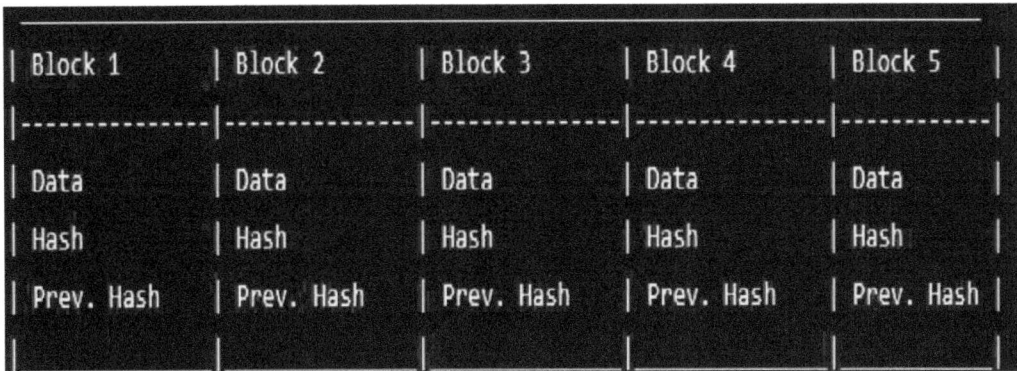

Fig. (1). The structure of the block.

BLOCKCHAIN *VS.* TRADITIONAL DATABASES

Blockchain and traditional databases provide different methods for managing data in healthcare systems [6]. Blockchain has decentralized control and uses encryption to protect data immutability and security. It offers great fault tolerance but has limited querying and familiarity. This new technology can integrate with Web 3.0 while improving the privacy and integrity of medical records. Traditional databases, on the other hand, provide well-known, dependable systems with broad SQL querying capabilities and a vast skill pool for management. However, they are centrally regulated and rely on optional encryption. Blockchain offers novel advantages for secure and immutable data management, possibly revolutionizing the handling and protection of healthcare information, while traditional databases benefit from their maturity and compatibility [7].

TYPES OF HEALTHCARE BLOCKCHAINS

In healthcare, blockchain can be implemented in both public and private settings. The choice depends on the specific use case and privacy requirements.

Public Blockchains

These are open, allowing anyone to participate in the network. However, they may not be suitable for storing private health information due to their transparency.

Private Blockchains

These are more appropriate for healthcare applications, as they offer controlled access and better privacy protection for sensitive medical data.

NEED OF BLOCKCHAIN IN HEALTHCARE

Blockchain technology in healthcare addresses several key challenges, including data transparency, traceability, immutability, audit, data provenance, flexible access, trust, privacy, and security, as shown in Fig. (**2**). By overcoming these obstacles, blockchain can transform healthcare data administration, establishing confidence in health data by enabling the tracking of changes from their source to their present form [8]. The application of blockchain in healthcare is still in its early stages. However, early solutions have shown the potential to reduce healthcare costs, streamline business processes, and improve access to information across disparate and diverse stakeholders working toward a common goal. As the technology matures, it promises to revolutionize how medical records are managed, enhance patient privacy, and streamline complex healthcare processes.

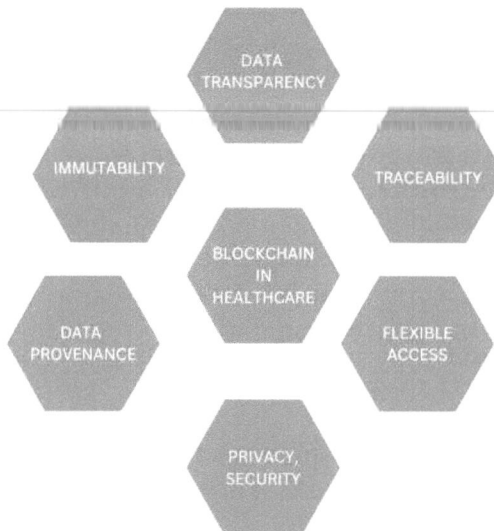

Fig. (2). Various challenges in healthcare addressed by blockchain technology.

REVOLUTIONIZING HEALTHCARE BY BLOCKCHAIN TECHNOLOGY

Blockchain technology has the potential to revolutionize patient-centric healthcare solutions by addressing long-standing challenges in data management, privacy, and patient empowerment. This section explores how blockchain is being applied to personal health records, consent management, and health data monetization. Fig. (3). shows the uses of Blockchain technology in healthcare.

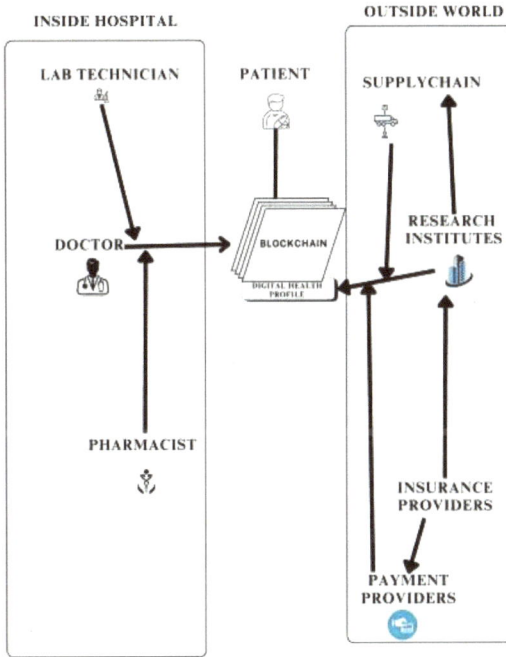

Fig. (3). Blockchain technology's potential uses in healthcare.

Personal Health Records

Blockchain-based Personal Health Records (PHRs) offer a novel approach to secure, transparent, and equitable data management. These systems enable patients to access, manage, and share their health information, leading to improved outcomes and reduced healthcare costs [9]. Unlike traditional electronic health records (EHRs), blockchain-based PHRs put data ownership and control in the hands of individual users, addressing privacy and security concerns that have hindered widespread adoption. Key benefits of blockchain-enabled PHRs include:

- Comprehensive single source of truth for patient medical records.
- Enhanced patient experience and improved healthcare provider interactions.
- Increased transparency, allowing patients to see every update to their records.

- Explicit consent management for data sharing.
- Time-limited access control for third parties.

One proposed solution involves creating a blockchain-based system that can be integrated with existing electronic medical record software. In this system, patient data is not stored directly on the blockchain. Instead, each new record is represented by a unique hash function, which can only be decoded with the patient's consent [10].

Consent Management

Blockchain technology offers significant improvements in consent management, a crucial component of healthcare operations. By leveraging blockchain, patient consent can be stored in a decentralized manner, giving patients greater control over their personal data [11].

Key features of blockchain-based consent management include:

- Immutable and tamper-proof storage of consent records.
- Enhanced accuracy and reliability of the consent management process.
- Secure and efficient sharing of consent between healthcare providers.
- Improved compliance with regulatory requirements (*e.g.*, HIPAA, GDPR).
- Enhanced patient experience through greater control over health data.

Platforms like MedRec utilize smart contracts to facilitate healthcare providers in validating and updating consent agreements, ensuring the security and availability of patient records [12]. However, it is important to note that some proposed reward systems, such as using patient data as incentives, may raise ethical concerns and require careful consideration of privacy protection mechanisms.

HEALTH DATA MONETIZATION

Blockchain technology presents an opportunity for patients to monetize their health data securely and privately. This approach allows patients to share their anonymized medical data with researchers or companies in exchange for compensation while maintaining control over their information [13].

Key aspects of blockchain-based health data monetization include:

- Secure and private data sharing.
- Patient control over data access and usage.
- Potential for patients to earn compensation for their data.
- Support for digital health application development and research.

Platforms like PatientSphere by Open Health allow users to connect with companies or research institutions and share their health records in return for a fee. This model uses blockchain technology to secure data exchange and address data governance and privacy concerns. As blockchain technology continues to evolve, it has the potential to transform patient-centric healthcare solutions by enhancing data security, privacy, and patient empowerment. However, challenges remain, including the need for regulatory frameworks and addressing potential trust issues between healthcare providers and patients.

Blockchain for Healthcare Providers and Institutions

With regard to some of the core issues, such as the safe sharing of patients' health data and adherence to data privacy acts, blockchain technology can disrupt the healthcare system to an extent [14]. In this way, the proposed distributed database system allows users to store and trade fragments of data safely and be sure that they will not be changed by other unauthorized persons. Blockchain technology offers new opportunities in several paramount fields for healthcare organizations and practitioners.

Interoperable Health Information Exchange

Patient data exchange between facilities is a major challenge in healthcare since current practices do not have optimal efficiency and safety. Some of the key challenges that blockchain addresses are inadequate data formats, data privacy, and security, thereby enabling the interchangeability of health data [15]. Due to distributed data architecture, several users can work simultaneously with the same table and do not require a single responsible person or a bottleneck.

There are various advantages of using blockchain technology for healthcare information exchange:

• Enhanced data availability and accessibility.
• Improved data integrity and transparency.
• Increased security through decentralization.
• Streamlined sharing of patient records across institutions.

Problems arising from poor data access response time, compatibility, and improvement in the quality of the data in health-related research are addressed by MedRec, a system developed to use blockchain technology for the storage of electronic medical records. The matters of data ownership and sharing have been contentious in the past. This solution empowers patients by allowing them to decide who should be allowed access to their data.

Credentialing and Privileging

It is worth stating that one can use blockchain technology to monitor and verify medical practitioners' credentials safely and efficiently. Blockchain technology has the quality of ensuring the credibility of credentials since the recorded information cannot be changed. As with both previous issuing and revocation, a healthcare expert's credential cannot be edited by an unauthorized party, and this subsequently ensures that the data retained remains correct.

The credentialing process is being made even better by the integration of artificial intelligence and even the blockchain. While the data is verified and stored on blockchain in an immutable manner, on the other hand, AI can easily analyze the big data for anomalies or peculiarities [16]. This combination greatly lowers errors and expedites the credentialing process by automating manual inspections.

Asset Tracking

In the case of its application to healthcare organizations, the functionality of the blockchain might revolutionize the monitoring of assets. Using the strong nature of blockchain technology, receptiveness of change, and decentralization, the healthcare sector may improve its monitoring of some properties, such as equipment, medicine, and supplies [17]. In the case of the pharmaceutical industry, the implementation of blockchain has the possibility of discouraging fake drugs since their journey will be recorded at the patient level. The deployment of blockchain technology may be valuable in multiple areas, which show its potential in enhancing the general operation of healthcare establishments and personnel, including credentialing and privileging and the exchange of health information. With more advancement, this technology can transform the current healthcare system, enhance the destiny of the patients, and transform all the related operational techniques.

These applications (Table **1**) illustrate how blockchain technology is being applied to address key challenges in healthcare, such as data security, interoperability, transparency, and efficiency. Each platform offers unique features and functionalities aimed at improving different aspects of healthcare delivery and management.

BLOCKCHAIN TECHNOLOGY'S BENEFITS FOR THE HEALTHCARE INDUSTRY

Integrated and enhanced data sharing among network participants and healthcare givers is seen as being revolutionized by blockchain, which is still an emerging technology. In the future, this innovation has the potential to accelerate the growth of the health sector in the manufacturing of cheap drugs and better treatments for several illnesses. The logistics industry has recently unveiled opportunities that also benefit the healthcare sector, given its direct impact on quality of life. As digital transformation progresses, innovations in healthcare are among the earliest and most impactful. Concurrently, blockchain technology is increasingly prevalent, particularly in finance, offering significant opportunities for the healthcare industry. These range from enhancing scientific research and logistics to improving relationships between healthcare practitioners and patients [18].

The vast uses of Blockchain technology in the healthcare industry are shown in Table **2**, which depicts how it can transform the management of data, patient records, clinical trials, financial processes, and other areas of the industry.

Table 1. A collection of blockchain applications developed in the healthcare industry.

Name	Description
Medicalchain	It relies on the blockchain technology solution in the storage and exchange of medical records. Encourages the planning of telemedicine sessions and increases the privacy of individuals and potential access to their health records.
ProCredEx	Facilitates the process of healthcare provider credentialing and verification by means of solutions based on blockchain. Enables the safe exchange of verified credentials between treatment givers, insurers, and other users.
Gem	Provides a blockchain application that is a marketplace and enables communication of healthcare data. Ensures the exchange of patient information content between the CPS and other healthcare personnel together with other health systems without compromising the patient information content.
SimplyVital Health	Coordinates a decentralized management approach to healthcare through blockchain. They are safe patient data exchange technology referred to as Connecting Care and other related results such as patient health benefits and healthcare systems' organizational gains.
Guardtime	Specializes in the protection of healthcare data and applying blockchain solutions to the issue. For it to not breach the highly sensitive information of the patient and not go against the regulations, it offers a way of storage, tracking of users' activities, and monitoring.
PokitDok	Applies blockchain technology to accelerate processes tangible to healthcare, for example, to work with insurance claims and payments. The flow of money in the healthcare industry is less problematic because all transactions made are very transparent and easy.
Tierion	Includes a blockchain platform, which is generally useful to build and validate any type of data – be it of a financial or medical nature. Offers resource information for healthcare transactions concerning well-structured regulation for records and necessities of proven audit trails.

Table 2. Significant applications of Blockchain in healthcare.

Applications	Description
Store information of an individual patient	Facilitates secure storage and seamless verification of patient data across various clinical phases, ensuring authenticity and accessibility for healthcare providers.
Analyze the effects of a particular procedure	Enables researchers to analyze treatment outcomes across large patient populations in real time, enhancing treatment precision and pharmaceutical innovation.
Validation	Ensures transactional authenticity through cryptographic validation, enhancing trust and security within healthcare operations.
Safety and transparency	Enhances data security and transparency, optimizing clinical trials and treatment protocols for improved healthcare outcomes.
Health record keeping	Centralizes and secures electronic health records (EHRs), streamlining data exchange and improving patient care coordination.
Clinical Trial	Improves integrity and transparency in clinical trials, ensuring accurate data collection and analysis for pharmaceutical advancements.
Display information	Verifies medication origins and authenticity, ensuring quality and safety for healthcare consumers.
Identification of false content	Facilitates easy verification of clinical trial results and medication authenticity, enhancing trust and reliability in healthcare treatments.
Reduces needless overhead expenses	Streamlines healthcare operations, reducing administrative costs and improving resource allocation for enhanced patient care.
Patient monitoring	Integrates IoT devices with Blockchain to monitor patient health metrics in real time, improving proactive healthcare management and emergency response capabilities.
Create research initiatives	Catalyzes new research initiatives by facilitating secure data sharing and collaboration among healthcare stakeholders.
Maintain financial statements in hospitals	Enhances financial transparency and efficiency in healthcare institutions, streamlining accounting processes and reducing administrative burden.
Improves safety	Ensures medication safety and traceability, improving overall patient safety and healthcare quality.
Minimise data transformation time and cost	Streamlines the verification and maintenance of medical qualifications and patient information while reducing processing times and expenses.

BLOCKCHAIN TECHNOLOGY IN MEDICAL RESEARCH AND DEVELOPMENT

With the help of blockchain, the field of medical research and development might be revolutionized due to the features of blockchain such as efficient data management, complete transparency, and cooperation. In clinical trial management, blockchain offers a tamper-proof system that enhances transparency and ensures the integrity of trial data and results. This includes a digital ecosystem centered around a blockchain-based clinical trial registry, where stakeholders interact through smart contracts to manage trial progress and protocol changes efficiently. As a result of privacy and control issues, genomic data exchange may benefit from utilizing blockchain's transparent and secure networking [19]. Tokenization helps the secure handling and, consequently, the sharing of user data, whereas LifeCODE.ai makes it possible to store genetic information safely. Furthermore, blockchain increases the efficiency of collaborative research platforms because it enables safe data sharing between institutions and researchers. This increases the credibility and the ability to replicate the results of scientific investigations while making an unalterable record of the research process. While these advancements promise to transform healthcare research and development, challenges such as standardization, regulatory frameworks, and scalability need to be addressed as blockchain technology continues to evolve.

Table **3** summarizes how blockchain technology is applied in clinical trial management, genomic data sharing, and collaborative research platforms within the context of medical research and development. Each application leverages blockchain's capabilities to enhance data security, transparency, and collaboration in the healthcare ecosystem.

Table 3. The applications of blockchain technology in medical research and development.

Application	Description
Clinical Trial Management	As for capturing trial data in a tampered-proof, transparent, and, thus, trustworthy manner, the best way is to use blockchain. The challenges, such as data validity, patients' enrollment, and other regulatory concerns, are discussed here. A framework includes a blockchain-based trial management system for stakeholders, a system for regulatory bodies, and a public view portal for transparency. Smart contracts manage interactions, data exchange, and trial progress synchronization with the registry.
Genomic Data Sharing	Blockchain secures and transparently manages sensitive genetic information, addressing concerns about data privacy, ownership, and control. Platforms like LifeCODE.ai offer decentralized data storage, giving users control over their data location, access permissions, and updates. Tokenization of genomic data (*e.g.*, Genecoin) enables users to trade data for tokens, enhancing user satisfaction and willingness to share data.
Collaborative Research Platforms	Blockchain facilitates secure and transparent data sharing among researchers and institutions, improving the credibility and reproducibility of research findings. It addresses challenges in data ownership, access control, and attribution of contributions. By providing an immutable record of research activities, blockchain promotes openness and collaboration while protecting intellectual property.

REGULATORY AND COMPLIANCE CONSIDERATIONS FOR BLOCKCHAIN IN HEALTHCARE

As blockchain technology gains traction in the healthcare industry, it brings forth a new set of regulatory and compliance considerations. These considerations are crucial for ensuring that blockchain implementations adhere to existing healthcare regulations while maximizing the potential benefits of this innovative technology.

Data Protection Regulations

One may infer that issues regarding the protection of patients' data could be solved by employing blockchain. Its decentralized nature and advanced encryption methods provide enhanced security for sensitive medical information [20]. By distributing data across a decentralized network, healthcare organizations can significantly reduce the risk of data loss and eliminate single points of failure [21].

Blockchain that supports data protection regulations include:

Immutability

Once information is added to the blockchain, it cannot be altered or removed, ensuring data integrity.

Encryption

Cutting-edge encryption methods protect data, guaranteeing that only authorized parties have access.

Smart Contracts

These self-executing agreements automate data exchange and access control processes, adding an extra layer of security.

Transparency

Blockchain promotes accountability by making data accessible to all network participants, potentially reducing fraud.

To comply with data protection regulations, healthcare organizations implementing blockchain solutions must demonstrate operational excellence through compliance standards such as SOC 2 and HIPAA. These standards focus on establishing measures to recognize and counter risks related to data availability, privacy, confidentiality, and security.

FDA COMPLIANCE

The United States Food and Drug Administration (FDA) has recognized the potential of blockchain technology in improving pharmaceutical supply chain management and drug traceability. In 2019, the FDA initiated a pilot program in support of the U.S. Drug Supply Chain Security Act (DSCSA) to explore blockchain's capabilities in addressing these challenges [22] To ensure FDA compliance, blockchain implementations in healthcare must adhere to the following principles [23].

- Establish common technical standards to enable interoperability and enhanced visibility for all supply chain participants.
- Develop a defined industry governance framework associated with the blockchain network and data standards for information exchange.
- Pursue blockchain-based solutions that enable DSCSA compliance while fostering new business models.

Blockchain Standards

As blockchain technology evolves in healthcare, the development of industry-wide standards becomes crucial for ensuring interoperability, security, and compliance. While specific blockchain standards for healthcare are still emerging, several key considerations have been identified:

Interoperability

Standards should enable seamless communication between different blockchain networks and existing healthcare systems.

Data Privacy

Standards must address the fundamental tension between cross-industry data sharing and the need to keep proprietary information private.

Governance Models

Equitable governance models are essential, ensuring that no single entity gains an undue advantage from controlling the blockchain network.

Integration Requirements

Standards should define how blockchain solutions integrate with existing healthcare IT infrastructure.

Solution Triggers

Clear guidelines on when and how blockchain solutions are activated within healthcare processes are necessary.

As the healthcare industry continues to explore blockchain applications, regulatory bodies and industry stakeholders must collaborate to develop comprehensive standards that address these considerations. This collaborative approach will help ensure that blockchain implementations in healthcare not only comply with existing regulations but also leverage the technology's full potential to improve patient care, data security, and operational efficiency.

CONCLUSION

Blockchain technology has a profound influence on healthcare, offering ground-breaking solutions to long-standing challenges. From enhancing patient data security to streamlining clinical trials and improving supply chain management, blockchain is causing a revolution in various aspects of the healthcare industry. Its ability to provide secure, transparent, and efficient systems has the potential to transform how healthcare is delivered, managed, and researched. As the healthcare sector continues to explore and implement blockchain solutions, it is crucial to address regulatory and compliance considerations. The development of industry-wide standards will be key to ensuring interoperability, security, and compliance across different blockchain implementations. To wrap up, while challenges remain, the future of blockchain in healthcare looks promising, with the potential to improve patient outcomes, enhance operational efficiency, and drive innovation in medical research and development.

AUTHORS' CONTRIBUTION

In Chapter 1, **Mandeep Kaur Sandhu** and **Mohit Angurala** jointly contributed to the conceptualization and writing. **Mandeep Kaur Sandhu** led the research and development of the chapter structure, focusing on exploring blockchain applications in healthcare and designing the theoretical framework. **Mohit Angurala** provided detailed insights into blockchain's technical aspects and applications, including data security and fraud prevention in clinical trials. Both authors collaborated on data collection and analysis of case studies, as well as the final drafting and revision of the chapter. Together, they aimed to provide a comprehensive introduction to blockchain's role in revolutionizing healthcare.

REFERENCES

[1]   Yaqoob I, Salah K, Jayaraman R, Al-Hammadi Y. Blockchain for healthcare data management: opportunities, challenges, and future recommendations. Neural Comput Appl 2022; 34(14): 11475-90.
[http://dx.doi.org/10.1007/s00521-020-05519-w]

[2]   Le Nguyen T. Blockchain in healthcare: A new technology benefit for both patients and doctors. 2018 Portland International Conference on Management of Engineering and Technology (PICMET). 2018 Aug 19-23; Honolulu, HI: IEEE 1-6.
[http://dx.doi.org/10.23919/PICMET.2018.8481969]

[3]   Pandey P, Litoriya R. Implementing healthcare services on a large scale: Challenges and remedies based on blockchain technology. Health Policy Technol 2020; 9(1): 69-78.
[http://dx.doi.org/10.1016/j.hlpt.2020.01.004]

[4]   Ismail L, Materwala H, Zeadally S. Lightweight blockchain for healthcare. IEEE 2019; 7(149935): 51.
[http://dx.doi.org/10.1109/ACCESS.2019.2947613]

[5]   Hussien HM, Yasin SM, Udzir SNI, Zaidan AA, Zaidan BB. A systematic review for enabling of develop a blockchain technology in healthcare application: taxonomy, substantially analysis, motivations, challenges, recommendations and future direction. J Med Syst 2019; 43(10): 320.
[http://dx.doi.org/10.1007/s10916-019-1445-8] [PMID: 31522262]

[6]   Singh D, Monga S, Tanwar S, Hong W-C, Sharma R, He Y-L. Adoption of blockchain technology in healthcare: challenges, solutions, and comparisons. Appl Sci (Basel) 2023; 13(4): 2380.
[http://dx.doi.org/10.3390/app13042380]

[7]   Moona G, Jewariya M, Sharma R. Relevance of dimensional metrology in manufacturing industries. MPAN J Metrol Soc India 2019; 34(1): 97-104.
[http://dx.doi.org/10.1007/s12647-018-0291-3]

[8]   Berdik D, Otoum S, Schmidt N, Porter D, Jararweh Y. A survey on blockchain for information systems management and security. Inf Process Manage 2021; 58(1): 102397.
[http://dx.doi.org/10.1016/j.ipm.2020.102397]

[9]   Agbo CC, Mahmoud QH, Eklund JM. Blockchain technology in healthcare: a systematic review. Healthcare (Basel) 2019; 7(2): 56.
[http://dx.doi.org/10.3390/healthcare7020056] [PMID: 30987333]

[10]   Zheng K, Liu Y, Dai C, *et al.* Model checking PBFT consensus mechanism in healthcare blockchain network. In: 2018 9th International Conference on Information Technology in Medicine and Education (ITME). Hangzhou, China. IEEE. 2018; pp. 877-1.
[http://dx.doi.org/10.1109/ITME.2018.00196]

[11]   Zhang P, Schmidt DC, White J, *et al.* Blockchain technology use cases in healthcare. In: Zelkowitz MV, Ed. Advances in computers. London: Elsevier 2018; 111: pp. 1-41.
[http://dx.doi.org/10.1016/bs.adcom.2018.03.006]

[12]   Fan K, Wang S, Ren Y, Li H, Yang Y. MedBlock: efficient and secure medical data sharing *via* blockchain. J Med Syst 2018; 42(8): 136.
[http://dx.doi.org/10.1007/s10916-018-0993-7] [PMID: 29931655]

[13]   Leeming G, Cunningham J, Ainsworth J. A ledger of me: personalizing healthcare using blockchain technology. Front Med (Lausanne) 2019; 6: 171.
[http://dx.doi.org/10.3389/fmed.2019.00171] [PMID: 31396516]

[14]   Gökalp E, Gökalp MO, Çoban S, *et al.* Analysing opportunities and challenges of integrated blockchain technologies in healthcare. In: Bider I, Ed. Information Systems: Research, Development, Applications, Education Lecture Notes in Business Information Processing. Cham: Springer 2018; 333: pp. 174-83.
[http://dx.doi.org/10.1007/978-3-030-00060-8_13]

[15]   Dagher GG, Mohler J, Milojkovic M, Marella PB. Ancile: Privacy-preserving framework for access control and interoperability of electronic health records using blockchain technology. Sustain Cities Soc 2018; 39: 283-97.
[http://dx.doi.org/10.1016/j.scs.2018.02.014]

[16]   Shah K, Chadotra S, Tanwar S, Gupta R, Kumar N. Blockchain for IoV in 6G environment: review solutions and challenges. Cluster Comput 2022; 25(3): 1927-55.
[http://dx.doi.org/10.1007/s10586-021-03492-0]

[17]   McGhin T, Choo KKR, Liu CZ, He D. Blockchain in healthcare applications: Research challenges and opportunities. J Netw Comput Appl 2019; 135: 62-75.
[http://dx.doi.org/10.1016/j.jnca.2019.02.027]

[18]   Haleem A, Javaid M, Singh RP, Suman R, Rab S. Blockchain technology applications in healthcare: An overview. Int J Intell Netw 2021; 2: 130-9.
[http://dx.doi.org/10.1016/j.ijin.2021.09.005]

[19]   Javaid M, Haleem A, Pratap Singh R, Khan S, Suman R. Blockchain technology applications for Industry 4.0: A literature-based review. Blockchain: Res Appl 2021; 2(4): 100027.
[http://dx.doi.org/10.1016/j.bcra.2021.100027]

[20]   Attaran M. Blockchain technology in healthcare: Challenges and opportunities. Int J Healthc Manag 2020; 15(1): 70-83.
[http://dx.doi.org/10.1080/20479700.2020.1843887]

[21]   Engelhardt MA. Hitching healthcare to the chain: an introduction to blockchain technology in the healthcare sector. Technol Innov Manag Rev 2017; 7(10): 22-34.
[http://dx.doi.org/10.22215/timreview/1111]

[22]   Le P, Grund L, Marwa J, Ojo W, Otts J Jr, Arab F. Combating substandard and counterfeit medicines by securing the pharmaceutical supply chain: The Drug Supply Chain Security Act (DSCSA) of 2013. Innov Pharm 2018; 9(2): 1–11.
[http://dx.doi.org/10.24926/iip.v9i2.966]

[23]   Jadhav JS, Deshmukh J. A review study of the blockchain-based healthcare supply chain. Soc Sci Humanit Open 2022; 6(1): 100328.
[http://dx.doi.org/10.1016/j.ssaho.2022.100328]

CHAPTER 2

Blockchain Applications in Healthcare

Vikas Kumar[1,*], Mushtaq Ahmad Rather[2] and Saptadeepa Kalita[3]

[1] *Department of AI & DS, Poornima Institute of Engineering & Technology, Jaipur, Rajasthan, India*

[2] *Department of CSE-IoT, Noida Institute of Engineering and Technology, Greater Noida, India*

[3] *Department of Computer Science and Engineering, Sharda University, Greater Noida, India*

Abstract: Blockchain technology has become an influential power in different areas, one of which is healthcare. Using Blockchain technology, the paperwork is reduced, and the information is secured in the database, which further aids research and development. Focusing on the healthcare industry, the patients and the doctors do not receive the complete medical record, which is the major challenge being faced. This issue has been very well addressed in Blockchain technology. Further, Blockchain helps securely share data across digital systems with the consent of the patients, which makes technology more robust. This chapter covers the manifold usage possibilities of blockchain in healthcare, focusing on aspects such as control over electronic health records, the safety of supply chains, conducting clinical trials, the functioning of the system for medical insurance claims, and telemedicine. The chapter aims to present a comprehensive review of how security, transparency, and efficiency can be improved in healthcare systems through the use of blockchain by considering its advantages, disadvantages, and future directions. Also covered are some issues relating to blockchain-based support for patient-oriented medical care, data interchangeability in the health sector, and lightening administrative burdens. Finally, the chapter discusses several case studies and currently available research that show practical implications and real-life applications of blockchain technology in healthcare operations. Moreover, there are also insights into regulatory considerations as well as the dynamic nature associated with blockchain adoption trends within the healthcare industry at large.

Keywords: Blockchain technology, Clinical trials, Electronic health records (EHR), Healthcare, Health insurance claims, Supply chain integrity.

INTRODUCTION

Digital technologies have evolved rapidly, and this has resulted in significant changes across different sectors of the economy, with healthcare being a major

---

* **Corresponding author Vikas Kumar:** Department of AI & DS, Poornima Institute of Engineering & Technology, Jaipur, Rajasthan, India; E-mail: vsangwan06@gmail.com

Mohit Angurala, Preet Kamal, Aryan Chaudhary, Rasmeet Singh Bali & Vijay Bhardwaj (Eds.)
All rights reserved-© 2025 Bentham Science Publishers

beneficiary. This chapter explores the possible uses of blockchain in healthcare and its potential benefits, emphasizing how it has reformed EHR management, supply chain integrity, clinical trials, health insurance claims, and telemedicine. In addition to data breaches, interoperability challenges, and ineffective management of information systems, among others, the industry is grappling with other struggles, including loss of data [1 - 3].

BACKGROUND AND FUNDAMENTALS OF BLOCKCHAIN TECHNOLOGY

At its core, cryptographic hashing ensures data integrity and transparency through consensus algorithms as well as immutable ledgers that exist within blockchain technology (Fig. **1**). In the healthcare setting, it enhances secureness; therefore, tamper-proofing systems that are also interoperable become increasingly significant. The existing traditional healthcare systems often face issues such as loss of data both in terms of breaches, which affect privacy policies in relation to confidentiality, especially when addressing patients' medical records, and poor communication between hospitals, leading to a lack of proper care coordination among providers or even prescribing unnecessary medications since doctors were not aware about last tests conducted on him/her by other physicians, *etc.* The above weaknesses can be solved by employing decentralization properties that blockchain offers, thereby enhancing robust security measures against unauthorized access attempts [4 - 8].

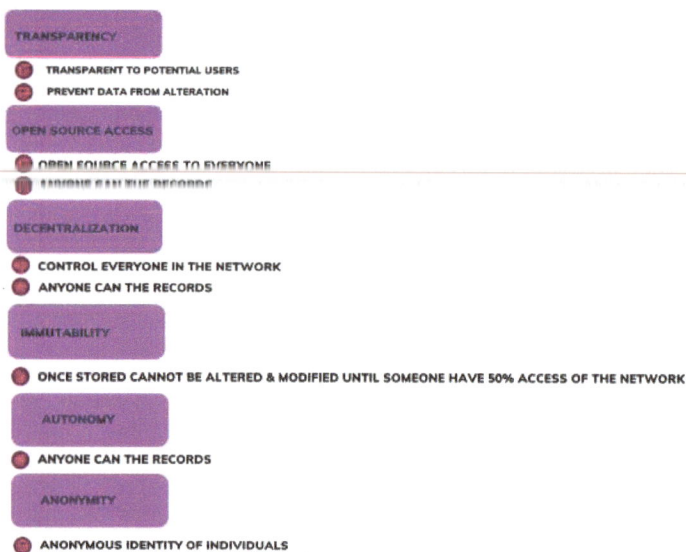

TRANSPARENCY
- TRANSPARENT TO POTENTIAL USERS
- PREVENT DATA FROM ALTERATION

OPEN SOURCE ACCESS
- OPEN SOURCE ACCESS TO EVERYONE
- ANYONE CAN THE RECORDS

DECENTRALIZATION
- CONTROL EVERYONE IN THE NETWORK
- ANYONE CAN THE RECORDS

IMMUTABILITY
- ONCE STORED CANNOT BE ALTERED & MODIFIED UNTIL SOMEONE HAVE 50% ACCESS OF THE NETWORK

AUTONOMY
- ANYONE CAN THE RECORDS

ANONYMITY
- ANONYMOUS IDENTITY OF INDIVIDUALS

Fig. (1). Key elements of blockchain.

EVOLUTION OF BLOCKCHAIN TECHNOLOGY

The evolution of blockchain can be categorized into three generations (Fig. **2**):

Blockchain 1.0 (Cryptocurrency)

Concentrated on electronic coins and specifically on Bitcoin.

Blockchain 2.0 (Smart Contracts)

Created programmable contracts that self-execute when a specific set of conditions exist on the blockchain. Ethereum is perhaps the quintessential example of this generation.

Blockchain 3.0 (DApps and Beyond)

Concerns itself with DApps and other Novum beyond financial uses such as healthcare.

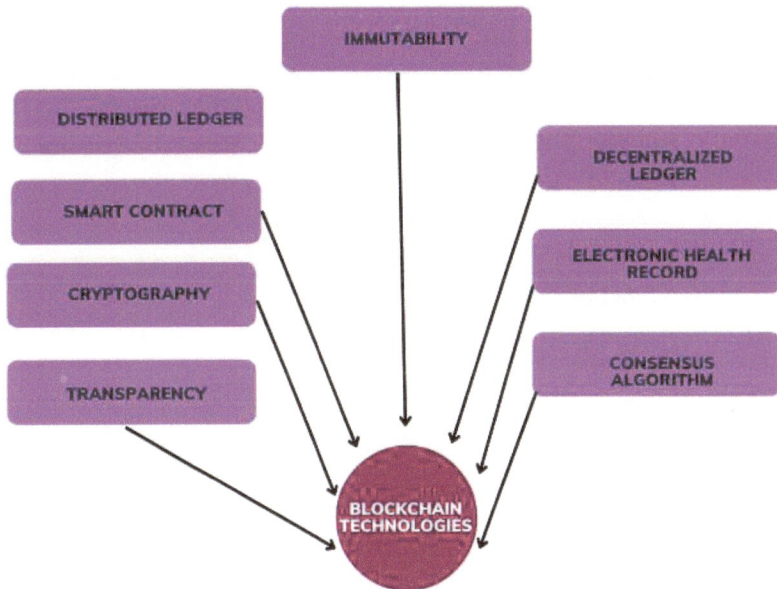

Fig. (2). Blockchain technologies.

BLOCKCHAIN TYPES AND RELEVANCE TO HEALTHCARE

In its broad sense, there are three types of blockchains [9]. Two of them are very distinct in their features that qualify them to be used in the different fields of healthcare.

Public Blockchain

Anyone can participate in it; it is managed by the system of nodes, which are also involved in the actual process [10 - 12]. Most suitable for the situation in which openness of results and endorsement by a community is necessary, for example, for the presentation of the results of clinical trials.

Private Blockchain

Limited to certain patients, increasing privacy and possible control. For patients in which access to patient records is of paramount importance [13].

Consortium Blockchain

Autonomous model of managing organized by a set of organizations. Appropriate for cooperation in healthcare, for instance, multiple scientific databases containing the results of studies [14 - 18].

BENEFITS OF DIGITIZATION OF MEDICAL HEALTH RECORDS

The digitization of health records through blockchain offers numerous benefits (Table 1):

- Data Security and Privacy.
- Interoperability.
- Data Integrity.
- Transparency and Traceability.

Table 1. Regulation and laws for medical data privacy.

Country	Regulations and Laws	Key Provisions
USA	Health Insurance Portability and Accountability Act (HIPAA)	Privacy, security, and breach notification rules
EU	General Data Protection Regulation (GDPR)	Data protection and privacy for individuals within the EU
Australia	My Health Records Act	Framework for the creation and management of HER

LITERATURE REVIEW

An excellent study by Tang and Ohno-Machado (2017) provides insight into the impact of blockchain on healthcare, highlighting its potential to improve information on security and interoperability. However, studies, as shown in Table

2, have shown that these findings need to be validated to be effective [19 - 21]. Another important topic, the use of electronic health records (EHRs), was examined by Chen *et al.* (2018), focusing on patient information management.

Table 2. Literature survey.

Paper	Approach	Strengths	Further Research
[12]	Qualitative	In-depth understanding of blockchain's impact	Need for quantitative validation
[33]	Decentralized EHR	Patient-centric data control	High implementation costs
[43]	Comparative Analysis	Comparison across different sectors	Focus on healthcare-specific outcomes
[48]	Systematic Review	Comprehensive review of existing literature	Emerging trends and technologies
[63]	Experimental	Empirical data on blockchain performance	Long-term effectiveness and scalability

BLOCKCHAIN USE CASES IN HEALTHCARE

To increase the level of security, transparency, and efficiency in several areas of healthcare, blockchain technology has a significant role to play (Table **3**). A good example is the MedRec system, which emphasizes health security through decentralized ledgers that secure patient data [22]. It provides a strong basis for safeguarding the privacy and integrity of medical records by exploiting the immutability and transparency of blockchain [23 - 26]. According to Patientory's website, "This application demonstrates how blockchain can be used as a tool to streamline data sharing among different healthcare providers while upholding patient confidentiality and integrity" [27].

Table 3. Use cases in healthcare of blockchain.

Paper	Healthcare Domain	Organization	Industry	Description
[27]	Health Security	MedRec	Blockchain	Securing patient data through decentralized ledgers
[28]	Medical Records	Patientory	Health IT	Managing patient records with blockchain for improved access
[39]	Medical Supply Chain	Chronicled	Pharmaceutical	Tracking pharmaceutical supply chain for authenticity
[50]	Genomic Market	Nebula Genomics	Genomics	Secure sharing and monetization of genomic data

APPLICATION OF BLOCKCHAIN IN HEALTHCARE

Blockchain technology has many uses in healthcare, including improving data security, transparency, and interoperability (Fig. **3**). Through leveraging decentralized ledger technologies, blockchain can enhance EHR management as well as accelerate clinical trials [28 - 31]. Inefficiencies are being minimized, data breaches are being avoided, and patients are receiving their own health information.

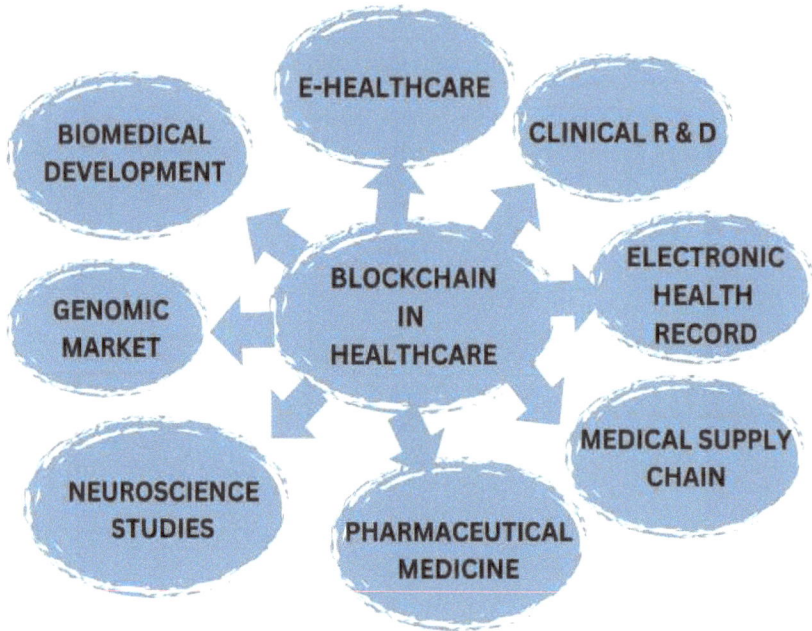

Fig. (3). Application of blockchain in healthcare.

EHR Management

Other examples include a blockchain-powered EHR system that offers robust security measures at the expense of interoperability as shown in Table **4**. Smart contracts can be used in managing EHR to automate who has access and who does not have access as well as those authorized to do changes on records only. Nevertheless, this method requires uniformity across different areas but is effective for complying with regulations.

Supply Chain Management

Blockchain technology revolutionizes supply chain management (SCM) in healthcare by helping trace and verify the genuineness of medical products (Table **5**). Traceability and transparency are improved by implementing blockchain; thus, all steps of the supply chain can be recorded and monitored [32].

Table 4. EHR management.

Paper	Implementation	Benefits	Issues	Further Research
[04]	Blockchain-based EHR	Enhanced security and privacy	Interoperability challenges	Integration with existing systems
[14]	Decentralized EHR	Patient-centric data control	High implementation costs	Cost-effective solutions
[21]	Smart contracts for EHR	Automated access permissions	Regulatory compliance	Standardization across regions
[44]	EHR with DLT	Immutable patient records	Scalability issues	Scalability improvements
[49]	Hybrid EHR systems	Balance of security and accessibility	Data migration from legacy systems	Efficient data migration strategies

Table 5. Supply chain management.

Paper	Implementation	Benefits	Issues	Further Research
[06]	Blockchain for SCM	Enhanced traceability and transparency	Complex integration with existing SCM	Simplified integration methods
[17]	Decentralized SCM	Reduction of counterfeit drugs	High operational costs	Cost reduction techniques
[18]	Smart contracts for SCM	Automated logistics and payments	Regulatory hurdles	Compliance frameworks
[29]	SCM with DLT	Real-time tracking of goods	Scalability concerns	Large-scale implementation studies
[51]	Hybrid SCM systems	Improved supply chain efficiency	Data interoperability issues	Standardization of data formats

Blockchain in Clinical Trials

In addition, clinical trials can be enhanced by blockchain through increased transparency, security, and efficiency (Fig. **4** and Table **6**). By implementing blockchain within clinical trials, it is possible to enhance transparency among stakeholders, thereby creating an immutable record of every trial data. However, this implementation faces challenges related to data privacy, which necessitate the development of privacy-preserving techniques [33].

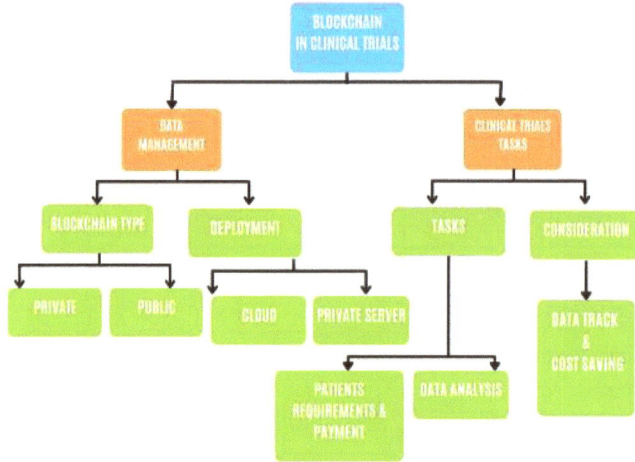

Fig. (4). Clinical trials with blockchain technology.

Table 6. Clinical trials.

Paper	Implementation	Benefits	Issues	Further Research
[11]	Blockchain for Clinical Trials	Increased transparency and trust	Data privacy concerns	Privacy-preserving techniques
[22]	Decentralized Clinical Trials	Secure patient data management	High setup costs	Cost-effective trial setups
[35]	Smart Contracts for Clinical Trials	Automated consent and data sharing	Regulatory compliance	Harmonization of regulations
[45]	Clinical Trials with DLT	Immutable trial data	Interoperability issues	Cross-platform integration
[55]	Hybrid Clinical Trials systems	Balance of security and efficiency	Scalability challenges	Scalable solutions for large trials

Health Insurance Claims

The insurance claim process using blockchain ensures secure handling through stages like document collection, claim initiation, verification, and payment initiation, while the underlying blockchain flow—starting from user login to ledger update—guarantees transparency, authentication, and immutability through smart contracts and mining (Fig. **5**).

Billing Management

This leads to reduced paperwork and timely billing with the help of smart contracts, where billing is automatically done on the blockchain (Fig. **6**).

The following (Table **7**) synopsizes the implementation enhancements, limitations, and further research directions of blockchain for billing management based on previous studies [34 - 37].

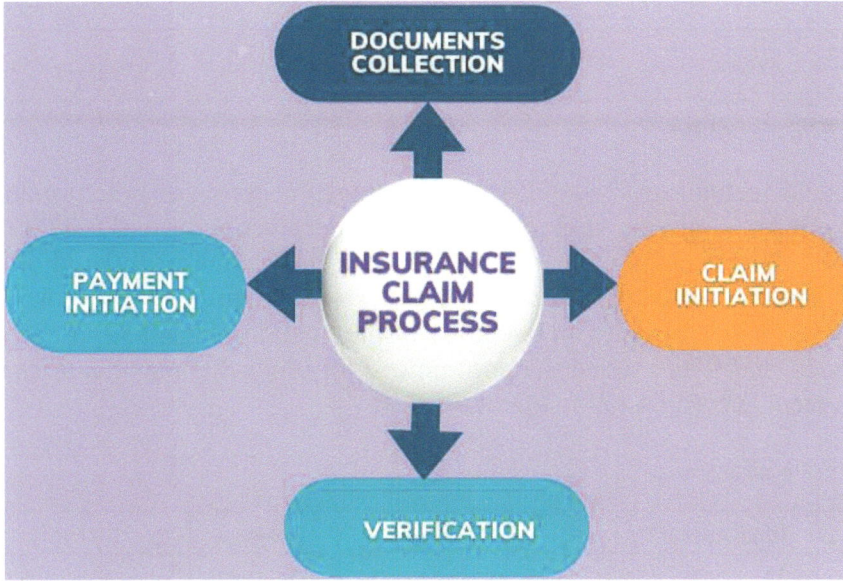

Fig. (5). Insurance claim process with blockchain.

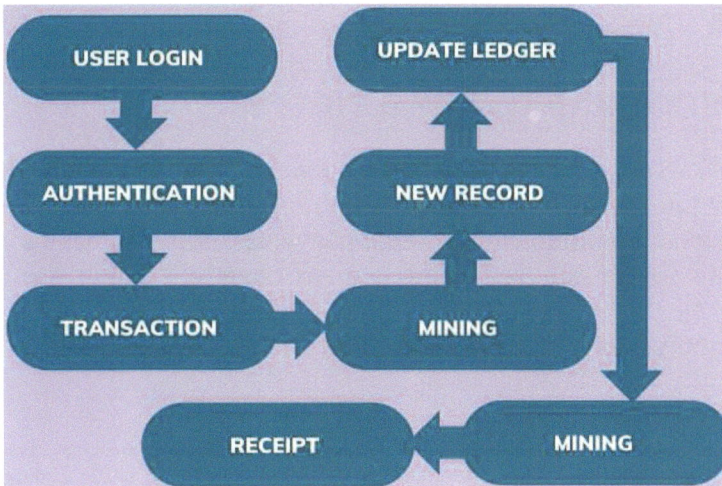

Fig. (6). Billing management with blockchain.

Table 7. Billing management.

Paper	Implementation	Benefits	Issues	Further Research
[13]	Blockchain for billing	Reduced fraud and errors	Integration with existing billing systems	Streamlined integration approaches
[26]	Decentralized billing	Enhanced billing accuracy	Regulatory hurdles	Compliance frameworks

Policy Management

Blockchain technology has multiple advantages in terms of policy management due to smart contracts and distributed ledger technology (DLT) [38]. This increases policy management from being done haphazardly and insecurely, making stakeholders more trusting and lowering the administrative costs involved [39 - 42]. Table **8** provides an overview of the main implementations, advantages, challenges, and future research opportunities for blockchain applications in policy management according to the literature.

Table 8. Policy management.

Paper	Implementation	Benefits	Issues	Further Research
[8]	Smart Contracts for Policy Management	Automated policy management	High initial setup costs	Cost-effective implementation
[19]	DLT in Policy Management	Secure and transparent policies	Data privacy issues	Privacy-preserving methods

TELEMEDICINE AND TELEHEALTH

Blockchain has the potential to transform telemedicine and telehealth by making sure of easy and efficient healthcare shipping [43, 44]. It can facilitate relaxed person-physician communications, enhance accessibility to healthcare offerings, and automate carrier delivery through smart contracts. Table **9** summarizes the key implementations, benefits, challenges, and further study directions for blockchain applications in telemedicine and telehealth based on diverse research.

Table 9. Telehealth and telemedicine.

Paper	Implementation	Benefits	Issues	Further Research
[10]	Blockchain for Telehealth and Telemedicine	Secure patient-doctor communications	Data privacy and security concerns	Enhanced security measures
[15]	Decentralized Telehealth and Telemedicine	Improved accessibility to healthcare	Scalability challenges	Scalable infrastructure solutions

(Table 9) cont.....

Paper	Implementation	Benefits	Issues	Further Research
[23]	Smart Contracts for Telehealth and Telemedicine	Automated service delivery	Regulatory compliance	Harmonization of regulations
[32]	Telehealth and Telemedicine with DLT	Transparent healthcare services	High operational costs	Cost reduction techniques
[46]	Hybrid Telehealth and Telemedicine systems	Balance of security and accessibility	Data interoperability issues	Standardization of data formats

RESEARCH IN HEALTHCARE WITH BCT

The blockchain era can extensively furnish research in healthcare by supplying a relaxed, transparent, and decentralized framework for fact sharing and collaboration. This ensures the integrity and accessibility of studies statistics while facilitating improved collaboration amongst researchers. Table **10** summarizes the important implementations, benefits, problems, and further research instructions for blockchain programs in healthcare research primarily based on various research [45 - 47].

Table 10. Healthcare research with BCT.

Paper	Implementation	Benefits	Issues	Further Research
[16]	Blockchain for healthcare research	Secure and transparent data sharing	Data privacy concerns	Privacy-preserving techniques
[36]	Decentralized healthcare research	Enhanced collaboration	High setup costs	Cost-effective research setups

ACCURATE MEDICAL DECISION

This more desirable data accessibility and integrity can result in extra knowledgeable and accurate scientific decisions [48 - 51]. However, integrating data from various resources and ensuring regulatory compliance are key demanding situations that need to be addressed [52 - 57]. Table **11** summarizes the key implementations, benefits, issues, and further study guidelines for blockchain applications in scientific choice-making based on diverse research.

Table 11. Medical decisions with BCT.

Paper	Implementation	Benefits	Issues	Further Research
[16]	Blockchain for Medical Decision-making	Enhanced decision accuracy	Data integration challenges	Seamless data integration techniques

(Table 11) cont.....

Paper	Implementation	Benefits	Issues	Further Research
[36]	Decentralized Medical Decision	Improved data accessibility	Regulatory compliance	Harmonization of regulations

HOSPITAL AND MEDICINE MANAGEMENT

The blockchain era can enhance health centers and medicinal drug control by improving operational efficiency and providing transparent tracking of medicines. The subsequent (Table **12**) summarizes the important implementations, benefits, problems, and similar study directions for blockchain programs in hospital and medication management based on diverse research.

Table 12. Hospital and medical management with BCT.

Paper	Implementation	Benefits	Issues	Further Research
[9]	Blockchain for Hospital and Medical Management	Improved operational efficiency	High implementation costs	Cost-effective solutions
[24]	DLT in Hospital and Medical Management	Secure and transparent medicine tracking	Data interoperability issues	Standardization of data formats

BLOCKCHAIN-ENABLED ACCESSIBLE ENCRYPTION

Blockchain generation offers progressive encryption answers, imparting stronger record protection *via* its decentralized nature. By means of integrating blockchain with encryption strategies, information may be secured more robustly against unauthorized entry and tampering [58 - 60]. However, this integration introduces complexities in managing encryption tactics and keys. Table **13** summarizes key aspects of blockchain-enabled encryption, along with its implementation, advantages, problems, and areas for additional research.

Table 13. Medical data encryption with BCT.

Paper	Implementation	Benefits	Issues	Further Research
[25]	Blockchain for Medical Data Encryption	Enhanced data security	Complexity of encryption	Simplified encryption methods
[31]	Decentralized Medical Data Encryption	Improved data privacy	Scalability concerns	Scalable encryption solutions

ISSUES RELATED TO BLOCKCHAIN IN HEALTHCARE

Following are the different types of issues related to the blockchain in healthcare:

Technical Issues

Storage Maintenance

Various use cases of blockchain in health systems, specifically supply chain and EHR, have varying storage solutions. These issues must be approached differently from application to application, and therefore, they have specific answers.

Security

For one healthcare application, like conducting clinical trials, the primary threat stems from unauthorized access; for another, like health insurance claims, the biggest problem is data privacy. Solving the mentioned problems requires implementing particular technologies and procedures aimed at preserving confidential information [61].

Scalability

The factor of scalability is of particular concern in healthcare applications. As shown with telemedicine or remote healthcare monitoring solutions, different uses face specific scaling issues. To this end, it implies that the selection and application of interventions hold incidental costs and can be used efficiently and by a large number of people.

Throughput

Another capacity of interest for the utilization of blockchain applications in healthcare is the throughput. Technological application areas like electronic EHRs face issues of throughput that are unique to their field such as in the field of supply chain. Solutions to overcome these challenges include improving the processing of transactions and cutting costs on operations.

Integrity

The integrity of the data that is stored in the blockchain must be maintained to ensure the reliability and credibility of blockchain solutions that will be used in the healthcare sector. Every application, for instance, clinical trials and health insurance claims, has unique issues when it comes to data accuracy.

Latency

This has implications for the speed of processing and access to data in most blockchain applications in healthcare on account of latency.

Confidentiality

Security and privacy, where the patient data is protected from access by third parties, remain the key considerations of blockchain applications in the healthcare sector. It is important to understand that various applications like EHR management and supply chain management have different kinds of confidentiality problems.

Non-Technical Issues

Adjustment Issues

The adoption of blockchain in the healthcare setting is changing, implying that, for the new systems to work, there is always the need to make changes. Even when it comes to each of the applications, for instance, clinical trials, health insurance claims, and so on, there are certain adjustment factors that are required to be understood and dealt with; if at all, the adoption of the concept is sought to be done in a proper manner. Measures reported include approaches to system change and costs.

Social Issues

Blockchain technology in healthcare can also face a number of social concerns that define its application and efficacy. The degree of social risks also varies from one application to another, such as patient acceptance and the general reluctance to change. In order to overcome these challenges, it is sometimes necessary to employ special approaches to make those changes acceptable and to facilitate transition.

Lack of Standard

One of the most important problems is the lack of a protocol and format that can simplify the application of blockchain solutions in the sphere of healthcare. All these aspects can be solved only with the help of the creation and utilization of strict standardization systems and data format specifications.

Regulatory Compliance

A challenge relevant to applications such as clinical trials and health insurance claims involves compliance with regulatory requirements. To overcome these challenges, mobilization of compliance structure and privacy-preserving instruments are required.

CONTRIBUTION AND NOVELTY

It is the intent of this chapter to give a brief of the work done and advancements adopted in the use of blockchain technology in the field of healthcare. It includes all the generic types and technologies of blockchain and their implementation in healthcare and concerns both technical and non-technical issues. Also, solutions to the problems highlighted, as well as future research recommendations, are provided for the field's development. The following (Table **14**) provides an overview of the chapter and the contribution/novelty of this work.

Table 14. Contribution and novelty.

Paper	Blockchain Types	Blockchain Technologies	Healthcare Applications	Challenges	Solutions	Future Directions
[10]	Public, Private	Cryptographic Hashing	EHR Management	Data privacy issues	Privacy-preserving methods	Integration with AI
[15]	Consortium	Smart Contracts	Supply Chain Management	High operational costs	Cost reduction techniques	Advanced interoperability solutions
[23]	Public, Private	Decentralized Ledgers	Clinical Trials	Regulatory compliance	Compliance frameworks	Cross-border regulatory harmonization
[32]	Consortium	Blockchain as a Service	Health Insurance Claims	Data integrity issues	Immutable records	Blockchain and big data integration
[46]	All	All	Comprehensive Healthcare Solutions	Technical and non-technical challenges	Comprehensive solutions framework	Future research on blockchain scalability and security enhancement

FUTURE DIRECTIONS

As blockchain technology continues to grow, more uses are set to be discovered and adopted within the healthcare sector. Here are some future directions for blockchain in healthcare: decentralized modern sampling and interconnected global health informatics, converging identities for EPC and decentralized patient authorization, blockchain-based health finance systems, self-executing smart health repositories, and government and regulatory embrace.

CONCLUSION

Blockchain technology has the potential to revolutionize the healthcare sector by boosting data security and data sharing and consolidating patients' power. However, this paper has named some technical and non-technical challenges that need to be solved for the adoption of the technology to prevail.

AUTHORS' CONTRIBUTION

In Chapter 2, **Mr. Vikas Kumar**, **Mushtaq Ahmad Rather**, and **Saptadeepa Kalita** collaboratively contributed to the chapter's conceptualization, research, and drafting. **Mr. Vikas Kumar** led the initial exploration of blockchain applications in healthcare, focusing on electronic health records, clinical trials, and supply chain management. **Mushtaq Ahmad Rather** conducted an in-depth analysis of blockchain's potential for telemedicine, insurance claims, and regulatory challenges, contributing significantly to the theoretical framework and technical details. **Saptadeepa Kalita** researched case studies and real-world implementations, emphasizing the practical implications of blockchain adoption in the healthcare industry. All authors contributed to reviewing and refining the chapter, ensuring clarity, coherence, and relevance to emerging trends and future directions in blockchain technology for healthcare.

REFERENCES

[1]   Nakamoto S. Bitcoin: a peer-to-peer electronic cash system 2008.

[2]   Kuo TT, Kim HE, Ohno-Machado L. Blockchain distributed ledger technologies for biomedical and health care applications. J Am Med Inform Assoc 2017; 24(6): 1211-20.
[http://dx.doi.org/10.1093/jamia/ocx068] [PMID: 29016974]

[3]   Wood G. Ethereum: a secure decentralised generalised transaction ledger 2014; 151: 1-32.

[4]   Zhang P, White J, Schmidt DC, Lenz G. Applying software patterns to address interoperability in blockchain-based healthcare applications. IEEE Blockchain 2018; 1: 1-41.

[5]   Hölbl M, Kompara M, Kamišalić A, Nemec Zlatolas L. A systematic review of the use of blockchain in healthcare. Symmetry (Basel) 2018; 10(10): 470.
[http://dx.doi.org/10.3390/sym10100470]

[6]   Engelhardt MA. Hitching healthcare to the chain: an introduction to blockchain technology in the healthcare sector. Technol Innov Manag Rev 2017; 7(10): 22-34.
[http://dx.doi.org/10.22215/timreview/1111]

[7]   Esposito C, De Santis A, Tortora G, Chang H, Choo KKR. Blockchain: a panacea for healthcare cloud-based data security and privacy?. IEEE Cloud Computing 2018; 5(1): 31-7.
[http://dx.doi.org/10.1109/MCC.2018.011791712]

[8]   McGhin T, Choo KKR, Liu CZ, He D. Blockchain in healthcare applications: Research challenges and opportunities. J Netw Comput Appl 2019; 135: 62-75.
[http://dx.doi.org/10.1016/j.jnca.2019.02.027]

[9]   Mettler M. Blockchain technology in healthcare: the revolution starts here IEEE. IEEE Access 2016; 4: 9974-84.
[http://dx.doi.org/10.1109/HealthCom.2016.7749510]

[10] Xia Q, Sifah EB, Smahi A, Amofa S, Zhang X. BBDS: blockchain-based data sharing for electronic medical records in cloud environments IEEE 2017; 6(39087): 97.
[http://dx.doi.org/10.3390/info8020044]

[11] Ivan D. Moving toward a blockchain-based method for the secure storage of patient records. Blockchain Healthc 2016; 3: 1-6.

[12] Azaria A, Ekblaw A, Vieira T, Lippman A. MedRec: using blockchain for medical data access and permission management. In: 2016 2nd International Conference on Open and Big Data (OBD). Vienna, Austria. IEEE. 2016; pp. 25-30.
[http://dx.doi.org/10.1109/OBD.2016.11]

[13] Ekblaw A, Azaria A, Halamka JD, Lippman A. A case study for blockchain in healthcare: "MedRec" prototype for electronic health records and medical research data. Proc IEEE 2016; 1(1): 1-7.

[14] Gordon WJ, Catalini C. Blockchain technology for healthcare: facilitating the transition to patient-driven interoperability. Healthcare (Basel) 2018; 6(2): 62-5.
[PMID: 29895767]

[15] Hylock RH, Zeng X. A blockchain framework for patient-centered health records and exchange (HealthChain): evaluation and proof-of-concept study. J Med Internet Res 2019; 21(8): e13592.
[http://dx.doi.org/10.2196/13592] [PMID: 31471959]

[16] Fan K, Wang S, Ren Y, Li H, Yang Y. MedBlock: efficient and secure medical data sharing *via* blockchain. J Med Syst 2018; 42(8): 136.
[http://dx.doi.org/10.1007/s10916-018-0993-7] [PMID: 29931655]

[17] Dubovitskaya A, Xu Z, Ryu S, Schumacher M, Wang F. Secure and trustable electronic medical records sharing using blockchain. AMIA Annu Symp Proc 2018; 2017: 650-9.
[PMID: 29854130]

[18] Roehrs A, da Costa CA, da Rosa Righi R, de Oliveira KSF. OmniPHR: A distributed architecture model to integrate personal health records. J Biomed Inform 2017; 71: 70-81.
[http://dx.doi.org/10.1016/j.jbi.2017.05.012] [PMID: 28545835]

[19] Patil M, Seshadri R. Big data security and privacy issues in healthcare. Int J Inf Secur 2014; 13(3): 245-60.

[20] Ivanov I. Implementing a blockchain-based system in healthcare. Blockchain Healthc 2019; 2: 1-8.

[21] Bennett B. Blockchain technology in healthcare: enhancing efficiency and privacy. J Med Syst 2018; 42(8): 140.
[PMID: 29956061]

[22] Lemieux VL. Trusting records: is Blockchain technology the answer?. Rec Manage J 2016; 26(2): 110-39.
[http://dx.doi.org/10.1108/RMJ-12-2015-0042]

[23] Badr S, Gomaa I, Abd-Elrahman E. Multi-tier blockchain framework for IoT-EHRs systems. Int J Adv Comput Sci Appl 2018; 9(6): 311-9.

[24] Wang H, Song Y. Secure cloud-based EHR system using attribute-based cryptosystem and blockchain. J Med Syst 2018; 42(8): 152.
[http://dx.doi.org/10.1007/s10916-018-0994-6] [PMID: 29974270]

[25] Sharples M, Domingue J. The blockchain and kudos: a distributed system for educational record, reputation and reward. Lect Notes Comput Sci 2016; 9891: 490-6.
[http://dx.doi.org/10.1007/978-3-319-45153-4_48]

[26] Underwood S. Blockchain beyond bitcoin. Commun ACM 2016; 59(11): 15-7.
[http://dx.doi.org/10.1145/2994581]

[27] Yue X, Wang H, Jin D, Li M, Jiang W. Healthcare data gateways: found healthcare intelligence on

blockchain with novel privacy risk control. J Med Syst 2016; 40(10): 218.
[http://dx.doi.org/10.1007/s10916-016-0574-6] [PMID: 27565509]

[28]   Mehta N, Pandit A. Concurrence of big data analytics and healthcare: A systematic review. Int J Med Inform 2018; 114(1): 57-65.
[http://dx.doi.org/10.1016/j.ijmedinf.2018.03.013] [PMID: 29673604]

[29]   Bashir I. Mastering blockchain: distributed ledger technology, decentralization, and smart contracts explained. Birmingham: Packt Publishing Ltd 2017.

[30]   Dixon BE, McGowan JJ, Grannis SJ. Electronic laboratory data quality and the value of a health information exchange to support public health reporting processes. AMIA Annu Symp Proc 2011; 2011(5): 322-30.
[PMID: 22195084]

[31]   Roman-Belmonte JM, De la Corte-Rodríguez H, Rivas-García A. Blockchain technology in the pharmaceutical industry. J Ind Eng Manag 2018; 11(3): 295-309.

[32]   Tang Q, Ohno-Machado L. Addressing gaps in consumer access and use of health information. JAMIA Open 2017; 4(2): 233-41.

[33]   Chen H, Xu B, Lu M, Chen N. Exploring blockchain technology and its potential applications for education. Educ Inf Technol 2018; 23(5): 1-8.

[34]   Szabo N. Formalizing and securing relationships on public networks. First Monday 1997; 2: 9.
[http://dx.doi.org/10.5210/fm.v2i9.548]

[35]   Davidson S, De Filippi P, Potts J. Economics of blockchain. J Econ Behav Organ 2016; 139: 1-13.

[36]   Fanning K, Centers DP. Blockchain and its coming impact on financial services. J Corp Account Finance 2016; 27(5): 53-7.
[http://dx.doi.org/10.1002/jcaf.22179]

[37]   Hinkes A. Blockchain technology in healthcare. J Healthc Manag 2017; 62(1): 10-3.

[38]   McCarthy J. What is blockchain and how is it changing the healthcare industry?. J Innov Health 2017; 7(4): 45-8.

[39]   Tapscott D, Tapscott A. Blockchain revolution: how the technology behind bitcoin is changing money, business, and the world. New York: Penguin 2016.

[40]   C. C. Agbo, Q. H. Mahmoud, and J. M. Eklund, "Blockchain technology in healthcare: a systematic review," in Healthcare, vol. 7, no. 2. Multidisciplinary Digital Publishing Institute, 2019, p. 56.

[41]   Steward M. Electronic medical records. J Legal Med 2005; 26(4): 491-506.

[42]   S. L. Cichosz, M. N. Stausholm, T. Kronborg, P. Vestergaard, and O. Hejlesen, "How to use blockchain for diabetes health care data and access management: an operational concept," J. Diabetes Sci. Technol., 2019, vol. 13, no. 2, pp. 248–53.

[43]   McClean S, Gillespie J, Garg L, Barton M, Scotney B, Kullerton K. Using phase-type models to cost stroke patient care across health, social and community services. Eur J Oper Res 2014; 236: 190-199.

[44]   Azaria A, Ekblaw A, Vieira T, Lippman A. MedRec: Using Blockchain for medical data access and permission management. Proc 2nd Int Conf Open Big Data (OBD) 2016: 25-30.

[45]   Yue X, Wang H, Jin D, Li M, Jiang W. Healthcare data gateways: Found healthcare intelligence on Blockchain with novel privacy risk control. J Med Syst 2016; 40(10).

[46]   Tschorsch F, Scheuermann B. Bitcoin and beyond: A technical survey on decentralized digital currencies. IEEE Commun Surv Tutor 2016; 18(3): 2084-2123.

[47]   Al-Janabi S, Al-Shourbaji I, Shojafar M, Shamshirband S. Survey of main challenges (security and privacy) in wireless body area networks for healthcare applications. Egypt Inform J 2017; 18(2): 113-122.

[http://dx.doi.org/10.1016/j.eij.2016.11.001]

[48]   Mettler M. Blockchain technology in healthcare: the revolution starts here IEEE 2016; 4: 9974-84.
       [http://dx.doi.org/10.1109/HealthCom.2016.7749510]

[49]   Xia Q, Sifah EB, Smahi A, Amofa S, Zhang X. BBDS: blockchain-based data sharing for electronic
       medical records in cloud environments IEEE 2017; 6: 39087-97.
       [http://dx.doi.org/10.3390/info8020044]

[50]   Kotz D, Gunter CA, Kumar S, Weiner JP. Privacy and security in mobile health: A research agenda.
       Computer 2016; 49(6): 22-30.

[51]   Chen Y, Ding S, Xu Z, Zheng H, Yang S. Blockchain-based medical records secure storage and
       medical service framework. J Med Syst 2018; 43(1).

[52]   Kish LJ, Topol EJ. Unpatients - why patients should own their medical data. Nat Biotechnol 2015;
       33(9): 921-924.

[53]   Azaria A, Ekblaw A, Vieira T, Lippman A. MedRec: Using Blockchain for medical data access and
       permission management. Proc 2nd Int Conf Open Big Data (OBD) 2016: 25-30.
       [http://dx.doi.org/10.1109/OBD.2016.11]

[54]   Zhang P, White J, Schmidt DC, Lenz G, Rosenbloom ST. FHIRChain: Applying blockchain to
       securely and scalably share clinical data. Comput Struct Biotechnol J 2018; 16: 267-278.

[55]   Omar AA, Bhuiyan MZA, Basu A, Kiyomoto S, Rahman MS. Privacy-friendly platform for healthcare
       data in cloud based on blockchain environment. Future Gener Comput Syst 2019; 95: 511-521.

[56]   Ren J, Li J, Liu H, Qin T. Task offloading strategy with emergency handling and blockchain security
       in SDN-empowered and fog-assisted healthcare IoT. Tsinghua Sci Technol 2022; 27(4): 760-776.
       [http://dx.doi.org/10.26599/TST.2021.9010046]

[57]   Gordon WJ, Catalini C. Blockchain technology for healthcare: Facilitating the transition to patient-
       driven interoperability. Comput Struct Biotechnol J 2018; 16: 224-230.

[58]   Brown MM, Brown GC, Sharma S, Landy J. Health care economic analyses and value-based
       medicine. Surv Ophthalmol 2003; 48(2): 204-223.

[59]   Zhang P, White J, Schmidt DC, Lenz G, Rosenbloom ST. FHIRChain: Applying Blockchain to
       securely and scalably share clinical data. Comput Struct Biotechnol J 2018; 16: 267-278.

[60]   Dhillon V, Metcalf D, Hooper M. The hyperledger project. In: Blockchain enabled applications. 2017:
       139-149.

[61]   Geng Q, Chuai Z, Jin J. An integrated healthcare service system based on blockchain technologies.
       IEEE Trans Comput Soc Syst 2024; 11(5): 6278-6295.
       [http://dx.doi.org/10.1109/TCSS.2024.3392591]

CHAPTER 3

Blockchain Technology in Healthcare: Uses and Challenges

Anita Tanwar[1,*]

[1] *Chitkara Business School, Chitkara University, Rajpura, Punjab, India*

Abstract: Blockchain is the amalgamation of encryption and noble technology for communication. By giving individuals precise, customized, and safe accessibility to their healthcare information, tailored electronic medical records may help patients take charge of their own care. Tailored health records facilitate the creation of an innovative system that integrates electronic interventions, medical data collection, and access to smart contracts. Blockchain retains every patient's complete medical history, providing a secure means to store and maintain detailed medical data for every patient. This technology can be used to ensure the safe transfer of private data, including records of patients, episode summaries, disease logs, test results, medical treatments received, and emergency medical services. The healthcare industry is now front and center as a potential use case for blockchain technology. We can see a high-level picture of blockchain pertaining to healthcare. The system is composed of many blocks that are interconnected using hash functions based on cryptography. The blockchain is an important yet resourceful technique for transmitting and receiving data in an efficient and highly secure manner. Anyone involved in a transaction initiates the process by creating a block. The system is composed of many blocks that are interconnected using hash functions based on cryptography. This chapter discusses the conceptual background of blockchain technology in healthcare, user's need for blockchain, and challenges in using blockchain technology in healthcare. Blockchain technology has produced a permanent record that many financial technology systems utilize to detect cryptocurrency double-spending in order to meet efficiency and security criteria.

Keywords: Blockchain technology, Decentralized ledger, Healthcare data management, Privacy, Security, Smart contracts.

INTRODUCTION

Blockchain technology is a decentralized platform that uses a collaborative distributed ledger system. It was initially created by Satoshi Nakamoto in 2008 for financial companies, but it has now become a fundamental technology for various decentralized applications [1]. Blockchain is the amalgamation of encryption and

---

[*] **Corresponding author Anita Tanwar:** Chitkara Business School, Chitkara University, Rajpura, Punjab, India; E-mail: anitatanwar.ggn@gmail.com

Mohit Angurala, Preet Kamal, Aryan Chaudhary, Rasmeet Singh Bali & Vijay Bhardwaj (Eds.)
All rights reserved-© 2025 Bentham Science Publishers

noble technology for communication. The system is composed of many blocks that are interconnected using hash functions based on cryptography. The blockchain is an important yet resourceful technique for transmitting and receiving data in an efficient and highly secure manner. Anyone involved in a transaction initiates the process by creating a block. A multitude of machines are distributed everywhere on the net that verify the block (Fig. **1**). The verified block is appended to a blockchain, which is subsequently distributed over the internet, creating both a singular and distinctive record with a unique historical trail. Therefore, in the context of blockchain technology, transactions are deemed genuine when there is a consensus among blocks, which is achieved through contractual agreements. The decentralized characteristics of blockchain technology result in the decentralization of trust, making trust between system users crucial for issuing keys [2].

Blockchain has undergone significant evolution throughout the years. We categorize blockchain into five distinct versions, referred to as blockchain technology 1.0 to 5.0. The initial iteration of the blockchain, known as blockchain technology 1.0, was developed by Nakamoto. It serves as a fundamental decentralized ledger system that facilitates transaction tracking and data storage across several devices. Simply put, the data stored in the original blockchains was limited to the intrinsic worth of an object that saw shifts in ownership during its lifespan. The entity we are alluding to was commonly a type of virtual currency, like dogecoin, ripple, and similar variants. Blockchain 2.0, commonly referred to as the emergence of Ethereum, is an upgraded iteration of cryptocurrency [3]. Ethereum was the pioneering blockchain that incorporated an integrated virtual technology for smart contracts. Smart contracts are an array of programs that are immediately performed when certain conditions are fulfilled, in a nutshell. These agreements let people or corporations conduct more intricate transactions beyond basic cryptocurrency trades. It is well-suited for applications that involve decentralized distribution and decentralized autonomous organizations. Blockchain 3.0 encompasses a broader series of applications, particularly in the realm of enterprise blockchain. Blockchain technology 3.0 encompasses several applications, such as healthcare, supply chain, cybersecurity, and manufacturing. Blockchain 4.0 now facilitates the implementation of industry and healthcare 4.0. Its objective is to optimize the experience of users inside the industry. Rchain and Metaverse are examples of blockchain technology 4.0 platforms. Blockchain technology 5.0 refers to the latest or current iteration of blockchain technology. The objective is to mitigate the conventional limitations and security concerns associated with blockchain technology. Relictum Pro, Hedra, and Hashgraph are typical applications of Blockchain 5.0 [4].

After traditional health information exchanges (HIEs) and health record-based exchanges failed to fulfill the claim of a common coalescent, blockchain technology presented a promising alternative. Various causes, including medical records that are electronic, competing goals, and others, keep bringing attention to the problem that comes with traditional health data exchange intermediaries [4, 5]. The healthcare industry is now front and center as a potential use case for blockchain technology. We can see a high-level picture of blockchain pertaining to healthcare. Patients and doctors are the data generators in the healthcare blockchain, together with medical cloud computing and the network of blockchain connections that houses the smart contracts. The worldwide Google Trends for the term "Blockchain - Healthcare" indicate a noticeable uptick in interest from academics.

Safety, interoperability, medical data transfer, and mobility are the different requirements of the healthcare division. The collection of healthcare statistics in the framework of the Industry 4.0 revolution takes place through files, devices with sensors, and various other applications. Electronic Medical Records, Health information technology, and Individual Health Records are the three types of digital health records. For such data, restricting access with suitable authentication is important. Additionally, the search performed for obtaining medical data needs to be tested with adequate access restriction to avoid management attacks [6]. Furthermore, encrypting is a poor method of protecting medical documents.

Also, encoding is a poor method of protecting medical papers. Interoperability difficulties arise when several encoding methods are designed to encode several types of medical records [7, 8]. Inadequate security of healthcare information also results in a number of privacy issues [9 - 11]. Another crucial prerequisite for healthcare records is interoperability. Interoperability is the ability to integrate and transfer data across diverse sources [12]. The utilization of central loading for data is the foundation of interoperability. Healthcare storage of data presents a challenge since centralizing all of the data might result in sluggish access, safety issues, and issues with privacy. Since healthcare data typically grows over time, it is not practical to send all of the data to central processing *via* untrusted networks. The centralized organization of the data makes it difficult to obtain in an efficient and safe way. Various scientific projects require the sharing of health-related information; thus, it is very tough to guarantee accessibility, consistency, and scalability when doing so [13, 14]. Patients havebecome more and more independent and demand that their medical information mobility becomes more and more important in the field of healthcare. With the increasing prevalence of sensors and smart devices linked to the internet, data transfer capacity is becoming more and more important.

USER NEEDS FOR BLOCKCHAIN

Because of issues with data sharing and usage policies, technological challenges, and privacy concerns, medical institutions are not working together effectively. Real-time access to healthcare information is frequently available to clients and other healthcare organizations. Fig. (2) illustrates and explains the most common and important customer demands of blockchain.

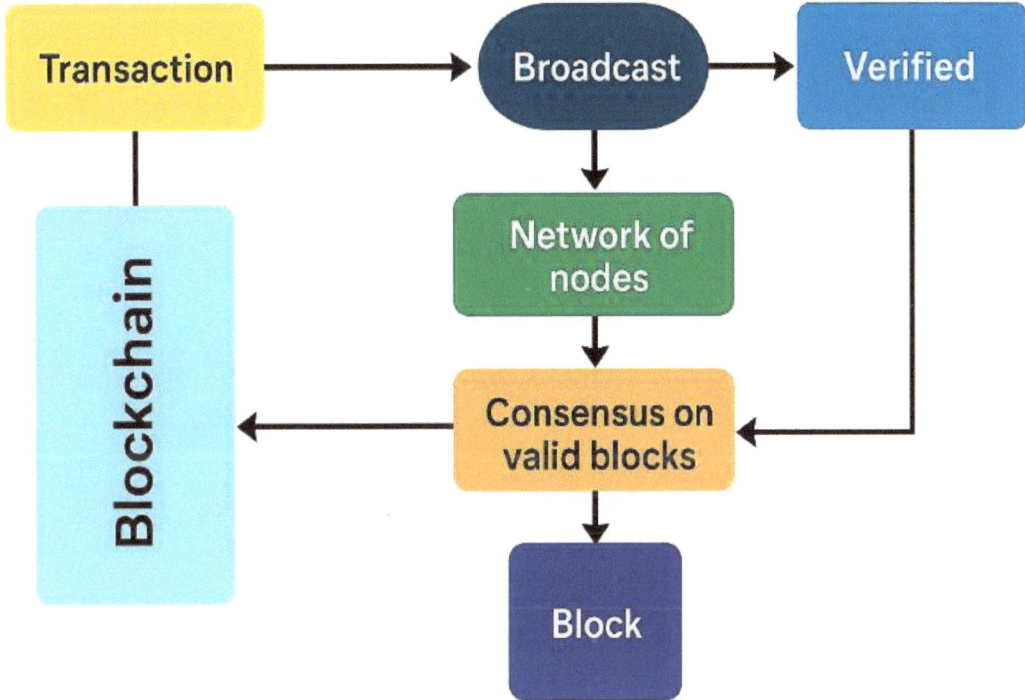

Fig. (1). BlockChain transaction and verification process.

2.1. Individualized medical records

2.2. Safety

2.3 Operational

2.4 Trustworthiness

2.5 Compatability

2.6 Management of Access

Fig. (2). Users' needs for blockchain.

Individualized Medical Records

Medical records include private information about therapies, surgeries, and recuperation. Traditional healthcare institutions still physically maintain such records on paper. Despite the increasing digitization of medical care distribution networks, electronic medical records remain fragmented and spread across different companies and geographical locations, with no wide-ranging structure in dwelling for updating and exchanging the information in actual time. Concerns around confidentiality and privacy of patients can make this scenario much more difficult. Equipment with Internet of Things features enables the rapid production of health-related information. Recent advancements in distributed database technology, sometimes referred to as blockchain or ledger technology, offer answers to problems pertaining to data interchange and access [15].

By giving individuals precise, customized, and safe accessibility to their healthcare information, tailored electronic medical records may help patients take charge of their own care. Tailored health records facilitate the creation of an innovative system that integrates electronic interventions, medical data collection, and access to smart contracts. The system provides strong consent processes for information transfer between different institutions and apps, and it intends to enable users to use their personal information to enhance their healthcare. Implementing an integration of driven-by-events health records, smart contracts, and patient control and monitoring systems requires the widespread acceptance of blockchain-based technologies for the modified healthcare record [15].

Safety

Healthcare plays a critical role in overseeing enormous volumes of record generation, exchange of information, storage spaces, and analysis at all levels of medical operation. In order to protect the system from losing information or misconduct, it employs additional state-of-the-art technological advances and offers robust, multiple layers of safety for every transmission of data online. The service frequently fulfills the most rigorous national confidentiality and data security laws. Because the medical facility's system runs on servers that are cloud-based and located external to the infrastructure, it is protected from hacking attacks. All things considered, the healthcare system promotes transparency, protects privacy, deters identity theft, and offers a secure and safe atmosphere in which hospitals can carry on with their business [15].

Operational

Healthcare systems built on blockchain significantly increase the speed, flexibility, and effectiveness of the system by streamlining and integrating several procedures. Due to its flexibility and intra-operability, it enhances the operational efficiency and patient-treatment capabilities of a healthcare facility. The features of the platform are specially designed to handle a range of duties, such as immediate medical action, billing and payment processing, activities, and administration of operational support departments, intensive care, and diagnostics. Users can use one or more functions, and the technology can provide role-based management, allowing users to monitor and track all the actions necessary to provide healthcare [15].

Trustworthiness

When it comes to technical disruptions, outages, or malfunctions that other systems of technology may encounter, the blockchain technology healthcare system is incredibly durable. With respect to the security of data, they are quite safe and have an easy-to-use, advanced graphical user interface. Upgrading does not take a lot of time, and maintenance chores can be separated into scheduled tasks in advanced phases according to how the tasks are least taxing. The remote updating and improvement of health information do not interfere with day-to-day activities. The framework's success depends on every asset and technology being available at all moments [15].

Compatibility

Some of the concerns raised by the shift to client-centered connectivity are the involvement of privacy, security, patients, consent, and governance. Blockchain technology offers an enticing way around these challenges by offering a structure for the secure transfer of data. To sum up, blockchain provides a basic structure that allows a patient to uniquely identify themselves to all institutions, interact securely with many parties, and collect their medical information in an enduring way [15].

Management of Access

Prior to obtaining the medical records of a patient, a physician had to obtain the patient's consent. If the healthcare professional takes no other action, the computer system will refuse entry. In the same way, if a patient requests regular availability, a physician should speak with them directly about allowing it. This means that in order for the individual to view his medical documentation, he needs to give authorization. Additionally, the patient has the autonomous ability to add or remove any user credentials from additional system clients as well as provide limited access [15].

CHALLENGES

Researchers and healthcare professionals struggle with incomplete data, delayed communications, and inequitable workflow tools. An additional concern is the lack of reliable connections that enable the establishment of a beginning-to-end accessible system by connecting all independent healthcare systems [16]. A digital medical record is difficult for medical professionals to administer and keep up to date [17]. Usage of the blockchain will enable decentralized, virtually anonymous transactions. It offers an unchangeable characteristic to stop data tampering from just one individual and duplicate entries. Blockchain technology can be used to enforce the safe transfer of private data, including records of patients, episode summaries, disease logs, test results, medical treatments received, and emergency medical services. These transactions must be confirmed by digital signatures for users and entered into the record as soon as possible [18]. Nevertheless, using blockchain technology presents a number of additional difficulties due to its complexity in the healthcare sector.

The Hyperledger Fabric [19] is a framework used in this digital health record to exchange data between enterprises through the utilization of blockchain technology as a distributed record of transactions among networks. Numerous platforms for Blockchain have been introduced by businesses like Ethereum, Ripple, NEO, Corda, and Quorum. The most common use of telemedicine is a technique [20] that enables a physician to do actual procedures with the aid of wireless communication equipment and robots. This reduces costs and saves time. It also helps address the physician shortage. Among the applications built on blockchain aiming to improve transparency in the healthcare sector and other industries is Medblocks [21]. In Fig. (**3**), challenges in blockchain technology in healthcare are mentioned.

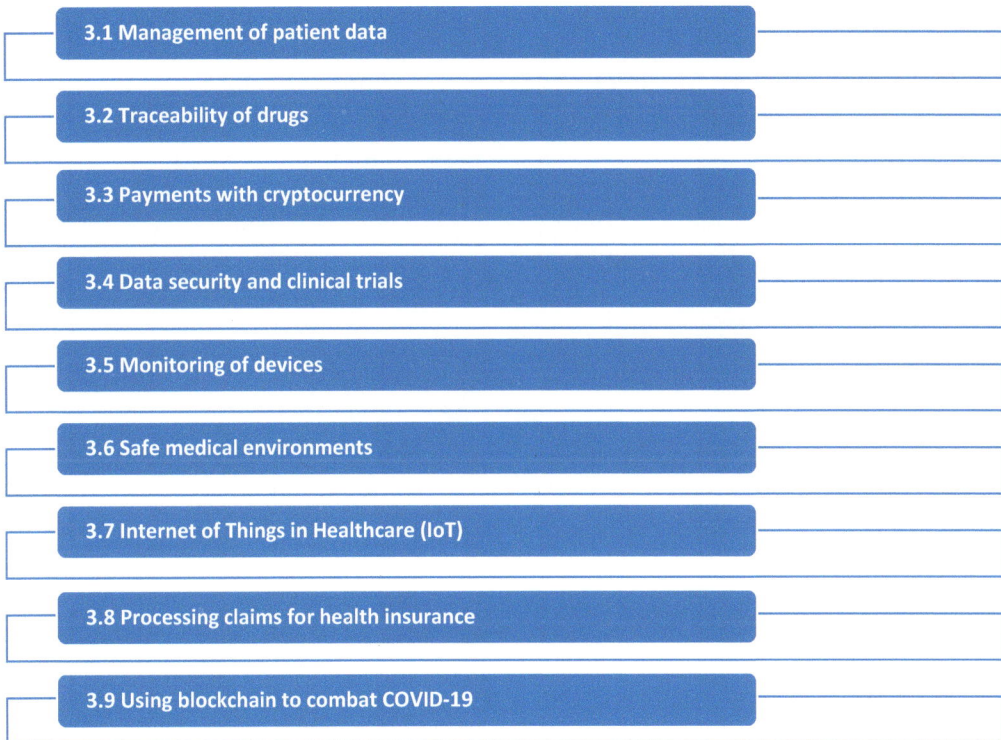

3.1 Management of patient data

3.2 Traceability of drugs

3.3 Payments with cryptocurrency

3.4 Data security and clinical trials

3.5 Monitoring of devices

3.6 Safe medical environments

3.7 Internet of Things in Healthcare (IoT)

3.8 Processing claims for health insurance

3.9 Using blockchain to combat COVID-19

Fig. (3). Challenges in blockchain.

Management of Patient Data

The key goals of blockchain's widespread application in handling patient information are cost- and security-effectiveness. Diagnostic tests are conducted, appointments for patients are scheduled, invoicing and finances are handled, and health information is digitally maintained [22]. Ensuring the delivery of secure, unalterable, and multiplatform health information is the primary objective.

Blockchain retains every patient's complete medical history, providing a secure means to store and maintain detailed medical data for every patient. It allows for several levels of administration by doctors, patients, authorities, medical facilities, insurance companies, and others.

Traceability of Drugs

A great deal of people suffer injuries or lose their lives each year as an outcome of using fake drugs. Counterfeiting pharmaceuticals results in serious economic and social consequences for the pharmaceutical industry. By eliminating fraud and imitation goods, blockchain technology medicine traceability improves manufacturing efficiency as opposed to using a conventional supply chain management framework. Musamih *et al.* established a system for tracking drugs [23] that allows stakeholders to collaborate with the medicine tracking mechanism and intelligent contracts. Stakeholders anticipate using software-based devices for accessing the intelligent contract, the decentralized file storage system, and the network resources. A d App serves as a front-end gateway, connecting the smart contract within the network products and services and distributed storage mechanism through an API. A G-coin network safeguards healthcare information and enables transparent medicine sales.

Payments with Cryptocurrency

The use of cryptocurrencies for transactions in healthcare has many advantages. A ledger records every transaction using blockchain technology. Most of the information regarding the proprietors of the currency is contained in the data that has been saved. This ensures the authenticity of the activities that are occurring. The decentralized nature of digital money means that neither the government nor the bank controls it. The owner of the digital money is still the person who produced it. Patients can communicate information thanks to blockchain. A central office's approval is not required in the absence of mediators such as banks, legislators, and shops in order to carry out the trades. It simplifies the charging procedure as a whole. The framework efficiently identifies the patients who attempt clinical activities [24]. It verifies the accuracy of the interactions and the truthfulness of the subtleties they provide.

Data Security and Clinical Trials

Accurate and true data collection is essential for clinical investigations. It is crucial to measure, correlate, and analyze this. Additionally, from the perspective of the patient, it provides an additional degree of security and safeguarding to the delicate and individually identifiable information, which the individual would be concerned with if it got into areas where theft of identity might take place.

Numerous scholarly investigations have examined the significance of blockchain technology in clinical research [25, 26]. Blockchain technology is making clinical trials more transparently available from the outset, including registration as well as informed consent, to the dissemination of data and the administration of drugs.

Monitoring of Devices

Following medical gadgets from their creation to their deactivation is a crucial step towards revolutionizing healthcare. Maintaining a pool of healthcare supplies used by various groups alongside patients is a challenge faced by hospitals everywhere. Finding the right materials for an illness requires time. In order to facilitate quick device recovery and prevent needless repurchasing fraudulent analysis from being transmitted to decommissioning, medical device surveillance and tracking are therefore essential [27]. Comparing a blockchain-based solution to traditional location monitoring techniques reveals a number of advantages. The invincibility and security of blockchain technology remain its most prominent characteristics. To support adherence to regulations using blockchain technology, an unchangeable record of the device's position and past whereabouts, along with its creator, reseller, and serial number, can be produced. A bad person cannot alter or erase the location of a device's records from its records thanks to this based on blockchain technology method. Blockchain gives us vital information concerning the way the healthcare equipment that is rented out is utilized, verifies that it is at an approved location, and ultimately ensures that clients make use of it. Easily finding equipment in a crisis, keeping a stock procedure log, and streamlining the usage process are a few advantages.

Safe Medical Environments

The field of intelligent healthcare has reached a high degree of competence in terms of effectively providing and prescribing healthcare for patients while protecting the confidentiality of the information they provide and also in providing medical professionals with real-time, reliable, and accurate information [28]. The Internet of Things has also done a fantastic job in the field of healthcare, making tracking patients and diagnosis easier.

Internet of Things in Healthcare (IoT)

IoT proposes a fully interconnected world in which objects can interact and communicate with one another through data. Numerous industries, including gadgets, smart towns, smart grids, smart houses, and the automobile sector, have adopted intelligent applications. The growth of IoT produces enormous amounts of data. One of the most important things to keep up with is making sure the data is credible. Blockchain-based technology can be used to ensure creditability in

Internet of Things data by offering a decentralized system that is approved by all parties involved and ensures that the information remains unchangeable. In the near future, blockchain-based technologies for hospitals may enable IoT productivity, adaptability, and standardization while simultaneously enhancing the security of data and accountability. Patients can now control those who have access to data that is collected by blockchain-enabled IoT devices utilized for healthcare, protecting those devices from hacking and keeping tabs on who has viewed the information. Blockchain-based applications driven by digital contracts can be used for automated supply chain settlements, contingent on the particular conditions observed by IoT devices [29].

Processing Claims for Health Insurance

One of the most annoying procedures is filing an insurance claim, as insurance processors must go through a vast amount of data to look for false claims, segmented information sources, and canceled policies that clients report. Insurance companies may now assume control over the assets they are insuring, and managing risks is transparent and hazard-free because of this advancement in technology [30]. These days, a lot of the insurance sector depends on transactions. Blockchain technology has produced a permanent record that many financial technology systems utilize to detect cryptocurrency double-spending in order to meet efficiency and security criteria [30].

Using Blockchain to Combat COVID-19

Every facet of humanity has altered due to the global COVID-19 pandemic. Information technology plays a major role in managing and controlling immunization, testing, and transmission. In order to address this unprecedented medical emergency, attention has turned to the online medical community, which is able to provide viable treatments to mitigate the effects of the pandemic [31 - 33]. The COVID-19 pandemic posed substantial challenges for the global medical community. It has come to light that digital healthcare is well-suited to provide innovative ways to tackle the pandemic. Developing healthcare, creative testing and medical decision-making tools, extending the application of smartwatches for monitoring physiological parameters, developing dependable monitoring systems, and developing interacting messaging applications to inform people about COVID-19 are a few of the possible solutions.

CONCLUSION

Blockchain is the amalgamation of peer-to-peer and encryption technology for communication. The system is composed of many blocks that are interconnected using hash functions based on cryptography. The blockchain is a fundamental yet ingenious technique for transmitting and receiving data in an efficient and highly secure manner. Anyone involved in a transaction initiates the process by creating a block. Because of issues with data sharing and usage policies, technological challenges, and privacy concerns, medical institutions are not working together effectively [34]. Real-time access to healthcare information is frequently available to clients and other healthcare organizations. Usage of the blockchain will enable decentralized, virtually anonymous transactions. It offers an unchangeable characteristic to stop data tampering from just one individual and prevent duplicate entries. Blockchain technology can be used to enforce the safe transfer of private data, including records of patients, episode summaries, disease logs, test results, medical treatments received, and emergency medical services. These transactions must be verified by digital signatures for each user and entered into the ledger as soon as possible.

AUTHOR'S CONTRIBUTION

In Chapter 3, **Anita Tanwar** was solely responsible for the conceptualization, research, and writing of the chapter. Anita Tanwar conducted an in-depth exploration of blockchain technology applications in healthcare, focusing on challenges such as data security, interoperability, and patient privacy. She examined blockchain's potential to transform healthcare through decentralized data management, secure patient information sharing, and integration with electronic health records. Additionally, she reviewed various blockchain versions and their relevance to healthcare and analyzed challenges specific to healthcare data privacy and accessibility. Anita also identified key user needs for blockchain technology in healthcare and evaluated its potential benefits and limitations through comprehensive literature and case studies.

REFERENCES

[1]   Wright CS. Bitcoin: a peer-to-peer electronic cash system. SSRN Electron J 2008; 3440802.

[2]   Iansiti M, Lakhani KR. The truth about blockchain. Harv Bus Rev 2017; 95(1): 118-27.

[3]   Buterin V. A next-generation smart contract and decentralized application platform. White Paper 2014; 3(37): 2-1.

[4]   McFarlane TD, Dixon BE, Grannis SJ. Client registries: identifying and linking patients. Health information exchange. Academic Press 2016; pp. 163-82.
        [http://dx.doi.org/10.1016/B978-0-12-803135-3.00011-6]

[5]   Andrew Onesimu J, Karthikeyan J. An efficient privacy-preserving deep learning scheme for medical image analysis. J Inf Technol Manag. Special Issue: The Importance of Human Computer Interaction: Challenges, Methods and Applications 2020; 12: pp. 50-67.

[6]   Suzuki S, Murai J. Blockchain as an audit-able communication channel. 2017 IEEE 41st Annual Computer Software and Applications Conference (COMPSAC). 2017 Jul 4-8; Turin, Italy: IEEE 516-22.
        [http://dx.doi.org/10.1109/COMPSAC.2017.63]

[7]   Xu JJ. Are blockchains immune to all malicious attacks?. Financ Innov 2016; 2(1): 25.
        [http://dx.doi.org/10.1186/s40854-016-0046-5]

[8]   Vithanwattana N, Mapp G, George C. Investigating an information security framework for mhealth
        data: Challenges and possible solutions. 2016 12th International Conference on Intelligent
        Environments (IE). London, UK. IEEE. 2016; pp. 258-61.
        [http://dx.doi.org/10.1109/IE.2016.40]

[9]   Andrew J, Karthikeyan J, Jebastin J. Privacy preserving big data publication on cloud using mondrian
        anonymization techniques and deep neural networks. 2019 5th International Conference on Advanced
        Computing & Communication Systems (ICACCS). Coimbatore, India. IEEE. 2019; pp. 722-7.
        [http://dx.doi.org/10.1109/ICACCS.2019.8728384]

[10]   Andrew J, Mathew SS, Mohit B. A comprehensive analysis of privacy-preserving techniques in deep
        learning-based disease prediction systems. J Phys Conf Ser 2019; 1362(1): 012070.
        [http://dx.doi.org/10.1088/1742-6596/1362/1/012070]

[11]   Onesimu JA, Karthikeyan J, Sei Y. An efficient clustering-based anonymization scheme for privacy-
        preserving data collection in IoT based healthcare services. Peer-to-Peer Netw Appl 2021; 14(3):
        1629-49.
        [http://dx.doi.org/10.1007/s12083-021-01077-7]

[12]   Azaria A, Ekblaw A, Vieira T, Lippman A. MedRec: Using blockchain for medical data access and
        permission management. 2016 2nd International Conference on Open and Big Data (OBD). Vienna,
        Austria. IEEE. 2016; pp. 25-30.
        [http://dx.doi.org/10.1109/OBD.2016.11]

[13]   Tseng JH, Liao YC, Chong B, Liao S. Governance on the drug supply chain *via* gcoin blockchain. Int
        J Environ Res Public Health 2018; 15(6): 1055.
        [http://dx.doi.org/10.3390/ijerph15061055] [PMID: 29882861]

[14]   Rohr CS, Vinette SA, Parsons KAL, *et al.* Functional connectivity of the dorsal attention network
        predicts selective attention in 4–7 year-old girls. Cereb Cortex 2017; 27(9): 4350-60.
        [http://dx.doi.org/10.1093/cercor/bhw267] [PMID: 27522072]

[15]   Sun J, Ren L, Wang S, Yao X. A blockchain-based framework for electronic medical records sharing
        with fine-grained access control. PLoS One 2020; 15(10): e0239946.
        [http://dx.doi.org/10.1371/journal.pone.0239946] [PMID: 33022027]

[16]   Xiang X, Zhao X. Blockchain-assisted searchable attribute-based encryption for e-health systems. J
        Systems Archit 2022; 124: 102417.
        [http://dx.doi.org/10.1016/j.sysarc.2022.102417]

[17]   Zhang P, Schmidt DC, White J, Lenz G. Blockchain technology use cases in healthcare. In: Zelkowitz
        MV, Ed. Advances in computers. London: Elsevier 2018; 111: pp. 1-41.
        [http://dx.doi.org/10.1016/bs.adcom.2018.03.006]

[18]   Zhang G, Yang Z, Liu W. Blockchain-based privacy preserving e-health system for healthcare data in
        cloud. Comput Netw 2022; 203: 108586.
        [http://dx.doi.org/10.1016/j.comnet.2021.108586]

[19]   Wutthikarn R, Hui YG. Prototype of blockchain in dental care service application based on
        hyperledger composer in hyperledger fabric framework. 2018 22nd International Computer Science
        and Engineering Conference (ICSEC). Chiang Mai, Thailand. IEEE. 2018; pp. 1-4.
        [http://dx.doi.org/10.1109/ICSEC.2018.8712639]

[20]   Vora J, Tanwar S, Tyagi S, Kumar N, Rodrigues JJ. Home-based exercise system for patients using
        IoT enabled smart speaker. 2017 IEEE 19th International Conference on e-Health Networking,
        Applications and Services (Healthcom) 2017; 1-6.
        [http://dx.doi.org/10.1109/HealthCom.2017.8210826]

[21]   Enescu FM, Bizon N, Cirstea A, Stirbu C. Blockchain technology applied in health: the study of

blockchain application in the health system (I). 2018 10th International Conference on Electronics, Computers and Artificial Intelligence (ECAI). Bucharest, Romania. IEEE. 2018; pp. 1-4.
[http://dx.doi.org/10.1109/ECAI.2018.8678988]

[22]   Shahnaz A, Qamar U, Khalid A. Using blockchain for electronic health records. IEEE Access 2019; 7: 147782-95.
[http://dx.doi.org/10.1109/ACCESS.2019.2946373]

[23]   Musamih A, Salah K, Jayaraman R, *et al.* A blockchain-based approach for drug traceability in healthcare supply chain. IEEE Access 2021; 9: 9728-43.
[http://dx.doi.org/10.1109/ACCESS.2021.3049920]

[24]   Kombe C, Dida M, Sam A. A review on healthcare information systems and consensus protocols in blockchain technology. Int J Med Inform 2018; 5(1): 18-27.

[25]   Jahankhani H, Kendzierskyj S. The role of blockchain in underpinning mission critical infrastructure. In: Abraham A, Bajaj A, Hanne T, Siarry P, Eds. Industry 40 and engineering for a sustainable future. Cham: Springer 2019; pp. 191-210.
[http://dx.doi.org/10.1007/978-3-030-12953-8_12]

[26]   Omar IA, Jayaraman R, Salah K, Yaqoob I, Ellahham S. Applications of blockchain technology in clinical trials: review and open challenges. Arab J Sci Eng 2021; 46(4): 3001-15.
[http://dx.doi.org/10.1007/s13369-020-04989-3]

[27]   Jafri R, Singh S. Blockchain applications for the healthcare sector: uses beyond Bitcoin. Blockchain applications for healthcare informatics. Academic Press 2022; pp. 71-92.
[http://dx.doi.org/10.1016/B978-0-323-90615-9.00022-0]

[28]   Chakraborty S, Aich S, Kim HC. A secure healthcare system design framework using blockchain technology. 2019 21st International Conference on Advanced Communication Technology (ICACT). PyeongChang, Korea. IEEE. 2019; pp. 260-4.
[http://dx.doi.org/10.23919/ICACT.2019.8701983]

[29]   Reyna A, Martín C, Chen J, Soler E, Díaz M. On blockchain and its integration with IoT. Challenges and opportunities. Future Gener Comput Syst 2018; 88: 173-90.
[http://dx.doi.org/10.1016/j.future.2018.05.046]

[30]   Raikwar M, Gligoroski D, Kralevska K. SoK of used cryptography in blockchain IEEE 2019; 7: 148550-75.
[http://dx.doi.org/10.1109/ACCESS.2019.2946983]

[31]   Kapoor A, Guha S, Kanti Das M, Goswami KC, Yadav R. Digital healthcare: The only solution for better healthcare during COVID-19 pandemic?. Indian Heart J 2020; 72(2): 61-4.
[http://dx.doi.org/10.1016/j.ihj.2020.04.001] [PMID: 32534691]

[32]   Malhan S, Tanwar A, Kaur M, *et al.* Integrating artificial intelligence and data analytics for enhanced healthcare management: innovations and challenges. In: Abraham A, Bajaj A, Hanne T, Siarry P, Eds. Intelligent systems design and applications Lecture Notes in Networks and Systems. Cham: Springer 2024; 1046.
[http://dx.doi.org/10.1007/978-3-031-64813-7_4]

[33]   Verma B, Tandon U. Modelling barriers to wearable technologies in Indian context: validating the moderating role of technology literacy. Global Knowledge, Memory and Communication 2024; 73(6/7): 984-1004.
[http://dx.doi.org/10.1108/GKMC-08-2022-0209]

[34]   Kaushal RK, Kumar N, Panda SN, Kukreja V. Immutable smart contracts on blockchain technology: Its benefits and barriers. 2021 9th International Conference on Reliability, Infocom Technologies and Optimization (Trends and Future Directions) (ICRITO). Noida, India. IEEE. 2021; pp. 1-5.
[http://dx.doi.org/10.1109/ICRITO51393.2021.9596538]

CHAPTER 4

The Application of Blockchain Technology in Medical Credential Verification and Fraud Prevention

Prabh Deep Singh[1], Riya Sharma[2,*], Kiran Deep Singh[3] and **Meenakshi Mandola[1]**

[1] *Department of Computer Science and Engineering, Graphic Era Deemed to be University, Dehradun, Uttarakhand, India*

[2] *Department of Commerce, Graphic Era Deemed to be University, Dehradun, Uttarakhand, India*

[3] *Department of Computer Science and Engineering, Chitkara University Institute of Engineering and Technology, Rajpura, Punjab, India*

Abstract: Blockchain technology is an innovative concept in the financial and computer fields. In view of medical treatment, medical information, and the authenticity of medical staff, it involves the vital interests of the personal and financial security of every patient diagnosed and treated in a medical institution. By sorting out the relevant research at the institutional level, it is found that blockchain technology has not yet been established as an industry standard, and there is significant room for development in the medical industry. Based on the advantages of advanced technology, the introduction of relevant application performance of blockchain technology in the latter part of this paper expounds the method and process of medical staff credential verification and medical fraud prevention. This chapter is based on the blockchain technology of avoiding the inconvenience, long time, and high cost of medical staff qualification review in a traditional management method with the advantages of tamper resistance, traceability, sharing, privacy protection, and new auxiliary to improve the traditional cross-independent credential verification mode. It further provides a method for preventing fraud in the cross independent medical diagnosis and treatment process. The significance of this research is to enhance the intelligent and digital level of medical management and increase the confidence of management decisions at the utmost. Finally, the conclusion and prospect are drawn, and at the same time, the application of blockchain technology in the field of transaction settlement, clearing, and other basic application fields is prospected.

Keywords: Auditing, Blockchain, Drug abuse, Efficient employment, Fraud prevention, Healthcare, Medical ID theft, Medical credential, Non-repudiation.

* **Corresponding author Riya Sharma:** Department of Commerce, Graphic Era Deemed to be University, Dehradun, Uttarakhand, India;
E-mail: riyasharma6568@gmail.com

Mohit Angurala, Preet Kamal, Aryan Chaudhary, Rasmeet Singh Bali & Vijay Bhardwaj (Eds.)
All rights reserved-© 2025 Bentham Science Publishers

INTRODUCTION

In the emerging digital economy, e-commerce transactions, electronic document signing, and online voting have become popular applications over the internet. Trust in the Internet has become a concern, especially in electronic business and transactions. In general, users seek secure systems in which to conduct their online transactions. The use of blockchain technology (BCT) can satisfy these needs. Currently, it has been actively applied in finance, supply chain, Internet of Things, energy, and other sectors. However, security issues of personal data have attracted much attention from the public. Medical personnel may provide fake diplomas or practice without certification. Patients can be harmed if they are treated by these unaccredited personnel. To prevent these problems, the verification of medical personnel should be established. Therefore, this research applies BCT to protect the personal data of certified medical personnel from being hacked and enables secure access to this data. In addition, when lying about diplomas to medical organizations or insurance companies to get paid, individuals with the wrong data can be verified quickly. The blurry coalition by threshold secret sharing (BCTSS) technology is applied to protect the diploma patient's decryption condition access structure key. The access control and authority flow are also utilized to manage the personnel's credentials. Finally, we propose a smart contract for rapid medical-credential verification. The proposed system enhances the security of the diploma, as shown by the experimental results. It prevents anyone from holding all decrypted data, and only the required number of appointed members can decrypt the data.

Definition and Key Concepts

Blockchain is a particular type of distributed ledger technology (DLT). Specifically, it refers to a shared, replicated, permissioned, append-only digital ledger that is secured by cryptography. Organizations use it as a tool for creating a database or ledger shared across multiple entities. Information is held in the ledger in packages known as blocks. Each block holds a set of data, and all are identified by a unique cryptographic identifier that links it to the previous block, creating the chain [1]. Information is publicly available, and no single entity controls the chain or data. Data is confirmed by consensus, meaning that all entities within the blockchain must approve data entries, preventing a single actor from introducing incorrect or fraudulent data. This makes blockchain information stored therein extremely difficult to tamper with and effortless to use. The range of potential applications for blockchain is considered significant [2]. Healthcare has been established as a plausible use platform for blockchain, offering many groundbreaking advantages such as a solution to mitigate disjointed patient data and maintaining accurate records for protection [3]. Since pharmaceuticals and medical devices are prone to and at risk of counterfeiting, blockchain can portray a mechanism to reduce the incidence rate and the negative effects of counterfeiting. Blockchain can be interestingly used to handle exclusive medical credential verification and avoid duplicate medical imaging datasets in this realm. Blockchain will be a possible platform for the validation of medical certification, prevention of fraud, and the abolition of duplication of radiological imaging datasets. The opportunities and challenges in the coupling of blockchain in the personalized medicine system are also discussed in this paper.

Fig. (**1**) represents the architecture of a blockchain-based healthcare credential verification system. The user interface and healthcare institutions interact with the blockchain network, which includes a smart contract layer. This layer manages the credential storage, verification, and access control modules, ensuring secure and compliant verification of healthcare credentials.

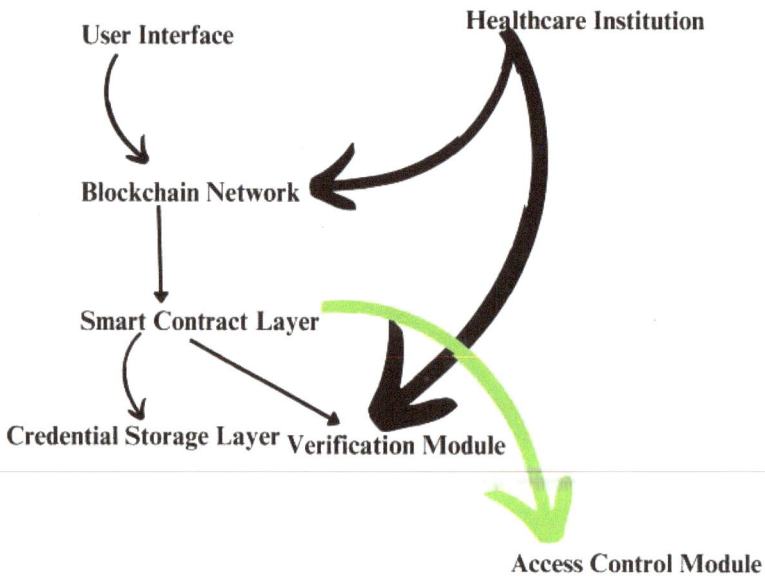

Fig. (1). Blockchain-based healthcare credential verification architecture.

BASIC PRINCIPLES AND FUNCTIONALITY

The basic concept is to create a distributed ledger through a network that operates under a certain consensus algorithm. This chain of blocks is ever-increasing, which directly solves the problem of single points of failure. Each new block contains within itself a reference to the previous block, creating a timeline through the blocks. Importantly, establishing consistency and integrity of data is the responsibility of multiple parties, rendering it difficult to alter any data once it has been included in the chain. The process of adding data to the blockchain is done by performing a study, also known as mining or logging. Not every participant on the network can log data on the blockchain; for some algorithms, only a single log is included within the blockchain. Once a study has been logged and the data has entered the blockchain, the owner of the study is awarded a certain number of cryptocurrency coins. This incentive of receiving coins is designed as compensation to the participants for the effort and energy spent in the logging process. In essence, a blockchain is a mechanism of coordination that provides standardization in a decentralized context. It ensures that everyone has the same data or at least has the guarantee that the data is immutable [4]. Moreover, it strengthens trust as it is not achievable to edit the previous result without modifying all subsequent ones. On top of these benefits, blockchain technology has the potential to make the need for centralized bodies in many industries unnecessary. This is typically worth exploring in a space in which several stakeholders need to share resources or authenticate the genuineness and integrity of the blockchain data. Indeed, many different blockchain applications are already in their initial state of development and have explored various use aspects in various industry domains.

CURRENT CHALLENGES IN MEDICAL CREDENTIAL VERIFICATION

One of the grave issues in the medical service arena is the number of falsified healthcare professionals, which increases administrative and financial burdens. Currently, most of the medical credentials rely on records that are held by the medical institution. During the process of obtaining a physician credential, the hospital may not be able to fully verify an applicant's background, such as the previous working experience, degree earned, or discipline supervised. For instance, it is common to have a fake letter of appointment or practice certificate. Fraudulent claims of practicing medicine have led to severe detriment to individual patients and sometimes caused public health crises [5]. In addition, medical institutions bear the risk of appointing someone using false credentials. They spend a considerable amount during the recruitment process as various credential screening tests might be needed, especially for some graduates from foreign countries. This process is cumbersome, time-consuming, and repetitive to a certain extent, with no references to confirm the integral information. Therefore, there is a need for a secure, generically applicable, and efficient verification mechanism for medical credentials to establish trust between organizations that seek qualified healthcare professionals. To ensure that only qualified healthcare professionals are being hired, the U.S. Centers for Medicare and Medicaid Services (CMS) have a requirement that hospitals complete the credentialing and privileging process in order to be eligible for reimbursement. The credentialing process for a practicing physician at the hospital can be very lengthy and complex. The credentialing process involves many verifications, such as recruits' educational background, specified training and skill, professional license, and medical malpractice history [6]. With advances in technology and other changes in healthcare fields, in the future, the healthcare system needs the ability to quickly access the credentials and qualifications of any healthcare worker at any time and in any location. Independent credential service companies who verify this data have been brought in to help other institutions or those who do not have a credentialing committee of rules for verification. However, these companies also rely on the documentation provided by individuals to verify qualifications.

Fig. (**2**) outlines the process of medical credential verification using blockchain technology. A medical professional submits their credential, which is stored encrypted on the blockchain. A smart contract validates the credential through the verification module, which then sends a verification response to the healthcare institution upon request.

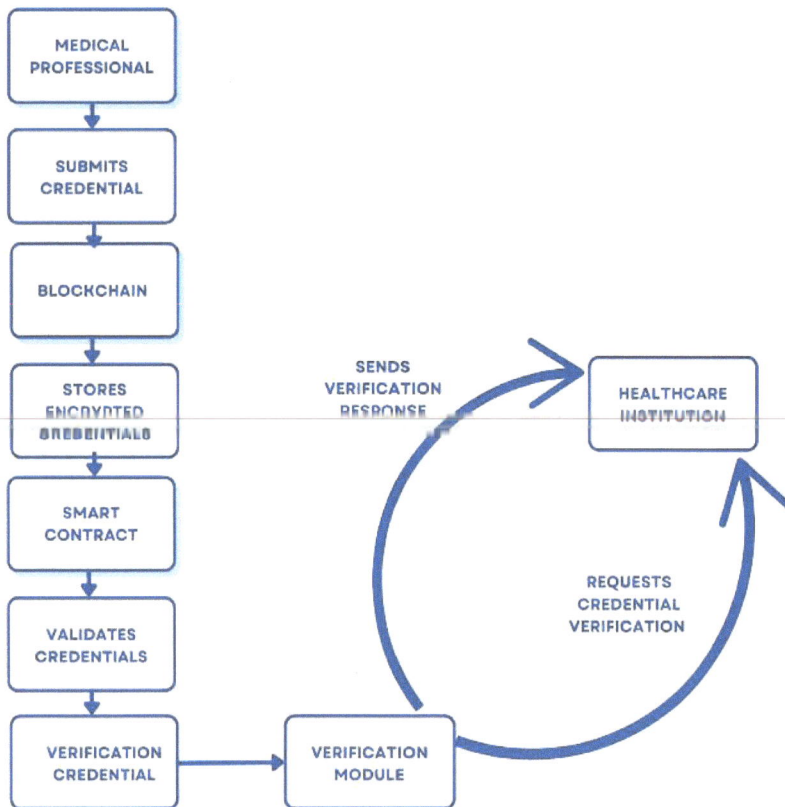

Fig. (2). Medical credential verification process.

Issues with Traditional Systems

Traditional credentialing methods, such as closed databases, paper certificates, and transaction verification schemes, are expensive to manage and highly susceptible to security threats. Higher education credentials are commonly verified using credential-issuing institutions [7]. However, medical education credentialing, which includes all the academic attainments necessary to become a licensed physician—premedical, medical school, and postgraduate training—is more complex and heavily influenced by the government *via* medical education accreditation. The recognition of a medical school's accreditation is the most crucial component in determining whether a physician completed post-secondary competence in medical school to treat patients in the U.S. This determines whether the medical school awarding the physician's diploma is recognized as an educational institution, which in turn can be crucial for licensure. Closed lists or open networks that are either religious or state-operated may be, in some cases, used to verify a medical school's accreditation but can have significant limitations and are occasionally slow to use.

Risks of Credential Fraud

There are three core categories of irregularities, which include medical expertise, professional ability and identity, and others. In medical expertise certification, practitioners often obtain multiple licenses and work across local jurisdictions. Given the frequent lack of trust between regional licensing bodies, many medical personnel are not punished or restricted by any means for medical errors. For industrial medical boards, large discrepancies exist in their evaluation standards, leading to the easy granting of licenses. In addition, some medical staff offer on-the-job training for medical examinations and help unreliable personnel pass various levels of licensing examinations in exchange for money [8]. This unlawful behavior can cause lasting problems, including the failure to acquire the same minimum competence for regaining personal health. There is also the problem of insufficient medical ethics. Unlicensed trainers sometimes have a moral disorder and record bribes in the form of inconsistent or counterfeited examination score certificates to facilitate a green channel for the recipient to pass the examination. The staff are not aware of the significance that saving lives and alleviating physical injury pose. As regards professional level and identity certification, some permanent tasks have a high chance of taking patients' lives or causing severe damage to their health. However, in the field of various types of staffing, certification boards decide to issue temporary certificates to non-qualified workers because they are debilitated by inactivity and do not provide a formal evaluation of these individuals. Also, many people use a counterfeit license for a short-term mission to an unknown ministry or organization. Once an accident occurs or differences are found, the fraudulent activities are impossible to track. The law regarding the use of guilty or invalid credentials is applied differently in different nations. In the third category, personnel certification creates a safety hazard, such as allowing unoccupied areas to be filled with zero allowance workers [9]. At this phase, customary strategies for dealing with counterfeit credentials consist of developing unified and regular operational systems and rules shared by different medical examination bodies. To construct decision-making and liaison boards of medical assessment organizations, the conventional verification technique includes a division by category and a variation of expert examination qualification types.

BENEFITS OF USING BLOCKCHAIN IN MEDICAL CREDENTIAL VERIFICATION

Medical credential verification helps to confirm the qualifications of healthcare personnel, confirming the intention for employment and identity. Failure to verify these credentials can lead to major long-term consequences. However, current verification methods depend on third-party platforms that are vulnerable to attacks. Assuming the breach of the third parties' network, a fraudster can redirect legal access to verify assets on the fake resources. The fraudster can obtain employment fraudulently, steal lives, access personal financial records, prescribe opioid medication, steal insurance payments, and sell illegal medical schemes [10]. To ensure the integrity and credibility of medical and employment verification processes through the establishment of new and novel unilateral methods of access control in order to maintain the current lifecycle of trust, which can positively reduce personal and informational risks for the individual and keep the health, personal, and financial records accurate for the employer and patient, this paper discusses the likelihood of integrating blockchain technology into the industry of medical credential verification [11].

Enhanced Security and Privacy

The use of blockchain inherently provides a certain level of security through cryptography. Hashes of the data are safely kept not just on one computer but on many different computers at the same time. A hacker would have to compromise the data simultaneously in multiple locations to perpetrate a fraud. This is the key principle underpinning blockchain ledgers. In this regard, security has been enhanced through immutable data [12]. Permission schema that allows only authorized entities to access the data is often designed in addition to blockchain to effectively manage what information can be put into the blockchain and what entities can have access to the information. While blockchain helps enhance security, in some aspects, it weakens privacy. Every transaction is transparent, and every entity's history of healthcare data can potentially be traceable over time. People are concerned about unauthorized parties or even unauthorized healthcare providers accessing their healthcare information. Data on the blockchain can be pseudonymized through encryption [13]. A research prototype has been developed to encrypt health data with attribute-based encryption (ABE) and store the encrypted data on a private blockchain. Only the persons possessing the right key can access the data. Homomorphic encryption has also been implemented to allow the operation of the data that will only reveal the results and hinges on the security of the inputs. According to research, the privacy of the healthcare data stored on the blockchain is maintained, and the integrity of the data is also guaranteed [14].

Increased Efficiency and Transparency

The use of blockchain enables the verification process to be executed in an efficient and reliable manner, thus increasing the possibility of productive use and promoting a sense of trust among medical staff and patients. In blockchain, the data is in a never-ending form of ledger known as blocks, and it is immutable as it cannot be altered once the entire blockchain has been established. This means preventing counterfeit information with the assistance of blockchain becomes an effective solution. Both the usability and ability of blockchain technology can be beneficial due to the immutability and decentralized nature by ascertaining the honesty of the involved medical staff [15]. Patients can always look for a second opinion to ensure that every input of information is verified for an improved and quality outcome before a medical procedure is to take place. Patients will perceive a sense of trust in the registered medical staff, and they will acquire the opportunity to determine who would be the most suitable and experienced medical practitioner to diagnose their medical issues, as all data is added with a timestamp once the recruitment and verification processes have been authenticated. Despite the potential advantage offered by utilizing blockchain technology in the field of medical credential verification, the healthcare ecosystem is compelled to undertake a more open, secure, scalable, and cost-effective infrastructure rather than the outdated and insecure existing system in use. The apparent advantage offered by utilizing blockchain technology in the field of counter-contraction and veracity of verified medical credential information should be implemented to promote and improve the attractiveness of the healthcare system to a better standard of potential medical personnel. It is anticipated that with the current trend being identified, healthcare fraud as a result of medical personnel practicing with unverified information will eventually be reduced, and fraud prevention will save time, money, and lives.

CASE STUDIES OF BLOCKCHAIN IMPLEMENTATION IN HEALTH-CARE

Despite numerous opportunities for blockchain in healthcare, the number of cases of blockchain technology application in real life is few. The real-life implementation of blockchain in healthcare is mainly seen in two use categories: functional blockchain solutions developed by highly individual healthcare teams for specific services/functions in the healthcare sector (*e.g.*, record keeping, medication prescription/sharing, supply chain management, and provider directory) and pre-developed blockchain technology-supported specialized healthcare services provided by single suppliers (*e.g.*, telemedicine and medical credential verification) [16]. Blockchain technology does have great potential in healthcare. However, most of the use of blockchain in healthcare is still in its infancy stage. Successful blockchain implementation remains a challenge for many healthcare organizations. The path for an organization to move toward successful blockchain technology implementation imposes many challenges from each angle, including but not limited to technology advancement, system implementation, and personnel involvement [17]. Even today, the most important benefit of blockchain still lies in optimizing the business model through streamlining, standardizing, and automating. No matter what kind of project, especially healthcare organizations, need collaboration, accountability, and effort once the decision for blockchain technology has been made. According to previous studies, the following points should be paid attention to for a successful blockchain technology implementation [18].

Example 1: Project MediChain

Blockchain in healthcare is aimed at developing carrier solutions, which will allow keeping all medical data strictly confidential while maintaining the necessary availability for timely treatment. The basic concept comes down to protecting this data and ensuring the integrity and confidentiality of the channels of data access, primarily by transferring the electronic medical record (EMR) to the blockchain network Ledger. The philosophy behind the project and the following problems is: "Project MediChain develops a decentralized system registry, securing a repository of medical data with controlled access. The patient provides permission for their medical views by all or by certain doctors, hospitals, insurance companies, researchers, *etc.* This record should consist of laboratory tests, reactions, diagnostics, prescriptions, imaging, and operations, as well as time sequences of the patient's activity." Our personal motivation for this section is to provide examples of existing blockchain projects that are aimed at solving specific medical care problems and trying to apply blockchain in a new field. BaseModel (adopted by almost all the projects below) is block storage, which includes only a very simple function (usually just the ID Protection function) and a function of the blockchain digest on the block. Data transmission is also quite capital intensive, representing the gas release to retrieve recreational, work, alarm, and vibration spectral data (machine acoustic) processing under time.

Example 2: Medicalchain

Medicalchain, a London-based company, has created a blockchain for supporting a platform to use electronic health records, allowing users to manage their own health records and share medical records with doctors and other medical professionals, wherever they are in the world. Physicians will have an opportunity to use Medicalchain to promote telemedicine and second medical opinion services. Medicalchain is collaborating with the Estonian e-Health Foundation, one of the most advanced e-Health systems globally, and should offer secure access to their citizens' health records. The application of blockchain technology provides a modern solution to a contemporary challenge: the illegal or unauthorized practice of medicine. Medicalchain is developing a secure platform to keep physician credentials, storing a record of the points along the education and training timeline where questions about fake diplomas could be asked, answered, and verified. Physicians who would like to become Medicalchain users must be thoroughly checked. The storage of 'verified' diplomas for licensed professionals can become an essential part of the Medicalchain platform.

REGULATORY CONSIDERATIONS AND COMPLIANCE IN HEALTHCARE BLOCKCHAIN

As domestic and international standards and requirements continue to evolve, systems may need to be capable of adapting to changing circumstances. Some regulations with data privacy provisions enforce data minimization principles, so it is important that blockchain systems are designed to comply with them. It is crucial that developers of blockchain technology factor in data privacy and confidentiality controls to ensure that their systems can facilitate the transfer of healthcare data in compliance with the current legal landscape [19]. This can include selective disclosure mechanisms, where users can reveal the data needed to be revealed to comply with the legal requirement or a type of data control technique that ensures the data is handled in a privacy-preserving manner. Since some blockchain-based systems in healthcare intrinsically require the availability of patient health data and health claims data for validation, stakeholders within the consortium and those responsible for ensuring data privacy should be actively involved in standards and ethics decisions and discuss what type of arrangements need to be made. These can include the codification of standards, both ethical and technical, and putting in place appropriate processes on data minimization and data linkage. If any data were to be provided by external parties for these consortiums to successfully request the sensitive data required for these blockchain systems, trust between these stakeholders and the consortium may need to be established. This trust may also require insurance to be taken out against nefarious actions, smart contracts enshrining the expected behaviors and breaches of privacy, and perhaps even banking arrangements to ensure that there are no financial pressures on those with possession of sensitive data [20]. The governance of negotiation and collaboration with external parties as potential data providers needs to be established. This should include specifying the ethical boundaries that the consortium can use as a decision-making framework, in conjunction with caveats and principles with regard to what type of entities could be involved. This becomes particularly important as not all healthcare organizations are able to reproduce the IT infrastructures required to comply with expected regulations or data-sharing agreements, and the incentives may require parties to join based on multinational legal, socioeconomic, and business models.

HIPAA and Data Protection Regulations

The Health Insurance Portability and Accountability Act (HIPAA), a data protection act in the United States, provides certain protections for appropriate electronic security of patients' personal health information (PHI) [21]. It also provides national companies covered by HIPAA that certain individuals must be permitted to request copies of their records of their digital health. Patients with limited exceptions and political interest in the organization have a duty to give access. Personal health information includes several data types, like clinical notes, lab outcomes, and billing data, since a lot of healthcare data tends to be private at the time of creation. Since the requisite important health information in patients' records is of such relevance, an extensive trade in private health information may exist [22]. Complete insurance in the US is combined with consideration of obtaining appropriate health advantages. Those trying to satisfy this regulatory prerequisite might quickly get access to exclusive health details of the entrepreneur's friends, who can be used to gain native benefits. Patients, friends, and even others in the contractors' electronic health records easily access this information [23]. Since requests are being made through privacy official applications, the friends of the employee do not search for them to trigger red flags or give the contact information for notification of such requests so they can manage the procedure on their health documents [24].

Legal Implications of Blockchain Use

The goal of credential verification in healthcare is to ensure that the medical staff is who they claim to be and to determine their current employment status and the nature of their relationship with the healthcare organization. Proper staff credentialing is a key enabler for accurate and safe patient care. Employers from the healthcare sector, such as hospitals, pharmacies, or ambulatory care clinics, must establish procedures for proper credential verification and maintenance of staff members' records of qualifications and competence. It is of paramount importance for every healthcare institution that their staff have recognized and qualified education and skills to ensure an appropriate level of quality for medical processes and patient care. Unfortunately, the verification process is commonly described as paper-based and is open to diverse types of fraud, therefore increasing the risk of misidentification errors or defensive medicine, where physicians pay too much attention to rules and regulations rather than the actual care of the patient. Currently existing systems and standards do not comply with or connect staff qualifications with the actual medical services provided or the achievement of successful medical practice. Such a system affects healthcare cost savings and the safety of patient care. The relevant professional qualifications reflect the level of advanced and specialized skills required to perform specialized medical procedures in regulated settings [25]. Further, satisfactory status and performance in previous work positions and satisfactory background checks confirm the staff member's suitability for the role and ongoing and regular background checks designed to identify staff with a history of alcohol or substance abuse, felony charges, or unethical conduct.

FUTURE TRENDS AND INNOVATIONS IN BLOCKCHAIN FOR HEALTHCARE

Current healthcare largely depends on intermediaries for data maintenance and validation. However, intermediaries bring their limitations in areas such as authentication and security of access, privacy protection, emergency centralization of data management, and extra cost. The blockchain technology may provide alternative solutions for these problems. In the healthcare context, the transaction record structures of blockchain can be used to hold reliable patient data. The security and decentralization of blockchain transactions enhance personal health information (PHI) protection.

Integration with AI and IoT Technologies

The reputation system can be constructed as well. As proposed in our previous work, the certificates of AI devices can be used for reference. Everyone who investigates AI models working in the medical area and has data of validation quality should be included in the certificate [26]. The higher the area and data quality of the model, the higher the reputation will be. All kinds of fraud, including the exchange of license numbers of the model between doctors, copying of doctor settings, or copying of specialized training quality certificates, can be easily detected and questioned if the doctor will be significantly more successful in treating patients than other doctors, indicating a high performance of his AI tools in comparison to other colleagues. Premium certificates can be used as recommendations on a high privacy level, and patients willing to exchange their data should do it only with these doctor AI services [27]. This concept can be combined with the applications from the above section. It can be realized by using smart contracts of Blockchain 3.0 like EOS, TRON, or Komodo. Trust in interacting AI devices is a difficult task that is already being tried to solve in the frame of the delegated training approach when the data is taken from different sources performing different tasks and then sent for the training of the model in an enclave. The smart contract of the fourth type can be used to delegate the work of analyzing secure data on the Core Network Node located inside AI on different devices. The certificate with the public key of this Core Network Node and the smart contract providing an AI service can be added to the blockchain as recommendations to use this AI service [28].

Scalability and Interoperability Solutions

Scalability is the biggest challenge facing current popular blockchains, even after the upgrade of Ethereum 2.0. Without sharding, Ethereum remains the most popular blockchain platform in the public domain, and its scalability is affected by the so-called scalability trilemma [29]. Different designs can prioritize any of the three but cannot provide all three at the same time. As a platform for medical data and services, the scalability problem limits the ability of blockchain. First and foremost, a growing number of participants and forks of the Ethereum blockchain help the platform process data transfer of a total size of 300GB as of Q3 2020. For medical IoT applications in a hospital, the ~45K TPS (transmission capacity) currently is still not enough. Heavy data work linked with more complex and reliable services and demand for tamper-resistant systems has warned us for years that fighting for zero-knowledge and supporting multi-functions are expensive, with high complexity, high hardware cost, and huge data transferred among trust parties [30]. Second, as introduced recently, the healthcare information system would localize with several closed healthcare blockchain networks due to the long confidentiality policy, which is an instance of heavy data work and high-cost service. High system latency, low failure, and waiting times much longer than the operation time would limit the further performance improvement of healthcare automation and robot-guided surgery. Third, an indirect scalability limitation comes from the energy cost in Blockchain and related P2P, which might affect the regulatory environment and technology application [31].

Blockchain technology has transformed many fields, including healthcare and pharmaceuticals. Using the inherent characteristics of blockchain-immutability, transparency, and decentralization-addresses long-standing problems, such as inefficiency in credential verification, safe patient data sharing, and preventing counterfeits in pharmaceutical supply chains. Further below, it details the applications and explores performance metrics, the process of implementation, and real-world outcomes.

Medical Credential Verification

Verifying medical credentials speedily and securely is considered to be one of the essential challenges in the healthcare industry. This would ensure patient safety and confidence and minimize fraudulent activities by being valid. The blockchain will enable tamper-proof credentials from healthcare providers.

Implementation Process

Blockchain-based credentials verification systems, like Medicalchain, enable health institutions to upload verified professional credentials of healthcare professionals in a blockchain ledger. Once encrypted and hashed, credentials become immutable and secure on the blockchain. Smart contracts automate the verification process with the system. If there is a need to verify a credential by a third party, such as an employer or regulatory body, then the smart contract will check for authenticity by cross-referencing the encrypted data on the blockchain. It thereby eliminates the requirement of an intermediary and saves administrative overhead.

Performance Metrics

Verification Time Reduced: According to research, blockchain-enabled credential systems can reduce the verification time for credentials by up to 50% [32].

Error Reduction: Blockchains have reduced administrative errors during credential validation processes to a certain level with their implementation [33].

Fraud Prevention: The cases of credential fraud have decreased by over 50% since records on the blockchain cannot be altered [34].

Real-World Outcomes

Such implementations of blockchain-based credential verification systems have exhibited significant outcomes. For instance, with a blockchain-enabled credentialing platform named ProCredEx, it now takes several hours for healthcare professionals to onboard in contrast to being onboarded for weeks previously. These developments have, therefore, led to speedy staff deployments in critical care areas while building trust in the patient and healthcare providers. Since the legitimacy of professionals is guaranteed, this contributes towards improved compliance with regulatory standards and the betterment of the patients.

CONCLUSION AND IMPLICATIONS FOR THE HEALTHCARE INDUSTRY

The healthcare industry is experiencing changes that require the adaptation of different stakeholders within it. While the popular focus is on cutting outside costs and improving the connectivity of the various stakeholders and other areas, the industry also needs solutions to improve operating efficiency and provide secure solutions for a new digital age. Transitioning from a paper-based system will significantly reduce the time taken to perform several, mostly administrative tasks, as well as reduce the temporal window for fraudulent activity to occur. Relying on certification issuers to confirm the authenticity of the documents submitted for validation is not a long-term solution. Blockchain technology provides a secure solution that has the potential to be the technology that the healthcare industry can rely on to provide secure medical credential verification in a manner that respects the privacy rights of the individuals whose documents are being verified. The collection of bad actors that will inevitably arise to take advantage of any new service, system, or process represents a significant threat to the medical credential verification process that is only going to increase over time if not controlled. Variation (delay due to limited range of original authorization), intentional misrepresentations of fact, and escalation across providers, which makes it more costly to perform medical credential verifications, all combine with the qualitative value to influence whether the overall verification systems are feasible to rely upon and budget for. Blockchain technology integrated with a personalized IDaaS-based solution can significantly reduce both the time to complete these necessary directives and reduce the false positive results providers receive when confirming credentials while improving security.

SUMMARY OF KEY FINDINGS

The number of blockchain research papers on medical credential verification and data access control is minuscule, highlighting the unfulfilled promise of blockchain technologies in this domain. The medical community widely agrees with this and has begun implementing pilot projects in practicing departments to explore the use of blockchain within the medical facility. The possible use cases and solutions have been outlined, with most literature focusing on expediting verification times and authenticating the true owner of medical records during data access. Most medical blockchain projects are in the proof-of-concept stage, and much work will need to be undertaken to encourage mass adoption from hospitals and a proliferation of blockchain applications within this industry. A potential problem that needs to be addressed is the central authority used to create digital IDs and validate true ownership of PII. As the role of new actors within the existing healthcare structure is questioned, the interest in valuing 'true ownership' through KYC standards and anchors that are utilized within health-related digital transformation plans will initiate partnerships that expand the extended reality of identities to anchor customers' existing identity in the collective environment. The majority of these papers do not deal with issues like the governance of the blockchain, and discussions on liability and compensation allocation in the event of patients' PII leaks and their resulting damage are also absent. This glaring omission is mostly glossed over or ignored in current research, where privacy and data security have been heatedly debated and discussed within the literature community for the past decade. Additionally, the issue of onboarding users has not been properly addressed. Developing a solution that reduces the identification workload at the onboarding phase is crucial in popularizing and scaling its use.

RECOMMENDATIONS FOR ADOPTION AND IMPLEMENTATION

Blockchain technology can play an integral role in decentralized medical credentialing. Its use can allow the establishment of a permanent, public record of a practitioner's certifications, which can be easily updated in real time. This system can also augment audit capabilities and provide a way to reduce the incidence of accidental or overt fraud. After reviewing the various types of blockchains, digital wallet technology, and various options for implementation, we provide a concrete methodology using Hyperledger Fabric to establish a blockchain network for the purpose of decentralized medical credentialing. We also examine how such an implementation would be received by patients and medical practitioners and present potential drawbacks and limitations of this system. For such a system to be implemented, we found that the blockchain should be a private/permissioned blockchain, that it is feasible and cost-effective to have various institutions hosting AAA server nodes, and that each user should control his/her own lightweight digital wallet with controlling access node(s) being operated by the practitioner and potentially others sharing the nature of the medical credential being used as well as patients requiring access to such credentialing information. The system has some potential limitations. Its cost-effectiveness assumes that hosting AAA nodes will not be expensive in terms of money or infrastructure. Cost-effectiveness is also reliant on an institution's desire to go through the implementation process as well as to share its stored medical credentialing data. The level of participation in this network is likely to be location-dependent, as not all practitioners, especially private practice providers or those who work in non-institutional settings, will have sufficient incentives or resources to join. The assumption that the use of this blockchain can help in reducing cases of careless or fraudulent issuance of medical credentials must be further researched and tested in diverse and real hospital settings. We also do not consider how much it may cost the patient to access the medical credential information stored on the blockchain *via* their digital wallet. We support some privacy considerations with respect to storing medical credentialing information, but more research is needed to establish whether a clearer and more practical guideline or incentive for practitioners and healthcare institutions may be necessary. Overall, however, harnessing blockchain technology has the potential to reinvent the way in which medical credentials are currently issued and shared by hospital, clinic providers, and their patients. Providing more uniform access to this information can be a major and impactful step in improving transparency within hospitals and clinics and more trust in the healthcare system.

AUTHORS' CONTRIBUTION

In Chapter 4, the co-authors **Prabh Deep Singh, Riya Sharma, Kiran Deep Singh,** and **Meenakshi Mandola** collaborated to explore the application of blockchain technology for medical credential verification and fraud prevention. **Prabh Deep Singh** focused on conceptualization and foundational research, covering blockchain technology's relevance to credential verification. **Riya Sharma** led the examination of challenges in traditional credential verification methods and the potential benefits of blockchain solutions. **Kiran Deep Singh** contributed to the analysis of real-world applications, particularly case studies that demonstrate blockchain's potential in the healthcare sector. **Meenakshi Mandola** reviewed regulatory considerations and compliance, addressing legal and ethical issues related to blockchain in healthcare. Together, the authors provided insights into future trends, including blockchain integration with AI and IoT technologies, as well as recommendations for implementation in healthcare systems.

REFERENCES

[1]   Singhal B, Dhameja G, Panda P. Introduction to blockchain. Blockchain applications. Springer 2018. Available from: https://link.springer.com/chapter/10.1007/978-1-4842-3444-0_1
[http://dx.doi.org/10.1007/978-1-4842-3444-0_1]

[2]   Haleem A, Javaid M, Singh R. Blockchain technology applications in healthcare: an overview. J Innov Health 2021. Available from: https://www.sciencedirect.com/science/article/pii/S266660302100021X

[3]   Halpin H. Introduction to security and privacy on the blockchain. 2017 IEEE Symposium on Security and Privacy 2017. Available from: https://ieeexplore.ieee.org/abstract/document/7966963
[http://dx.doi.org/10.1109/EuroSPW.2017.43]

[4]   Radanović I, Likić R. Opportunities for use of blockchain technology in medicine. Appl Health Econ Health Policy 2018; 16(5): 583-90.
[http://dx.doi.org/10.1007/s40258-018-0412-8] [PMID: 30022440]

[5]   Namasudra S, Sharma P. Blockchain-based medical certificate generation and verification for IoT-based healthcare systems. 2022 Int Conf Cloud Comput 2022. Available from: https://ieeexplore.ieee.org/abstract/document/9669123

[6]   Haleem A, Javaid M, Singh RP, Suman R, Rab S. Blockchain technology applications in healthcare: An overview. Int J Intell Netw 2021; 2: 130-139.

[7]   Bittins S, Kober G, Margheri A, Masi M. Healthcare data management by using blockchain technology. Blockchain for healthcare. Springer 2021.
[http://dx.doi.org/10.1007/978-981-15-9547-9_1]

[8]   Arenas R. CredenceLedger: a permissioned blockchain for verifiable academic credentials. In: 2018 International Conference on Emerging Technologies 2018. Available from: https://ieeexplore.ieee.org/abstract/document/8436324
[http://dx.doi.org/10.1109/ICE.2018.8436324]

[9]   Harrell D, Usman M. Technical design and development of a self-sovereign identity management platform for patient-centric healthcare using blockchain technology. J Innov Health 2022. Available from: https://www.ncbi.nlm.nih.gov/pmc/articles/PMC9907400

[10]   Ghazali O. A graduation certificate verification model *via* utilization of the blockchain technology. Telecomm J 2018. Available from: https://jtec.utem.edu.my/jtec/article/view/4707

[11]   Reddy TR, Reddy PP. Proposing a reliable method of securing and verifying the credentials of graduates through blockchain. J Innov Health 2021. Available from: https://link.springer.com/article/10.1186/s13635-021-00122-5

[12]   Hossein K. Blockchain-based privacy-preserving healthcare architecture. 2019 IEEE International Conference on Cloud Computing 2019. Available from: https://ieeexplore.ieee.org/abstract/document/8861857/?casa_token=zkhZcEDMdmkAAAAA:xIw1Qhz6t54zSZScMO7RyG4iEf0yDtbLi L-726WpeRk_79kmcjUqHPWhYCVu_QdSFAAVPB-o
[http://dx.doi.org/10.1109/CCECE.2019.8861857]

[13]   El Majdoubi D, El Bakkali H, Sadki S. SmartMedChain: a blockchain-based privacy-preserving smart healthcare framework. J Healthc Eng 2021; 2021: 1-19.
[http://dx.doi.org/10.1155/2021/4145512] [PMID: 34777733]

[14]   Jiang Y, Wang C, Wang Y, Gao L. A privacy-preserving e-commerce system based on the blockchain technology. IWBOSE 2019 - 2019 IEEE 2nd International Workshop on Blockchain Oriented Software Engineering 2019; 50-5.
[http://dx.doi.org/10.1109/IWBOSE.2019.8666470]

[15]   Andrada G, Clowes RW, Smart PR. Varieties of transparency: exploring agency within AI systems. AI Soc 2022; 38(4): 1-11. Available from: https://link.springer.com/article/10.1007/s00146-021-01326-6
[PMID: 35035112]

[16]   Chang S. Blockchain in healthcare innovation: literature review and case study from a business ecosystem perspective. J Med Internet Res 2020. Available from: https://www.jmir.org/2020/8/e19480

[17]   Hussien H, Yasin S, Udzir N. Blockchain technology in the healthcare industry: trends and opportunities. J Innov Health 2021. Available from: https://www.sciencedirect.com/science/article/pii/S2452414X21000170

[18]   Ben Fekih R. Application of blockchain technology in healthcare: a comprehensive study. In: 2020 7th International Conference on Blockchain Technology 2020; 268-76.
[http://dx.doi.org/10.1007/978-3-030-51517-1_23]

[19]   Filatova N. Smart contracts from the contract law perspective: outlining new regulative strategies. Int J Law Inf Technol 2020; 28(3): 217-42.
[http://dx.doi.org/10.1093/ijlit/eaaa015]

[20]   Institute KD. Case studies on the regulatory challenges raised by innovation and the regulatory responses. Regulatory Studies in Tech Innovation 2021; 3-30. Available from: https://books.google.com/books?hl=en&lr=&id=XpJUEAAAQBAJ&oi=fnd&pg=PA3

[21]   Exploring the intersection of HIPAA compliance and blockchain technology in health information

systems. 2024 IEEE Conference on Health IT 2024. Available from: https://scholar.google.com/scholar?start=10&q=Exploring+the+Intersection+of+HIPAA+Compliance +and+Blockchain+Technology+in+Health+Information+Systems&hl=en&as_sdt=0,5

[22]   DeLeon C. Blockchain and the protection of patient information in line with HIPAA. Health IT Innovation. IGI Global 2021.
[http://dx.doi.org/10.4018/978-1-7998-5351-0.ch076]

[23]   Elkourdi F, Wei C, Xiao L. Exploring current practices and challenges of HIPAA compliance in software engineering: scoping review. 2024 IEEE International Conference on Software Engineering 2024. Available from: https://ieeexplore.ieee.org/abstract/document/10506964/
[http://dx.doi.org/10.1109/OJSE.2024.3392691]

[24]   Ettaloui N, Arezki S. An overview of blockchain-based electronic health record and compliance with GDPR and HIPAA. 2023 IEEE International Conference on Artificial Intelligence and Telecommunication 2023. Available from: https://link.springer.com/chapter/10.1007/978-3-0-1-48573-2_58
[http://dx.doi.org/10.56294/dm2023166]

[25]   Elsa J, Ahmed S. Data privacy and security in sustainable healthcare: navigating legal and ethical challenges. 2024 Healthcare Privacy Conference 2024. Available from: https://easychair.org/publications/preprint_download/Qt42

[26]   Available from: https://scholar.google.com/scholar?hl=en&as_sdt=0%2C5&q=Integration+with+AI+and+IoT+Technologies&btnG=

[27]   Raut R, Narkhede BE, Shee H, *et al.* Review on the adoption of AI, blockchain, and IoT in sustainability research. Sustainability 2022. Available from: https://www.mdpi.com/2071-1050/14/13/7851

[28]   Knickerbocker J, Budd R. Heterogeneous integration technology demonstrations for future healthcare, IoT, and AI computing solutions. 2018 IEEE Int Conf Heterog Comput 2018. Available from: https://ieeexplore.ieee.org/abstract/document/8429744/

[29]   VK . Challenges and solutions of interoperability on IoT: how far have we come in resolving the IoT interoperability issues. 2017 Int Conf IoT Syst 2017. Available from: https://ieeexplore.ieee.org/abstract/document/8358436/

[30]   Mahmud M, Koch F, Buyya R. Cloud-fog interoperability in IoT-enabled healthcare solutions. 2018 ACM Int Conf Cloud Comput 2018.
[http://dx.doi.org/10.1145/3154273.3154347]

[31]   Albouq S, Sen AA, Almashf N. A survey of interoperability challenges and solutions for dealing with them in IoT environment. 2022 IEEE Conf IoT Interoperability 2022. Available from: https://ieeexplore.ieee.org/abstract/document/9741799/
[http://dx.doi.org/10.1109/ACCESS.2022.3162219]

[32]   Kaul . Blockchain in education: Revolutionizing academic verification and resource access. Medium 2024. Available from: https://medium.com/liveplexmetaverseecosystem/blockchain-in- education-revolutionizing-academic-verification-and-resource-access-aa631760087f

[33]   Psicosmart . How is blockchain technology revolutionizing compliance in global talent management processes. Psicosmart 2024. Available from: https://psicosmart.net/blogs/blog-how-is- blockchain-technology-revolutionizing-compliance-in-global-talent-management-processes-217950

[34]   Mohammad A, Vargas S. Challenges of using blockchain in the education sector: A literature review. Appl Sci (Basel) 2022; 12(13): 6380.
[http://dx.doi.org/10.3390/app12136380]

CHAPTER 5

The Impact and Implementation of Blockchain-Based Solutions for Efficient Electronic Health Record (EHR) Management

Kiran Deep Singh[1], Sharon Christa[2,*], Pardeep Kumar Jindal[3] and Garima Sharma[4]

[1] *Department of Computer Science and Engineering, Chitkara University Institute of Engineering and Technology, Rajpura, Punjab, India*

[2] *Department of Computer Science and Engineering, MIT Art Design and Technology University, Pune, Maharashtra, India*

[3] *Department of Electronics and Communication, Chandigarh Engineering College, Mohali, Chandigarh, India*

[4] *Department of Computer Science and Engineering, Graphic Era Deemed to be University, Dehradun, Uttarakhand, India*

Abstract: An electronic health record (EHR) system can facilitate complete and accurate patient information to authorized users and can help organizations and service providers gain improved productivity. Furthermore, the doctors can effortlessly access the records of the patients, including medicines, medical records, and laboratory results, resulting in more conversant decisions along with improved care. The EHR technology improves patient care, which allows for better patient engagement by the medical practitioners. With this technology, patients can easily get their medical records, which further aids in taking active care of their own health. The technology of EHR permits real-time availability of scientifically-proved tools, permitting providers to make better decisions on the health of the patient. EHRs improve patient safety by reducing the likelihood of duplicate tests and medication errors. However, the global implementation of EHR systems is still facing multiple challenges due to the underlying issues related to security, data integrity, and privacy preservation. Several EHR security issues are mainly associated with centralized data storage systems and their integrators/providers. The decentralized control and access capabilities of blockchain can offer a suitable solution to EHR security and data management issues. This paper examines the challenges associated with EHR systems and solutions based on blockchain, which can be used to overcome the barriers related to data security, integrity, and patient ownership. Finally, through the review of two EHR blockchain application areas, it is illustrated how research can provide various applications and propose openings for related debates and research to highlight future directions.

* **Corresponding author Sharon Christa:**Department of Computer Science and Engineering, MIT Art Design and Technology University, Pune, Maharashtra, India;
E-mail: sharonchrista@gmail.com

Mohit Angurala, Preet Kamal, Aryan Chaudhary, Rasmeet Singh Bali & Vijay Bhardwaj (Eds.)
All rights reserved-© 2025 Bentham Science Publishers

Keywords: Blockchain, Electronic health record, Patient information, Security.

INTRODUCTION

The rise in corporate data breaches, cyber-warfare, and quickly evolving sophisticated hacking methods is alarming, enabling the fast passage of regulation and enforcement that carries significant costs in terms of compliance, risk mitigation, and the policing of the digital economy. Further complexity is generated through the increased globalization of business and society. The primary strategies that have emerged to meet these challenges are centralization in all forms, such as data centers and cloud storage solutions, and the excitation of cyber security and information assurance at the system, software, hardware, and network levels [1]. Unfortunately, these strategies result in the creation and operation of data silos through restricted centralization methods that prohibit distributed management practices and threaten the privacy and sovereignty of the data's owners, creators, and subjects, as well as every intermediary actor involved in their access, processing, and distribution. On the other hand, the secondary field of cryptography is derived primarily from mathematics and involves the application of computational systems for the transformation of data in order to achieve selective information disclosure and the mathematical modeling and automatization of 'trust' and the design of 'secure' systems [2]. However, this field remains conceptually complex as it embroils the following elements: distributed parties that communicate; long-standing promises of collision resistance, security, and identity of electronic and virtualized objects; automation, identification, and encryption tools; and the properties of 'simplicity' and 'reliability' that are based on mathematical algorithms. Notably, these privacy practices are highly valued in economic terms, which generates demand [3]. In the more general context of computer science and distributed systems, there is an inability to deploy, enact, and manage the explicit, ongoing function adhesion of those properties at the scale of complexity and diversity required to be seamlessly interoperable with the vast range of existing systems and actors.

Background and Significance of EHR Management

Electronic Health Record (EHR) management is a critical function in healthcare. One of its primary benefits is that it provides authorized users with access to their patients' health information at all times [4]. It enables real-time, secure, and accurate access to health information required for the management of care delivery services. The access may involve patients themselves, health professionals, and other healthcare providers within and outside the facility where the patient received care services. They can quickly and securely retrieve and review the patient's health information to diagnose and treat the patient accordingly. In addition, in any case that requires immediate attention for critical diagnoses and treatment, authorized health professionals can quickly access patient health information [5]. Moreover, EHR is a critical source for clinical research and population health management. Properly formatted patient data in electronic health records can advance evidence-based research and contribute to the creation of effective healthcare solutions optimized for patients' specific treatments, medications, and protocols. These benefits mean that the management of EHR should emphasize efficient, secure, and real-time accessibility, integrity, and reliable information. To meet these requirements, the traditional central server-based EHR systems are not suitable. An EHR central server-based solution is implemented that has encountered significant challenges, both in addressing user on-demand real-time access to health information and concerns about health record data ownership, integration, security, auditability, and interoperability in the main system [6].

Overview of Blockchain Technology

Blockchain, by its most useful definition, is a collective agreement method with which the global state of networked message contents can be maintained. The participants interact by either using a network protocol with which aggregated data services can be performed, updating its network, and/or confirming the addition of a new work or message. What makes blockchains really special is that anyone can download a complete state of the network, and the reader of a complete state, hereafter a node, will locally validate the state [7]. The main drivers of this and the success of blockchains are the automatic completeness, correctness, security, and integrity of the replicated database that the nodes together maintain, the cryptographic chaining of blocks of transactions to ensure the integrity of the network combined with ensuring their public, global uniqueness, and the ability to create hierarchical blockchains using Positional Based Navigation (PBN) to bootstrap the management of the initial database that was initially applied to create the first blockchain of Bitcoin. Blockchain technology is notable because it is self-contained; the implications propagated through the blockchain to all participants generally hold – since we assume the link installers of the blocks to be trustworthy [8]. If we use a commonly accepted mechanism, we can use any blockchain effectively without having to rely on a third party in order to administer it. Since this feature is mandatory, we can isolate the design of the inserting mechanism and consider independent blockchains within the same system, allowing us to focus on their contents.

UNDERSTANDING ELECTRONIC HEALTH RECORDS (EHR)

An electronic health record (EHR), or a personal health record (PHR), refers to the container that is prepared for documenting and preserving health-related information of an individual. This EHR solution, as per the law, should include the capability of the owner to transfer all or any portion of the information that is under such person's control in a machine-readable format when encountered with specific situations such as meeting a healthcare provider or changing an insurance company [9]. This document is a compilation of compliant information from multiple healthcare providers or other entities. As per case-specific documentation with greater specificity in further law, the term may include treatment history, doctor's visit notes, medications, allergies, and advertisement of advance directives. It also helps in patient care by collaborating information from multiple different healthcare providers. If agreed by the healthcare provider and the patient, it will allow the patient to share all or portions of their EHR with other entities [10].

As a digital document containing each patient's personal healthcare account, EHR is able to hold information related to any disease, diagnosis, or treatment, care plans or medical problems, as well as history, care management, liabilities, education, progress, and counseling information. It also contains the latest medication and allergies list. Not just restricted to these, EHRs incorporate information about long-term treatment such as immunization rates, the risk of coronary disease, smoking, and other characteristics of health, which makes it easy for all healthcare providers to provide value-based healthcare benefits. Individual hospitals use EHRs, and patient care improvements can be achieved by means of decreasing medication errors, making healthcare easier for patients, supporting decisions with evidence-based guidelines, strengthening health services and personal capacity, and making it easier to give patients safe, effective care. In meaningless visits by a patient and doctors, this system may even reduce duplication of diagnostic tests, thereby conserving money.

Definition and Components of EHR

Electronic Health Records remain a relevant topic in the medical world. They can improve efficiency, reduce costs, reduce errors, and provide better and more personalized customer service [11]. Blockchain has been present as a framework for medical records protocols for Electronic Health Records (EHRs), relying on the strong base it can provide in several aspects, such as data privacy and secure transactions. However, their implementation has not been massive, and a few practical examples can still be found in the world. There are still some discussions and questions to answer concerning its usage and abstinence at large-scale operations. This article's objective is not to replace existing state-of-the-art studies but rather to perform a qualitative analysis of current intelligence based on academic research publications on blockchain and EHRs [12]. Fig. (1) outlines the process of managing Electronic Health Records (EHR) using blockchain technology. The process starts with the patient visiting the doctor, followed by the doctor updating the EHR. The EHR data is then encrypted and stored on the blockchain. Subsequent steps include data access requests, smart contract validation, and access granting, ensuring secure and compliant management of health records.

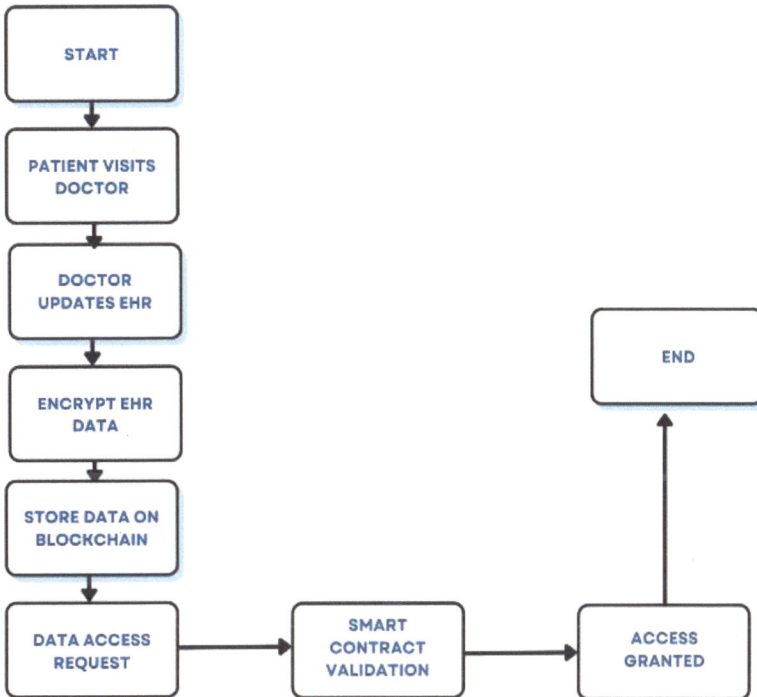

Fig. (1). EHR management process flowchart using blockchain.

Electronic Health Records (EHR) define the next generation of medical records that exchange and transmit the information exchanged with patients, health professionals, organizations, and other stakeholders, such as insurance companies, laboratories, and people who need health information [13]. The EHRs include a combination of data, documents, voices, images, signals, and other media for the health of individuals. These EHRs can be created, managed, and consulted by authorized entities in the patient's interest. However, participants in the healthcare industry need to constantly evolve and improve information systems as well as the governance and the mode of EHR management [14]. There is also a growing interest in the use of blockchain technology attributes to support data security, immutability, and reliability in the EHR's business management process. Developments in technology over the past five years have proven that blockchain is a technology that can meet the expected performance standards, including scalability and privacy.

Current Challenges in EHR Management

Merging the numerous disease cases of millions of patients creates an enormous volume of raw data in EHR that has traditionally been difficult to interpret. Information developed out of this lack of comprehensive analysis in the healthcare system increases the long-term risk of negative healthcare outcomes, including increased mortality and morbidity [15]. To restore the relationship between patients and their healthcare providers, EHRs must grow into an unimpeded mechanism for comprehensive clinical documentation that offers effortless information retrieval, identification, visualization, knowledge translation, and patient engagement. EHRs must be accessible, scalable, and sustainable in order to achieve these objectives. As part of the design and analysis techniques of EHRs, this necessitates a re-evaluation of the current architecture and heuristic analysis. On the one hand, many EHR systems and patient healthcare databases exist, but they are not referred to care providers and health patients. The purpose of the implementation of these systems is, instead of offering real-time information, to help plan and govern the healthcare system. Rigidly built, complex, and networked are characteristics of these systems. However, they face difficulties in incorporating assorted, high-quality data and supplying users with valuable expertise at the point of care. To transform into enlightened systems of health record management for individual patients, the requirements of EHRs must be realigned [16]. One possible model is a shared blockchain. This ensures shareholder control among all core army stakeholders: healthcare staff, patients, hospitals, researchers, and insurance firms, as well as scalable high-function middleware. This digital cooperation system, focused on the use of protected EHR data of citizens, will allow patients to choose where and how health services are delivered and offered. This ensures that physicians gain individual personal data gain.

BLOCKCHAIN TECHNOLOGY IN HEALTHCARE

Blockchain is a distributed ledger technology whose origins can be traced back to the invention of digital currency – Bitcoin. Blockchain works based on a distributed peer-to-peer network, and it enables peer-to-peer transactions for digital currency without the need for a trusted central authority [17]. This technology can enhance the security and privacy of existing systems that are used to manage electronic health records. The security of this technology is made possible by the fact that all transactions are recorded in chronological order and linked together as records through cryptographic chains. These records are stored in multiple physical locations in the network [18]. To add additional records to the blockchain, a cryptographic algorithm known as hash is used. When a node adds records to the chain, the algorithm creates a hash value from the first part of the records and the newly added records. Each record also contains the hash value of the previous record, so this makes it very difficult for attackers to tamper or try to insert records into the system.

Key Features and Advantages of Blockchain in Healthcare

Immutability, data integrity, security, and interoperability are the essential benefits of blockchain. Because of blockchain's salient features, the healthcare community's interest is growing steadily in spite of blockchain's original association with Bitcoin. Hence, let us investigate how these key features impact record management. Once the record is posted to the blockchain with timestamped blocks, these are cryptographically linked for identification and reference [19]. The block hashes are used to link the following block in a linear and chronological order. Once the content is added to the ledger system, it becomes very difficult for a single party to alter that particular record. This characteristic of blockchain greatly benefits the parties involved, who want to ensure high integrity and unchanged endorsement of the data. The system type of ledger change *via* the immutability of the crypto-based keys is one of the major security objectives addressed by blockchain. Data can be related to the ownership of a good. Customers can digitally own products that are certified by a digital transaction for the product's history and other underlying components belonging to encrypted digital assets. People in this way can also hold these products in specific domains such as identity verification, ownership of VR (Virtual Reality) content, digital voting cards, allocation of entitlements and privileges, and even digital certificates [20]. Blockchain is a secured way for digital ownership and autonomous systems. Immense trust is in the distribution of ownership because it is in individual identities; therefore, the individuals and participants keep digital assets and digital identities themselves. Blockchain applications make data actualized and sustainable. The blockchain is not just technology; it is a social entity that can provide us with the various core capabilities of trust, privacy, security, authentication, and ownership.

INTEGRATION OF BLOCKCHAIN IN EHR MANAGEMENT

Considering the issues mentioned above, it is evident that EHR management needs a robust solution to solve these problems. Unfortunately, we have not seen any such solution. To address the barriers to EHRs, in this chapter, we propose an integration of blockchain technology for EHR management. Blockchain technology is, without a doubt, one of the most intriguing computer technologies in our world today [21]. Blockchain, at its core, is a distributed ledger that is secure, transparent, and difficult to compromise. Each type of blockchain has its own unique set of advantages that make it the most appropriate option for specialized scenarios. We chose the Ethereum blockchain because of its consensus mechanism, PoW, which protects the network from cyberattacks, and the Solidity smart contract technology for its ability to include custom applications that interact with blockchain-stored data [22]. The smart contract functionality is designed to address complex scenarios in healthcare, including dynamic access control and multi-party protocols. Dynamic access control is implemented using the blockchain's inherent decentralized architecture and role-based permissions encoded within the smart contracts. This functionality allows for real-time adjustments to data access permissions based on predefined rules or triggers, such as changes in the role of a healthcare provider or the urgency of a patient's condition. For instance, in emergency situations, a patient's sensitive health data can be temporarily made accessible to an attending physician who previously did not have permission, with all actions logged immutably on the blockchain. The Ethereum blockchain is utilized for these functionalities because it supports programmable smart contracts through the Solidity programming language, enabling developers to create logic for dynamic permissions and automated workflows.

The other functionalities included in the smart contract are multi-party protocols, which play an important role in secure collaboration with multiple stakeholders in the health sector, including patients, insurers, healthcare providers, and researchers. These functionalities ensure collaboration between several stakeholders, including the patients, insurers, healthcare service providers, and researchers, with a minimum possible risk and trustworthiness across processes like claims for medical covers or even clinical tests. For instance, in the insurance claim process, a smart contract can automatically check whether the conditions of the claim are met, verify necessary documents, and perform payment if the agreed conditions are fulfilled. Such scenarios utilize the Proof of Authority consensus protocol, as it provides the advantage of being efficient and fast in contrast to Proof of Work, which is considered an energy-intensive consensus method, making it ideal for private or consortium blockchains in which the validators have already built up trust with one another.

These smart contracts work according to this workflow:

Dynamic Access Control: The smart contract stores data access permissions as variables for the patient. Upon a request for data, the smart contract checks the credentials and context of the requester, such as role, time, or location, against the stored permissions. Upon meeting the conditions, access is granted, and the event is recorded on the blockchain, thus allowing for auditability and compliance.

Multi-Party Collaboration: Each stakeholder communicates with the smart contract *via* their blockchain node. For example, in a clinical trial, patients may agree to provide particular health information, which the researchers are only allowed to view if pre-specified conditions such as approval by the ethics committee or a non-disclosure agreement have been met. The smart contract ensures the conditions are met without having to involve any intermediary, minimizing the chances of data breaches and disputes.

The blockchain-based technology ensures immutability, and the system is secure to the extent that the requirements for scenarios involving sensitive healthcare information are met. The participation of these protocols increases further trust among all the actors because blockchain's decentralized nature gets rid of the necessity to have a single central authority.

Conclusion: This chapter's given design will provide a relevant framework to handle the complex situations related to healthcare in general and those that require more dynamic and multi-party scenarios to ensure regulatory compliance coupled with operational efficiency.

Fig. (**2**) depicts a blockchain-based Electronic Health Record (EHR) management system. The system involves user interfaces for healthcare providers and patients, which interact with the blockchain network. The blockchain network integrates a smart contract layer and an EHR storage layer, which further utilizes an encryption module and an access control module to ensure secure and compliant management of health records. The aforementioned issues with EHR systems currently make it excessively costly for individuals and entities to protect patient medical records [23]. These barriers prevent the appropriate usage of medical records in different departments and research projects that require it. In this study, we argue that blockchain technology would be a game-changer in this area. We propose an open-sourced EHR management solution for the storing and managing of patient medical records. The aim is to ensure the integrity of the files and, at the same time, make the data appropriate for the initiation of automated transactions, enforced access control, and data-sharing. This solution provides a secure and private way to link with personal health data, enabling interactions with it using secure, transparent, and auditable usage features of blockchain technology without relying on any central authority.

Use Cases and Success Stories

Through multiple institutions and individuals incorporating blockchain technology into the health sector, various ongoing use cases and success stories have brought to light the tremendous potential of blockchain in improving participants' efficiency and operations. In this section, we will convey first-hand information about the uses and real benefits of blockchain technology in the healthcare field. Specifically, we have underlined applications consisting of EHR management or the reinforcement of the access that individuals can hold over their health-related data. From each use case, we summarize current initiatives, summarize learnings from the technology deployment, and represent any lessons learned or potential improvements to ameliorate or scale the current solution. In the last part of this section, we compare the strengths and limitations of all introduced concepts for all the blockchain-based solutions in health and consider potential future explorations in the direction of addressing the limitations.

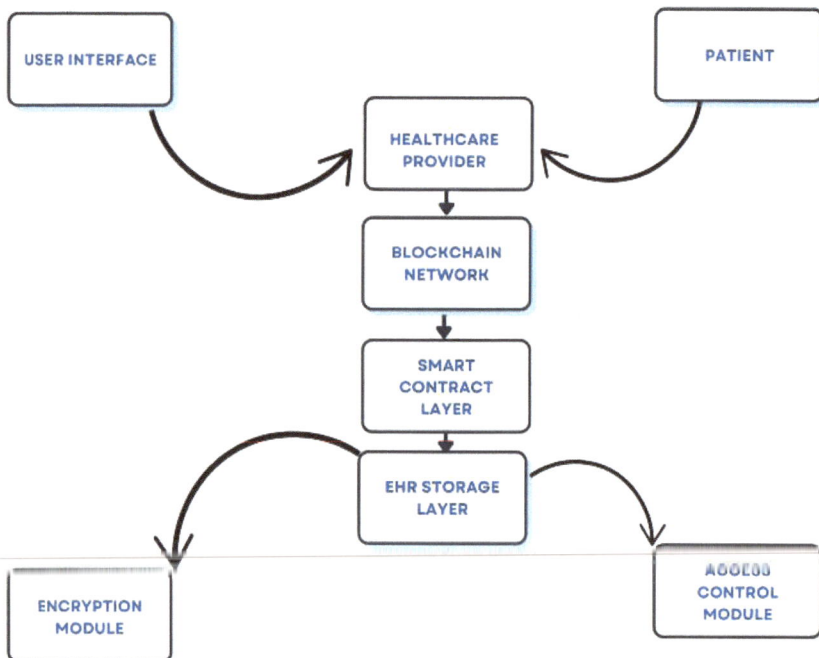

Fig. (2). Blockchain-based EHR management architecture.

The Swiss company MTIP, founded in 2019, supports health innovations by leveraging blockchain technology. The use cases are to provide total oversight of healthcare data to individual patients and to optimize medical data quality for clinical patients. For patients to take full advantage of their rights and specified democratic rights, the blockchain should give individuals power over and access to their healthcare data. On the other hand, for inspection and treatment purposes, after the data has been given to an assigned person or institution, cryptographic data should not be seen publicly. This means that privacy and data security must be made possible while the medical data to be utilized can be confirmed by an authorized institution.

CHALLENGES AND LIMITATIONS OF BLOCKCHAIN IN EHR MANAGEMENT

Most user-centric blockchain-based systems implement integration with a central trusted third party, which contains the identification and other user's relevant information. This poses legal, regulatory, authentication, standard, privacy, and confidentiality risks. Currently, blockchain technology has some development bottlenecks, such as the cost of joining a chain, simple attacks, and forgers. TPS (Transaction per second)is improved by pruning unnecessary data and using sharding technology. In fact, Ethereum, Cosmos, and Zilliqa currently use them to improve TPS. However, performance lags behind in terms of distribution and overall speed. Compounding the performance problem involves having a large number of stalled transactions after a service. There are also design bottlenecks and gaps in how healthcare information is shared among the participants of a clinical study, such as matching the ledger from a specific trial result with a patient's. Technical and administrative difficulties include obtaining patients' consent, storing data, randomizing patients, tracking the stages of the tests, managing the progress of data, and monitoring the credibility of the findings during clinical tests conducted at multiple clinical centers. There are no natural supports for handling unexpected and flexible application events that are necessary for the underlying process of electronic medical records. Additionally, there is a relatively limited regenerative chain space and a long confirmation time of ledger records for patients' hospital record updates. Fast interaction and up-t--date ledger records are expected, but they require paying a fee. Ethics, including trust, safety, dependence, guidance, and other important data considerations, are also a concern. Legal concerns include liability, data ownership, identity, and resolving disputes related to access to justice. Regulatory issues also need to be addressed. The consequences for healthcare include centralization, security, fraud, hacking risks, and biased treatment of health data. While blockchain technology is widely used, there are realistic and focused concerns that need to be addressed. The key is to focus on hypothetical issues. Using blockchain health options that do nothing for evidence-based practice is not sufficient. Organizations, including the government and other low-trust entities, will likely have to work especially hard to build patient confidence and become truly valuable.

REGULATORY AND ETHICAL CONSIDERATIONS

Regulation is defined as a rule or directive made and maintained by an authority. In this context, regulatory refers to the standards and policies that should be followed within the blockchain and EHR environment, which can also refer to legal-related regulations that have to be met. Examples are the General Data Protection Regulation (GDPR) for compliance with data privacy laws in the EU health records system(s) environment [24]. In the discussion on using blockchain to manage EHRs, where user access is deemed private and confidential, the concept of regulatory is aimed specifically at how to apply blockchain principles in a manner that is ethical and meets the legal requirements to end up with a working model at the lowest cost [25]. This largely refers to the concepts of confidentiality and data handling by prescribed policies and standards. Here, the concept of regulations and policies for the things that can be done uses some identifiable tools and processes; where these tools and processes include wallet setup, audit, and user management processes. An audit mechanism is examined for integrity checking, and dictated policies for the use of the system are key in achieving this. International legal concepts like the data subject and data controller are observed with respect to the EHR blockchain environment. From both the regulatory and ethical standpoints, decisions have to be made on what is personal, anonymous, and confidential. Existing prescriptive standards and policies that can be used in a blockchain EHR management system are listed, noting some exceptions or deficits: Regulatory, GDPR, blockchain, anonymization, Wallet API, asynchronous and direct messaging, and Patient Management System (PMS) [26].

FUTURE TRENDS AND INNOVATIONS IN BLOCKCHAIN-BASED EHR MANAGEMENT

Consequently, by exploring the themes expounded upon in the seven chapters, the volume underscores the potential advantages of blockchain in EHR management and encourages varied stakeholders to play a pivotal role in contributing to the creation of enhanced enabling multi-level environments utilizing the presented criteria. The themes offer technology and policy practitioners detailed technical information interlocked with strategic and operational frameworks that concern them and motivate them to take innovative strategic actions to enhance interactions between EHR and blockchain. In advanced technologies, EHRs are plagued by various issues predominantly governed by information exchange and management problems. Despite the push by health data interoperability requirements, the growth in EHR systems, and changes in organizational infrastructures, concerns over accessibility, security, privacy, and data management among stakeholders remain challenging to address. To mitigate these concerns, similar to other sectors, particularly financial services that have witnessed transformative gains through blockchain, EHR can be managed, shared, and created effectively, efficiently, and securely through blockchain technology.

The impact and implementation of blockchain-based solutions for efficient electronic health records (EHR) management provides innovative insights into the exploitation of EHRs through blockchain in varied public health centers effectively. Various new themes and trends relating to electronic health records are sketched out in the monograph. The study targets multi-stakeholders (healthcare providers, health technology solution designers, and health system managers) who believe that EHR management can effectively improve healthcare globally. The monograph aims to encourage discussions around innovative exploitation of policies, standards, and governance strategies relating to EHRs in varied healthcare systems and recommend the adoption and utilization of these pioneering technological solutions to electronic health records globally. It highlights future trends and breakthroughs by pointing out the four major areas where blockchain can improve EHR management. The volume presents several future breakthroughs derived from the use of blockchain in EHR management and the parameters that enable/block their breakthrough. The rise of blockchain technology has paved the way for innovative methods of EHR creation, management, and sharing.

CONCLUSION

Additional research that explores administrative and technical approaches to using blockchain technologies for generating and managing EHRs is definitely needed. Proof-of-concept projects should be performed to check potential use cases and to show the practicability and benefits of blockchain in the management of health information. Also, QIS can help to measure the impact of technological and infrastructural innovations such as blockchain on the effectiveness of mental health treatments. Future research should examine how blockchain can facilitate the wider sharing of personal experiences relevant to the management of complex multi-morbidity patients with the sharing of information between consumers, providers, and decision-makers. Our study shows that clinical blockchain technologies offer benefits in records administration, security, and patient privacy, but they also involve a number of constraints. We have implicitly contributed to fostering the initial stages required by hospitals' news on the well-known potential of blockchain technologies for addressing EHR management privacy, safety, and interoperability issues.

Media apparatuses remain crucial in the implementation of any blockchain technology in healthcare, which will also increase its adoption. The optimal educational outreach is when this information is presented clearly and efficiently to a broad audience, targeted to the specifics of the audience, and promoted and informed about its ease of use. This can improve the collaboration of all stakeholders in building QIS by aligning expectations. There is an understanding that this implementation represents not just a technical solution but a reconfiguration of incentive models, increased patient engagement, and an enhancement of patient control and privacy, making them the gatekeepers of their records. Also important is an international agreement on future legislation, government rules, and compliance determinations, as well as future needs funding that encourages the transfer of usable technologies of blockchain into health systems. With the convergence of privacy and security concerns, users will need guidance from information security professionals, such as health information management professionals and better evidence-based governance.

AUTHORS' CONTRIBUTION

In Chapter 5, **Kiran Deep Singh, Sharon Christa, Pardeep Kumar Jindal, and Garima Sharma** collaborated to provide insights into blockchain-based solutions for EHR management. **Kiran Deep Singh** initiated the study, focusing on EHR management challenges and the application of blockchain technology for improving data security and patient control. **Sharon Christa** conducted a comprehensive analysis of blockchain features in healthcare, contributing to the exploration of current use cases and success stories in EHR systems. **Pardeep Kumar Jindal** addressed the technical challenges and limitations of blockchain in EHR management, providing regulatory insights. **Garima Sharma** researched future trends and ethical considerations in blockchain-enabled EHR systems. Together, the authors proposed strategic recommendations for implementing blockchain solutions to optimize EHR management and patient data security.

REFERENCES

[1]   Reegu F, Daud S, Alam S. Blockchain-based electronic health record system for efficient Covid-19 pandemic management. Academia 2021. Available from: https://www.academia.edu/download/ 67322950/19_preprints202104.0771.v1_2_.pdf

[2]   Mahajan, H.B. Emergence of healthcare 4.0 and blockchain into secure cloud-based electronic health records systems: Solutions, challenges, and future roadmap. Wirel. Pers. Commun. 2022; 126, 2425-46. Available from: https://link.springer.com

[3]   Shahnaz A, Qamar U. Using blockchain for electronic health records. IEEE Access 2019. Available from: https://ieeexplore.ieee.org/abstract/document/8863359/
       [http://dx.doi.org/10.1109/ACCESS.2019.2946373]

[4]   Quaini T, Roehrs A, Da Costa C, Da R, Righi R. A model for blockchain-based distributed electronic health records. IADIS Int J Web Interfaces 2024; 16(2): 66-79. Available from: https://www. iadisportal.org/ijwi/papers/2018161205.pdf
       [http://dx.doi.org/10.33965/ijwi_2018161205]

[5]   Jabbar R, Fetais N. Blockchain technology for healthcare: enhancing shared electronic health record interoperability and integrity. IEEE 2020. Available from: https://ieeexplore.ieee.org/abstract/ document/9089570/
       [http://dx.doi.org/10.1109/ICIoT48696.2020.9089570]

[6]   Alam MGR, Munir MS, Uddin MZ, Alam MS. Edge-of-things computing framework for cost-effective provisioning of healthcare data. J Parallel Distrib Comput 2019; 123: 54-60.

[7]   Shukla R, Agarwal A. Blockchain-powered smart healthcare system. Blockchain research. Elsevier 2020. Available from: https://www.sciencedirect.com/science/article/pii/B9780128198162000101
[http://dx.doi.org/10.1016/B978-0-12-819816-2.00010-1]

[8]   Kumar V, Ali R, Sharma PK. A secure blockchain-assisted authentication framework for electronic health records. Int J Inf Technol 2024; 16(3): 1581-93.
[http://dx.doi.org/10.1007/s41870-023-01705-w]

[9]   Majdoubi E, El Bakkali H, Sadki S. SmartMedChain: a blockchain-based privacy-preserving smart healthcare framework. Wiley Online Library 2021. Available from: https://onlinelibrary.wiley.com/doi/abs/10.1155/2021/4145512
[http://dx.doi.org/10.1155/2021/4145512]

[10]   Porsdam Mann S, Savulescu J, Ravaud P, Benchoufi M. Blockchain, consent and prosent for medical research. J Med Ethics 2021; 47(4): 244-50.
[http://dx.doi.org/10.1136/medethics-2019-105963] [PMID: 32366703]

[11]   Wang S, Ouyang L, Yuan Y. Blockchain-enabled smart contracts: architecture, applications, and future trends. IEEE Syst Man Cybern 2019. Available from: https://ieeexplore.ieee.org/abstract/document/8643084/
[http://dx.doi.org/10.1109/TSMC.2019.2895123]

[12]   Verma P, Rao CM, Chapalamadugu PK, Tiwari R, Upadhyay S. Future of electronic healthcare management: blockchain and artificial intelligence integration 2024; 179.218.
[http://dx.doi.org/10.1007/978-981-97-1249-6_9]

[13]   Verma P, Rao CM, Chapalamadugu PK. Future of electronic healthcare management: blockchain and artificial intelligence integration. In: Kaushik, K., Sharma, I. (eds) Next-Generation Cybersecurity. Blockchain Technologies. Springer, Singapore 2024.
[http://dx.doi.org/10.1007/978-981-97-1249-6_9]

[14]   Vardhini B, Dass S. A blockchain-based electronic medical health records framework using smart contracts. IEEE 2021. Available from: https://ieeexplore.ieee.org/abstract/document/9402689/

[15]   Holmes J, Beinlich J. Why is the electronic health record so challenging for research and clinical care?. Thieme Connect 2021. Available from: https://www.thieme-connect.com/products/ejournals/html/10.1055/s-0041-1731784
[http://dx.doi.org/10.1055/s-0041-1731784]

[16]   Seymour T, Frantsvog D. Electronic health records (EHR). ResearchGate 2014. Available from: https://www.researchgate.net/profile/Dr-Tom-Seymour-2/publication/267226700_Electronic_Health_Records_EHR/links/57594e9508ae414b8e43a316/Electronic-Health-Records-EHR.pdf

[17]   Shukla M, Lin J. BlockIoT: blockchain-based health data integration using IoT devices. NCBI 2021. Available from: https://www.ncbi.nlm.nih.gov/pmc/articles/PMC8861710/

[18]   Quzmar A. Reducing counterfeit drugs with blockchains: a survey. IEEE 2021. Available from: https://ieeexplore.ieee.org/abstract/document/9491695/
[http://dx.doi.org/10.1109/ICIT52682.2021.9491695]

[19]   Hasan H, Salah K, Jayaraman R. Blockchain-enabled telehealth services using smart contracts. IEEE 2021. Available from: https://ieeexplore.ieee.org/abstract/document/9605640/
[http://dx.doi.org/10.1109/ACCESS.2021.3126025]

[20]   Naresh VS, Pericherla SS, Murty PSR, Reddi S. Internet of Things in healthcare: Architecture, applications, challenges and solutions. Comput Syst Sci Eng 2020; 35(6): 411-421.

[21]   Griggs KN, Ossipova O, Kohlios P, Baccarini AN, Howson EA. SmartMedChain: a blockchain-based privacy-preserving smart healthcare framework. Wiley Online Library 2018. Available from: https://onlinelibrary.wiley.com/doi/abs/10.1155/2021/4145512

[22]   Bacon L, Tarr J. Distributed ledger technology and blockchain: insurance. Taylor & Francis 2024.

Available from: https://www.taylorfrancis.com/chapters/edit/10.4324/9781003319054-5/distributed-ledger-technology-blockchain-lee-bacon-julie-anne-tarr

[23]   V. S, E. O. Martinson, N. S, and P. M. An efficient secure sharing of electronic health records using IoT-based hyperledger blockchain. Int. J. Intell. Syst., 2024: 2024, 1–16. Available from: https://search.ebscohost.com

[24]   Yeoh, P. Regulatory issues in blockchain technology. J. Financ. Regul. Compliance, 2017; 25 No. 2, 196-208. Available from: https://www.emerald.com/insight/content/doi/10.1108/ JFRC-08-20-6-0068/full/html

[25]   Choudhury O, Sarker H, Rudolph N, Foreman M, Fay N, Dhuliawala M. Enforcing human subject regulations using blockchain and smart contracts. Blockchain Healthc Today 2018. Available from: https://www.blockchainhealthcaretoday.com/index.php/journal/article/view/10 [http://dx.doi.org/10.30953/bhty.v1.10]

[26]   Hossein KM, Esmaeili ME, Dargahi T, Khonsari A. Blockchain-based privacy-preserving healthcare architecture. Proc IEEE Can Conf Elect Comput Eng (CCECE) 2019: 1-4.

CHAPTER 6

The Impact of Blockchain Technology on Streamlining Insurance Claims

Riya Sharma[1,*], **Sharon Christa**[2], **Deep Mann**[3] and **Rajbir Kaur**[4]

[1] *Department of Commerce, Graphic Era Deemed to be University, Dehradun, Uttarakhand, India*

[2] *Department of Computer Science and Engineering, MIT Art Design and Technology University, Pune, Maharashtra, India*

[3] *Department of Computer Science and Engineering, Thapar Institute of Engineering & Technology, Patiala, Punjab, India*

[4] *Department of Electronics and Communication Engineering, Punjabi University, Patiala, Punjab, India*

Abstract: Blockchain technology has witnessed a significant level of curiosity from several industries, including the insurance sector, in relation to extensive applications in claims management processes. In the present study, a blockchain-distributed system for the insurance sector is proposed, which utilizes smart contracts to create valid insurance policies. Blockchain, being a distributed ledger, has several advantages and disadvantages, which are explained in detail. This system provides mechanisms that automate the complex processes of claim settlements, ensuring appropriate compensation to claimants and verifying the conditions and terms of insurance policies on the occurrence of a specific unforeseen event. Data retrieved from a real case has been used to consolidate the assessment of the approach proposed here. The profitability and sustainability of the insurance sector are underpinned by a smooth claims process. Traditional techniques for the adjustment of insurance claims are responsible for high administrative costs and the payment delays that occur after unforeseen events have occurred. Inefficient communication channels lead to conflict and civil fragility in the sector. However, traditional models have shown that the efficiency of the claims process can be improved by the adoption of modern digital technologies, notably the use of blockchain protocols. Blockchain is expected to streamline the end-to-end operations of insurers, thereby reducing the churn rate and enabling value-based partnerships. This chapter develops a reference framework with functional and non-functional requirements for Blockchain-based Accredited Parametric Insurance (Blake) that will ensure the on-time payment of rightful beneficiaries.

Keywords: Blockchain technology, Claims management, Insurance claims, Insurance, Smart contracts.

---

* **Corresponding author Riya Sharma:** Department of Commerce, Graphic Era Deemed to be University, Dehradun, Uttarakhand, India; E-mail: riyasharma6568@gmail.com

Mohit Angurala, Preet Kamal, Aryan Chaudhary, Rasmeet Singh Bali & Vijay Bhardwaj (Eds.)
All rights reserved-© 2025 Bentham Science Publishers

INTRODUCTION TO BLOCKCHAIN TECHNOLOGY

The insurance business has a long and storied history, having existed in some form, at least since the early days of the written word. For millennia, the fundamental mechanisms underlying insurance have remained remarkably consistent [1]. But today, we stand poised on the precipice of an inevitable, remarkable change. With time, what elements of traditional insurance models will remain intact for the duration will be revealed. Blockchain technology is a distributed ledger that is spearheading a revolution in the financial world today, providing an unparalleled level of trust among untrusted parties. We look at how it is uniquely positioned to bring radical efficiencies to insurance, particularly in the claims and billing processing area. The basis of Blockchain technology can be traced to an article written by two researchers titled "Blockchain – A Brief Introduction" and "Blockchain – A Supporting Technology in Case of Supply Chain Finance?" in 2011. Blockchain technology is a distributed ledger that is secure, transparent, and immune to fraudulent changes [2]. Entries are highly secured using a cryptographic hash. Any new entry created uses the hash of the previous entry. It is used across continents, bridging supra-national borders. There is no central location or a central trust anchor in the blockchain. A list of records – blocks- is used to track transactions across all the ledgers. A sharp token or a cryptographic hash is used to define the previous block. Blockchain is secured using cryptographic techniques. Specially designed consensus algorithms are used to elect a controller among the blockchain transactions [3]. It can be implemented through distributed or decentralized models. The blockchain system is open for participation, which enables innovations and technical developments through community participation. Small agents and the general public are provided with enormous benefits through consumer digital services. Blockchain, being a distributed ledger, has several advantages and disadvantages, which are explained in detail.

Definition and Key Concepts

Millions of work hours are spent working with manual, paper-intensive processes in the insurance industry. Fortunately, emerging technologies such as blockchain have the potential to address these challenges by streamlining and automating separate insurance processes, from claims, billing, and investing to reporting and compliance [4]. This particular report examines the use of blockchain technologies in streamlining the insurance industry's claim and billing process. It discusses the advantages provided by blockchain technology and the challenges that need to be understood and resolved. The report also includes prototype models and application patterns used to deploy blockchain to streamline the claim and billing processes. Blockchain provides new technologies for solving this problem and uses a decentralized platform to update transactions from stakeholders. Blockchain applications in the insurance industry can help speed up and automate certain processes, eliminate the need for trust building between parties in a deal, reduce the number of compliance violations, and decrease costs and complexity [5]. It is possible to release resources from these calls so they can be used with expertise. Blockchain is an implementation of this concept. This technology enables network participants who do not know each other to establish a decentralized information exchange process, create control among participants, and avoid planned activities that would otherwise take place between participants and third parties (such as shareholder registration agencies, banks, and operations). Due to these advantages, insurers see the value of embedding it into their business processes.

CHALLENGES IN INSURANCE CLAIMS AND BILLING PROCESSES

Since the earliest times of human civilization, people have always faced unexpected possible losses or damages in their lives, leading to the creation of contractual relationships to exchange economic risk. Insurers assume a variety of risks of loss due to hazards and perils. Insurance services have become essential for individuals and organizations globally, providing coverage for possible losses in defined conditions. They can be inclusive of life, health, property, accident, and liability insurance. Various contractual relationships can be created between insurers and respective individuals or organizations to provide insurance services [6]. Claims and billing management are essential processes for the insurance industry. Quick and precise claims and billing management processes can be differentiators for an efficient and excellent insurance company. These processes become fundamental to be performed in hours or days to prevent dissatisfaction and reputational risks. Claims are intended to compensate insured parties for the accidental loss of covered hazards. After incidents happen, the insureds or their representatives inform the insured insurers about those happenings, starting the claims management process. For valid claims, the insurers provide an indemnity payment to the insured and, if applicable, to the third-party claimants [4]. Claims are not only linked with charges but can also link insurers with sophisticated law litigations. Therefore, insurers often have claim units specialized in claims management and, if necessary, in the assurance of appropriate trials. However, not all claim reports may result in a claim file; sometimes, these can just represent fake or unqualified claims. Billing management is the process by which insurance consumers receive and handle invoices from insurers, mainly regarding policy renewals or the invoicing of additional premiums. These invoices shall be received, supervised, and paid when the insurance contract is adjusted. When an insurer discovers errors in previous payments, refunds or charges are invoiced and processed. Both claims and billing management processes are administrative and require different types of human resources to be performed. Although good systems and mechanisms will necessarily ensure the objectivity and automation of those processes, paperwork still represents a considerable part of them. Because various insurance transactions that lead to claims and billing incidents can be any vertical value in the insurance value chain, a large number of processes have been relying upon partnerships that can sponsor specific insurance activities.

Complexity and Inefficiency

Each individual insurance and financial services-related party manages its own data servers, network computer systems, or cloud network services, further accounting for consistent transaction data or different computer system data variations among parties during information updating processes. Insurance-pertinent structured information or data bear a cross-sector nature, consisting of detailed policy-related data (including policy status and information on the terminal point as well as the premium to be paid each year), settlement-related data (including benefits to which the beneficiary is entitled and the insured individually benefits from and who receives the insurance money), and additional service content data. The joint management system of claim and settlement multi-agent processes is imperfect; there is a lack of a supervising approach in the multi-agent node alliance and a lack of ability of different administrative alliances to simultaneously supervise and perform operations [4]. In addition, the dominance of controlling and stacking by the leading nodes has generated significant trust problems among the various participating nodes. With regards to intelligent claim and automated settlement, the multi-agent data landscape and intelligent service architecture and space contain a custodial-based and immutable blockchain ledger-tamper-proof function. The insufficiencies of traditional insurance claim and accounting processes have previously attracted the attention of many scholars and experts who suggest using blockchain's automated settlement functions to improve claim filing efficiency, a smooth claim process, and instant settlement. By combining blockchain technology with intelligent smart contract code, the insurance company is able to immediately investigate accidents, verify basic external evidence with the automated data query function, verify, validate, and settle claims, automatically support basic claim processes and automated data check and justify denials, and provide more extensive claim options and centralize unified management [3]. This way, the overall automated claim settlement function is significantly improved. The goal is to achieve a cryptographic hash transition blockchain, further utilizing a customer-activated blockchain network to facilitate blockchain-installed insurance policy credential management systems and multi-agent joint management decision-making integrity service platforms. In this regard, a preferred design for an insurance claim and automated billing process through smart contracts was proposed.

BENEFITS OF IMPLEMENTING BLOCKCHAIN IN INSURANCE

Blockchain is the key technology in cryptocurrencies such as Bitcoin and Ether. It is simply a shared public ledger on which the entire Bitcoin network relies. All confirmed transactions are included in the block. It allows Bitcoin wallets to calculate their spendable balance so that new transactions can be verified, thereby ensuring that they are actually owned by the spender [2]. The integrity and chronological order of the blockchain are implemented with cryptographic hashes. Blockchain technology is perceived as a disruptive force in numerous sectors. It supports efficient data management and trading in multi-party situations by removing the need for trusted third parties. Blockchain is a decentralized, digital, and secure way to store data and confirm transactions. DLT can streamline operations and processes for the insurance ecosystem, from policy creation and administration to claims submission and verification. The technology also forms the basis for creating a new business model in which third parties can access client data for specific policy incentives. Deploying DLT can reduce costs and risks for insurers and policyholders while also improving trust, transparency, and customer experience [7]. First, blockchain provides improved security and greatly reduces the risk of data breaches and fraudulent transactions. The technology is based on cryptology and often implemented in a permissioned framework to confirm identities and validate incoming data. Data is stored digitally and cryptographically and then distributed across numerous connected devices. All participants in this network are aware of any changes made, mitigating unauthorized changes. The broadband ledger is maintained using synchronization protocols and cryptographic keys for decentralizing data management. Unlike traditional database customers and insurers, decentralized blockchain infrastructure can be maintained and updated independently. By using smart contracts, users can perform specific insurance operations and processes. This independent verification method reduces fraudulent transactions and, thus, potential losses. Smart contracts execute when users are aware of external events, and once deployed on the network, results can never be altered. The general consensus or policy rules take precedence, and only predetermined participants can launch specific contracts. Insurers can automatically designate specific smart contracts, and policyholders are more likely to trust their claims to be processed quickly and securely. Moreover, insurers and their shareholders benefit from substantial cost savings [8]. Insurers can automate processes and manage requests in different data streams without human intervention by using DLT. Furthermore, blockchain reduces administrative costs related to ensuring data immutability and process transparency and validity. Blockchain technology, in particular, has the potential to create a wide variety of platforms and ecosystems. By leveraging the decentralized nature of the blockchain to create new insurance models, these systems provide carriers with new revenue and growth opportunities. Insurers can use valuation methods and smart contracts to develop policies that reward individuals for proven claims behavior [9]. Platform behavior can be confirmed and validated using third-party data streams. These new business models allow insurers to improve customer trust, form new customers, and subsequently increase sales and market share. Blockchain-enabled drug traceability system, through end-to-end transparency and authenticity, helps reduce risks due to counterfeit drugs and inefficient supply chains, as shown in Fig. (**1**).

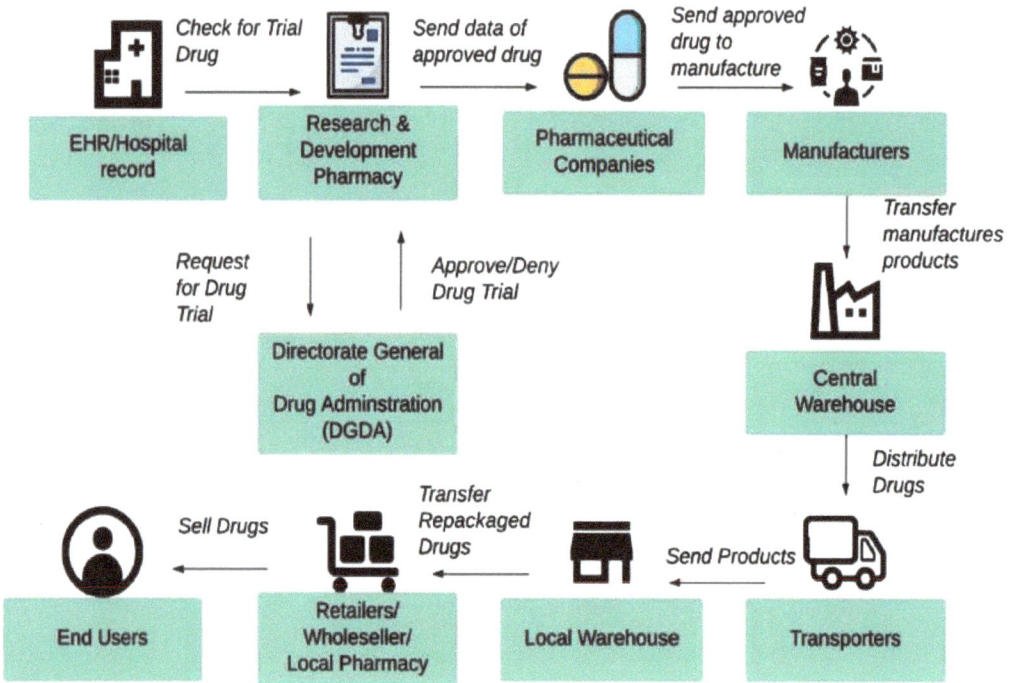

Fig. (**1**). Blockchain-enabled drug traceability system [29] .

This system will start by attaching a singular digital identifier with each drug batch at manufacturing, registered immutably on a blockchain. Going forward along the supply chain- from distributor and storage house to a pharmacy and onward to its end users- every transaction is then securely logged, forming a new block of transactions traceable in a blockchain-based ledger. Smart contracts are placed into the blockchain, which validates and approves them at every level by the predefined conditions to fulfill the regulatory standards. Through this, it ensures timely tracking, providing up-to-date information on location, condition, and ownership status to the stakeholders involved in the process. The system increases trust among stakeholders by using blockchain's decentralized and tamper-proof nature, which greatly reduces the chances of fraud and inefficiencies in the delivery of drugs to patients.

Transparency and Trust

For insurance companies, trust and relationships with their customers are key for sustaining profitable business. In creating rules and permissions for different roles of participants, coding legal and business rules, and preservation of permissions for all system adaptation and configuration, with mechanisms providing logical confidentiality and physical integrity, blockchain provides for the institutional requirements of a business ecosystem. Guarantees of fairness include cryptographic consensus, supplementations provided by smart contracts, immutable and tamper-evident records, and democratic, fair governance [10]. Trust in a blockchain platform, providing strategic information to all participants and allowing automation within a trusted system's border, is gained by cryptographic and logical integrity of information with functions of reputation and protection with predetermined rules for any kind of participation. Such value includes the guarantee of fair terms and equal opportunities for all concerned elements, resulting in suggesting that participants get their best interests activated to align four major expenditures of transaction costs. These are the costs of searching and information collection, costs of bargaining and negotiation, costs of contract monitoring, and policing costs. Equally, trust contributes to opposing increased opportunism due to the fact that parties have legal obligations and take the risk of future trespasses openly. Parties involved have a mutually agreed understanding of commonality and rules while having a long-term continuous cooperative venture [11].

Transparency, in combination with control, leads to trust. The incentives for telling the truth are enhanced when property rights are clearly defined. Transparency contributes to the production of objectivity through verifiability. The relative success of transparency can be explained as a mechanism that promotes trust. Increased transparency and decentralization of information, reducing cost and ability to asymmetrically control and make decisions, and the ability to create trust in a system can lead to potential lower costs and increased speed in execution [12]. Fig. (**2**) depicts the insurance claim processing workflow using blockchain technology. The process starts with the customer submitting a claim to the insurance company, which updates the claim status. The blockchain network then stores the encrypted data and executes a smart contract to validate the claims. The access control module subsequently notifies both the customer and the insurance company about the claim status, ensuring a transparent and secure process.

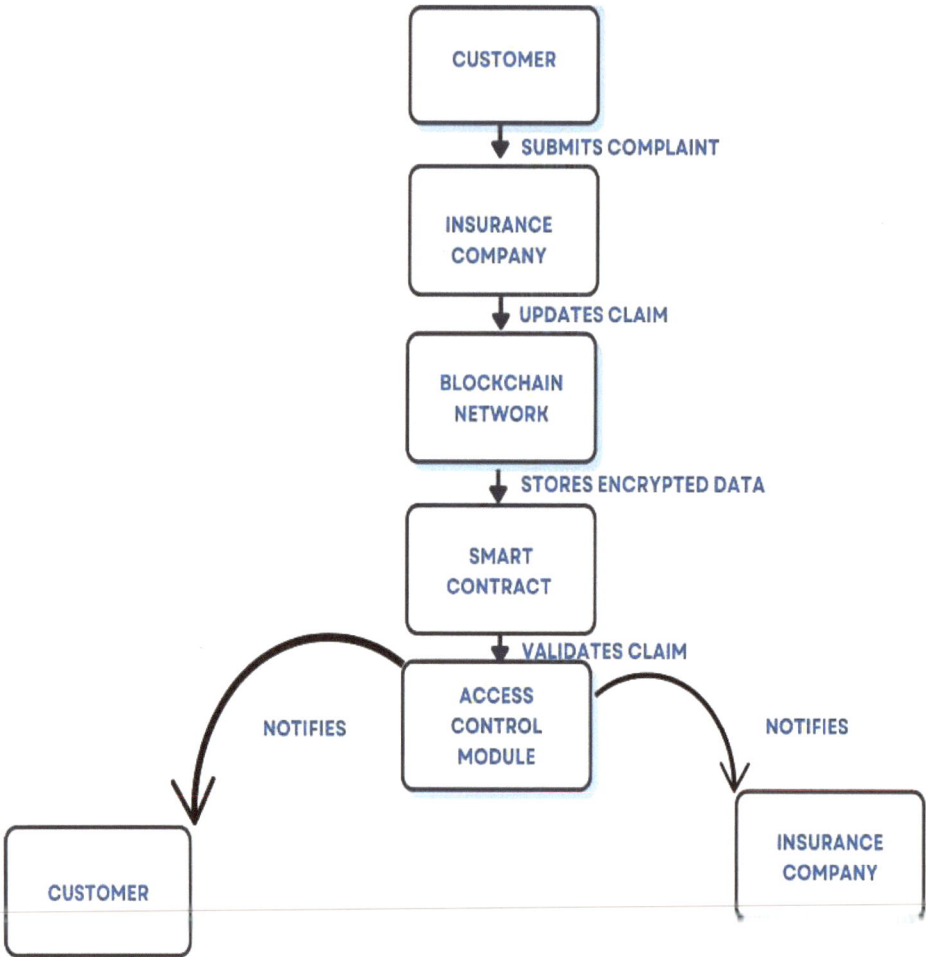

Fig. (2). Insurance claim processing workflow using blockchain.

CASE STUDIES OF SUCCESSFUL IMPLEMENTATIONS

In this section, in-depth and real case studies of blockchain technology applications in the insurance industry are discussed. The reason for doing so is that blockchain has been hyped in the industry and regarded as a new solution for overcoming some issues related to the insurance industry. However, blockchain technology is still new and mostly applied to the financial and supply chain sectors. In these various cases of blockchain applications in the industry, only a few cases are related to insurance services, though blockchain technology's characteristics provide a perfect pathway for the insurance industry to make use of the opportunities. The successful cases included herein have cost-saving results and a significant decrease in processing times as their outcomes when compared to traditional channels [13]. These cases demonstrate how insurance industry players address pain points or optimize business processes. In January 2017, DLA Singapore (hereafter referred to as DLA) announced that they introduced blockchain technology in the insurance industry by launching the DLA Claimchain [14]. The first successful example of such technology integration with insurance occurred in China. The technology aims to reduce administration and processing costs for the claims and health insurance sector. Along with Chain of Things, a Hong Kong-based distributed application development company, DLA slightly modified the underlying cryptocurrency client, using blockchain technology to provide verification of medical records. It involves obtaining the patient's consent to share their medical information, submitting an insurance claim, securely transmitting an encrypted medical report, and providing a hospital attendance record documented through timestamps [15]. The secure and encrypted transmission is done as a form of decentralized notarization of "the completion of medical procedures, rather than actual storage".

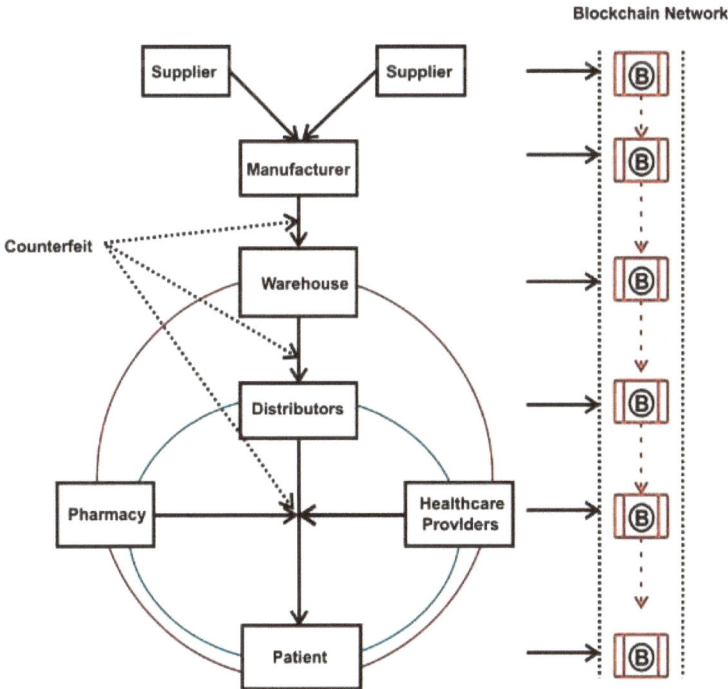

Fig. (3). Blockchain applications in the medical supply chain. [https://appinventiv.com/blog/blockchain-in-medical-supply-chain/].

The Fig. (**3**) depicts a blockchain-enabled system of the healthcare supply chain by making tracking and verification effortless at each step from supplier to end-users, ensuring transparency and authenticity. It starts when the raw materials are taken to the manufacturer by the supplier. The products are allocated a unique identifier that is entered on the blockchain immutably. These identifiers allow drug batches to be traced as they move through each subsequent process: warehousing, distributing, and dispensing to the pharmacies and the healthcare services before reaching the patient.

The blockchain network allows transactions at every level to be securely recorded and prevents the alteration of those records or identifies drugs entering the chain as counterfeit. Smart contracts enforce essential checks like proper storage conditions, authenticity checks, and whether they are handled appropriately through compliance. Blockchain's decentralized, tamper-proof feature of blockchain strengthens the resilience of the supply chain by having timely updates on the drug location and condition, along with details on handling.

This means that the integration of blockchain in the health supply chain mitigates fraud, reduces inefficiencies, and provides a secure mechanism of provenance verification. As such, only authentic and safe drugs will reach patients, thus instilling a culture of trust across industries, improving patient safety as well as overall integrity within the supply chain.

Industry Examples

Blockchain technology has dramatically changed the nature of insurance, especially the claim-processing process, for higher efficiency, transparency, and automation. The next section adds more detailed coverage of applications of blockchain in insurance; that is, specific performance metrics of insurance fields, implementation procedures, and real-world output results. One of the salient applications is the claim processing of smart contracts. Platforms such as Allianz's pilot blockchain project use Hyperledger Fabric to make travel insurance claims much easier, which has resulted in a reduction of claims settlement time by 50% [16] and the removal of errors in manual processing. It uses smart contracts that automatically validate conditions of claims—such as flight delays—and execute payments directly to policyholders' accounts, thereby removing delays due to intermediaries and ensuring timely compensation.

Allianz Allianz, a multinational financial services company, recently started testing a claims platform that uses blockchain in the travel insurance sector. Allianz uses Hyperledger Fabric and Ethereum in its test environment. Hyperledger is the main blockchain product used by Allianz in their pilot projects. The system allows customer claims to be processed faster without requiring claims decisions. All an insured person has to do at the time of his visit abroad is to report the claim through a mobile device about the detected travel deficiency [16]. Location determination is important since flight delays will not be paid for until the roads are closed to traffic to the airport. The customer's insurance company is connected to the system we developed. Customers' payment transactions are carried out over blockchain or, if necessary, in bank card transactions. When their insurance company's system becomes active at the time of the records, the identity details of the customer will be verified by the insurance company and their mobile device will be recognized. The identity verification service will be limited to the policies that the insurance company will make payments it receives from the customers. The patient's travel documents and the time and place of any incidents (accident, disease) are considered to be the genetic information the insurance companies are interested in, considering anti-money laundering (AML) and investment taxation applications of transmission requirements [17]. Secondly, Allstate has taken a huge step forward in the direction of blockchain technology used by the North American construction home services provider. Because this is a product of blockchain media, you cannot find a lot of information about this work. .. MetLife, as the sponsor of the "Spirit of Service Awards", is connected to blockchain technology. It relies on "the wisdom to inspire more people to adopt blockchain". Since 1875, the corporation has been backing its symbol, which is a particular peacock.

Another case study highlighted is the AXA Flight Delay Insurance program, which utilizes Ethereum's blockchain to automate payouts for delayed flights. The smart contracts on Ethereum integrate with an Oracle service to fetch real-time flight status. When a delay is confirmed, the smart contract automatically triggers payouts without requiring claim filing by the user. Further, AXA is the first product to have aroused public interest in the insurance industry. This is why we are interested in filling out our survey of block applications. The product offered by a French insurance group named AXA is Flight Delay Insurance, which is a partnership with Ethereum. The Ethisphere insurance agreement, based on the smart contract offered by the public blockchain network, is fully automated to provide real-time information about an airplane's flight temperature. After the arrival of the airplane, the profit can be paid out in a matter of minutes. There are no payment facilities when using an arsenal [18]. Fig. (4) shows a generalized blockchain-enabled insurance claim processing workflow adapted from all the case studies presented. The customer provides claim data to the insurance company, which then updates the claim status. The blockchain network stores the encrypted data and executes a smart contract to validate the claims. Third parties can access the claim data for validation, ensuring transparency and security in the claim processing process [19].

Customer ——Provides Claim Data—▶ Insurance Company ——Updates Claim Status—▶ Blockchain Network

Stores Encrypted Data—▶ Smart Contract Execution ——Validates Claims

Third Party

——Accesses Claim Data——

Fig. (4). Blockchain-enabled insurance claim processing.

REGULATORY CONSIDERATIONS AND COMPLIANCE

Adapting traditional insurance laws to the broader use of democratizing technologies presents several challenges. Regulators need to have sufficient knowledge of emerging technologies. They must also ensure the security and privacy of personal information and maintain the stability and effectiveness of the insurance market [20]. Legislators must address issues of ownership, incentivization, AI accountability, and the legal limitations of current regulation in the context of fintech automation and decentralized networks. As blockchain expands into decentralized applications, effectors of physical or proprietary rights, or changing contracts and building machines, we demonstrate the technical features of blockchain-based insurance (smart contract enforcement) that require integration with laws that may not yet exist. Anticipating and planning legislative responses is a challenge [21]. Legal systems are generally created reactively and struggle to keep pace with technological innovation. A proactive response to blockchain's potential beneficial and potentially harmful effects includes the formulation of legal interventions. Insurance laws often focus on registered insurance companies. The way the claims management function of insurance is transformed by blockchain requires insurers to modify statutes that reside in a decentralized data structure that avoids the need for traditional businesses. An example is the signature of the federal prosecutor in the USA, which creates a foreign verdict. Mutual government and mutual corporations are formed, which can act as private regulatory agencies in the insurance and other industries [22].

Legal Frameworks

Federal law regulates the registration of vehicles in Canada. All vehicles must be inspected and registered. In most provinces, claims for injuries resulting from a vehicle accident are compensated by provincial-run insurance programs. A body of case law with respect to the issuance of policies and claims resulting from accidents handles regulation within this industry. All of these are functions not inherently affected by blockchain technology [23, 24]. Naturally, there are operational processes supported by such technologies, but these processes do not comply with the liability regime. The paper "How Can Blockchain Technology Benefit the Insurance Industry in Emerging Markets" claims that any potential benefit from blockchain technology in the insurance space will ultimately be capped by the ability to claim funds on an insurance policy – something that the technology on its own is unequipped to do [25]. The requirements surrounding the principles of insurable interest and the principle of utmost good faith will remain vital to maintaining the insurance contract.

FUTURE TRENDS AND INNOVATIONS IN BLOCKCHAIN FOR INSURANCE

The integration of blockchain technology in the insurance sector has opened numerous opportunities to streamline and innovate business processes. Blockchain has gained interest mostly in cost reduction, fraud prevention, and payment processes, setting automating accountability, notary, and payment validation functions as a priority. To take advantage of its full potential, future developments must prioritize enhancing operational aspects such as blockchain design, infrastructure management, current systems integration, and transition costs. In this paper, a forensic-level analysis reveals how blockchain can greatly contribute to streamlining this Business Process Management stream: insurance claim and billing services. The current gap in the literature, which shows few studies focused on these essential services and low use percentages in the insurance sector, makes this study a crucial and exploratory preliminary step to open up new innovative IT applications in the insurance industry [26]. The present study strives to provide a practical analysis by professionals and in-depth knowledge that highlights the innovations and benefits experienced through blockchain technology and verifies that the performance measurement level meets the expected high standards. Further steps should deepen the benefits with specific metrics or service level standards and gap improvements. Breaking down blockchain features can facilitate the decision-making tools for transformation. This reduction simplifies the process of determining the actions or tasks that blockchain performs compared to current structures. While the literature focuses on generic and explorative studies, few practical and operational empirical accounts point out some innovative use cases to improve insurability in assets property and liability insurance. The world of insurance still has many unexplored aspects that require analyzing and focusing on specific insurance services [27]. Empirical research on innovative use case studies may provide easy-to-observe design principles, identifying viable blockchain-able insurance process characteristics to help insurance companies implement this technology effectively. The implications highlight future developments in the integration of blockchain in techniques for high-quality forensic-level decisions. Finally, in the next section, the research context, design, material, and model are described, followed by discussion and conclusion topics.

Smart Contracts

Although the potential of smart contracts arouses unmatched interest from many different industries, the concept itself is overly difficult to understand. A smart contract, also known as a self-executing contract or computerized contract, is a program that manages the transfer of digital assets between parties when the pre-agreed conditions that exist in its code are fulfilled. This feature of smart contracts makes them the best instrument for designing escrow services and identity management services for verifying the conformance of clients, multi-factor authorization, activation of access to resources, dispute resolution, and the use of oracles for checking external actions that affect the fulfillment of the condition for carrying out an operation [28]. Despite the increased efficiency that both industries and users derive from the use of such algorithms, smart contracts with full programming capability contain inherent security flaws. If it is realized without employing safety strategies, code logic and additional factors can be exploited by one of the parties to execute actions contrary to the spirit of the agreement. Thus, vulnerable smart contracts expose the involved parties to economic loss and legal risk.

CONCLUSION

The future of insurance carriers will become reliant on their success in harnessing the power of blockchain to streamline insurance claims and billing processes. Blockchain technology can create a positive and substantial impact on automating, streamlining, and enhancing the claims management process and billing across the insurance carriers' business lines. The innovation offered by blockchain, remodeling the billing and insurance claim process, promises systemic improvements in the insurance system. The broad array of difficulties that are confronted by the firms should stimulate technology, which will encourage reforms to the utilization and implementation of blockchain technology. We hope that the new opportunities predicted to arise from the use and implementation of this innovative blockchain resolve some of the most extensively acknowledged issues. There are hundreds of use cases for blockchain in insurance, and we can expect that, just like other financial services industries, the insurance sector will test and adopt blockchain in a variety of these different use cases. However, it remained at the early stages of exploration and adoption compared with use in CHs such as R3, the Hyperledger Project, and Digital Asset Holdings. It is vital that insurance firms understand the technology potential and prepare themselves to pursue the technologically associated risks as well.

AUTHORS' CONTRIBUTIONS

For Chapter 6, **Riya Sharma, Sharon Christa, Deep Mann,** and **Rajbir Kaur** contributed to the examination of blockchain's role in enhancing the efficiency of insurance claims and billing processes. **Riya Sharma** led the study's development, focusing on the challenges and benefits of blockchain integration in insurance claims management. **Sharon Christa** provided detailed insights into the regulatory considerations and compliance requirements essential for blockchain in the insurance sector. **Deep Mann** analyzed existing case studies and real-world applications of blockchain technology, illustrating successful implementations and industry impact. **Rajbir Kaur** contributed to identifying future trends and smart contract innovations, enhancing the understanding of blockchain's evolving role in the insurance industry. Together, the authors proposed a framework that highlights the potential of blockchain to revolutionize insurance claims and billing processes.

REFERENCES

[1]   Shetty A, Shetty AD, Pai RY, *et al.* Blockchain application in insurance services: A systematic review of the evidence. SAGE Open 2022; 12(1): 21582440221079877. Available from: https://journals.sagepub.com/doi/abs/10.1177/21582440221079877 [Internet]. [http://dx.doi.org/10.1177/21582440221079877]

[2]   Chetna L, Deepika S, C. Komalavalli. Applications of blockchain technology. Elsevier 2020; 213-43. Available from: https://www.sciencedirect.com/science/article/pii/ B9780128198162000095

[3]   Hans R, Zuber H, Rizk A, Steinmetz R. Blockchain and smart contracts: Disruptive technologies for the insurance market. In: Proceedings of the 23rd Americas Conference on Information Systems (AMCIS) 2017. Available from: https://core.ac.uk/download/pdf/301371768.pdf

[4]   Tarr, Julie-Anne. Distributed ledger technology, blockchain and insurance: Opportunities, risks and challenges. J. Technol. Insur. Law 2018; 29(3), 254-68. Available from: https://eprints.qut. edu.au/122862.

[5]   Oliver B. Transforming the insurance industry with blockchain and smart contracts: Enhancing efficiency, transparency, and trust. TechRxiv [Internet] 2023; 1(2), 105-110. Available from: https://www.techrxiv.org/doi/full/10.36227/techrxiv.24006237.v1

[6]   Narikimilli N, Kumar A, Antu A. Blockchain applications in healthcare—a review and future perspective. Springer 2020. Available from: https://link.springer.com/chapter/10.1007/978-3-0-0-59638-5_14

[7]   RKJ . AI-enhanced claims processing: Streamlining insurance operations. J Res Adm 2021. Available from: http://journalra.org/index.php/jra/article/view/1449

[8]   Trivedi S. Blockchain technology as an emerging technology in the insurance market. Emerald Insight 2022. Available from: https://www.emerald.com/insight/content/doi/10.1108/978-1-80262-605-620221006/full/html

[9]   Available from: https://scholar.google.com/scholar?hl=en&as_sdt=0%2C5&q=+Blockchain+Technology+on+Streamlining+Insurance+Claims+&btnG=

[10]   Okoampah E, Takyi K. RGA. Adoption of blockchain technology to streamline the claims settlement in the health insurance industry in Ghana. SSRN 2023. Available from: https://papers.ssrn.com/sol3/papers.cfm?abstract_id=4424646

[11] Bordekar JA, Gupta SK, Kumar A. Insurance claiming process based on blockchain technology using smart contracts. Int J Adv Res 2019. Available from: https://www.academia.edu/download/59123408/V5I1-120120190503-12928-inwpxt.pdf

[12] Trivedi S, Malik R. Blockchain technology as an emerging technology in the insurance market. Big Data: A Game Changer for Insurance Industry. 2022; pp. 81-100.
[http://dx.doi.org/10.1108/978-1-80262-605-620221006]

[13] Popovic D, Avis C, Byrne M, Cheung C, Donovan M, Flynn Y. Understanding blockchain for insurance use cases. Br Actuarial J 2020. Available from: https://www.cambridge.org/core/journals/british-actuarial-journal/article/understanding-blockchain-for-insurance-use-cases/3F0FBE7A633CE3EAC2CEA0DD98A63286

[14] Sun R, Garimella A, Han W. Transformation of the transaction cost and the agency cost in an organization and the applicability of blockchain—a case study of peer-to-peer insurance. Frontiers in Blockchain 2020. Available from: https://www.frontiersin.org/articles/10.3389/fbloc.2020.00024/full

[15] Pagano A, Romagnoli F. Implementation of blockchain technology in insurance contracts against natural hazards: A methodological multi-disciplinary approach. Environ Clim Technol 2019. Available from: https://sciendo.com/article/10.2478/rtuect-2019-0091

[16] Spydra . Unleashing the power of hyperledger fabric in insurance: Revolutionizing the blockchain landscape. Medium 2023. Available from: https://medium.com/@spydra/unleashing-the-power-of-hyperledger-fabric-in-insurance-revolutionizing-the-blockchain-landscape-827f2528a4c2

[17] Laroiya C, Saxena D. Applications of blockchain technology. Elsevier 2020. Available from: https://www.sciencedirect.com/science/article/pii/B9780128198162000095

[18] Hassan A, Ali MI, Ahammed R, Khan MM, Alsufyani N, Alsufyani A. Secured insurance framework using blockchain and smart contract. Scientific Programming 2021; 2021.
[http://dx.doi.org/10.1155/2021/6787406]

[19] Kar A. Diffusion of blockchain in the insurance industry: An analysis through the review of academic and trade literature. Elsevier 2021. Available from: https://www.sciencedirect.com/science/article/pii/S073658532030191X

[20] Bacon L, Tarr JA. Distributed ledger technology and blockchain: Insurance. Taylor & Francis 2024. Available from: https://www.taylorfrancis.com/chapters/edit/10.4324/9781003319054-5/distributed-ledger-technology-blockchain-lee-bacon-julie-anne-tarr

[21] Amponsah A. Blockchain in insurance: Exploratory analysis of prospects and threats. Semanticscholar 2021. Available from: https://pdfs.semanticscholar.org/1e3f5f71u72u68bb28120203 8u0u69617 735285e.pdf

[22] Popovic D, Avis C, Byrne M, Cheung C. Understanding blockchain for insurance use cases. Br Actuarial J 2020. Available from: https://www.cambridge.org/core/journals/british-actuarial-journal/article/understanding-blockchain-for-insurance-use-cases/3F0FBE7A633CE3-EAC2CEA0-DD98A63286

[23] PYJ . Regulatory issues in blockchain technology. Emerald Insight 2017. Available from: https://www.emerald.com/insight/content/doi/10.1108/JFRC-08-2016-0068/full/html

[24] Chen CL, Deng YY, Tsaur WJ, Li CT, Lee CC, Wu C-M. A traceable online insurance claims system based on blockchain and smart contract technology. Sustainability (Basel) 2021; 13(16): 9386.
[http://dx.doi.org/10.3390/su13169386]

[25] Charles W, Marler N, Long L. Blockchain compliance by design: Regulatory considerations for blockchain in clinical research. Front Blockchain 2019. Available from: https://www.frontiersin.org/articles/10.3389/fbloc.2019.00018/full

[26] RBJ . Blockchain and insurance: A review for operations and regulation. Emerald Insight 2020. Available from: https://www.emerald.com/insight/content/doi/10.1108/JFRC-09-2018-0127/full/html

[27]   Shetty A, Shetty AD, Pai RY, *et al.* Blockchain application in insurance services: A systematic review of the evidence. SAGE Open 2022; 12(1): 21582440221079877.
[http://dx.doi.org/10.1177/21582440221079877]

[28]   Shah M, Li C, Sheng M, Zhang Y. Smarter smart contracts: Efficient consent management in health data sharing. Springer 2020. Available from: https://link.springer.com/chapter/10.1007/978-3-030-60290-1_11

[29]   Gomasta SS, Dhali A, Tahlil T, Anwar MM, Ali ABMS. PharmaChain: Blockchain-based drug supply chain provenance verification system. Heliyon 2023; 9(7): e17957.
[http://dx.doi.org/10.1016/j.heliyon.2023.e17957] [PMID: 37483827]

CHAPTER 7

Smart Contracts and Healthcare Transactions

Keesara Sravanthi[1], P. Prasant[2,*], Rajeev Kumar Bedi[3] and Navneet Kumar Rajpoot[4]

[1] *Department of Information Technology, VNRVJIET University, Hyderabad, Telangana, India*

[2] *Department of Computer Science, AIPH University, Bhubaneswar, Odisha, India*

[3] *Department of Computer Science and Engineering, I. K. Gujral Punjab Technical University, Jalandhar, India*

[4] *Department of Computer Science & Engineering, Graphic Era (Deemed to be University), Dehradun, India*

Abstract: This chapter delves into the transformative role of smart contracts within healthcare transactions, emphasizing their potential to streamline processes, enhance data security, and optimize patient engagement. Built on blockchain technology, smart contracts automate agreements with embedded terms in code, offering a more secure, efficient, and transparent alternative to traditional methods. This study highlights the benefits of smart contracts in patient record management, insurance claim processing, and supply chain logistics, addressing critical challenges like high implementation costs, technical integration, and regulatory compliance. By exploring both opportunities and hurdles, this chapter provides insights into the future of smart contracts in the healthcare sector. This chapter is aimed at bringing a comprehensive view of smart contracts and their potential to transform healthcare transactions. The objectives of this chapter include exploring business opportunities of smart contracts and enhancing health products and services in the areas of electronic health records and processing of insurance claims. Further, the deployment of smart contracts will be evaluated with respect to risks, challenges, and ethical considerations for data privacy and regulatory compliance. It also evaluates the cost-benefit analysis that deals with financial implications and return on investment. Examples from the real world, along with future trends of applicability, practice, and novelty in this area, are addressed at the end of the chapter on the use of smart contracts in healthcare.

Keywords: Automation, Blockchain technology, Data privacy, Healthcare efficiency, Healthcare innovation, Healthcare transactions, Insurance claims, Patient data security, Regulatory compliance, Smart contracts.

---

* **Corresponding author P. Prasant:** Department of Computer Science, AIPH University, Bhubaneswar, Odisha, India; E-mail: pprasant@aiph.ac.in

Mohit Angurala, Preet Kamal, Aryan Chaudhary, Rasmeet Singh Bali & Vijay Bhardwaj (Eds.)
All rights reserved-© 2025 Bentham Science Publishers

INTRODUCTION

Smart contracts, developed on blockchain technology, represent a radical development associated with the management of healthcare transactions. They are self-executable contracts with directly embedded terms in code, thus making them efficient, secure, and transparent. Considering that the sector is heavily burdened by administrative complexities, high costs, and data privacy problems, smart contract implementation is likely to be very effective. Smart contracts have already established themselves in areas like patient record management, insurance claims, supply chain logistics, and other processes that have many intermediaries involved and are prone to errors. This chapter reviews smart contract capabilities to make a change in healthcare, explaining the technical grounds of their diverse applications and related benefits and addressing the challenges and future directions in this innovative field.

Structure

The chapter first discusses the opportunities and challenges in healthcare transactions, followed by enhancements to healthcare products and services, risks and challenges of implementing smart contracts, ethical and regulatory considerations, and utilization and cost analysis of smart contracts.

Potential of Blockchain in Healthcare

Blockchain holds immense potential to reshape healthcare by enhancing security, transparency, and efficiency in managing sensitive data and transactions. At its core, blockchain offers a decentralized, tamper-resistant system that can transform how patient records, insurance claims, and supply chains are managed, reducing reliance on intermediaries and lowering administrative costs. Smart contracts, a key feature of blockchain, can automate processes like insurance payouts and consent management, allowing instant, secure actions based on pre-set conditions. For patients, this means greater control over personal health data and assurance that information is securely stored and accessible only with permission.

Opportunities and Challenges in Healthcare Transactions

Opportunities

Streamlined Operations through Automation

Smart contracts in the operations of healthcare can revolutionize operations through a lot of routine procedures that make workflow easier and reduce many burdens of administration. Conventional health systems are characterized by manual operations, especially in areas such as patient registration, billing, and record keeping. These activities are very time-consuming, besides being prone to human error, hence giving rise to inefficiencies and inaccuracies.

These processes are automated using self-executing code under smart contracts. In the case of patient registration, smart contracts can automatically verify insurance details, fix appointments, and update the records of patients without human intervention [1]. The automation guarantees that all the steps involved in the process are efficiently followed, thus avoiding delays and reducing administrative workload.

One practical example of this is in the area of billing and insurance claims. Today, underwriting processes within the insurance industry are very hands-on; every claim made requires submission, verification, and subsequent reimbursement, which generally goes through a wide number of intermediaries, and involves a great deal of paperwork and information control. With smart contracts, once the healthcare service is rendered, the contract is executed—that is, a claim is automatically generated, with all the details verified against the patient's insurance policy for its viability, and upon approval, payment is then made. It reduces the time taken for reimbursement and also minimizes fraudulent cases involved in claims since everything is recorded on the blockchain and is transparent and immutable [2].

Enhanced Data Security and Privacy

Security and privacy in healthcare, with regard to the sensitivity of the patient's information, are paramount. Any traditional health system is easily prone to data breaches and undesired access, leading to huge financial and reputation losses.

Hybrid coordination, in which the Proof of Work (PoW) and proof of Stake (PoS) layers cross-verify each other's outputs, just adds another layer of redundancy to prevent manipulation by the entire system from one single entity. Implementations in the real world of hybrid consensus mechanisms have shown a potential yet still a considerable area of improvement. Ethereum 2.0 would replace the traditional PoW consensus algorithm and function as a hybrid system, adding more layers of security, while the scalability of Komodo, a blockchain application, would rely on its notarized checkpoints alongside PoW.

Looking forward, hybrid consensus mechanisms must balance scalability and security trade-offs such that increasing the capacity of transactions does not weaken the robustness of the system. Moreover, energy efficiency continues to be a significant challenge for hybrid models because they want to reduce the energy-intensive demands of PoW while ensuring reliability and decentralization, which is the foundation of blockchain security. Further research and innovation in technology will be required as it progresses in order to exploit hybrid consensus mechanisms and their inherent challenges fully.

Hybrid consensus mechanisms provide scope for improving the security and trustworthiness of blockchain systems by combining PoW with PoS. PoW, given that it is resistant to tampering due to its requirements on computational power, will also provide a solid base of block validation, and it is in PoS where energy efficiency becomes beneficial and active participation is made possible through staking by stakeholders. This dual-layered method ensures that attacks are highly costly and impossible without exerting both computational and economical efforts to breach the network. However, integrating these two mechanisms introduces complexity since, for seamless communication and interaction between the PoW layer and the PoS layers, it has to work out. With this, proper design and implementation of hybrid models are inevitable to avoid inefficiencies in hybrid designs, which may cause block validation to go slow or dispute between both components that can weaken the whole system.

Moreover, hybrid consensus mechanisms have significant implications for industries beyond cryptocurrency, particularly in sectors requiring high levels of data integrity, security, and transparency. For example, supply chain management systems can use hybrid consensus models to ensure the immutability of transactional data while benefiting from the scalability and energy efficiency of PoS. Similarly, in healthcare, these systems can protect sensitive patient data by leveraging PoW's tamper-proof characteristics alongside PoS's dynamic validator selection to secure access and ensure compliance with privacy regulations. As blockchain technology gains broader adoption, hybrid models will likely become increasingly relevant, offering tailored solutions to meet the diverse requirements of different applications. However, achieving widespread adoption will require addressing interoperability challenges, establishing standardized protocols, and ensuring compliance with evolving regulatory frameworks. By continuing to refine hybrid consensus mechanisms, blockchain technology can unlock new possibilities for secure, efficient, and scalable solutions across industries.

Smart contracts increase the security and privacy of the data through blockchain technology, a distributed and immutable ledger of data storage. Every single transaction on the blockchain is encrypted and then subsequently 'chained' to the one prior to it, effectively making all data alteration or hacking practically impossible.

For example, the creation and storage of EHRs *via* smart contracts allow their secure storage and management. Every time a patient's record is accessed or updated, the transaction gets recorded on the blockchain. This means there will be a clear audit trail of events regarding 'who accessed the data and when.' This ensures access to sensitive information of the patient by only authorized personnel, all the while rendering any unauthorized attempt easily detectable [3].

Moreover, smart contracts can also be used in the enforcement of privacy policies and consent management. This is developed by smart contracts that manage patient consent logic and enable fine-grained and revocable consent for access to health data. The respect of patient choice in sharing data only with authorized entities will ensure the protection of their data from unauthorized leakage or access. In this respect, trust and compliance with regulations like HIPAA will increase due to protection against unauthorized use.

Without proper engagement of the patient, it is not possible to deliver effective healthcare. Smart contracts can boost patient engagement through transparent, secure, and efficient means for managing the interactions of patients and their consent.

One of the major problems in healthcare includes collecting and managing patient consent for various treatments and data sharing. Traditionally, this involves the manual filling of forms and paperwork that can sometimes be very tedious to handle and mistake-laden. Smart contracts mechanize this process by digitization of consent in forms stored on the blockchain.

For example, a patient may consent to a surgical procedure through a smart contract that activates a sequence of subsequent care activities—such as scheduling the surgery, notifying treating health care providers, and updating the EHR—that ensures appropriate, extremely transparent consent.

It can also increase patient engagement due to real-time status updates and notifications. For instance, a smart contract can be programmed to send reminders to patients regarding upcoming appointments, medication schedules, and test results. Keeping patients up-to-date with regard to these things makes them informed and engaged in their care, which results in better health.

Challenges

<u>High Implementation Costs</u>

While there are many benefits, implementing smart contracts in healthcare has significant associated costs. These include not only the preliminary investments linked to the blockchain infrastructure and the development of smart contracts but also their continuous repair, renovation, and upgrade.

Specialized technical expertise is required for the development of smart contracts; the costs may be expensive. Healthcare organizations will have to bear the costs of hiring or training developers who are equipped with blockchain technology and the nuts and bolts of smart contract coding [4]. The development also requires the integration of smart contracts with the prevailing systems of healthcare and accomplishment of interoperability in the absence of any hassle, which can also be complex and costly.

For example, if a hospital wants to introduce smart contracts in its EHR management, it will have to build blockchain infrastructure, then develop smart contracts that will align with its mission, and finally integrate such contracts with its existing EHR system. All this is very time-consuming and expensive; it becomes a fact that turns into a barrier for many healthcare organizations, especially the smaller ones with limited budgets.

Furthermore, smart contracts need investments in maintenance and updating. As regulations and healthcare practices evolve over time, smart contracts have to be updated accordingly so as to remain compliant and effective. In such a way, this can turn into a cycle of continuous development, as it strains resources and makes budgeting complicated on the part of a healthcare provider.

Integration with Existing Healthcare Systems

One of the biggest challenges will be how smart contracts are going to be integrated into the existing healthcare systems. For instance, most healthcare organizations are running various types of legacy systems in managing their respective patient records, billing, claims, and other operational works. Most of these systems are outdated, fragmented, and not designed to work with blockchain technology.

Healthcare organizations wanting to implement smart contracts must, therefore, have the assurance of the possibility of communication between their existing systems and the blockchain network. That is realized by the development of interfaces and protocols between old systems and smart contracts that can support seamless data exchange. The integration process at this point may be highly complex or easy, depending on how varied and old the existing systems are.

For example, if smart contracts are to be allowed to interact with an EHR, this would involve mapping data fields from the EHR onto the blockchain and maintaining consistency in those data, creating workflows that enable the execution of smart contracts based on updates to the EHR. Such technical processes might prove very challenging, time-consuming, and heavy in coordination between IT teams, developers, and healthcare professionals.

Interoperability between different healthcare organizations is the most critical factor in the success of smart contracts. There must be common standards and protocols accepted by all participating entities—the healthcare providers, insurers, and other actors—and adhered to if the seamless exchange of information is to take place over the blockchain network. This kind of interoperability is hard to achieve because of the different standards and practices used by different organizations.

Regulatory Compliance

The healthcare industry is highly regulated in terms of the use, storage, and sharing of patient information, with strict laws and standards. In using smart contracts in healthcare, their regulations have to be put into consideration in order to ensure compliance.

Compliance of smart contracts to data protection laws, for example, under the HIPAA in the United States or the GDPR in Europe, is one of the major challenges relating to regulation [5]. It dictates very stringent controls around processing patient data, thereby providing for data encryption, access controls, and audit trails. Smart contracts will need to be designed with these provisions in mind. For instance, HIPAA wants all the patients' data in motion and at rest encrypted. Smart contracts in charge of EHRs should ensure that all data is well-encrypted, not only while resting on the blockchain but also while in transmission to varied healthcare providers. In addition, smart contracts must offer robust access controls that would bar the possibility of accessing a patient's information by unauthorized people.

Another regulatory challenge is the need to ensure that smart contracts are capable of being audited and checked for compliance. Regulators should be in a position to review smart contract codes and transaction records to ensure that healthcare providers meet legal standards. This will call for the development of auditing tools for smart contracts and the institution of procedures that give transparency to their execution.

Suppose a smart contract has been deployed for the automation of insurance claim processing; regulators would want to inspect the said contract to enforce policies strictly and evaluate insurance claims transparently. This could be realized through the examination of source code for smart contracts, transaction logs, or the output from executed contracts.

Another degree of complexity finally arises from the fact that healthcare regulations continue to evolve. Every time new laws and standards are defined, smart contracts have to be redefined to abide by those laws. Consequently, a health organization must keep itself updated regarding changes in laws and standards and, based on those changes, update its implementation of smart contracts.

Although smart contracts show great opportunities for healthcare transaction optimization, data security improvement, and patient empowerment, there are also numerous challenges to the high costs of implementation, integration into legacy systems, and regulatory compliance. A healthcare organization should, therefore, carefully weigh opportunities and challenges, strategically develop plans for implementing these digital solutions, and invest in technical and regulatory expertise to make the best use of smart contracts in operations. Only if the challenges are addressed will the healthcare sector exploit the potential of smart contracts in healthcare delivery and bring positive change to patient outcomes.

Enhancements to Healthcare Products and Services

EHR: More efficient management and security in patients' health records sharing electronic health records are the keystone of every healthcare information system. They harbor a patient's digital record of their complete medical history, treatments, and diagnoses. Combining EHR systems with smart contracts will help bring automation and security into management and sharing.

Automated Management

Smart contracts automate processes within EHR management, hence making it easy. For example, when a healthcare provider changes a patient's record by adding a new diagnosis or treatment plan or updating medication to the prescription, the smart contract checks this update against predefined rules and records the event on the blockchain. This serves to reduce administrative burdens and minimize errors, ensuring all updates are transparent and temper-proof.

Secure Sharing

Buttressing secure sharing of patient records is very important if the privacy of patients is to be protected and healthcare regulations implemented. Smart contracts secure data sharing through the encryption of sensitive information and management of permission by access to the blockchain. For instance, if a patient had visited different healthcare providers or specialists, a smart contract would help facilitate controlled access to different parts of the patient's EHR according to preset conditions and permissions.

Example: This is the case if a patient is transferred to another hospital for specialized treatment:

- Scenario: Patient X is transferred from Hospital A to Hospital B for surgery.
- Smart Contract Action: A request for transfer is given by Hospital A by updating Patient X's EHR with a transfer authorization note. It checks the request for predefined criteria, including consent and medical necessity, and then proceeds with recording this transfer transaction in a secure form on the blockchain.
- Results: Timely and secure access to all of Patient X's medical history and treatment plans will be available to Hospital B, and therefore, the continuum of care is preserved without losing time in re-designing or reproducing information.

Insurance Claim Processing: Faster and fraud-resistant claim processing.

The process for insurance claims involves checking the services availed by the customer against the terms of the policy and processing them immediately for reimbursement. Smart contracts have proven to be able to optimize this multi-step process by making it faster, more transparent, and resistant to fraud.

Faster Processing

Smart contracts automate the validation of an insurance claim and its further processing. Hence, it saves time from normally conducting manual reviews. If a healthcare provider submits a claim for reimbursement, then the information will be checked by the smart contract against the terms and conditions that a patient has agreed to as part of his or her insurance policy. Provided that such a claim corresponds to all the criteria, a smart contract is enabled to approve the payment automatically and initiate it, which enables faster retribution to healthcare providers.

Example: A patient is admitted and operated in Hospital C:

- Scenario: Patient Y is operated in Hospital C.
- Smart Contract Action: The healthcare provider submits an insurance claim to the smart contract, which matches the claim against predetermined criteria such as procedure codes and coverage limits. It checks on the patient's blockchain-stored insurance policy for coverage and thus automatically approves a claim.
- Output: The amount, after being validated, is automatically paid to Hospital C, ensuring that the money will be efficiently reimbursed without one party delaying or disputing the other.

Fraud-Resistant Claims

Smart contracts enhance security by establishing a non-deniable and transparent record of every transaction that involves claims. It is recorded on a blockchain through which smart contracts reduce the risk of fraudulent activities related to double billing or the falsification of treatment records. It deters fraudulent behaviors because data manipulation would be detected and traceable.

Supply Chain Management: Enhanced Transparency and Traceability

Healthcare requires effective supply chain management so that drugs, medical devices, and supplies are delivered on time without affecting quality or safety in the process. In this respect, smart contracts enhance transparency and traceability in the healthcare supply chain—from procurement to distribution.

Enhanced Transparency

Smart contracts allow visibility in real-time into the movement of supplies within healthcare and the status regarding the shipment and delivery of those supplies. Each interaction, from ordering to shipping and delivery, gets recorded on the blockchain. It creates an immutable record for all authorized parties. This reduces discrepancies in the supply chain while ensuring that ripples with the inventory are accurate and also aids efficiency in procurement processes.

Example: Consider the management of COVID-19 vaccines during a global vaccination campaign:

- Scenario: A healthcare facility orders COVID-19 vaccines from a pharmaceutical supplier.
- Smart Contract Action: The amount, due date, and conditions for the delivery of that order are registered in a smart contract. As the vaccines are shipped, each curveball milestone (*e.g.*, leaving supplier, received at the facility) is registered as a transaction on the blockchain.
- Output: Healthcare administrators and regulators will trace the entire supply chain process on a real-time basis to ensure safe distribution without any lack of documentation to the national network of vaccination centers.

Smart contracts allow each product batch or shipment to be linked to its origin and journey through the supply chain. In case of a product and quality issue, this provides support for fast batch recall, aiding with the swift tracing of affected batches. It supports rapidly affected health providers in this junction to be able to take the necessary actions to maintain patient safety and execute regulatory compliance.

Telemedicine Services

Telemedicine has been a critical part of healthcare delivery, enabling patients to receive medical services from any location through the use of digital communication technologies. It optimizes the transactions pertaining to telemedicine with increased efficiency, security, and respect towards the regulatory requirements by using smart contracts.

Efficient Transactions

Smart contracts self-execute the scheduling of appointments, management of patient consent for virtual consultations, and secure payment processing, making telemedicine transactions absolutely frictionless. For example, when a patient books an appointment for a telehealth consultation, the smart contract checks on physician availability, confirms patient eligibility, and successfully logs this appointment on the blockchain. This whole process helps in improving operational efficiency and raising patient satisfaction.

Example: Consider a telemedicine appointment booking:

- Scenario: Patient Z schedules a virtual consultation with a physician.
- Smart Contract Action: A patient selects an open time slot for a visit *via* an online platform, which triggers the verification of the physician's availability and patient eligibility by the smart contract. Post verification of the same, it will ensure all appointment details are securely captured by the smart contract and take prior consent from the patient for telehealth services.
- Output: The telehealth consultation happens smoothly; all transactional details get securely documented on the blockchain for audit and compliance purposes.

Smart contracts certainly rank among the most disruptive technologies in healthcare today, given the huge strides they are making in EHR management, insurance claims processing, supply chain transparency, and telemedicine services. By automating the process, smart contracts increase security, hence increasing efficiency in enabling care organizations to provide greater and more patient-oriented care [6, 7]. As healthcare continues to break frontiers, smart contracts will contribute to that innovation by driving better operational workflow and ensuring better health outcomes for patients across the globe.

RISKS AND CHALLENGES OF IMPLEMENTING SMART CONTRACTS

While smart health care is full of promise, there are several risks and operational challenges that have to be dealt with when applying smart contracts in healthcare.

Technical Risks

Vulnerabilities in Smart Contract Code

One of the significant technical risks is that the smart contract code itself may be vulnerable. Smart contracts are realized with programming languages like Solidity, and as with any other type of coding error or oversight in a program, they give rise to security vulnerabilities. For instance, this may lead to severe bugs where malicious attackers may take advantage of such loopholes, therefore compromising data integrity or executing unwanted transactions. Auditing and rigorous testing are necessary for spotting these dangers and mitigating them before deployment.

This construes that the scalability of smart contracts remains an open challenge, in particular within the healthcare sector, where transactions are run into large volumes of data every day. As the number of transactions grows, smart contracts may be faced with scalability issues, which may lead to delays or an increase in cost per transaction [8]. Moreover, another technological challenge that needs to be addressed is interoperability: ensuring smart contracts can interoperate seamlessly with existing healthcare information technology systems and external platforms.

Operational Challenges

- Resistance to change from stakeholders.
- Integrating smart contracts into healthcare operational workflows takes a great deal of buy-in and cooperation from various stakeholders [9]. These stakeholders include healthcare providers, administrators, and regulatory bodies.
- Some amount of resistance to the change can be because the technology underlying smart contracts is complex; disruption of current workflows can happen, with possible job loss. Addressing these concerns through education, training, and demonstration of tangible benefits is very key to acceptance and adoption.

Need for Ongoing Maintenance and Updates

Smart contracts require constant monitoring, maintenance, and updating processes to counter evolving cybersecurity threats, regulatory changes, and technological advancement. In this regard, smart contracts are run autonomously immediately after deployment, so implementing updates or fixes without careful planning and adherence to governance protocols is quite a challenge compared to traditional software applications. Smart contracts can, over time, expose healthcare organizations to security vulnerabilities or compliance problems if not frequently maintained and updated (Fig. **1**).

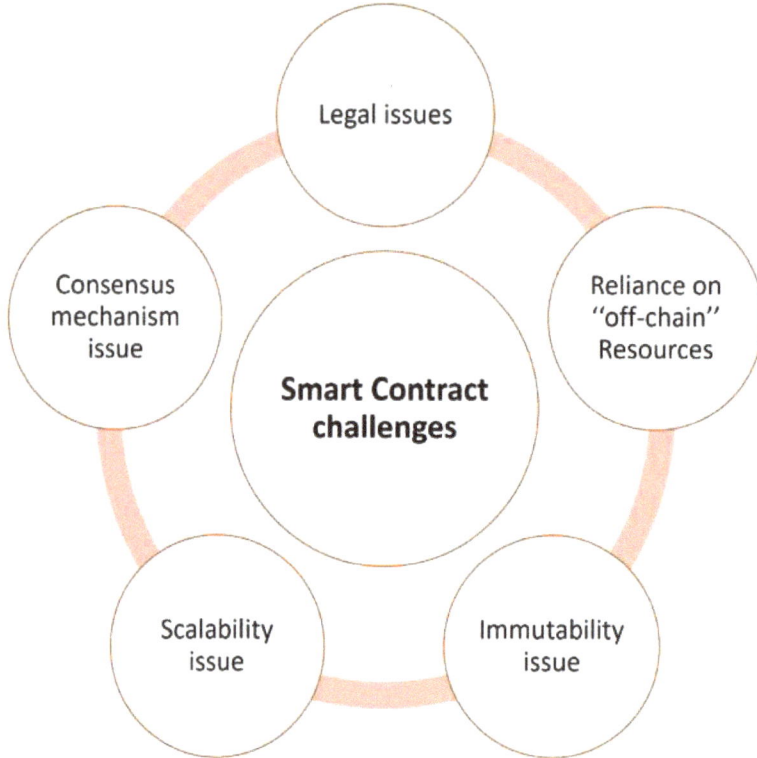

Fig. (1). Challenges in smart contract implementation.

Mitigating Risks and Overcoming Challenges

The organization must adopt a systematic approach for effectively mitigating risks and successfully handling challenges during the implementation process of smart contracts within the health sector. This involves:

- **Thorough Code Audits and Testing:** Conduct comprehensive audits and rigorous testing of smart contract code to identify and rectify vulnerabilities before deployment.
- **Scalability Planning:** Plan scalability needs by making scalable smart contracts and research layer-two protocols or sidechain solutions for higher transaction volumes.
- **Stakeholder Engagement and Education:** This involves the early involvement of all stakeholders during the implementation process and communicating to them the benefits of the smart contracts with several various training programs/workshops [10].

- **Robust Governance and Compliance Frameworks:** Establish governance frameworks to oversee smart contract deployment, maintenance, and updates, ensuring adherence to regulatory requirements and industry standards.
- **Continuous Monitoring and Maintenance:** Implement robust monitoring tools and protocols to detect anomalies, ensure data integrity, and promptly address security incidents or operational issues.
- **Collaboration and Interoperability:** Foster collaboration with industry peers and technology partners to promote interoperability standards and integrate smart contracts with existing healthcare IT infrastructure seamlessly.

Provided that healthcare organizations are proactive in taking all necessary measures to realize the risks and challenges, the full transformative power of smart contracts can be tapped for efficient, transparent, and effective health management. This would further improve the quality of patient outcomes and avoid the fall into potential pitfalls in the process of their implementation.

Ethical and Regulatory Considerations

The implementation of smart contracts in healthcare puts forth a set of ethical and regulatory issues, given that adequate caution should be taken to protect patient's rights, the dignity of health services, and compliance with law standards. This section addresses salient points on ethical and regulatory issues about privacy, transparency, and accountability.

Patient Data Privacy: Safeguarding Data

Data privacy forms one of the foundations of good ethical healthcare practice. With health records being digitized and smart contracts implemented, the need for protecting patient data becomes more critical than ever. Smart contracts are implemented in such a manner that access to huge amounts of personal and medical data is inevitable to execute their functions, hence bringing the data security and privacy aspects into question.

Security Measures for the Protection of Data

Such techniques include robust methods of encryption to guard patient information. All data REST and in transit, stored and processed by smart contracts, should be encrypted. Secure multi-party computation and zero-knowledge proofs can be implemented on top of this to provide more privacy. These methods confirm and process data without the actual exposure of sensitive information.

Example: Patient data sharing for consultation with specialists:

- Scenario: A primary care physician intends to share patients' health information to get a second opinion from the specialist:
- Smart Contract Action: The smart contract authenticates the request to ensure the intended specialist has requisite authorization and relevance to the data shared and limitation of data shared to the needs of the consultation.
- Results: Sharing of patient data in a secure setting, which is opened only to the intended specialist, hence maintaining their privacy while securing effective healthcare delivery.

Regulatory Compliance

Compliance with the Health Insurance Portability and Accountability Act in the United States, General Data Protection Regulation in Europe, and regional laws on data protection is very important [11]. Smart contracts should be designed such that these regulations are addressed by establishing and providing a record of informed consent by patients for sharing their data and for access to it, which should only be possible by authorized personnel, and it should be auditable.

Transparency: Clearly stated, understandable terms of the contract.

The transactions occurring in healthcare need transparency to instill trust between patients and care providers, especially other stakeholders. Smart contracts can improve this transparency by having clearly defined immutable transaction and contract terms records. However, the complexity of smart contract code makes it difficult to be understood by non-technical stakeholders.

Simplification of Terms in Smart Contracts

This should be done with supporting plain language around the smart contract's terms and conditions so that all parties to it — patients, healthcare providers, insurers and regulators — know what the contract has in store for them. This can further be improved with user-friendly interfaces and dashboards to depict activities underway on smart contracts.

Example: Use case of insurance claim processing:

- Scenario: A patient brings in an insurance claim for a medical surgery treatment.
- Smart Contract Action: The smart contract processes the claim based on predetermined conditions. It is available within a dashboard with full transparency with a view of the present state of claims, their process of approval, and the expected time for reimbursement.

- Outcome: More importantly, by using real-time monitoring, patients and healthcare providers are able to trace every step, reduce uncertainty, and lower administrative overhead.
- Ethical Implications.
- Ethically, transparency would ensure that patients are fully informed on how their data is used and the terms of any smart contract they have entered. An environment will be thus based on trust, empowering patients to make decisions regarding their health.
- Accountability: Making responsibility for smart contract execution and possible failures.

Need for Accountability Mechanisms

Accountability in smart contract execution is a must to ensure that errors or failures have a response to them, and there is no doubt as to who is responsible for the management of the contract. In healthcare, with the stakes being very high, accountability mechanisms need to be very robust and well-defined.

Smart Contract Audits

This is an indication that the smart contracts go through reviews from time to time to ascertain if they perform the intended operation and align with jurisdictional requirements. Audits thus detect loopholes and areas that require upgrading so that smart contracts will remain true to their reliability and safety attributes with an elapse of time [12].

Example: Mistake in the execution of a smart contract:

- Scenario: A smart contract refuses to pay for the claim due to a fault in the programming.
- Smart Contract Action: The Audit system flags the error and exercises the dispute resolution mechanism at hand [13].
- Results: The error is investigated, the claim gets manually re-evaluated and corrected, and the audit log serves as a transparent record of the incident and the resolution process.

Legal and Ethical Accountability

This would apply to the establishment of clear accountability in the events of deployment and management of smart contracts. From a legal point of view, healthcare providers, software developing companies, and insurers must be liable for their activities. In ethical terms, this ensures that patients have a redressal mechanism in case the smart contracts go wrong or give undesired results.

Governance and Dispute Resolution

Governance frameworks are important in the operationalization of smart contracts in cases of dispute or error detection. They should detail clear procedures for updating the contract, addressing discrepancies, and resolving disputes. This way, a transparent and just mechanism for the resolution of disputes lays the foundation for maintaining trust in smart contract systems.

Practical Implementation Considerations

<u>Integrating Smart Contracts with Existing Systems</u>

- The practical difficulties seen in the implementation of smart contracts in health are those devices being integrated with already existing healthcare information systems, electronic health records, and other legacy systems [14, 15]. This needs a firm octal of interoperability standards and protocols.
- Healthcare entities need to follow standards of interoperability, like HL7 FHIR (Fast Healthcare Interoperability Resources), for hassle-free interaction of smart contracts with the existing systems. Such standards allow for the interchange of healthcare information; therefore, smart contracts can also access information from a broad range of sources to process the same.
- Standardization of data formats and protocols is a big requirement in the actualization of smart contracts. It focuses on ensuring that data to be handled by smart contracts is consistent and accurate and can thus be shared by several health systems. Data standardization at this level ensures that there is a reduction in probability errors while making operations efficient for the smart contract [16 - 18].

Example in Real-life: Interoperability in the management of EHRs:

- Scenario: In a hospital where smart contracts are used to automate the process of sharing patients' data among departments.
- Its Smart Contract Action: Smart contracts are implemented that automatically fetch and share, if needed, patient records from the hospital's EHR system with radiology and laboratory departments using HL7 FHIR standards.
- Its Outcome: Sharing patient data interdepartmentally has been so simplified that it has bettered care coordination, trimming all kinds of administrative burdens associated with it.

Complying and Ensuring Ethical Use

Ethical Guidelines and Best Practices

These guidelines and best practices should be mandated in an ethical way in healthcare organizations. The guidelines should handle issues on patient consent acquisition, data privacy issues, and the ethics involved when a decision is taken by automation. Such use of smart contracts should follow ethical practices relating to the interest of the patients in question.

Obtaining consent and managing it vis-a-vis the patient is one of the main ethical and regulatory requirements. Through the use of smart contracts, patient consent can be automated in a way that affects the acquisition, recording, and management of the same in a transparent manner [19]. The patients should understand and be in control of how the data is used and who has access to it.

Example: Automated patient consent:

- Scenario: A patient reports to the health facility and is supposed to give consent to start a new line of treatment.
- Smart Contract Action: The smart contract shall detail the treatment plan to the patient *via* an interactive interface, record his consent, and update the EHR of the patient.
- Outcome: The consent of the patient will be openly recorded and managed for compliance with ethical and regulatory requirements.

Applying smart contracts in healthcare has to drive through a complex scenario of ethical and regulatory considerations. Data privacy, transparency, and accountability are essential elements of any successful implementation strategy. On such fertile ground, health organizations, by addressing the existing challenges and following good practices in their application, will successfully deploy smart contracts to bring about increased efficiency, security, and patient trust in their transactions. As the technology continues to evolve, work on the refinement of ethical guidelines, improvement of interoperability, and assurance of compliance will be paramount to the full realization of the potential that smart contracts have for healthcare transactions.

Use and Cost Analysis of Smart Contracts

The health transaction smart contract holds a great deal of future in convenience, security, and cost reduction. A complete utilization and costing study would be better understood for its financial implications, the measure of effectiveness, and the return on investment (Fig. **2**). It gives an in-depth analysis of the cost-benefit, utilization metrics, and ROI, supported by technical insights and real-life examples.

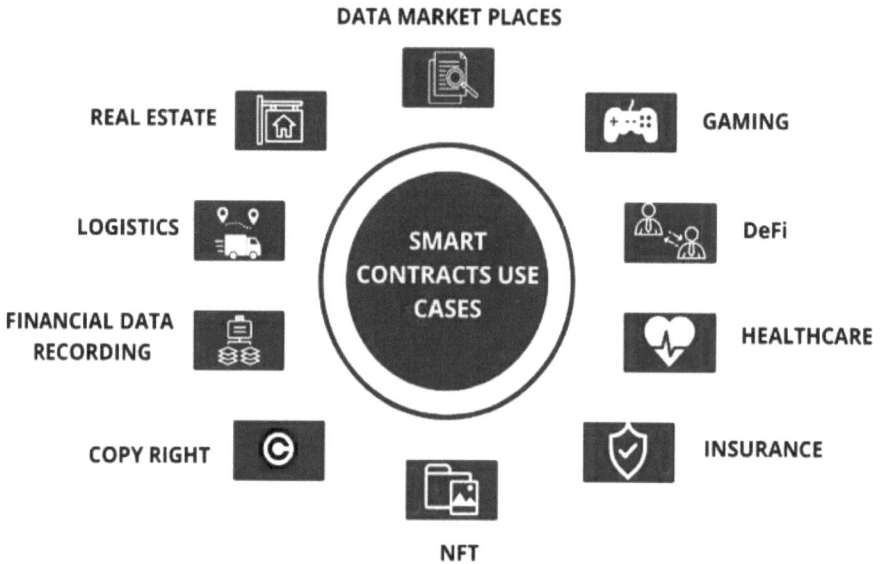

Fig. (2). Smart contract use and expenses.

Cost-Benefit Analysis

The initial investment for a smart contract includes:

- Development Costs: It requires hiring blockchain developers to develop and deploy smart contracts.
- Setting up Blockchain Infrastructure: Setting up nodes and cloud services as blockchain infrastructure.
- Integration Costs: Smart contracts are supposed to be integrated with traditional healthcare information technology systems.
- Training Costs: These costs are incurred to enlighten the staff and stakeholders on using and managing smart contracts.
- These can be very expensive, particularly for large healthcare organizations with their invariably complicated IT environments. However, such upfront investments are required to put in place the foundations for efficient and secure smart contract operations.

Operational Costs

Some of the ongoing operational costs include:

- Maintenance and Updates: The actual updating of smart contracts regularly in reaction to vulnerabilities and regulatory changes.
- Transaction Fees: The costs for executing the transactions on the blockchain itself.
- Security and Monitoring: Configuration of security elements with monitoring tools that would ensure the integrity of smart contracts and their performance.
- Notwithstanding, these recurrent costs will result in saving the smart contract from costs contributed by huge administrative overheads and operational inefficiencies in the long term.

Cost Savings and Efficiency Gains

A few of the potentials for cost savings and efficiency gains that surround smart contracts include (Table **1**):

Table 1. Cost-benefit analysis overview.

Cost Type	Description	Estimated Impact
Initial Setup Costs	Development, infrastructure, integration, training	High
Operational Costs	Maintenance, transaction fees, monitoring, and security	Moderate
Cost Savings	Reduced administrative costs, improved data accuracy, fraud prevention	High

- **Lower Admin Costs:** It can reduce administrative costs with the automation of insurance claims, patient data management, and billing, which would reduce the need for manual intervention.
- **Greater Accuracy of Data:** Smart contracts reduce costs associated with correcting errors and reconciling discrepancies by reducing errors in data entry and processing.
- **Better Fraud Prevention:** The immutable nature of blockchain technology helps avoid fraud, which could save millions of dollars for healthcare organizations.

UTILIZATION METRICS: MEASURING THE EFFECTIVENESS AND EFFICIENCY IMPROVEMENTS BROUGHT BY SMART CONTRACTS

Key Utilization Metrics

The following utilization metrics can, in general, be tracked to denote the effectiveness of smart contracts in healthcare:

- **Transaction Volume:** This refers to the volume of the different transactions processed using a smart contract.
- **Processing Time:** The time taken for processing any particular transaction through smart contracts as compared to traditional processes.
- **Error Rate:** The frequency of errors in transactions handled by smart contracts as opposed to manual processes.
- **Compliance Rate:** The percentage of transactions in adherence to regulatory standards.
- **Stakeholder Satisfaction:** Feedback from patients, healthcare providers, and insurers regarding the user-friendliness and efficiency of smart contracts.

Transaction Volume and Processing Time

Smart contracts are capable of processing volumes of transactions with minimal delay. For instance, smart contracts can reduce the weeks it takes to process insurance claims to mere minutes. Such a vast reduction in time enhances operational efficiency and cash flow for healthcare providers.

Example: Insurance claim processing:

- Traditional Method: Processing the claim manually requires data entry, validation, and approval procedures sometimes take several weeks (Table 2).
- Smart Contract Method: A smart contract will automate these tasks of validation and approval, reducing the time to minutes.

Table 2. Comparison of processing time.

Process	Traditional Method	Smart Contract Method
Insurance Claims	2-4 weeks	10-20 minutes
Patient Data Sharing	1-3 days	Instant
Billing and Payments	3-5 days	Instant

Error Rate and Data Accuracy

Smart contracts eliminate errors due to human blunders in data entry and processing. Assuring that all the transactions will take place according to the pre-defined terms of smart contract optimizes data accuracy, lowering the chance of errors that cost so much to be corrected and disputed.

Compliance Rate

The healthcare industry has very strict regulations regarding data protection, billing, and reporting standards. Smart contracts can be programmed to comply with these regulations automatically, thereby ensuring a high rate of compliance and reducing the possibility of fines and litigation.

Stakeholder Satisfaction: Healthcare regulations are strict in terms of data protection, billing, and reporting standards. This will help in high compliance rates and reduce the risks of fines and litigation.

The efficiency and transparency that smart contracts can bring to the value chain will increase the satisfaction of all the stakeholders. Patients will benefit from faster services and more transparent billing, while healthcare providers and insurers appreciate a reduced administrative burden and better cash flow (Table 3).

Table 3. Utilization metrics overview.

Metric	Description	Impact
Transaction Volume	Number of transactions processed	High
Processing Time	Time taken to execute transactions	Reduced by 90%+
Error Rate	Frequency of errors in transactions	Reduced significantly
Compliance Rate	Adherence to regulatory standards	High
Stakeholder Satisfaction	Feedback from patients, providers, and insurers	Improved

Example: Patient satisfaction:

- Scenario: A patient uses a smart contract-enabled telemedicine service.
- Outcome: The patient experiences seamless appointment booking, instant data sharing with the physician, and immediate billing and payment processing, leading to higher satisfaction.

Return on Investment (ROI)

Healthcare organizations, however, have to consider the initial and recurrent costs against the long-term benefits of knowing the ROI of smart contract implementation. Thus, considering the above definition of a basic smart contract, the ROI is computable using the following formula:

$$ROI = \frac{\text{Net Benefits}}{\text{Total Costs}} \times 100$$

Where:

Net Benefits = Total Savings + Efficiency Gains − Total Costs

Total Costs = Initial Setup Costs + Operational Costs

Example Calculation

Now, assume that the following costs and savings are incurred by a healthcare organization over a year:

Initial Setup Costs: $500,000

Annual Operational Costs: $200,000

Annual Savings from Reduced Administrative Costs: $300,000

Annual Savings from Improved Data Accuracy: $150,000

Annual Savings from Fraud Prevention: $100,000

The total savings are $550,000 per annum; the total costs in the first year are $700,000. The net benefits in the first year are:

Net Benefits=$550,000−$700,000=−$150,000

The ROI in the second year and beyond would be:

$$ROI = \frac{\$350,000}{\$200,000} \times 100 = 175\%$$

Long-Term Benefits

Long-term benefits of smart contracts in healthcare go beyond financial savings, including:

- Improved Patient Outcomes: Faster and more accurate data sharing and processing lead to better clinical decision-making and patient care.
- Enhanced Trust and Transparency: Immutable records of transactions and clear contract terms build trust among patients, providers, and insurers.
- Regulatory Compliance: Automated adherence to regulatory standards reduces the risk of non-compliance and associated penalties.

CASE STUDY: SMART CONTRACTS IN TELEMEDICINE

Consider a healthcare provider that implements smart contracts for telemedicine services. The following are the benefits that the provider experiences (Table **4**):

Table 4. Long-term benefits analysis.

Benefit	Description	Impact
Improved Patient Outcomes	Better data sharing and processing	High
Enhanced Trust	Transparent and immutable transaction records	High
Regulatory Compliance	Automated adherence to standards	High
Reduction in No-Show Rates	Automated reminders and rescheduling	20% reduction
Increased Revenue	Faster billing and payment processing	Improved cash flow
Patient Retention	Higher satisfaction and seamless services	15% increase

Reduction in No-Show Rates: Automated appointment reminders and easy rescheduling through smart contracts reduce no-show rates by 20%.

Increased Revenue: Faster billing and payment processing increase revenue collection efficiency, improving cash flow.

Patient Retention: Improved patient satisfaction due to seamless service delivery enhances patient retention rates by 15%.

The utilization and cost analysis of smart contracts in healthcare portray a very promising landscape of efficiency gains, cost savings, and improved patient outcomes [20]. Though the initial setup and operational costs are big, the long-term benefits and high ROI justify the investment. It is only by carefully assessing the financial implications, measuring effectiveness through utilization metrics, and assessing ROI that a healthcare organization would be better positioned to make decisions for the implementation of smart contracts. These efforts will not only be operationally efficient and secure but also lay down the groundwork for trust and transparency between all entities involved in a healthcare ecosystem. By using these insights, healthcare organizations can move away from traditional systems and start using innovative blockchain-based solutions that will create an environment where patient care is synchronized with technologocal advancements. When smart contracts are used and aligned with strategic goals as well as stakeholder collaboration, they can change the future of healthcare delivery. Recent developments, such as decentralized consent management for safe sharing of health records [21], attribute-based models of data access in blockchains [22], and new integrity management systems for electronic medical records [23], indicate the importance of blockchain technologies in the development of next-generation healthcare ecosystems.

CONCLUSION

Smart contracts represent a significant advancement in healthcare transactions, offering solutions that simplify complex administrative processes, bolster data security, and improve patient engagement. By automating tasks like patient registration and insurance claims processing, they reduce administrative burdens and minimize errors. Despite their potential, challenges such as high implementation costs, integration with legacy systems, and meeting regulatory requirements must be addressed. As healthcare organizations navigate these complexities, a strategic approach to adopting smart contracts can unlock long-term benefits, including increased operational efficiency, enhanced trust among stakeholders, and improved patient outcomes. The future of smart contracts in healthcare holds promise, contingent on addressing these challenges with continued innovation and adaptation.

AUTHORS' CONTRIBUTION

For Chapter 7, Keesara Sravanthi, P. Prasant, Rajeev Kumar Bedi, and Navneet Kumar Rajpoot collaboratively contributed to the exploration of smart contracts in healthcare. Keesara Sravanthi led the analysis of the technical structure and the transformative potential of smart contracts within healthcare transactions. P. Prasant provided insights on the operational challenges, high implementation costs, and integration issues with existing healthcare systems. Rajeev Kumar Bedi focused on regulatory compliance and ethical considerations, addressing data privacy and patient consent management. Navneet Kumar Rajpoot examined case studies, real-world applications, and future trends, enhancing the practical insights of smart contract adoption in healthcare. Together, the authors developed a comprehensive view of smart contracts' role in optimizing healthcare transactions.

REFERENCES

[1]   Hewa TM, Hu Y, Liyanage M, Kanhare SS, Ylianttila M. Survey on blockchain-based smart contracts: Technical aspects and future research. IEEE Access 2021; 9: 87643-62.
       [http://dx.doi.org/10.1109/ACCESS.2021.3068178]

[2]   Velmovitsky PE, Bublitz FM, Fadrique LX, Morita PP. Blockchain applications in health care and public health: increased transparency. JMIR Med Inform 2021; 9(6): e20713.
[http://dx.doi.org/10.2196/20713] [PMID: 34100768]

[3]   Shafiq M, Gu Z, Cheikhrouhou O, Alhakami W, Hamam H. The rise of "Internet of Things": Review and open research issues related to detection and prevention of IoT-based security attacks. Wirel Commun Mob Comput 2022; 2022: 1-12.
[http://dx.doi.org/10.1155/2022/8669348]

[4]   Chang V, Baudier P, Zhang H, Xu Q, Zhang J, Arami M. How Blockchain can impact financial services – The overview, challenges and recommendations from expert interviewees. Technol Forecast Soc Change 2020; 158: 120166.
[http://dx.doi.org/10.1016/j.techfore.2020.120166] [PMID: 32834134]

[5]   Politou E, Alepis E, Virvou M, Patsakis C. Privacy and data protection challenges in the distributed era. Springer 2022; p. 26.
[http://dx.doi.org/10.1007/978-3-030-85443-0]

[6]   Chen CL, Deng YY, Tsaur WJ, Li CT, Lee CC, Wu CM. A traceable online insurance claims system based on blockchain and smart contract technology. Sustainability (Basel) 2021; 13(16): 9386.
[http://dx.doi.org/10.3390/su13169386]

[7]   Aslan Ö, Aktuğ SS, Ozkan-Okay M, Yilmaz AA, Akin E. A comprehensive review of cyber security vulnerabilities, threats, attacks, and solutions. Electronics (Basel) 2023; 12(6): 1333.
[http://dx.doi.org/10.3390/electronics12061333]

[8]   Zheng Z, Xie S, Dai HN, *et al.* An overview on smart contracts: Challenges, advances and platforms. Future Gener Comput Syst 2020; 105: 475-91.
[http://dx.doi.org/10.1016/j.future.2019.12.019]

[9]   Kannengieser N, Lins S, Sander C, Winter K, Frey H, Sunyaev A. Challenges and common solutions in smart contract development. IEEE Trans Softw Eng 2022; 48(11): 4291-318.
[http://dx.doi.org/10.1109/TSE.2021.3116808]

[10]   Pólvora A, Nascimento S, Lourenço JS, Scapolo F. Blockchain for industrial transformations: A forward-looking approach with multi-stakeholder engagement for policy advice. Technol Forecast Soc Change 2020; 157: 120091.
[http://dx.doi.org/10.1016/j.techfore.2020.120091]

[11]   Bakare SS, Adeniyi AO, Akpuokwe CU, Eneh NE. Data privacy laws and compliance: a comparative review of the EU GDPR and USA regulations. Computer Science & IT Research Journal 2024; 5(3): 528-43.
[http://dx.doi.org/10.51594/csitrj.v5i3.859]

[12]   Singh A, Parizi RM, Zhang Q, Choo KKR, Dehghantanha A. Blockchain smart contracts formalization: Approaches and challenges to address vulnerabilities. Comput Secur 2020; 88: 101654.
[http://dx.doi.org/10.1016/j.cose.2019.101654]

[13]   Vieira G, Zhang J. Peer-to-peer energy trading in a microgrid leveraged by smart contracts. Renew Sustain Energy Rev 2021; 143: 110900.
[http://dx.doi.org/10.1016/j.rser.2021.110900]

[14]   Taherdoost H. A critical review of blockchain acceptance models—blockchain technology adoption frameworks and applications. Computers 2022; 11(2): 24.
[http://dx.doi.org/10.3390/computers11020024]

[15]   Nakamoto S, Nakamoto S. Bitcoin: A peer-to-peer electronic cash system. Decentralized Bus Rev 2008; 21260. Available from: https://bitcoin.org/en/bitcoin-paper

[16]   Androulaki E, Barger A, Bortnikov V, *et al.* Hyperledger fabric: a distributed operating system for permissioned blockchains. In Proceedings of the Thirteenth EuroSys Conference (EuroSys '18). Association for Computing Machinery, New York, NY, USA 2018, 30, 1–15.

[17]   Buterin V. A next-generation smart contract and decentralized application platform. White Pap 2014; 3: 2-1.

[18]   Sklaroff JM. Smart contracts and the cost of inflexibility. Univ Pa Law Rev 2017; 166: 263.

[19]   Macrinici D, Cartofeanu C, Gao S. Smart contract applications within blockchain technology: A systematic mapping study. Telemat Inform 2018; 35(8): 2337-54.
[http://dx.doi.org/10.1016/j.tele.2018.10.004]

[20]   Madanchian M, Taherdoost H. The impact of digital transformation development on organizational change. Driving Transformative Change in E-Business through Applied Intelligence and Emerging Technologies. Hershey, PA, USA: IGI Global 2022; pp. 1-24.
[http://dx.doi.org/10.4018/978-1-6684-5235-6.ch001]

[21]   Madine MM, Salah K, Jayaraman Ret. Fully decentralized multi-party consent management for secure sharing of patient health records. IEEE Access 2020; 8: 225777-91.
[http://dx.doi.org/10.1109/ACCESS.2020.3045048]

[22]   Satheesh KKSVA, Sree TK. AB-DAM: attribute-based data access model in blockchain for healthcare applications. Multimedia Tools Appl 2022; 81(17): 23567-88.
[http://dx.doi.org/10.1007/s11042-022-12674-w]

[23]   Hang L, Choi E, Kim DH. A novel EMR integrity management based on a medical blockchain platform in hospital. Electronics (Basel) 2019; 8(4): 467.
[http://dx.doi.org/10.3390/electronics8040467]

CHAPTER 8

The Role of Smart Contracts in Ensuring Regulatory Compliance in Blockchain Healthcare Systems

Riya Sharma[1,*]**, Prabh Deep Singh**[2]**, Rohan Verma**[2] **and Deep Mann**[3]

[1] *Department of Commerce, Graphic Era Deemed to be University, Dehradun, Uttarakhand, India*

[2] *Department of Computer Science and Engineering, Graphic Era Deemed to be University, Dehradun, Uttarakhand, India*

[3] *Department of Computer Science and Engineering, Thapar Institute of Engineering & Technology, Patiala, Punjab, India*

Abstract: In the last decade, blockchain technology has evolved in various applications, especially in healthcare systems where decision-making needs to be reliable, secure, and transparent. In these applications, the main concern is the storage and transfer of the patient's medical data to offer solutions for data privacy, user control over their data access, and satisfying regulatory compliance. Moreover, due to the need for security assurance and integration with other systems, *i.e.*, traditional healthcare systems, the platform needs a system that, in addition to storing the data, can be able to simplify exchange and manage patient data records through collaboration with smart contracts. This chapter considers the constraints surrounding the role and growth of blockchain smart contracts in promoting healthcare regulatory compliance, positional questions that are yet to be resolved or explored, and boundaries in the underlying structure of international regulatory policies. The chapter introduces the methodological issues inherent in the process of resolution of regulatory compliance. The main purpose is to help system designers understand how to systematically evaluate how blockchain-based systems comply with General Data Protection Regulation (GDPR) requirements. Further the study proposes a set of smart contracts for a blockchain-based healthcare data exchange aimed at the resolution of regulatory compliance accounting issues.

Keywords: Blockchain technology, Decision making, Data privacy, Healthcare systems.

* **Corresponding author Riya Sharma:** Department of Commerce, Graphic Era Deemed to be University, Dehradun, Uttarakhand, India; E-mail: riyasharma6568@gmail.com

Mohit Angurala, Preet Kamal, Aryan Chaudhary, Rasmeet Singh Bali & Vijay Bhardwaj (Eds.)
All rights reserved-© 2025 Bentham Science Publishers

INTRODUCTION

Blockchain technology is intended as an advanced tool with the ability to resolve difficulties linked to safety, data sharing, and compliance with regulatory standards across healthcare organizations, jointly offering the essentials necessary for current electronic health records and management systems and trying to mitigate electronic healthcare data transfer and access constraints [1]. In essence, a public record is used by multiple nodes to collectively record a range of operations by forming a digital sequence. A blockchain is a decentralized and distributed ledger. Each portion of this sequence, known as a block, is connected to the preceding one, constructing a lengthy and untampered lineage chain [2]. The chain serves both as an anchor and archive of transactions' history, safeguarding contributed contents against internal or external cyber threats. Many healthcare utilizations have been recommended. Given the different blockchain abilities to establish and maintain longevity and protect or verify transmitted data, as well as its ability to automate and validate various procedures, these plans can result in substantial advances in healthcare data management.

The blockchain's custom-designed smart contracts might address several compliance issues and extend assured advantages to healthcare, including healthcare providers and patients. Intended regulatory measures are required for management and information structures that blockchain can automate. Furthermore, smart contracts might also create opportunities and consequences for non-compliance, resulting in potentially increased data integrity through enhanced consistency of process control and the capacity to disclose reliable results [3].

Fig. (1) illustrates the process of managing healthcare data using blockchain technology. The patient provides health data to the healthcare provider, who encrypts and stores the data on the blockchain. A smart contract is executed to ensure compliance, validate data access, and notify authorized entities.

Background and Significance

Several interdisciplinary studies [4, 5] on regulatory guideline level approaches permit integration with blockchain systems that influence the laboratory medicine environment. The usage of smart contracts in the defined scope of regulatory compliance in healthcare blockchain systems or mechanisms to ensure data integrity or even proof for longer than a year remains a gap that will not be addressed by existing research in the current field [6].

Looking exclusively from the standpoint of the blockchain operational integrability with a specific, national eHealth system development, they have also identified that immediate policy change support is required from additional legislative documents, linking the activities with international priorities such as the Digital Single Market Strategy published by the European Commission" [7].

The usage of blockchain in healthcare is on the rise due to the underlying principles such as security and anti-tampering, confidentiality, distributed verification, and storage of data or event provenance. However, the need to comply with different data protection laws and regulations indicates that the adaptation must be highly intricate or intricate in a well-defined manner. More concretely, research indicates that smart contracts are decentralized, transparent, and secure tools, capable of automatically resolving the actions that are predefined by the contract parties without any intermediaries at a very low cost. This study can also support the understanding of strategic adoption, system audits, or blockchain conceptualization and design work.

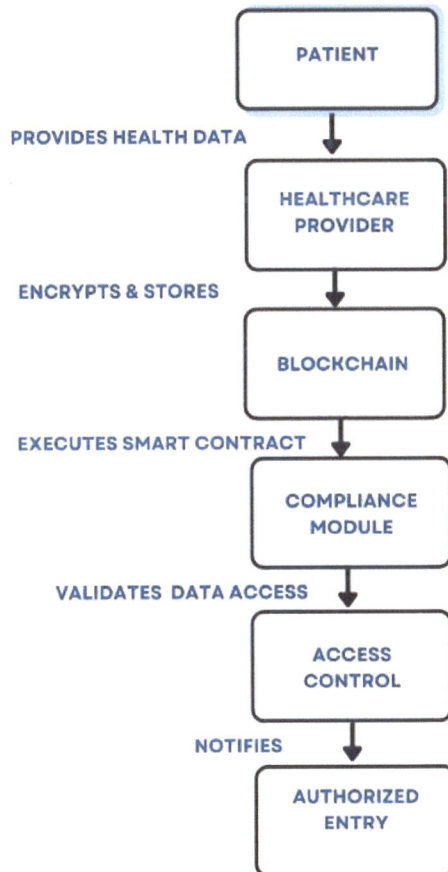

Fig. (1). Blockchain-enabled healthcare data management.

Research Objectives

Based on the above discussion regarding smart contracts in the context of healthcare with related concepts and principles in blockchain, there is still a lack of research on this topic. The main aim of this study is to review the literature on the governance of smart contracts in blockchain-based projects or platforms implemented within the healthcare industry context. Further, the governance of smart contracts is analyzed using the Smart Contract Governance Cycle comprising three dimensions (allocating control rights, managing accountability, and managing risk) within the blockchain-based projects or platforms implemented within the healthcare industry context. The study also aims to investigate the capacity of these smart contracts to respond to the trade-offs of a multiplex project by aligning the interests of involved parties, ensuring regulatory compliance as well as the established smart contracts' specifications, and managing the funding scheme of these projects. Lastly, suggestions are provided that are innovative in the sense that they look across the entire project for improving institutional mechanisms dealing with contractual solutions designed to enhance the ability of smart contracts to ensure governance functions within the multiplex project.

Structure of the Paper

Research dealing with blockchain in healthcare has commonly concentrated on the obvious advantage of providing guarantees and ensuring the reliability and authenticity of healthcare-related data. Despite an innovative idea, it is not enough to solve all problems. The use of blockchain technology in healthcare systems simultaneously raises several challenges, closely connected with privacy challenges, lack of regulatory support, and lack of standardization, but also the challenge of effective enforcement of GDPR and providing functions and services connecting existing healthcare systems to the network that are efficient and convenient for the end user. As presented, the research focuses deeply on the challenges mentioned and the problem of blockchain healthcare systems' compliance with legal norms with IT tools that not only guarantee the legal requirements but also facilitate management and implementation processes.

FOUNDATIONS OF BLOCKCHAIN TECHNOLOGY

Blockchain technology offers to address these fundamental issues mentioned. Blockchain technology is a decentralized system that can help to build trust mechanisms between two potential transactors by providing transparency and accountability. Blockchain technology has been seen as a potential game-changer in various application domains, such as supply chain management, financial transaction management, identity management, e-voting, and healthcare systems

[8]. This technology employs cryptographic functions and data immutability, making it ideal for data storage and transparency handlers. Every day, new decentralized services are built upon a blockchain foundation. These decentralized services, also known as decentralized applications (dApps), employ Smart Contracts to operate. Smart Contracts' purpose is to enforce or detect various regulations related to the operation or use of distinct blockchain systems. Blockchain-fueled healthcare systems that utilize smart contracts can enforce regulations in alliance with existing governmental agencies, regulating healthcare data usage governance. Such cooperation can help blockchain-based healthcare systems to ensure different levels of compliance (*e.g.*, GDPR, HIPAA) [9] to those who enroll, maximizing transparency and accountability. The cooperation can additionally help governmental authorities to detect illicit activities and thus penalize non-compliance [10].

Fig. (**2**) provides an overview of how blockchain technology and smart contracts are utilized in healthcare. Blockchain technology incorporates decentralized ledgers and smart contracts, enabling healthcare data management with a focus on security, privacy, and immutable records. Additionally, smart contracts enforce compliance and create audit trails to ensure transparent and secure data handling.

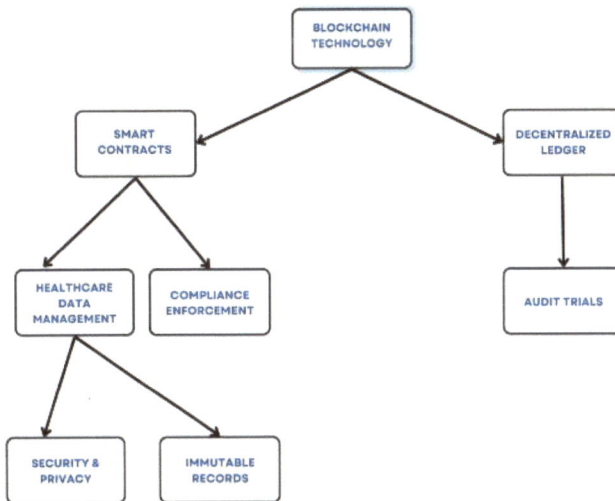

Fig. (2). Overview of blockchain and smart contracts in healthcare.

Healthcare systems have been in place for decades or even centuries in certain cases. Traditional healthcare systems, however, suffer from several challenges related to trust, security, and data ownership. Traditionally, healthcare systems are prone to expose patients' sensitive health records to information adversaries, who may misuse them for identity theft or other malicious modes [11]. Data stored in traditional health systems may be manipulated, deleted, or injected with bogus information, making the data in question unreliable for use. Such occurrences may further lead to a decrease in trust in the health system in place. Furthermore, it is well known that global healthcare systems are prime targets for advanced persistent threat actors to enter and steal data. Healthcare systems are prime targets due to the significant value of health records in dark markets. Centralization of worldwide health systems further facilitates a tidier process of theft for malicious individuals, as adversaries can focus on a few large targets in comparison to many smaller ones.

Definition and Characteristics of Blockchain Technology

A blockchain is a type of database containing a "chain" of "blocks" - a linear sequence of records called "transactions", designed to be secure and resistant to data theft, tampering, and/or double spending [12]. Transactions included in blocks are considered as confirmed by all participants in a blockchain network since adding them to blocks and verification ensures that it is computationally infeasible to alter and/or delete them without detecting such unauthorized changes [13]. Blockchain technology may function as a decentralized, democratic, immutable, transparent, and fully accessible distributed ledger. Besides, permissioned blockchains, relying on the consortia of verified institutions, help preserve privacy, data protection, and regulatory compliance [14]. Such decentralized and distributed cryptographic features offer transparency, traceability, and trust between parties interlinked and exchanging assets, such as digital currency, physical goods, electronic health records (EHRs), patient-generated healthcare data (PGHD), and laboratory results. As a result, blockchain technologies interest stakeholders in various sectors, including healthcare, public administration, banking and finance, professional services, insurance, agriculture, tourism, supply chain management, logistics, and energy [15].

Key Components of Blockchain Technology

Blockchain smart contract technology is a computer protocol intended to replace a traditional contract. These contracts make possible the transactions of different blockchain stakeholders with security or credible transactions. The term 'smart contract' was first proposed by Nick Szabo in 1997 [16]. He then described it as "a computerized transaction mechanism that implements the terms of the contract which can be activated and written to contract." These transactions are traceable, irrevocable, and complete. Moreover, it decreases the need for many centralized authorities, which are used as brokers to confirm, validate, and approve the process.

Therefore, smart contracts can decrease the transaction costs of building a secure transaction agreement between users, even if the contracting members are either entirely strange or not entitled to carry out transactions without a conventionally trustworthy intermediary [17]. Blockchain technology is a decentralized network of computers that share a public, transactional network, creating an online database. The backbone of the technology is developed through a chain of 'data blocks' that contain transactional data, data about the equipment or devices that support the transaction, the intended users of the equipment, and other types of information that facilitate authorization of all transactions on the network [18]. Each block contains a time stamp and a link to the previous block, forming the blockchain, while the data it holds is checked and encrypted such that any changes are easily identified, localized, and refused. Since transactions have a time stamp every time that they occur, the system functions as a unique database entry; once any information is found, it is then easily traceable.

Applications of Blockchain in Healthcare

To tackle the issue of fake drugs, the use of blockchain technology has also been proposed. By using blockchain technology to improve the logistics and traceability of drug products, the drug supply chain can be secured. This possibility presents an instance of how blockchain technology can be used to tackle drug counterfeiting in the pharmaceutical industry. Moreover, blockchain technology has also been proposed for use in ensuring health data reliability. Furthermore, concerns have been raised about the use of blockchain technology to ensure regulatory compliance in healthcare [19]. However, Feijóo explained how regulatory compliance in healthcare can be secured using smart contracts executed on a blockchain. Specifically, the authors proposed a framework that can facilitate health information authorization based on smart contracts. It has been acknowledged that blockchain technology offers a wide range of applications in healthcare [20]. For instance, the use of blockchain technology in healthcare has been proposed to solve data privacy challenges.

Blockchain technology has also found applications in improving the transparency and security of health data exchange and managing medical records in healthcare [21]. Research has also shown that the use of smart contracts can help to improve the security of medical records stored on a blockchain. Another area in healthcare where blockchain technology has been applied is patient information sharing in at-home care. In this application, blockchain technology enables a patient and a healthcare provider to securely share patient information within the home care service. This is achieved by modeling patient information sharing using smart contracts.

REGULATORY COMPLIANCE IN HEALTHCARE

Healthcare is a highly regulated sector to ensure the safety of consumers, for example, through drug laws to control the marketing and control of therapeutic products. Hence, companies and organizations in this sector must demonstrate regulatory compliance to operate legally in the market [22]. However, regulatory compliance is a significant burden as it requires exhaustive documentation and often complex procedures. Failing to satisfy regulatory requirements and manage risks will result in consequences, including fines and halting of operational practices [23]. With smart contracts, however, it is possible to automate the verification of companies and organizations according to the regulatory compliance criteria, therefore saving both time and effort to minimize the risk [5]. Blockchain may have different roles and the workflows in which it is involved focus on each participant's obligations and expectations. The feature of blockchain technology allows either two parties to review, discuss, and agree with each other on whether a contract has been completed before delivering a digital asset. Other forms of chain contracts, such as partially intelligent contracts or intelligent contracts, realize regulatory requirements verification on blockchains, creating an abundant decentralized applications ecosystem [24]. Fig. (**3**) illustrates the data-sharing workflow in healthcare using blockchain technology. The patient provides health data to the healthcare provider, who encrypts and stores the data on the blockchain network. A smart contract is executed to validate access requests, enabling authorized third parties to access the health data securely.

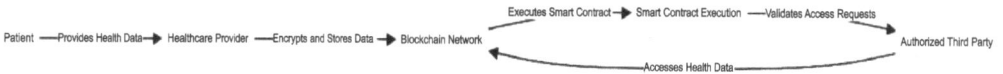

Fig. (3). Data sharing workflow using blockchain in healthcare.

Importance of Regulatory Compliance in Healthcare

In recent years, smart contracts have been proposed and adopted in various applications, such as financial instruments, digital rights management, and supply-chain management, to name a few. Previous research has focused on examining the nature and scope of smart contracts and mainly on the legal challenges raised by them. This study extends the scope of smart contracts and examines how they can be employed to solve an important problem related to blockchain healthcare systems, that is, how to ensure regulatory compliance. In healthcare, the term 'compliance' refers to processes, policies, and actions that healthcare institutions, healthcare professionals, and patients follow to conform to stipulated rules and regulations. Compliance may relate to a wide range of areas across different countries [25]. It may be legal, such as following legislation and regulations issued by a country's health authorities. Healthcare as a sector requires products and services to comply with many regulations, thus ensuring a baseline level of quality and safety of care guaranteed to consumers. Those who fail to comply with these regulations are generally subject to significant penalties. In healthcare, it is important to protect the interests of parties who may not be able to comprehend all the risks they face, yet they are required to exchange high-quality and safe services. Smart contracts are an appropriate solution for ensuring regulatory compliance in blockchain-based healthcare ecosystems, as they can implement policies across decentralized systems with a high level of automation [26].

Challenges of Ensuring Regulatory Compliance

Despite the numerous advantages and opportunities that blockchain offers to the healthcare industry, it is important to note that there is no existing legislation on the compliance requirements of how medical data and healthcare services should be accessed, stored, and transmitted by blockchain technology in most countries. The lack of regulatory frameworks for blockchain healthcare may be linked to the fact that most countries are still coming to terms with national strategies to prepare for implementing the technology. Healthcare regulations dictate the processes to be followed in providing or receiving healthcare. Establishing compliant blockchain healthcare systems may require healthcare applications to be radically changed to ensure that vital healthcare infrastructure, middlemen, and compliance rules are not discredited or surpassed. For instance, existing requirements specified by healthcare regulations may necessitate healthcare systems to implement variations of smart contract handling rules and business logic distinct from what is directly provided by the default blockchain platforms. While recombining a single blockchain enterprise can be administratively feasible without sacrificing data limits or data transport constraints, this solution is not scalable. Blockchains that can improve healthcare privacy and compliance requirements may need to evolve through a meta-operational model, expanding to multiple specialized blockchains, each supporting specific kinds of clinical and administrative services]. Despite the strength and potential profession of the proposed solution, shifting from a single blockchain to several autonomous blockchains is not a trivial task. Existing regulations and guidelines that call for healthcare data protection through authentication, encryption, and transfer of medical information between consumers, providers, and other stakeholders are missing in guidance specific to blockchain systems. Adherence to global data protection laws such as the Gramm-Leach-Bliley Act (GLBA), Health Insurance Portability and Accountability Act (HIPAA) [28], the Data Protection Directive (95/46/EC), and others is increasingly seen as barriers to entry into the healthcare sector, particularly when patient trust and confidentiality are essential for the health information exchange to be successful.

SMART CONTRACTS: CONCEPT AND FUNCTIONALITY

Smart contracts are self-executing contracts with the terms of the agreement between buyer and seller being directly written into lines of computer code [29]. The code and the agreements contained therein exist across a distributed, decentralized blockchain network. These contracts permit trusted transactions and agreements to be carried out among disparate, anonymous parties while avoiding the services of a middleman. They render transactions traceable, transparent, and irreversible.

A smart contract is executed when, as a self-run computer program, it validates the fulfillment of certain conditions and causes the execution of certain predetermined tasks. These contracts involve data and the digital "transfer" and "management" of money. In terms of blockchain transactions, the contract rules or guidelines can be verified, enforced, or performed by a blockchain network. Each smart contract aims to bring off an anticipated outcome through the systems of checks or signs, which it can accomplish. The transactions and the fulfillment of conditions are traceable, transparent, and irreversible since the program code is observable and understood by the participants inside the network. The determinations are run on an automatic basis without human oversight and supervision. They are approaching the true potential as a way to practice and react to money, properties, work, or the performance of any object of value relentlessly and effortlessly. In addition, smart contracts can reduce transactional costs and guarantee the certainty, autonomy, and dependability of cybersecurity. The development of smart contracts for various legal practices is the core innovation of blockchain.

Definition and Characteristics of Smart Contracts

SCs (also known as self-executing contracts, blockchain contracts, or digital contracts) are prototypical applications that take inputs—usually a series of pledged commitments—and translate them into conditional rules that actuate the pledged commitments when specified parameters are achieved. They are characterized by characteristics issued from different technological perspectives, *e.g.*, the validation process. Despite the frequently occurring confusion, one should note that SCs are neither smart nor contracts in a strict legal sense. They are pieces of code [30]. First, to write, deploy, or call for an SC, a person should, in the first place, access the corresponding blockchain network. Consequently, when the blockchain network adopts an RDBMS, SC can mimic the validation process but not other characteristics. Also, SCs are applications that can be attached to blockchain-based systems and thereby trigger various types of blockchain operations. Therefore, the SC implementation includes the logic of operation and the corresponding interaction patterns. Note that different types of blockchain systems imply different types of operation.

Key Features of Smart Contracts

Smart contracts are self-executable agreement units with self-governance logic coded on a blockchain network. Smart contracts hold enormous potential for a global revolution of business by converting increasingly complex transactions into code, automating away the bank, retail middleman, and other custodial services, and providing tamper-proof agreements with guaranteed rule execution. The normal contract is constructed to encapsulate event-driven contractual provisions or proofs, which can be resolved only by referring to a human third party, and therefore, smart contracts are self-governing. This characteristic means that the need to depend on a third party for the performance or adjudication of a contract is removed. Thus, their appeal to crypto-market transactions intensifies. The direct program execution substitutes any encryption of virtual tiles or reality that confounds users with worries of mapping each paper or legal contract with an on-chain cryptocurrency. Many times, it is necessary to combine legal and conditional logic to any decision outcome to validate a contract. In common terms, many signatures are required for all involved parties based on the decision outcome, which confirms the legality of the signatures under the validation context with respect to a particular agreement unit. In a scenario of open signatures on a predetermined platform with many participants, all involved parties can bind to a public ledger by using open signatures in constructive ways. This form of binding was first addressed as a smart contract in this paper. Our definition requires the smart contract to build upon the construction of a single signature (or proof of the decision result needed for signature generation). The non-repudiable process has the same force as the stacking of the paper-based claim. Furthermore, it is necessary for a smart contract to automatically validate each decision outcome unrestricted to trusted third parties over the coded agreement. The smart contracts are typically deployed in a public network which enforces an identical and tamper-evident version of a smart contract to provide a valid and reliable public record of the agreement execution.

Benefits of Smart Contracts in Healthcare

Smart contracts can greatly benefit blockchain healthcare systems by ensuring that the various stakeholders within the sector uphold critical roles mandated by law, are duly licensed, and, wherever required, hold particular certifications to sell or offer medical services. In the delivery of healthcare services, verification and credentialing of professionals in the industry are mandatory [31]. By using a blockchain, a high level of confidence in the integrity of the information shared is possible. With smart contracts, transactions that occur on the blockchain can be programmed with business rules for each stakeholder relationship. Hence, in this paper, we posit that smart contracts are a catalyst in ensuring that the functionaries within the blockchain healthcare systems implement the right legal obligation as well as adhere to the power conferred by law, provided due process has been followed. Another fundamental benefit of smart contracts is that they ensure customers' rights are respected. The process of digitizing human rights helps lessen the opacity that exists in traditional systems. It makes the rights easier to represent and enforce. In digital healthcare marketplaces, patients should have the right to know the performance records of medical professionals while having informed consent over their data. Smart contracts manage and enforce patients' rights and obligations as well as those of third-party services. In fact, a blockchain-based smart contract will not admit a careless user agreement that involves disclosing patient health secrets without the user's concern. This is in line with the concept of autonomy, one of the key elements of bioethics. Furthermore, autonomous consent avoids transactions such as taking advantage of exposing information deemed unacceptable to a third party, leading to situations where the benefits of the other in the process generate revenue sharing that the patient lacks returns.

INTEGRATION OF SMART CONTRACTS IN BLOCKCHAIN HEALTHCARE SYSTEMS

Currently, smart contracts are used to implement many business processes, such as the acquisition of IT services, the assignment of copyrights, *etc.* Such contracts can be used in healthcare systems where there is a need for the principles of the contract, especially when implementing business logic and the need for automated fulfillment or failure of the contract conditions. The concept presented in this paper may control the correctness and completeness of data added to the healthcare blockchain. Such an algorithm configuration is formulated using the EVM code templates. The developed concept is implemented using smart contract object-oriented cloud regress trading contracts. Therefore, smart contracts are used to automate and encapsulate healthcare regulations in blockchain systems, taking into account the principles of Federal Law No. 323-FZ "On the Basics of Health Protection in the Russian Federation", and the regulation modules based on plans for the principle of distribution, which will facilitate data insertion, update, and access control monitor the possible abnormal actions. The exploration of various scientific papers confirmed the purpose of the smart contract in ensuring the transfer of regulations of government laws and regulations in blockchain data. In the paper "The Role of Smart Contracts in Ensuring Regulatory Engineering Blockchain Healthcare Systems", healthcare regulation is the regulation that must be applied in the healthcare system, and that cannot be violated. Healthcare regulations are federal health and safety laws.

Use Cases of Smart Contracts in Healthcare

Despite the potential benefits, industry-specific blockchain-based systems in healthcare are still limited. The gap in blockchain-based systems for the healthcare sector is mainly due to technical challenges such as the efficiency, scalability, and regulation compliance of key technological enablers such as smart contracts. One of the main enablers for blockchain adoption in healthcare is smart contracts. In addition to routine automation, some of the recent advancements in smart contract research and deployment suggest the potential of new analytics and machine learning medical research services delivered through blockchain-based systems in the future. Independent of specific applications, research on smart contracts in healthcare is expected to gain major momentum once rich and heterogeneous datasets are collected from operational blockchain-based healthcare systems, in addition to the custom-defined blockchain transactional attributes.

The heterogeneity of countries and institutions in healthcare suggests that a wide range of use cases is possible with smart contracts. Beyond standalone actions, smart contracts can further decentralize, automate, and execute low-level health policies. Through specific rules embedded in their code, smart contracts can evaluate complex constraints or conditions and implement key health policies. Healthcare surveillance, identity management, medication adherence monitoring, patient common protocol implementation, and access control-audit compliance are some of the existing or possible use cases for smart contracts in healthcare.

Technical Implementation Considerations

Vital to implementing and enforcing the rules embedded in smart contracts are private data management and confidentiality. Blockchain technology offers secure and decentralized storage, processing, and management of private data, but both public and private blockchains require secure and efficient methods of managing access to the stored data. Recently, we leveraged Amazon's Managed Blockchain service to implement a fully functional blockchain network to verify physicians' identities. Smart contracts store a physician's certification information, which includes the physician's full name, National Provider Identifier (NPI), and the time that the contents were published. Physicians wishing to verify another physician's identity first submit the NPI of the physician to be verified. The smart contract returns the physician's name, NPI, and the date the physician was added or removed from the certification contract, along with a certification status: Certification, Pending Certifications, and Revoked Certification. Setting up a blockchain network *via* the manual method directly provided on AWS or following a cloud setup can be achieved. The study crafted it programmatically using AWS CLI scripts. Securely provisioned physician IDs in a blockchain network managed access control to the enrolled data, stored medical records as per HIPAA regulations, ensured the transparency of the rules *via* the smart contracts, and accounted for access reasons to enhance the overall trustworthiness with the blockchain. Discernment of a physician's identity is accomplished through a process that is agnostic to the blockchain network(s) and the associated participants (querying physician and queried physician). The high-level process is outlined in the following section. We focused on Hyperledger as the framework of our choice to securely provision physician IDs in a blockchain network, manage access control to the enrolled data, store medical records as per HIPAA regulations, ensure the transparency of the rules *via* smart contracts, and account for access reasons to enhance the overall trustworthiness with the blockchain.

ENSURING REGULATORY COMPLIANCE WITH SMART CONTRACTS

Even though smart contracts self-execute on the agreed terms and conditions and guarantee trust and transparency through blockchain technology, there are gaps in this technology that need to be addressed in order for healthcare and regulatory compliance to assure and rely on using smart contract-based systems. Smart contracts are a powerful tool that connects business requirements and executable business processes. In crossing blockchain technology with business process management, smart contracts can be generated from a business process model and can be checked against the model. Smart contracts represent business-process-level exportable executable business processes that can be run on blockchain systems. This opens the door to a range of new opportunities to ensure transparent, autonomous, trust-free interactions on blockchain systems. Even better, the conversion process from a business process model to a smart contract may perform some of the checks required by regulatory compliance models. By doing so, the healthcare provider network may be reassured that they can meet the terms and conditions of contracts that represent regulatory compliance. Smart contracts can be generated from business process diagrams. Through mapping, running a business process will involve posting some data on the blockchain. Data posting is governed by the smart contract to be created. Smart contracts can be validated against business process models in isolation. Thus, their functionality can be checked, including the poster on the blockchain before deployment, and some regulatory compliance functionality can be checked by inspection on the blockchain before any money or cryptocurrencies are allowed to travel.

Let us assume that a PoC network model involving a group of healthcare providers has a business process management model in place. The development of smart contracts involved in the PoC must ensure that the business model of the provider network is supported. By providing the process ontology views, smart contract views in support of oncological best practice clinical pathways will be part of PoC design. For this PoC, an organization will have to have as many of the process ontological viewpoints as possible. As a result, the PoC will test the PoC's proof of principle for specific patterns of cross-organization conformation management, document acceptance rules, and steps representing the top of the process onto pathways.

Role of Smart Contracts in Addressing Regulatory Compliance

Smart contracts are self-executing contracts that can be executed in an automatic and decentralized manner without human intervention. The underlying implications of smart contracts have the capability to significantly revolutionize the way how blockchain ecosystems are currently functioning. These contracts can potentially replace the storage of human-readable terms with machine code that can be executed automatically. With the advancements in technology development, engineers have successfully implemented frameworks that utilize smart contract features to perform automated computations and digital agreements. As smart contracts are programmed to automatically execute when the contractual criteria have been met, they can be effectively deployed in blockchain ecosystems to automate the process of trust in digital form. Smart contracts can also be developed to interact with blockchain healthcare information. These smart contracts can be directly deployed in the blockchain and compute the distributed data in an efficient way. Smart contracts can be utilized to automate trust relations between various entities, including organizations, individuals, and devices, in the blockchain structure of healthcare systems. The utilization of smart contracts will be particularly useful in ensuring regulatory compliant blockchain healthcare systems. A set of multistakeholder smart contracts can be developed depending upon the roles of regulatory compliance in a similar manner to the ones in the business use cases. Some of the applications of smart contracts in ensuring regulatory compliance within blockchain healthcare systems include the automation of existing regulatory standards, operationalization of various guidelines within the blockchain environment, and development of advanced regulatory standards using blockchain features.

Legal and Ethical Considerations

Extensive use of smart contracts can give rise to legal and ethical issues in both the applicable jurisdiction and extraterritorially. Smart contracts can effectively enter into contracts on their own, and all contractual relations generated by the computer code can potentially generate legal obligations that must be fulfilled.

The status of smart contracts within a legal system is still uncertain. Lack of legal recognition for smart contracts may lead to legal uncertainty about their enforceability and the absence of traditional legal safeguards. Questions arise as to what rights and obligations smart contracts have and how courts can enforce and interpret these agreements. It is still not clear whether the legal treatment of smart contracts should recognize a new contractual entity, handle smart contracts through existing legal rules, or propose a mix of legal principles and self-executing contract design. With smart contracts, parties agree to the rules of the contract code, not to the subjective intent of the software developer or the public perception of the contract terms. Although the "contractual negotiations" between the two parties are mediated by the programmer's legal expertise and the developer's technical skills, the code should reflect the actual commitments between the parties. Since the underlying code is visible for inspection and audit by the parties, a key part of contractual performance takes place ex ante. Shortcomings in contract formation are not played out, and legal mechanisms for the post-contractual stage are limited. A concrete problem associated with this ex ante nature is that parties might discover bugs and other defects in the designed smart contract during its operation.

CASE STUDIES AND EXAMPLES

This study considers a health insurance company that wants to provide health insurance to a group of employees. We assume that the company does not trust the employees to send only correct claims and that the employees want to ensure their privacy about their claims. The study presents a healthcare consortium where all participants have constant easy access to data they have permission to see while ensuring that healthcare data, among the most heavily regulated kinds, stay put and visible to only a small group of people. Some participants, healthcare providers, in this case, do not control the computers of others, their patients, and would make them peers in an open blockchain network. We also use a use case in the same scenario with similar or better outcomes. Proxy re-encryption with verifiable delegation of the decryption for linear functions is an efficient privacy-preserving mechanism for delegating decryption of the encrypted claims(31). We determine if a set of claims can be decrypted to a value within a determined range but without revelation of the claim. This can be applied to minor, simple expenses. Employees can sum up these non-revealing changes and send them to health insurance without revealing private information about health status or other claims. Casual inspections by the health insurance are possible. It is possible to detect fraud attempts if the consolidated claims are above the predefined limits for each of the registered employees.

Real-world Applications of Smart Contracts in Healthcare Compliance

Real-world applications of smart contracts in the healthcare field are usually related to the automation of payment procedures to save resources and money for patients. For example, professionally executed medical monitoring can help a patient to make a faster recovery and will make it possible for him or her to be released from the hospital earlier and with better progression. Home monitoring programs need qualified medical professionals who are self-employed entrepreneurs who partner with specific medical practices, clinics, or hospitals in larger urban areas. These healthcare professionals provide day-to-day monitoring of vital signs associated with chronic illnesses (*e.g.*, diabetes, hypertension, kidney or heart failure, significant viral or bacterial infections) in a patient at home. The usage of smart contracts as a pay-per-use system offers significant advantages since it can automatically pay for medical services for the remote monitoring of home care patients for individuals with one or more particular types of illnesses. The processing payments can be scheduled at various levels of granularity at different times during the day or night, each additional scheduled time of constant attendance at each variable time, such as the specific observation of, and interaction with, patients who have obligations to measure and return specific types of medical parameters in order to conform to the proper procedure. In addition to high-precision patient data, payment plans can also be determined by considering other data that can be shared and used within intelligent smart contracts implementing the system.

FUTURE DIRECTIONS AND CHALLENGES

Surveying the potential of blockchain-based markerless systems in healthcare revealed manifold insights and ideas for future research work. Traditionally, a smart contract has been considered as the "Legal Prose" expressing the parties' intent. It contains the rules of the agreement between the parties and describes the obligations, benefits, and penalties that are included in the contract [27]. This perspective contributes an important layer of understanding when trying to define the "smart" digitized clinical protocols directly involving the regulatory governance of healthcare systems. Interest in digitized clinical guidelines mentioned can ensure that all intermediaries in the shared system make legal decisions and ensure that the digitized protocols are executed.

Improving the performance of smart contracts in HCOs with rights: Aligning smart contracts with their contribution rights has significant implications. It is important that the creation of the new clinical evidence upon which the clinical guidelines are based in each HCO is appropriately compensated. As a possible solution, it is important that additional formalisms be adopted. Currently, the penalty conditions of smart contracts are the only rules that need to be enforced.

Improving performance and the AccountExempt smart contract: The smart account exemption is a system that collects privacy-sensitive personal clinical information. The patient agrees to use their own health data free of charge for insensitive information, and it is a part of the advertising model-related incentives of the Tappydo app. The concept can be further developed into a clinical data compensation mechanism.

The smart contract error recovery: The conditions of the smart contract can be very complex. The error will bring unwanted additional costs to all parties. Therefore, creating a method to eliminate human error in implementing and enforcing the smart contract requires appropriate attention.

Potential Innovations in Smart Contracts for Healthcare Compliance

Payer tests the economic interests of individuals and the healthcare system support. Scalars that manage smart contract deals and the market for healthcare, as presently organized, are responsible for the smart contract designs. Even in a prominent legal tradition, smart contracts appear to be endorsed in ways that create legal norms. Indeed, in a recent report on contract legality, much emphasis was placed on the party raising and responding to concerns about smart contracts and their effects. Despite an increase in widespread use, they can be problematic for both parties involved due to the lack of a natural pricing mechanism.

The contacting part that exists on most smart contracts of IoT only becomes inaccurate and more complex as it has a non-intentional no-reply clause occurring mostly from the human factor, increasing the risks of being manipulated (illegally or unintentionally). And, over the years or due to the changes the specific regulations bring, the risk of a smart contract agent no longer containing the criteria standard evolves. Randomization or best-practice organizational criteria cannot fully define every behavioral rule of the smart contract that best aligns with the search criteria. Particularly, there is a direct economic benefit of negating intent in the capacity of responsibility of a particular variety of contracting. Certain departments in the Ministry of Health may radically change, dampening the current emphasis on market relations with and within the system. The more accurate signing of the smart contract may encourage authorized organizations to challenge order-map regulation to prevent the potential side effects.

An independent arbitrator is one way of ensuring more confidence in smart contract compliance. Smart contracts for healthcare will have as one of their main functions the regulation of the exchange of health-specific information and health-related data required to fulfill the regulatory requirements of Decree

2.134/96. The smart contract on-ground may exist between the health operator, the healthcare professional registered by the National Health Oversight Agency (ANS), and the autonomous health professional. The purpose of this contract would be, through data transfer from the platform to the ANS, to provide all information required, with legal aspects internally involved with these professionals, such as their legal and/or labor registration, working hours worked, patient care guaranteed, and attributions performed according to objectives publicly disclosed on the platform. The same records would validate the support provided to the on-demand healthcare professional in complying with its obligation. The term "support" refers to solving the possible questions related to professional practice and duty, providing experts (medical scholars or clauses in the hospital procedures they created), and contributing to the medical procedure, among others. The resources available in current smart contract models are useful but ultimately as limited as their scope. The implementation of these new solutions is intended to bypass inaccuracies and difficulties in contracting. These third-party solutions sometimes are not totally independent of the parties that may have contractual disputes and, therefore, would probably not solve the incentive-incompatibility problem in contracts in the healthcare space.

Key Challenges and Limitations

The most paramount technical challenges closely associated with smart contract utilization in healthcare, as well as other domains, heavily revolve around addressing security issues and data privacy protection. This research, therefore, seeks already available solutions to address these highlighted challenges when developing smart contracts in blockchain-based healthcare platforms. The most fundamental proposed mitigation strategies to address these security issues involve the integration of proven data privacy protection methodologies and applicable novel data privacy protection techniques to provide a solid protection framework that intersects all tenets of information security. To properly highlight and address the identified challenges by proposing best-in-class solutions, it is prudent to carefully consider each challenge and, if necessary, classify each by employing valid classification strategies. It is vital to follow strategies that clearly elucidate the challenges and the proposed robust solutions that are integrated into the smart contracts. This is the recommended approach to follow to alleviate these concerns while implementing final smart contract-based blockchain healthcare systems.

CONCLUSION

This chapter analyzed the regulatory challenges posed by blockchain-enabled smart contracts in healthcare systems. We have developed a four-layer architecture for healthcare compliance to enable secure and compliant smart contracts in healthcare. We have also discussed its possible implementation using an example of an innovative blockchain healthcare system for the procurement and prescription of rare drugs and medication adherence monitoring. Therefore, we have provided the first step towards a full privacy-aware, GDPR (General Data Protection Regulation)-compliant, blockchain and smart contract-enabled healthcare data transaction ecosystem. Such a Dispute Resolution Protocol will address the need for regulated smart contracts in healthcare that are not only privacy-aware but also provide dispute resolution in situations of unforeseen outcomes. Additionally, in cases of fraudulent users (such as the use of snooping participants or uploads of fake health records) involved in the procurement of rare drugs, it is proposed to use a consortium (instead of public) permissioned or hybrid blockchain. This will be based on the proof-of-authority consensus algorithm to ensure judicial security for regulated smart contracts. As a result of this process, the implemented protocol will validate and verify each participant's identity in the procurement process. This is to ensure that each prescription of rare drugs strictly follows the authorized and legal prescriber orders. Furthermore, the next steps in this journey may involve the use of privacy-aware blockchain solutions to ensure data privacy and detect data privacy leaks in the novel architecture. This includes the implementation of zero-knowledge proofs within the healthcare compliance protocol and digital contracts. Also, the unwanted consequences of failure for smart contracts when the treatment outcome is not satisfactory and the potential creation of an automated dispute resolution mechanism have also been introduced.

SUMMARY OF FINDINGS

This chapter articulated research questions within the context of blockchain business transformations. The questions interrogated the nature of blockchain transformations and their implication for smart contract research and practice. A mixed methods research strategy was adopted, including expert interviews and a pilot source code analysis. Regulatory smart contracts are blockchain-based code artifacts that embody both the law itself and a set of predicates that verify the satisfaction of the law's legal conditions. This chapter started the process of constructing a formal model of blockchain regulatory smart contracts by identifying the most important (from the perspective of healthcare and other industries) attributes of regulatory smart contracts. The types of regulatory smart contracts identified by this study are legalization, legality, self-execution, self-enforcement, information gathering, notifications, and dispute resolution. In addition to traditional smart contract vulnerabilities, blockchain regulatory smart contracts suffer from mistakes in legal translation, mistakes in encoding statutory law, mistakes in implementing legal checks, vulnerabilities stemming from the interaction with external actors, and vulnerabilities stemming from unwanted external authorities gaining control of the smart contract.

This chapter described the potential role of smart contracts in ensuring regulatory compliance in blockchain healthcare systems within the specific context of transformational blockchain solutions. The presence of transformations affecting existing and new stakeholders, underlying business logic, business processes, and business infrastructure put smart contracts in a particular spotlight. The presence of both cryptographic and smart code vulnerabilities is a serious concern that requires the attention of developers and researchers alike. The study identified the most important attributes of regulatory smart contracts, namely legality, self-execution, and self-enforcement. These attributes are currently underexplored and under-theorized. The study then described how existing smart contracts contribute to regulatory compliance at the level of transformative healthcare processes, enabling transformational healthcare logistics and services. The study described the three most disruptive force chains, showing how they interact with each other and with smart contracts. The study's results showed the differences in the use of smart contracts within the three force chains, showing that the patient force chain has the smallest positive externalities. The main contributions to theory and practice are discussed.

IMPLICATIONS FOR FUTURE RESEARCH AND PRACTICE

The rapidly growing body of smart contract research has been mostly carried out in the cryptocurrency and blockchain industries. Consequently, in contrast with their transformative potential, the true role of smart contracts in supporting regulatory compliance in healthcare blockchain systems remains largely unexplored. In the healthcare industry, a better understanding of smart contracts for ensuring regulatory compliance and enhancing interoperability for different digital healthcare tools and platforms is crucial. Although integrating smart contracts in many digital healthcare solutions can ensure many trust and choice problems, in an open community market, it may not always be widely desirable. Accordingly, we advocate that more empirical research should be conducted on how blockchain technology, in general, and smart contracts in particular, can ensure regulatory compliance and interoperability across unique digital healthcare systems, platforms, solutions, and tools in practice. Such empirical evidence will offer sufficient ethical and social rationales to persuade healthcare systems and providers to invest in blockchain technology to manage the growing healthcare supply chain. For example, administrative burdens on physicians and other healthcare practitioners can be alleviated in case management or the vast management of other phone calling systems through the automatic execution of smart contracts into a blockchain network, especially in large patient populations.

Alternatively, smart contracts can be designed as part of a built-in monetization model, including the concept that can stimulate genuine regulatory change much needed in the current healthcare industry that frequently supports higher administrative remunerations than actual patient care.

AUTHORS' CONTRIBUTION

In Chapter 8, **Riya Sharma, Prabh Deep Singh, Rohan Verma,** and **Deep Mann** collaboratively explored the role of smart contracts in regulatory compliance within blockchain healthcare systems. **Riya Sharma** led the research on the integration of blockchain and smart contracts in healthcare, particularly in ensuring compliance with regulations like GDPR. **Prabh Deep Singh** analyzed the challenges of implementing smart contracts in healthcare systems, focusing on issues of data privacy and security. **Rohan Verma** contributed to the examination of technical and operational frameworks that facilitate compliance through smart contracts, including use case studies. **Deep Mann** provided insights into future directions, innovative applications, and the ethical and legal considerations of smart contract usage in healthcare. Together, the authors created a comprehensive overview of regulatory compliance facilitated by blockchain and smart contracts in healthcare.

Glossary of Key Terms

In support of the non-expert readers, a glossary of key terms is presented as follows:

- Blockchain: A digital log that records transactions across different computers in a secure and transparent manner that cannot be changed. It can be seen as a digital logbook that is shared by a group of users.
- Consensus Mechanism: A process that will ensure all participants in blockchain systems agree on the validity of certain transactions. Common methods of consensus mechanisms include:
- Proof of Work (PoW): A method whereby computers solve complex puzzles to verify transactions.
- Proof of Stake (PoS): A system where participants validate transactions based on the number of coins they own.
- Data Encryption: A security technique that converts data into unreadable code to prevent unauthorized access. Only those with the correct key can decode and access the original data.
- Distributed Ledger Technology (DLT): A distributed system of data storage across many places (or nodes) other than a central server for the purpose of improving security and minimizing the chances of data loss.

- Smart Contract: An in-blockchain self-executable program that automatically enforces a set of rules and conditions agreed upon by parties. It can, for instance, only release funds if a set of conditions is met.
- Hash: A unique string of characters produced from data through some mathematical function. Any alteration made in the original data generates a different hash, which can make it useful for proving that the data has not been altered.
- Immutability: A characteristic in the blockchain whereby, once data is fed, it cannot be updated or deleted. It enhances the accuracy and reliability of the records.
- Decentralization: It refers to the lack of central authority in a system. Blockchain has its data distributed over a network, reducing the dependence on a single point of control.
- PKI (Public Key Infrastructure): A type of cryptographic system that utilizes two keys to facilitate encrypted communication and data exchange—public for encryption and private for decryption.
- IoT (Internet of Things): A network of physical devices such as wearables and medical sensors that collect and share data *via* the internet
- Throughput: The number of transactions that a blockchain system can make per second, showing efficiency
- Latency: The time between the sending of a transaction and its confirmation on the blockchain. Less latency is very important to real-time applications
- Scalability: This is the ability of a blockchain system to handle increased numbers of transactions or users without suffering performance degradation
- Fault Tolerance: The ability of a blockchain to continue working even if several nodes fail or are attacked.
- Sharding: A technique to achieve scalability in blockchain by creating smaller, more manageable groupings called "shards" that work independently for processing transactions.

REFERENCES

[1]   Griggs KN, Ossipova O, Christopher P, Kohlios P, Baccarini AN, Howson EA, *et al.* A blockchain-based smart contract system for healthcare management. Electronics (Basel) 2018; 42(7): 130. Available from: https://www.mdpi.com/2079-9292/9/1/94

[2]   Hu C, Li C, Zhang G, *et al.* CrowdMed-II: a blockchain-based framework for efficient consent management in health data sharing. World Wide Web (Bussum) 2022; 25(3): 1489-515. [http://dx.doi.org/10.1007/s11280-021-00923-1] [PMID: 35002477]

[3]   Jaiman V. Consent model for blockchain-based health data sharing platforms. IEEE Xplore 2020. Available from: https://ieeexplore.ieee.org/abstract/document/9159120/

[4]   Omar IA, Jayaraman R, Salah K, Simsekler MCE, Yaqoob I, Ellahham S. Ensuring protocol compliance and data transparency in clinical trials using Blockchain smart contracts. BMC Med Res Methodol 2020; 20(1): 224. Available from: https://link.springer.com/article/10.1186/s12874-020-01109-5 [http://dx.doi.org/10.1186/s12874-020-01109-5] [PMID: 32894068]

[5]   Choudhury O, Sarker H, Rudolph N, *et al.* Enforcing human subject regulations using blockchain and smart contracts. BHTY [Internet] 2018 Mar. 23; 1. Available from: https://www.blockchain healthcaretoday.com/index.php/journal/article/view/10

[6]   Paper S, Rupasinghe T, Burstein F, Rudolph C. Blockchain-based dynamic patient consent: A privacy-preserving data acquisition architecture for clinical data analytics. Monash University Research 2019. Available from: https://research.monash.edu/en/publications/blockchain-based-dynamic-pati-nt-consent-a-privacy-preserving-dat

[7]   Adams CA, Hill WY, Roberts CB. Corporate social reporting practices in Western Europe: Legitimating corporate behaviour?. Br Account Rev 1998; 30(1): 1-21. [http://dx.doi.org/10.1006/bare.1997.0060]

[8]   Wang S, Ouyang L, Yuan Y. Blockchain-enabled smart contracts: Architecture, applications, and future trends. IEEE Xplore 2019. Available from: https://ieeexplore.ieee.org/abstract/document/8643084/

[9]   Ettaloui N, Arezki S. An overview of blockchain-based electronic health records and compliance with GDPR and HIPAA. Springer 2023. Available from: https://link.springer.com/chapter/10.1007/978-3-031-48573-2_58

[10]   Shukla R, Agarwal A. Blockchain-powered smart healthcare system 2020. Available from: https://www.sciencedirect.com/science/article/pii/B9780128198162000101

[11]   Wang L. Big data, cybersecurity, and challenges in healthcare. IEEE SoutheastCon 2019. Available from: https://ieeexplore.ieee.org/abstract/document/9020632/?casa_token=wBhsDTcWz1MAAAAA

[12]   Garzik J., Donnelly J.Blockchain 101: An introduction to the future. Academic Press 2018; 179-186. Available from: https://www.sciencedirect.com/science/article/pii/B9780128122822000085

[13]   Halpin H. Introduction to security and privacy on the blockchain. IEEE Int Symp 2017. Available from: https://ieeexplore.ieee.org/abstract/document/7966963/

[14]   Chen L. A brief introduction to blockchain economics. World Sci 2021; 1-14. Available from: https://www.worldscientific.com/doi/abs/10.1142/9789811220470_0001

[15]   Singhal, B., Dhameja, G., Panda, P.S. Introduction to blockchain. In: Beginning Blockchain. Apress, Berkeley, CA 2018. Available from: https://link.springer.com/chapter/10.1007/978-1-4842-3444-0_1

[16]   Khan SN, Loukil F, Ghedira-Guegan C, Elhadj Benkhelifa A, Bani-Hani AB. Blockchain smart contracts: Applications, challenges, and future trends 2023; 14(5): 2901-5. Available from: https://link.springer.com/article/10.1007/s12083-021-01127-0

[17]   Vetrivel S. Blockchain health: Smart contracts transforming healthcare operations. IGI Global 2024. Available from: https://www.igi-global.com/chapter/blockchain-health/344185

[18]   Distributed IPC. Introduction to blockchain technology. Wiley Online Library 2019. Available from: https://onlinelibrary.wiley.com/doi/pdf/10.1002/9781119488330#page=111

[19]   Narikimilli N, Kumar A, Antu A. Blockchain applications in healthcare: A review and future perspective 2020. Available from: https://link.springer.com/chapter/10.1007/978-3-030-59638-5_14

[20]   Knickerbocker J, Budd R. Heterogeneous integration technology demonstrations for future healthcare, IoT, and AI computing solutions. IEEE SoutheastCon 2018. Available from: https://ieeexplore.ieee.org/abstract/document/8429744/

[21]   Sreedevi A, Harshitha T. Application of cognitive computing in healthcare, cybersecurity, big data, and IoT: A literature review 2022. Available from: https://www.sciencedirect.com/science/article/pii/S0306457322000176

[22]   Filatova N. Smart contracts from the contract law perspective: outlining new regulative strategies. Int J Law Inf Tech 2020; 217-42. Available from: https://academic.oup.com/ijlit/article-abstract/28/3/217/5897086

[23]   Sharma P, Moparthi NR, Namasudra S, Shanmuganathan V, Hsu C-H. Blockchain-based IoT architecture to secure healthcare system using identity-based encryption. Expert Syst 2022; 39.

[24]   Institute KD. Case studies on the regulatory challenges raised by innovation and the regulatory responses 2021. Available from: https://books.google.com/books?hl=en&lr=&id=XpJUEAAAQBAJ& oi=fnd&pg=PA3&dq=Decentralized+ledger+Smart+contracts+Compliance+automation+Regulatory+ compliance+Startup+innovations+Case+studies&ots=IBSSLpGSX5&sig=HNA304c0TZxeF3BsSUTh QsYGB0s

[25]   Charles W, Marler N, Long L. Blockchain compliance by design: Regulatory considerations for blockchain in clinical research. Front Blockchain 2019. Available from: https://www.frontiersin. org/articles/10.3389/fbloc.2019.00018/full

[26]   Charles W, Marler N, Long L, Manion S. Blockchain compliance by design: Regulatory considerations for blockchain in clinical research. Front Blockchain 2019; p. 2.

[27]   Yaqoob I, Salah K. Blockchain for healthcare data management: Opportunities, challenges, and future recommendations 2022. Available from: https://link.springer.com/article/10.1007/s00521-020-055-9-w

[28]   Ettaloui N, Arezki S, Gadi T. An overview of blockchain-based electronic health record and compliance with GDPR and HIPAA. Lecture Notes Netw Syst 2024; 838 LNNS: 405-12.2024;

[29]   Xu Y, Chong HY, Chi M. A review of smart contracts applications in various industries: A procurement perspective. Adv Civ Eng 2021; 2021.
        [http://dx.doi.org/10.1155/2021/5530755]

[30]   Vardhini B, Dass S. Blockchain-based electronic medical health records framework using smart contracts. IEEE Xplore 2021. Available from: https://ieeexplore.ieee.org/abstract/document/9402689/

[31]   Dal Mas F, Dicuonzo G, Dell V. Smart contracts to enable sustainable business models: A case study. Emerald 2021. Available from: https://www.emerald.com/insight/content/doi/10.1108/MD-09-20-9-1266/full/html

Exploring the Intersection of HIPAA Compliance and Blockchain Technology in Health Information Systems

Prabh Deep Singh[1], Kiran Deep Singh[2], Riya Sharma[3,*] and Sharon Christa[4]

[1] *Department of Computer Science and Engineering, Graphic Era Deemed to be University, Dehradun, Uttarakhand, India*

[2] *Department of Computer Science and Engineering, Chitkara University Institute of Engineering and Technology, Rajpura, Punjab, India*

[3] *Department of Commerce, Graphic Era Deemed to be University, Dehradun, Uttarakhand, India*

[4] *Department of Computer Science and Engineering, MIT Art Design and Technology University, Pune, Maharashtra, India*

Abstract: The healthcare industry's transformation into an information-rich world has led to an unprecedented level of data availability and data sharing, thus encouraging the development of sophisticated information-sharing platforms facilitated by technologies such as blockchain systems. Standard health data models like Fast Healthcare Interoperability have been raising issues more crucially regarding data security, managing and controlling different types and levels of access privileges, and ensuring that sensitive health data is access-controlled according to HIPAA regulations. A trusted blockchain maintains its decentralized and tamper-proof characteristic and enables its participating stakeholders to share and/or store information. Consequently, it is anticipated that this technology may have a fruitful effect on healthcare applications. These distributed systems, which are comprised of ever-growing unchangeable transaction records, ensure security in data storage and exchange processes. However, the advantages gained from applying blockchain to healthcare create fundamental challenges in terms of security and privacy. To date, discussions focused on the intersection of the private healthcare sector with blockchain technology have been quite limited. This research, therefore, examines how the principles of the Health Insurance Portability and Accountability Act (HIPAA) can be aligned with blockchain technology in health information centers. Consequently, the research not only has implications for companies, especially health information centers and blockchain developers, but will also inform regulatory bodies as they deliberate on updating the rules governing privacy, healthcare technology, and use.

* Corresponding author Riya Sharma: Department of Commerce, Graphic Era Deemed to be University, Dehradun, Uttarakhand, India;
E-mail: riyasharma6568@gmail.com

Mohit Angurala, Preet Kamal, Aryan Chaudhary, Rasmeet Singh Bali & Vijay Bhardwaj (Eds.)
All rights reserved-© 2025 Bentham Science Publishers

Keywords: Blockchain systems, Data availability, Data security, Distributed systems, Healthcare transformation, Information sharing.

INTRODUCTION

Health information systems (HIS) are becoming more integrated and centralized with the advances in technologies and regulations such as the Health Insurance Portability and Accountability Act (HIPAA). The access control framework of HIPAA has some security requirements that make this control in HIS more complex, difficult, and sensitive [1]. Moreover, the frauds and breaches of privacy in the healthcare system are increasing, and the importance of HIS for humans in preserving their health has been growing with new care available, preserving secret health data, like self-aware systems, that provide consultation and automated healthcare. This paper discusses the Health Information System's security problem using the concept of Hyperledger, a hybrid permissioned blockchain as private, private-permissioned or permissioned-public, which possesses high alteration and confidentiality in local access and a sustainable level of decentralization [2].

The adopted approach uses the Hyperledger Caliper from the Hyperledger project, which is a benchmark program to assist clients in calculating their capacity to use blockchain in a transactional system, supporting developers to choose the best framework through benchmark comparisons, and the FlexSCIB, a two-level Sensitive Information Model that makes it easier to understand and operate with healthcare information and its sensibilities, furthering its correct model and enabling improved access control [3]. The computational replica used was implemented through Blockchain Explorer, a live demo tool of Hyperledger. The obtained results showed that all requirements established by the benchmarking target were met and surpassed with successful compliance with access controls and sensibilities of patient history data. The response time to the transaction was 100% of committed transactions, and the ratio of private transactions remained less than 1% for both in the current configuration (high performance) for the considered blockchain. The system resiliency was reached with no partition. The observer (compared to the verifier) results were consistent and reliable (consistency test passed).

This paper follows the following structure: In Section 2, the background and research problem are discussed, followed by state-of-the-art and related work in blockchain and HIPAA and the adopted methodology and Hyperledger Framework in Section 3. In Section 4, the Sensitive Information Model is depicted, and the experimental setting is exposed. Section 5 reports the obtained results, and Section 6 ends with our outlook on the results and future work.

Background and Significance

ProgressHUD is a lightweight and easy-to-use HUD for iOS. This demonstrates how to use it on NimbleHQ's latest jobs, and it only takes a couple of minutes to install and set up. It is about the installation of technology in a hospital facility. When a change in the measured features is detected, the cardiac device's wireless transmission of the patient's vital signs becomes a sequence of alert alarms [4]. Physicians, an important target of the alerts, cannot access any of these data on any of the hospital's PCs while still on the hospital campus. The protection of electronic health records and data in health information systems is in line with the Health Insurance Portability and Accountability Act (HIPAA) of 1996, which safeguards the confidentiality, integrity, and availability of an individual's health records. Blockchain technology, on the other hand, is a relatively new concept that is garnering attention from various fields. It has the potential to provide a secure layer for electronic health record access in decentralized environments and address security, integrity, data management, and many of the existing challenges in health information systems [5]. However, the capability of blockchain with respect to the implementation and compliance of HIPAA standards has not been researched thoroughly in the current literature. Additionally, as blockchain is not fully regulated, it is particularly essential to pay attention to data privacy and confidentiality regulations when deploying it in healthcare. In this paper, we review HIPAA compliance with telecommunications, storage, and blockchain basics and then explore the intersection of HIPAA compliance with the current capabilities of blockchain technology in enabling the secure sharing of electronic health records.

Purpose of the Study

This examination using the grounded theory method was performed because of its ability to develop theoretical frameworks based on data derived and validated from intense research within a domain. The results' quality comes from the methodological fact that inquiries rely on the industriousness in the research laboratory to construct useful and interesting explanations of how non-technical people working at an organization with mission-critical information security responsibilities construct, tack up, and evaluate their internal audit staff to support their chief executive's, board's, and shareholders' intent. They are given the opportunity to face the realities of actual corporate practices by laptop tests to test models that dissatisfy the attractiveness of theoretical and postulated hypotheses through qualitative research. The use of case-oriented methodologies in the inquiry permits what has not been allowed to date in hypothesis testing in broad general classificatory studies. This rigorous inquiry asks radical questions about what a relatively little-studied population in information security is. The purpose of this interpretative case study is to examine the strategy formation processes used by senior information security officials at the nation's financial institutions. The technological capabilities of banks to support customer demands for a variety of new, always accessible, worldwide electronic banking services have significantly changed banking strategy priorities since a number of banking mergers and acquisitions and the deregulation of telecommunications. Furthermore, the study will identify which environmental and organizational management concerns are prompting strategic changes to be made in the data security function, a function that the study found has similarities to being a key service element that defines a bank. Lastly, the study will evaluate the security function's impact on security-sensitive user satisfaction with international banking automated delivery systems. The investigation's goal is to learn by highly valuing the stimulating knowledge of why people (the senior officers) act as they do in designing security policies. Results appear to be descriptive and tentative and extend the present understanding of non-technical security managers.

UNDERSTANDING HIPAA COMPLIANCE IN HEALTH INFORMATION SYSTEMS

HIPAA's combination of privacy, security, and standardization provisions goes much further than before in changing the healthcare industry. In particular, unlike previous US healthcare laws, HIPAA has significant penalties for violation and does not allow states to undertake a less comprehensive scheme. This paper discusses HIPAA in some depth because compliance with this law will have significant long-term effects on any system that transmits, provides, secures, and/or exchanges personal health information (PHI) [4]. HIPAA applies to these entities in their electronic exchange of transactions related to healthcare services and the management of PHI.

Any system that involves at least one covered entity transmits private health information in the electronic exchange of transactions and allows external systems to obtain information is affected by HIPAA. HIPAA also applies to businesses providing services to covered entities, contractors, and trading partners.

These different categories are briefly described. No other existing federal law or regulation in the United States has transformed industries the way the Health Information Portability and Accountability Act (HIPAA) has transformed the US healthcare industry [5]. HIPAA was originally passed to "provide for the development of uniform national standards for electronic healthcare transactions and code sets, and for unique health identifiers for providers, health plans, and employers." In 1996, the Kennedy-Kassebaum Act (KLA) extended HIPAA to "protect the privacy, foster trust, be highly adaptable, and designed to secure access to data, increase the value of data exchange, protect personal data yet allow it to be monetized, not monopolized but help create rather than suppress competition, and most importantly, transform customer service." HIPAA established complex security standards, standardized health information and the secure flow of this information, and established standards for the storage of this information [1].

Overview of HIPAA Regulations

The Health Insurance Portability and Accountability Act legislation is composed of three sections. The first section, called the Health Insurance Reform, poses for the purposes of administering COBRA (the Consolidated Omnibus Budget Reconciliation Act) and title X (Grants and Coverage for Family). The second section is called administrative simplification, which deals with standardizing transactions and specifies that group health plans and certain other organization's sponsors assume certain operations regarding privacy and the protection of records (portability).

Finally, the third section outlines the Internal Revenue Code for health insurance and the tax deduction for employer-provided health benefits. Of interest in the HIPAA legislation is the administrative simplification's provisions concerning coverage and portability of data. Since its inception nearly a quarter of a century ago, compliance with the Health Insurance Portability and Accountability Act (HIPAA) has become a central concern for stakeholders in the ever-increasing network of electronic health information systems. While the intentions of the law are irreproachable, organizations subjected to its provisions are failing to demonstrate compliance with the law's mandates and secure sensitive patient data as required [6]. It may, therefore, be necessary to look at emerging technologies developed to maintain patient privacy, prevent data tampering, and ensure business continuity for the framework necessary to maintain compliance with HIPAA regulations under an increasingly dynamic and complex network of health information systems [7].

Key Requirements for HIPAA Compliance

HIM processes support the objectives of allowing authorized use of patient information while keeping information confidential. The HIM field is changing very rapidly because of the rapid changes in digital storage capabilities. Health information management is critical because patients expect information to be protected. CHKD primarily manages information using at-rest encryption technologies, secure backup and restoration technologies, and secure session services. CHKD has duplicative server services with independent backup technologies [8].

For instance, CHKD fielded a project that harnessed Pure Storage FlashBlade technology to contain Hadoop workloads and to ensure that we met HIPAA requirements for large datasets. Our department worked with CHKD's HIM leader to ensure compliance and, as with other challenges in healthcare, HIM is a concern that should be frequently revisited to ensure not only that technology processes are effectively addressing concerns but also that privacy goals are being consistently met.

For those entering the health information systems domain and seeking confidence as well as a clear understanding of HIPAA compliance, several key components are required [9]. First, understanding the three rule-making bodies in health information systems: the US Congress (public law), the US Department of Health and Human Services (HHS clarifications and penalties), and the Health Information Technology for Economic and Clinical Health Act (HITECH) (state statutes that reinforce HIPAA). Second, CHKD's health information systems team should fully respect patients as individuals and the rights of patients and guardians to have discrete discussions. Specifically, in situations that involve separating guardians from the patients themselves, CHKD's legal team is an invaluable partner. Information systems cannot address HIPAA compliance on their own. HIPAA-compliance discussions often require complex considerations such as those that arise when parents and patients divorce, when different perceptions regarding appropriate care are identified, and in other sensitive situations. These encounters require assistance from CHKD's legal department. Third, Health Information Management (HIM) is the practice of ensuring patient privacy [10].

BLOCKCHAIN TECHNOLOGY IN HEALTHCARE

Blockchain technology has already achieved some level of implementation within the healthcare industry. Large electronic medical record (EMR) companies and some health systems are partnering together to develop patient-centric and longitudinal health records that would incorporate information from commercial or independent systems [11]. As the Patient-Centered Data Home (PCDH) model increases, the problem of lack of informed consent within healthcare is slowly removed. Patients can potentially provide their approval through a phone app and have their blockchain-based consent tracked along with their medical records, allowing them to take a more active role in their own healthcare [12].

Permissioned blockchains can directly address the problem of telemedicine and prescription fraud. Discussions concerning the potential problems with gainsharing contracts, as well as those about terms of compensation, can also be tracked using permissioned blockchains.

With respect to social determinants of health, the use of blockchain technology can help emphasize the importance that these determinants represent to overall health and wellness [13]. Therefore, further exploration of the technology and healthcare can provide additional insights concerning the differences in blockchain technology compared to mainstream technology and the advantages that blockchain can provide when properly developing information systems. Fig. (1) outlines the process for integrating blockchain technology with HIPAA compliance in healthcare. It starts with analyzing HIPAA regulations, identifying security requirements, evaluating blockchain capabilities, designing and implementing a blockchain solution, testing for HIPAA compliance, deploying the solution, and concluding with ongoing monitoring and maintenance of compliance.

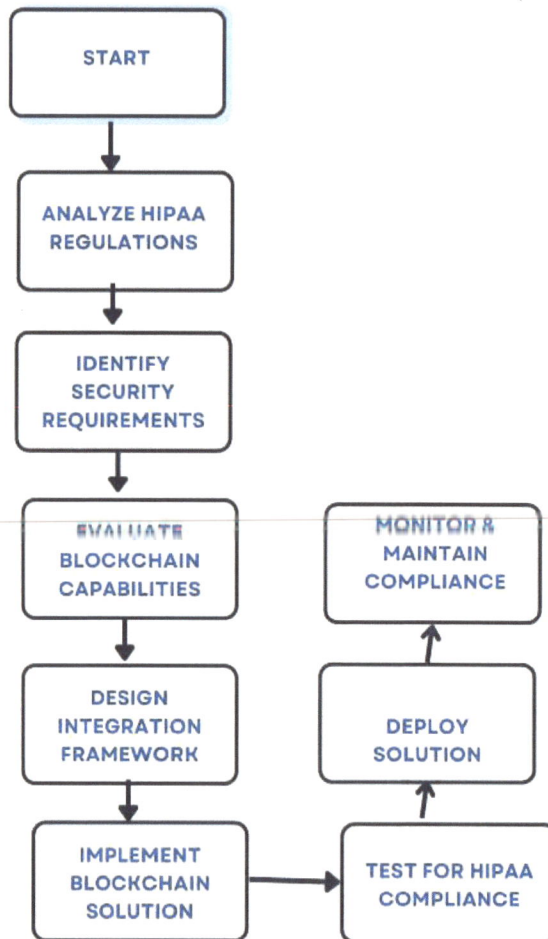

Fig. (1). HIPAA compliance and blockchain integration flowchart.

There are numerous uses for blockchain technology within the healthcare industry. Some potential use cases that are under development include patient identity validation, patient engagement, data exchange, claims adjudication in insurance, pharmaceutical integrity, electronic prior authorization, and monitoring and reporting of clinical quality measures. In addition, consent management, medical billing, secure prescription drug ordering and fulfillment, decentralized web-based electronic medical records (EMR), rural health, supply chain integrity for medical supplies, telemedicine, and health information exchanges may also benefit from blockchain technology [14].

These potential use cases can provide some innovative disruptions in the industry by increasing data integrity, decreasing costs, removing administrative barriers, streamlining cooperation, or increasing security. Moreover, patient options can be expanded to allow for self-guided care and to have medical records be accessed or transmitted based on the needs of these patients. With patient access to their own medical data, patients can provide consent and revoke consent while others discuss the secondary use of their data within the healthcare industry. Ultimately, the use of blockchain technology can help make medical records more patient-centered [15].

Fundamentals of Blockchain Technology

Blockchain development is driven by formal software and system design, cryptographic building blocks, and standard bodies that develop the building blocks for internet communication and collaboration. In co-sponsored meetings and publications, the National Institute of Standards and Technology (NIST) and the Department of Health and Human Services have incorporated blockchain technology into their guidance materials and standard publications in recognition of the potential of blockchain technology in health information management [16].

Blockchain technology uses cryptographic techniques to create security and functionality by processing and representing information about transactions [17]. These transactions can represent things beyond the transfers of the tables of accounts of financial ledgers in a currency system or in a modern enterprise resource planning system [18]. They can represent the movement and transfer of any things that can be digitally described, including the activities of patients in a healthcare environment.

Blockchain technology is often used to create digital, distributed databases. The core digital components of a blockchain include a cryptographically secure identity (a hash) assigned to each "block" of data, a reference to an earlier block in the blockchain, a set of confirmed transactions, a set of consensus rules to govern how new blocks in the chain are validated and committed, and a distributed network that shares in the commitment to the blockchain so that no single entity can monopolize control of the system.

Blockchain databases can contain any information that can be digitized, and consensus rules can be incorporated into private blockchains that are validated by trusted entities [19]. Cryptocurrency systems use blockchain technology and have been in use for more than a decade. Larger software projects have recognized the potential and problems in using blockchain technology to maintain secure records of any type of transaction. Blockchain first made its mark as the technology underlying the digital currency, Bitcoin, which has been in continual use since its creation in 2009 [20]. Since then, blockchain technology has gathered significant attention across many industries because of the interesting properties it promises: distributed, tamper-resistant, append-only, and peek-only records. These properties have led many individuals and organizations to explore the potential of blockchain technology in industries like supply chain management, public records, online voting, and real estate.

Fig. (**2**) represents the architecture of a Health Information System, divided into three layers: Data Storage Layer, Application Layer, and Blockchain Layer. Each layer consists of specific components such as electronic health records and encrypted databases in the data storage layer, user interface and access control services in the application layer, and blockchain network and consensus mechanism in the blockchain layer.

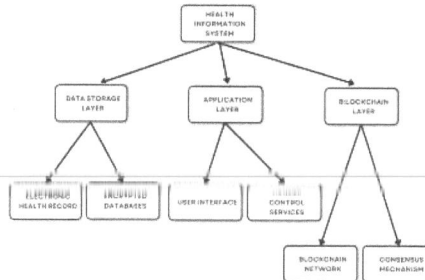

Fig. (2). Health information system architecture diagram.

Fig. (**3**) illustrates the class diagram, which manages sensitive data and access controls. The FlexSCIB class contains lists of sensitive data and access control objects and includes a method for compliance checks. The Sensitive Data class holds patient information such as patient ID, health records, and encryption key, while the access controls class manages role-based access, permissions, and audit logs.

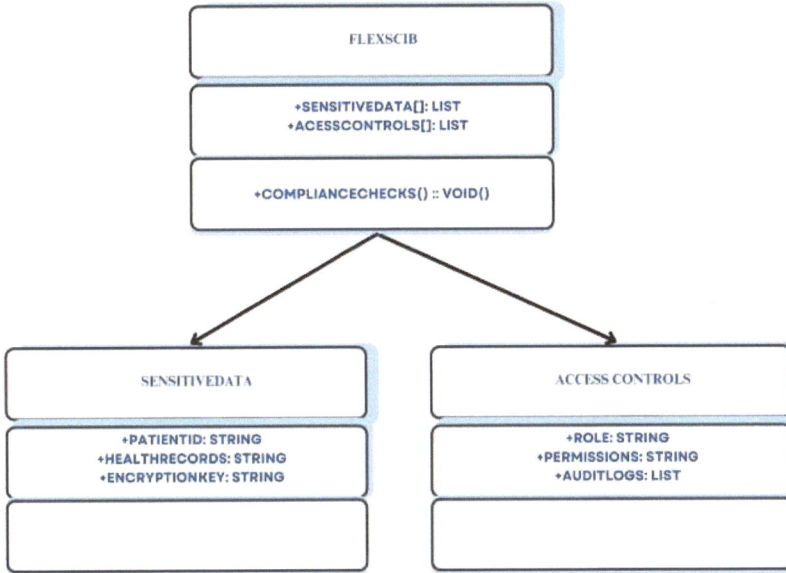

Fig. (3). Sensitive information model.

Applications of Blockchain in Healthcare

Ohno-Machado *et al.* (2018) present a list of applications where the blockchain can be utilized in healthcare: (1) indexing EHRs, (2) prescription tracking, (3) supply chain integrity, (4) research reproducibility, and (5) refuting or detecting fake news and a list of features attributed to the blockchain with possible security implications that can make interoperability of EHRs for data sharing and secondary activities more secure.

Holzinger *et al.* (2017) suggest application areas for EHRs by utilizing the benefits of blockchain technology, such as monitoring and controlling attendance and accessed health information, IPR-related issues in data security, data integrity versus data agility, health information benchmarks for big data analytics for precision medicine and smart data analytics, and mastering privacy regulations according to data regulations. A study [21] suggests that blockchain can be a disruptive enabler of healthcare by enabling processes such as EHR management, the healthcare system, processes and policies, IDs, tracking, IoT security, and patient-data security.

Raj *et al.* (2019) state that blockchain can be very beneficial in regulating fraud, digitally automating identification, simplifying patient data exchange, providing tamper-proof databases for public health, ensuring interoperability, yielding patient-focused longitudinal health records, supporting health-system financial processes, providing structured data for public health surveillance, and regulating data disruptions in their research on the applicability of blockchain in the healthcare industry [22].

According to a study conducted by Mohanta and Jena (2019), blockchain technology is effective in areas of healthcare such as EHR and efficiency optimization, medical supply chain, controlled sharing of medical records, the security of IoT-based medical devices, personalized healthcare data exchange, robust health information exchange, implementation of a tamper-proof database, healthcare fraud detection, and computational health.

CHALLENGES AND OPPORTUNITIES OF INTEGRATING BLOCKCHAIN AND HIPAA COMPLIANCE

Exploring the intersection of HIPAA compliance and blockchain technology (Block HIPAA) reveals that healthcare organizations can leverage the benefits offered by an unchangeable, time-stamped record that is transparent and secure. The chapter, however, discusses the vulnerabilities that arise from a fully implemented blockchain since the technology is unable to detect or prevent attacks that compromise the factual integrity of the data input into the system or of the model itself. Prior security literature is then summarized, and a research agenda is presented at the end of the chapter.

This gives rise to significant challenges that healthcare organizations must address to employ a weakened blockchain effectively for HIPAA compliance. Since the blockchain creates an unchangeable, time-stamped record that is transparent and secure, this study discusses the benefits that legitimate users can harness against adversaries [23]. This study, however, also cautions against the vulnerabilities presented by the blockchain itself. While the blockchain can ensure high-quality data, it cannot detect or prevent attacks that compromise the veracity of the data input into the system. As a result, one can create large-scale tampering to fool a particular machine learning model into making deceptive decisions and actions. This study discussed four different permutations of manipulated data to fool a model, thus making blockchain systems susceptible to attacks.

Privacy and Security Concerns

The suggestion is to utilize blockchain and smart contracts to promptly update the Modified Early Warning Survey (MEWS) that combines patients' vital signs. To accommodate blockchain, privileged blockchain is initiated, allowing only the authorized healthcare supplier to acknowledge service requests once commitment documents of the earlier agreements are successfully finished. By working on Ethereum, such a proposed system is tested, and their result extends the trustworthiness of the innovative blockchain system. By using a fast and privacy-preserving protocol, an approach to caring for the remarkably efficient data updates of the study emerges. This dual-centered off-blockchain storage of personal privacy attributes and healthcare data can become an answer to privacy concerns within healthcare management systems.

The security of encrypted data in solidity contracts that manage sensitive and confidential data is analyzed in the Ethereum environment. Third parties are given access to data using a permissioned blockchain. At least 80% of nodes are required to unanimously agree to all access requests back to the node that is able to authorize permission granting. This method attempts to reduce the threat by limiting the acceptance of suicidal code by a single node. A remote procedure call serializes RPC to ensure that all peers have access to the other peers' requests. A proposed blockchain-based protocol that allows patients to obtain ownership of the existing health information represented in SMART.

Anti-cryptographic tools such as "Zero-Knowledge Proofs" and "Private Information Retrieval" can be used to challenge a participant's claims regarding the amount of data included in the blockchain, which does not benefit the participant. Zero-knowledge proofs are valuable tools that blockchain enthusiasts believe may overcome any privacy concerns and can be exploited to work out the privacy of the inner layers of the blockchain (Fig. **4**). It also provides privacy within a blockchain. Allowing this level of privacy may not sit well with regulators who strive for the importance of transparency. The sharing of patient's health information with other authorized healthcare management systems or patients across the globe must be secure against external malicious programs or unauthorized access. The Total Health Record of the patient, including all diagnostic reports and examination images, can be distributed across an off-blockchain directory with the use of a private certain permission blockchain for pointer management and data reference.

Privacy and security are the bedrocks of HIPAA rules and regulations. They guard the confidentiality of individuals' health information and regulate healthcare organizations' manipulation of Electronic Health Records. Technically, proper maintenance of cryptography keys for each participant can potentially overcome the issue of public and private key cryptography. Whenever a participant wants to send encrypted data, he or she can encrypt the data with the recipient's public key, and the recipient can use his or her private key to decrypt the encrypted data. Since the recipient is the only one who can decrypt the encoded data, this system ensures the privacy of protecting personal health records. However, within the blockchain community, public key cryptography has always been compromised. With advances in quantum computing technology, current cryptographic methods will have the capability to be broken, therefore inherently violating the privacy of the participant. Additionally, unauthorized access to public patient health information within a healthcare organization must be the main focus of the owners of these healthcare organizations. Because the same level of trust is needed for patients to authorize the use and disclosure of their data established by the traditional healthcare management processes using blockchain technology.

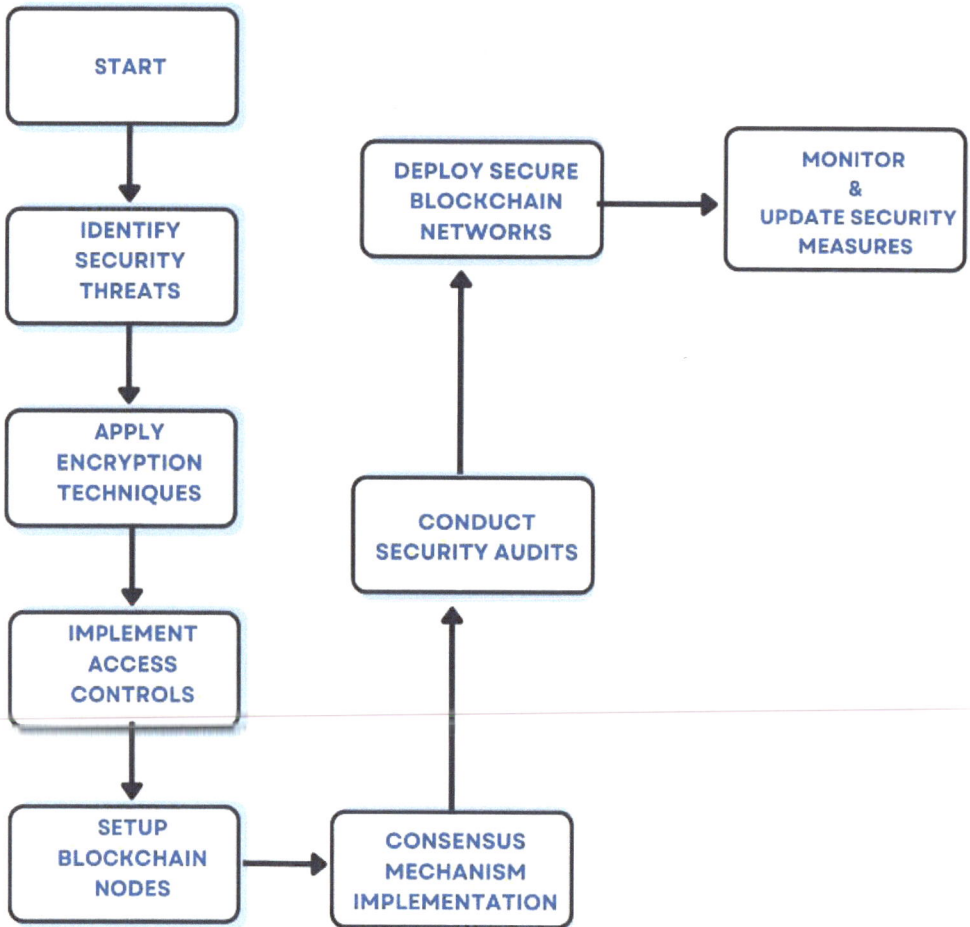

Fig. (4). Blockchain security measures.

Interoperability Issues

Interoperability typically requires a central data repository, where all data-sharing entities contribute and extract PHI from. However, as was discussed, if PHI is locked into a proprietary central data repository, this achieves the opposite of interoperability, *i.e.*, IID. Emerging blockchain solutions demonstrate PHI interoperability and advantage, not of one or two entities, but rather the whole network, *i.e.*, HIN. Each entity thus has equal access to the input and extraction of PHI, usually through API gateways or similar entities, which can provide the right environment to ensure the prior authorization controls remain in place.

Interoperability in healthcare is the primary goal of HIPAA, so PHI can flow between authorized entities as required. The HIPAA Privacy Rule helps ensure the flow of PHI, including proper protection of patient privacy. Both are necessary complements. Interoperability can be enhanced, making PHI use more efficient, but this cannot be at the expense of privacy and security. This is a natural tension. To fulfill the demands of both HIPAA compliance needs and, at the same time, the drive for interoperable PHI, robust filters are required to ensure patient privacy is upheld at all times.

CASE STUDY

The potential of health information system technology is neither theoretical nor untapped. It is a rich investment for the nation. In 2016, the Deloitte Center for Health Solutions predicted a growing move toward more consumer-centered care, combining new technologies, informatics, digital tools, and data analytics, which aligns with our roadmap for the next 10 years. Knowing these strengths in health information technology, the Department of Health and Human Services (HHS) sought concepts for the development of a national blockchain technology that could potentially change the advancement of technology throughput for meaningful use of health IT. To better use electronic health information and to better inform patients of their care plans and the results of their care, HHS developed a health IT mission statement in support of its mission of promoting the use of health IT to transform many important functions and promote the health of the patients and the sources of the right products to manage their health effectively.

Successful Implementations of Blockchain in Healthcare

Given the rapidly evolving research in this area, the structure of the proven applications of blockchain technology in health informatics will likely change. Nevertheless, many potential applications have surfaced that can be valuable for healthcare organizations—especially regarding the security and privacy of electronic health record exchanges. A combination of HIPAA requirements and blockchain advantages in solving potential cryptographic problems can be found in the implementation of the following use cases. Cryptographic problems can be classified into three categories: access control, privacy, and encryption. Electronic health record access logs have been frequently abused by healthcare insiders, even though this is a major violation of HIPAA [24]. EHR tamper-proof access logs based on blockchain technology have been proposed to prevent unauthorized data access, trace the history of EHR access, and thereby act as a broker for a trusted health data exchange.

The value of blockchain in healthcare is in its ability to deliver better security, traceability, and privacy. The uniquely trusted characteristics of blockchain technology are interconnected consensus, content integrity, peer-to-peer cybersecurity, and tamper resistance within the boundaries of the healthcare system. Five primary categories have been identified in which healthcare has already seen successful implementations of blockchain technology, which are included in conjunction with meeting HIPAA privacy and security regulations. Beyond these commonly discussed applications, healthcare is also experimenting with new ways blockchain technology can be used in clinical data exchange, wearable data management, and clinical trial recruitment, with new discoveries in this area being published with increasing frequency.

BEST PRACTICES FOR ENSURING HIPAA COMPLIANCE IN BLOCKCHAIN-ENABLED SYSTEMS

The following are viewed as extremely important for health information systems using blockchain technology: enhanced security at the endpoints, always-on encryption, strong and transparent authentication, an advanced data integrity and consensus algorithm, a mechanism of providing legal immutability while still providing for right-to-be-forgotten requirements of the patient, and ongoing re-evaluation of the blockchain network security to make sure that the requirements of the health system in 2022 are being met. Various additional blockchain-specific security controls are suggested, such as the use of the strongest encryption form, strong user identification and authentication, automated or manual detection of access to record data, and specialized application programming for interfaces (PIPs). The purpose of a PIP is to provide a simplified list of commands for the underlying operating system and allow these commands to be used without going through the complex protocol structure.

Given the potential for increased sharing of medical information and HIPAA breaches through blockchain technology, security features should be built into the infrastructure to comply with current laws and guidelines. It is essential that systems and applications designed to utilize blockchain technology acknowledge and plan for the additional requirements and regulations in health information systems that include HIPAA. The Office of Civil Rights, Department of Health and Human Services, issued a fact sheet on blockchain and HIPAA to help the application of the law. The Office of the National Coordinator for Health

Information Technology (ONC) commissioned a two-phased challenge to come up with new ideas for guaranteeing security in health information systems using blockchain technology. They advised the use of effective security safeguards to ensure that the patient information in health information systems built on blockchain technology is fully protected.

Data Encryption and Secure Access Controls

Assured encrypting data is on a surge, with blockchain technologies increasingly being developed and used for this purpose. Public key encryption is particularly vital to the advancement and security of blockchain technology. The same aspect also dictates the requirements for a feasible key-storage solution for such public keys. One way to present a key storage for distributed ledger technologies is by integrating with blockchain. That is, blockchain solutions can be utilized to store public keys and respective certificates. Individuals attempting to encrypt a message can then use existing stored public keys, thus alleviating the need to provide secure and performant public key distribution points. The most noteworthy way to raise the issue of methods for secure access controls is to emphasize the business impact of security breaches and the need for robust security measures to protect valuable assets. Currently, due to the permission-less, decentralized creation of blockchain content, blockchain technology can be realized as a novel data store that offers immutability, thus enabling more robust cybersecurity tracing and forensics history logs, protecting such logs from ill-intended individuals who can copy it to prevent future forensic analysis and perform fraud detection and prevention.

Data encryption, a technology that ensures that stored or transmitted information cannot be modified or accessed by an unauthorized party, forms an integral part of data security and constitutes an essential requirement for compliance with the Security Rule. Nevertheless, the Security Rule does not generally specify unique encryption requirements outside of some general considerations. First, the Security Rule does not explicitly require any specific kind of encryption while recognizing the fact that some implementations of encryption are more secure than others. It does provide guidance and flexibility to those regulated under the Security Rule in selecting encryption implementation. Second, the Security Rule does not mandate the amount of information that must be encrypted, and the hospital can decide to include specific details about the data items it encrypts.

REGULATORY CONSIDERATIONS AND FUTURE DIRECTIONS

As of now, HIPAA generally applies to "individually identifiable health information", including demographic data collected from an individual that is created or received by a healthcare provider, health plan, employer, or healthcare clearinghouse that relates to past, present, or future physical or mental health or conditions of an individual or the provision of healthcare to an individual. This information must be transmitted or maintained in electronic media or any other form or medium. To be considered PHI, the information must identify the individual or have the potential to reasonably identify the individual. Blockchain can also store value transaction data accompanying commands applied to digital assets.

In response to blockchain technology, the Office of the National Coordinator for Health Information Technology issued a fact sheet addressing a few regulatory considerations and permitted entities to share a patient's electronic health information across different networks using blockchain technology without violating the Health Insurance Portability and Accountability (HIPAA) Privacy Rule. The Office of the National Coordinator for Health Information Technology concluded that blockchain may generally share patient information either directly or *via* a hyperlink to the record that complies with the HIPAA Privacy Rule. The purpose of the blockchains is to improve data integrity, but content must allude to a "distributed ledger" or a "log-based technology" anywhere in the blockchain.

Legal Implications of Blockchain in Healthcare

While in healthcare, the main goal of blockchain technology solutions is to help manage and improve the accuracy and security of sensitive data, they do present a set of legal implications regarding the application of certain rules. Hence, to ensure the promising benefits of blockchain in healthcare, there is a need to address and solve potential legal issues such as secure workflow optimization in the network, patient privacy, sanctions for improper use, and risk management, as the lack of legal guidance can hinder the interoperability of solutions. All emerging blockchain-based healthcare solutions need to follow a certain set of guiding principles, such as a patient-centered approach, trust, transparency, security, privacy, and cost-effectiveness. Many existing national and international laws and regulations consider technology as a tool to provide evidence of efficiency. As a result, we believe blockchain systems can be positioned as a legal equivalent of existing business practices, as the regulations and compliance methods are likely to evolve. In fact, the use of blockchain technology in healthcare processes may contribute to improving patient trust in the health data exchange.

The advent of blockchain technology is said to be as significant as the establishment of the internet, impacting most, if not all, industries. As of now, blockchain is predominantly known as the technology underpinning virtual currencies like Bitcoin. Under the radar, blockchain is disrupting other industries, too. Healthcare is one of those industries that is predicted to be positively influenced by blockchain technology by providing the group with innovative solutions. However, using blockchain technology in the healthcare industry comes with its fair share of challenges, primarily due to existing legal frameworks, like the Health Insurance Portability and Accountability Act. Legislation must keep up with technological advancements for industries to harness the full potential of new technologies.

CONCLUSION

With the help of improved computing techniques and continuously developing optimization algorithms, the performance of blockchain has been more acceptable. Research on blockchain, health information systems, and HIPAA compliance has matured from the phase of discussion of concepts and principles, exploration of possibilities, and overcoming limitations. The reviews of the most recent research describe the state-of-the-art contributions in these areas. HIPAA remains effective in its framework as time passes by, and it is still not outdated. Blockchain technology in health information systems is among the most important promising solutions for more cost-effective, safer, and efficient health information exchange and management. Despite ongoing efforts, no final solution that combines blockchain and HIPAA currently exists. In future research, ongoing pilot works, and the consensus on blockchain, health information systems, and HIPAA compliance, the future of the healthcare ecosystem is promising.

Blockchain technology is an evolving technology, and its capabilities and potential are still under exploration. The challenge of HIPAA compliance in the domain of health information systems is a critically essential problem to solve. This paper explored how blockchain technology is utilized in HIPAA-compliant solutions for health information systems. Researchers are still working on the interoperability of health information systems to encourage data sharing across healthcare providers. Blockchain will change health information systems into detailed, useful, and accurate systems that are helpful both for individuals and institutions. The efforts and explorations are still ongoing, and there are still significant challenges to overcome. With the results from current research, especially the exploration of novel cryptographic and distributed computing techniques, the future utilization of blockchain in health information systems can be even broader and more diversified, leading to a spontaneous and failsafe health ecosystem.

SUMMARY OF KEY FINDINGS

The inherent security of electronic health records (EHRs) and blockchain features enable HIPAA compliance. Blockchain requires modifications to traditional health information systems. Research studies focused on the delegated administration for HIPAA rules, risk management through access control by the blockchain technology, cryptographic anonymous electronic health records with rights management, secure de-daemon establishment in healthcare IoT, secure data management when using an interoperable identity service, and a risk-adaptive decision-making framework for actionable risk sensing and mitigation in healthcare social networks. Amid the ongoing pandemic, blockchain technology is also being applied to contact tracing by using an interoperable identity service customized for a user-centric P2P IoT architecture that addresses the HIPAA delegation of data to secure remote health monitoring. Measurements include a consensus algorithm, practicality, accountability, background, and security in studies that have performed performance evaluations. Finally, threats and their relative significance according to the blockchain characteristics have been addressed in each study.

This chapter explored the intersection of HIPAA (the Health Insurance Portability and Accountability Act of 1996) compliance and blockchain technology in health information systems. The Health Insurance Portability and Accountability Act (HIPAA) establishes legal requirements for the use of electronic medical records, also known as protected health information (PHI). Several IT solutions have implemented blockchain technology to infer HIPAA's intrinsic requirements. The confidentiality, availability, and integrity of electronic protected health information (EPHI) in electronic medical records are improved while eliminating the risk of a single point of failure by having a decentralized and unalterable healthcare data record.

AUTHORS' CONTRIBUTIONS

In Chapter 9, **Prabh Deep Singh, Kiran Deep Singh, Riya Sharma, and Sharon Christa** collaborated to explore the convergence of HIPAA compliance and blockchain technology in health information systems. **Prabh Deep Singh** led the research on HIPAA's requirements and the challenges of implementing compliance in blockchain-enabled healthcare systems. **Kiran Deep Singh** contributed to analyzing technical frameworks, focusing on interoperability and security issues related to blockchain in healthcare. **Riya Sharma** examined potential applications and use cases of blockchain technology for ensuring HIPAA-compliant data management, including patient data privacy. **Sharon Christa** provided insights into the legal implications and future research directions for integrating blockchain technology with HIPAA standards. Together, the authors offered a comprehensive assessment of how blockchain can support HIPAA-compliant health information systems.

REFERENCES

[1]   Ettaloui N, Arezki S. An overview of blockchain-based electronic health records and compliance with GDPR and HIPAA Lecture Notes in Networks and Systems 2023. Available from: https://link.springer.com/chapter/10.1007/978-3-031-48573-2_58

[2]   Ettaloui N, Arezki S, Gadi T. An overview of blockchain-based electronic health records and compliance with GDPR and HIPAA. Lecture Notes in Networks and Systems 2024; 838: 405-12. [http://dx.doi.org/10.1007/978-3-031-48573-2_58]

[3]   DeLeon C, Choi Y. Blockchain and the protection of patient information: Using blockchain to protect the information of patients in line with HIPAA (work-in-progress). IEEE Xplore 2018. Available from: https://ieeexplore.ieee.org/abstract/document/9092292/

[4]   Elkourdi F, Wei C, Xiao L, Zhang Y. Exploring current practices and challenges of HIPAA compliance in software engineering: Scoping review. IEEE Xplore 2024. Available from: https://ieeexplore.ieee.org/abstract/document/10506964/

[5]   DeLeon C. Blockchain and the protection of patient information in line with HIPAA. IGI Global 2021. Available from: https://www.igi-global.com/chapter/blockchain-and-the-protection-of-patient-information-in-line-with-hipaa/268666

[6]   Ettaloui N, Arezki S. An overview of blockchain-based electronic health records and compliance with GDPR and HIPAA. Lect Notes Netw Syst 2023. Available from: https://link.springer.com/chapter/10.1007/978-3-031-48573-2_58

[7]   Available from: https://ieeexplore.ieee.org/abstract/document/10224728/

[8]   Payne DM, Watson K, Milovich M, Kowalski A, Coren JS, Schoen EJ. Policy integrated blockchain to automate HIPAA Part 2 compliance. IEEE Xplore 2021. Available from: https://sjbe.s3.us-east-2.amazonaws.com/SJBE_Volume_13_2021.pdf#page=44

[9]   Ettaloui N, Arezki S, Gadi T. An overview of blockchain-based electronic health records and compliance with GDPR and HIPAA. Lect Notes Netw Syst 2024; 838: 405-12. [http://dx.doi.org/10.1007/978-3-031-48573-2_58]

[10]   Charles W, Marler N, Long L. Blockchain compliance by design: Regulatory considerations for blockchain in clinical research. Frontiers in Blockchain 2019. Available from: https://www.frontiersin.org/articles/10.3389/fbloc.2019.00018/full?trk=article-ssr-frontend-pulse_x-social-details_comments-action_comment-text

[11]   Kumar V, Ali R, Sharma PK. A secure blockchain-assisted authentication framework for electronic health records. Int J Inf Technol 2024; 1-13. Available from: https://link.springer.com/article/10.1007/s41870-023-01705-w

[12]   Hossein K. Blockchain-based privacy-preserving healthcare architecture. IEEE Xplore 2019. Available from: https://ieeexplore.ieee.org/abstract/document/8861857/?casa_token=zkhZcEDMdmkAAAAA

[13]   Shukla M, Lin J. BlockIoT: Blockchain-based health data integration using IoT devices. PubMed Central 2021. Available from: https://www.ncbi.nlm.nih.gov/pmc/articles/PMC8861710/

[14]   Yu Y, Li Q, Zhang Q, Hu W. Blockchain-based multi-role healthcare data sharing system. IEEE Xplore 2021. Available from: https://ieeexplore.ieee.org/abstract/document/9399028/

[15]   Reegu FA, Abas H, Gulzar Y, Xin Q, Alwan AA, Jabbari A. Blockchain-based framework for interoperable electronic health records for an improved healthcare system. Sustainability 2023. Available from: https://www.mdpi.com/2071-1050/15/8/6337 [http://dx.doi.org/10.3390/su15086337]

[16]   Mohana M, Ong G. Implementation of pharmaceutical drug traceability using blockchain technology. Inti J 2019; 20: 35. Available from: http://eprints.intimal.edu.my/1308/

[17]   Angraal S, Krumholz HM, Schulz WL. Blockchain Technology. Circ Cardiovasc Qual Outcomes 2017; 10(9): e003800.
[http://dx.doi.org/10.1161/CIRCOUTCOMES.117.003800] [PMID: 28912202]

[18]   Angraal S, Krumholz H. Blockchain technology: Applications in healthcare. American Heart Association 2017. Available from: https://www.ahajournals.org/doi/abs/10.1161/CIRCOUTCOMES.117.003800

[19]   Bacon J, Michels J, Millard C. Blockchain demystified: A technical and legal introduction to distributed and centralized ledgers. HeinOnline 2018; 25: 1. Available from: https://heinonline.org/hol-cgi-bin/get_pdf.cgi?handle=hein.journals/jolt25&section=4

[20]   Mohana M, Ong G. Revolutionizing health data management with blockchain technology: Enhancing security and efficiency in a digital era. IGI Global 2024. Available from: https://www.igi-global.com/chapter/revolutionizing-health-data-management-with-blockchain-technology/339350

[21]   Payne DM, Watson K, Milovich M, Kowalski A, Coren JS, Schoen EJ, *et al.* Is blockchain the answer for healthcare records of the future? A promising intersection of law and technology. South J Bus Econ 2021; 13 Available from: https://sjbe.s3.us-east-2.amazonaws.com/SJBE_Volume_13_2021.pdf#page=44

[22]   Balasubramanian R, Prakash E, Khan I, Platts J. Blockchain technology for healthcare. Cardiff Metropolitan University 1996. Available from: http://pstorage-cardiffmet-6926567247.s3.amazonaws.com/28060653/AMI2021_paper_47.pdf

[23]   Azbeg K, Ouchetto O. BlockMedCare: A healthcare system based on IoT, blockchain, and IPFS for data management security. Elsevier 2022. Available from: https://www.sciencedirect.com/science/article/pii/S1110866522000160

[24]   Szczepaniuk H. Cryptographic evidence-based cybersecurity for smart healthcare systems. Elsevier 2023. Available from: https://www.sciencedirect.com/science/article/pii/S0020025523012185

CHAPTER 10

Securing Healthcare Data: Privacy and Regulatory Compliance Through Blockchain

Sandeep Singh[1], Sonal Rattan[2,*], Varinder Pabbi[3] and **Navneet Kumar Rajpoot[4]**

[1] *Department of Computer Science Engineering, SGT University, Gurugram, Haryana, India*

[2] *Department of UCRD and Apex Institute of Technology, Chandigarh University, Mohali, Punjab, India*

[3] *Department of Computer Application, I. K. Gujral Punjab Technical University, Phagwara, Punjab, India*

[4] *Department of Computer Science & Engineering, Graphic Era (Deemed to be University), Dehradun, India*

Abstract: Blockchain technology has a solid base to improve privacy and compliance in healthcare. Its basic features—immutability, decentralization, and transparency—are most of the issues related to the management of sensitive health information. The health sector has been swamped with many challenges to the assurance of privacy and regulatory compliance. This chapter, with an insight into the basic concepts and types of blockchains, elaborates on the ability of healthcare organizations to make use of this technology for protecting data security by ensuring compliance with set regulations and creating trust among stakeholders. Blockchain technology will be central in the evolving healthcare sector for protecting patient data while increasing quality care. This chapter explores the vital role of privacy and regulatory compliance in the healthcare sector, focusing on the protection of sensitive patient data in an increasingly digital world. As healthcare providers adopt technologies like blockchain, safeguarding data from unauthorized access and ensuring regulatory adherence become paramount. Key regulations such as HIPAA, GDPR, and the HITECH Act are examined alongside challenges posed by cybersecurity threats, data breaches, and fragmented health records. Blockchain technology is proposed as a transformative tool for enhancing privacy, security, and compliance through mechanisms like encryption, access control, and automated compliance checks. The chapter also discusses future trends, including the convergence of blockchain with artificial intelligence (AI) and the Internet of Things (IoT), offering a forward-looking perspective on how healthcare can leverage these innovations for improved data protection and regulatory compliance.

*** Corresponding author Sonal Rattan:** Department of UCRD and Apex Institute of Technology, Chandigarh University, Mohali, Punjab, India; E-mail: sonal.e15123@cumail.in

Mohit Angurala, Preet Kamal, Aryan Chaudhary, Rasmeet Singh Bali & Vijay Bhardwaj (Eds.)
All rights reserved-© 2025 Bentham Science Publishers

Keywords: Artificial intelligence, Blockchain technology, Compliance automation, Cybersecurity, Data security, Encryption, GDPR, Healthcare, HIPAA, HITECH Act, Internet of Things, Patient data, Privacy, Regulatory compliance.

INTRODUCTION

The intersection of privacy and regulatory compliance in the health sector seeks to protect patient data and uphold trust in healthcare systems. Given that this industry is becoming digital, the integrity of data and its security become matters of greatest concern. Privacy ensures that patients' information is safeguarded from unauthorized access or breaches, and compliance refers to various legislations and regulations set out to ensure this protection. Data integrity is a guarantee of the accuracy, completeness, and reliability of records, all of which are essential in effectual diagnosis and treatment. This technology also offers a decentralized, immutable ledger that enhances data security and transparency at the very core level of blockchain. Thus, blockchain aids healthcare providers in ensuring the security of their patients' data and that it is maintained accurately and only accessed by those who have proper authorization, adhering to strict privacy and regulatory requirements. This chapter reviews critical aspects of privacy and regulatory compliance in healthcare and explores how blockchain technology can be a transformative tool in their accomplishment.

Structure

The following topics are covered in this chapter:

- Regulatory Landscape in Healthcare.
- Challenges in Ensuring Privacy and Compliance.
- Blockchain Technology: An Overview.
- Leveraging Blockchain for Privacy and Compliance.
- Implementing Blockchain in Healthcare Systems.
- Comparative Analysis.
- Future Trends and Opportunities.

Objectives

The chapter "Privacy and Regulatory Compliance" deals in detail with how privacy should be protected and regulatory requirements implemented in healthcare. This chapter aims to give a realistic overview of the current regulatory environment, showing essential regulations like HIPAA, GDPR, and the HITECH Act and their bearing on healthcare providers. It seeks to locate challenges in ensuring the integrity and security of data amidst rising cyber threats and data breaches. To that end, the chapter will further explore ways in which blockchain technology may improve privacy and compliance. This is through strong mechanisms for data encryption, access control, and automated compliance checks. The chapter is aimed at providing real-world case studies and best practices to equip healthcare professionals with practical insights and strategies to achieve the effective implementation of blockchain for protecting patient data and delivering regulatory compliance.

Regulatory Landscape in Healthcare

This section gives an overview of the key regulations and standards that set a minimum threshold for data privacy and security in healthcare, including the precise compliance requirements that organizations must put in place. Regulatory compliance is important in the health sector since this protects patients' information and the general trustworthiness of health providers.

Key Regulations and Standards

HIPAA (Health Insurance Portability and Accountability Act)

The Health Insurance Portability and Accountability Act was enacted in 1996 to protect the health information of patients. HIPAA contains several key provisions:

- **Privacy Rule:** This is part of the HIPAA legislation that creates national standards to protect individuals' medical records and other personal health information. It applies to healthcare providers, health plans, and healthcare clearinghouses [1]. It demands that appropriate safeguards on protecting the privacy of PHI be in place, limits on its use, and disclosure without patient authorization. Patients retain the right to receive a copy of their medical records and request corrections.
- **Security Rule:** This rule sets certain standards to maintain the security of electronic PHI (ePHI) that must be assured of confidentiality, integrity, and security. This requires the covered entities to develop and implement administrative, physical, and technical safeguards under the Security Rule. Administrative safeguards are policies and procedures that manage the selection and development, as well as the implementation and maintenance of security measures. Whereas physical safeguards are concerned with controlling physical access to protect ePHI, technical safeguards concern the technology and policies for protecting ePHI and controlling access to such information [2].
- **Breach Notification Rule:** This requires a covered entity to notify affected individuals, the Secretary of Health and Human Services (HHS), and, at times, the media when there is a breach of unsecured PHI. A business associate must also notify the covered entity in case of a breach [3, 4].

GDPR (General Data Protection Regulation)

- The GDPR is a wide-ranging law on the protection of personal data from 2018 within the European Union. Any organization that handles the personal data of European Union citizens must adhere, irrespective of its geographical location. Some major points on the GDPR are:
  - **Consent:** Controllers must obtain full and explicit consent from the subjects before collecting their data for processing. Such consent must be free, specific, informed, and unambiguous.
  - **Rights of a Data Subject:** Many rights for individuals may be exercised under the GDPR with respect to their data, from the right of access to correction of inaccuracies and erasure of personal data —to the rights of data portability, objection to data processing, and protection from automated decision-making.
  - **DPO:** The controller or processor is required to have an appointed data protection officer who shall oversee compliance with the provisions of the GDPR in cases of large-scale processing of personal data or certain types of data processing activities.
  - **Data Breach Notification:** It places an obligation on organizations to notify data breaches to the concerned supervisory authority within 72 hours of becoming aware of it unless the breach is unlikely to result in a risk to the rights and freedom of individuals. In case of high risk associated with the breach, affected individuals must also be informed about it.

HITECH Act (Health Information Technology for Economic and Clinical Health Act)

The HITECH Act—Title XIII of the American Recovery and Reinvestment Act of 2009—increases the adoption and meaningful use of health information technology. To the extent that such business associates operate in a manner best considered as interactions with the consumer, this set of rules enhances the protections afforded under HIPAA by adding new rules for creating such protection, as described below:

- **Meaningful Use:** The HITECH Act provides incentives for healthcare providers toward the adoption of electronic health records and toward meaningful use of the HIT. Meaningful use would involve using certified EHR technology to improve quality, safety, and efficiency, reduce health disparities, engage patients and their families, and provide privacy and security protections of PHI.
- **Breach Notification:** HITECH mandates that covered entities and business associates send a notification regarding unsecured PHI breaches. It also mandates notifying the HHS and the media of breaches affecting 500 or more individuals.

- **Increased Penalties:** HITECH strengthens the penalties for non-compliance with the rules of HIPAA. It introduces tiered penalty structures based on the level of culpability. The penalties would be between $100 to $ 50,000 for each violation, with an annual maximum of $1.5 million for identical violations.

Compliance Requirements

Several compliance requirements need to be met by healthcare organizations for the protection of data about patients and the setting of standards under the regulatory framework. The major compliance requirements are patient consent and rights, access and control of the data, security measures, and notification of breach.

Patient Consent and Rights

As emphasized in a Compliance Core Requirement, it is necessary to get informed consent from patients regarding how their health information is used and shared [5]. Patients should be made aware of how their data will be used, to whom it will be accessible, and the purposes the data will be shared. Specific requirements include:

- **Informed Consent**: Patients must be explicitly taken through consent procedures before information on their health status can be collected, used, or shared. Consent forms are expected to be written in clear and broad terms to cover much of the processing.
- **Patient's Right to Access their Health Information**: The patient is entitled to easy access to their health information, which will include reviewing or getting copies of the medical records. The access request shall be promptly responded to by the healthcare providers and enabled in a method that is readily available, understandable, and user-friendly.
- **Right to Correction:** The patient has the right to ask for correction of his health information if he finds it to be inaccurate or incomplete. This application for rectification shall be responded to and acted upon by the health professionals in due course.
- **Right to Erasure:** Sometimes there is a right of the patient for the erasure of health information. The much-hyped "right to be forgotten" applies when such information is no longer required for the purposes for which it was taken or if the consent for the same information gathering was from the patient.

Patient Consent and Rights

Patients consents and rights can be defined using the following points:

- **Data Access and Control**

Healthcare organizations must implement adequate access controls to ensure that only legitimate staff members gain access to patient information. Some of the key requirements are:

- **Access Controls:** Organizations should create and implement access control policies regarding health information access based on staff members' roles and responsibilities in ensuring the protection of the sensitive information of the patients. It also provides a means of user authentication, such as a password, biometrics, or multi-factor authentication, that verifies the identity of a person with access to such information.
- **Role-Based Access**: Information should be accessed on a need-to-know basis, meaning that whoever accesses it does so based only on their qualification for a given task. Role-based access controls (RBAC) help to implement this consideration by assigning access rights according to job roles.
  - **Audit Trails:** Organizations are required to maintain audit trails for monitoring and tracking access to health information. The audit logs should have the capability to record information such as who accessed, when, and what was done. Audit trails frequently provide an opportunity for identifying unauthorized access and ensuring the policies for access control are followed. There should be strong security provisions to protect health information from unauthorized access. Major measures in security and breach notification requirements include:
- **Administrative Safeguards**: These are policies and procedures at the epicenter of handling the selection, development, and maintenance of security measures for the protection of health information. This includes carrying out risk assessments at regular intervals, developing security training programs, and developing incident response plans.
- **Physical Safeguards**: These are concerned with determining physical access systems to protect facilities and equipment that store health information. Examples are the security of workstations, control over access in data centers, and appropriate disposal of physical records, including health information.
- **Technical Safeguards**: It includes using technology to protect health information and control access to it. Technical safeguards pertain to technical environment implementations, including data encryption in motion and at rest, implementation of secure communication protocols, and performing regular updating of software and systems for vulnerabilities.
- **Breach Notification:** In the event of a breach, an organization is required to follow its breach notification procedures to the letter. Affected individuals, regulatory authorities, and, in some situations, the media should immediately be contacted. In these notifications, the breach, the data elements involved, the

corrective action taken, and the process to prevent it from happening again should be described.

To protect patient data, health organizations must navigate the regulatory landscape and comply with key regulations and standards. This includes HIPAA, GDPR conformance, and the HITECH Act—plus adhering to patient consent and rights, data access and control, security measures, and breach notification. Using blockchain, healthcare providers will be able to offer enhanced privacy and compliance that assures the integrity and security of a patient's data.

CHALLENGES IN ENSURING PRIVACY AND COMPLIANCE

Digitalization of health records and increasing cyber threats pose a danger to the privacy and security of the data of patients (See Fig. **1**). Maintaining the integrity and accuracy of the data while balancing the need for data utilization adds more complexities [6]. It calls for in-depth attention to data breaches and issues of cybersecurity threats, data fragmentation, and synchronization issues, as well as ethical considerations and trade-off constraints to sharing data and privacy.

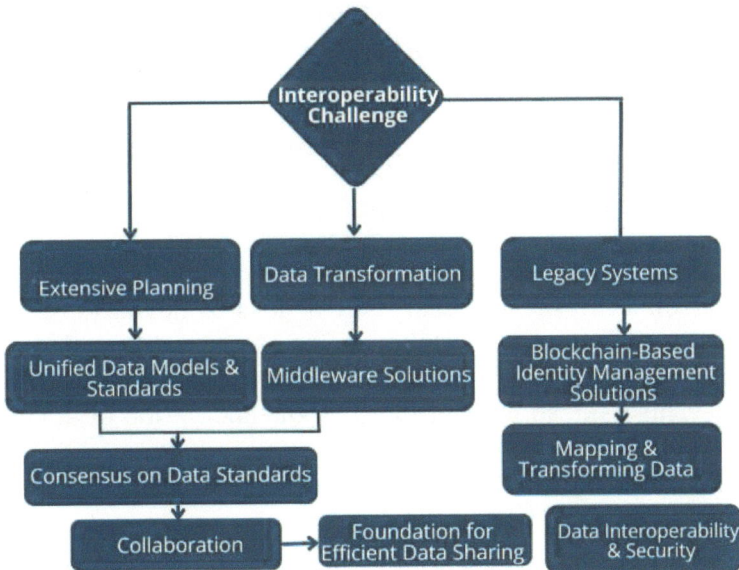

Fig. (1). Privacy and compliance challenges.

DATA BREACHES AND CYBERSECURITY THREATS

Data breaches and cybersecurity threats are the highest risks in the general process of assuring privacy and compliance in healthcare. Health information is another area under heavy fire due to its sensitive nature.

Common Types of Breaches for Data

The common types of breaches include:

Hacking and IT Incidents

The incidents of data breaches related to cyber-attacks resulting from hacking and IT incidents continue to top the list in health care. Most of these attacks are performed because of vulnerabilities resident within software packages or network infrastructure that allow unauthorized access to sensitive data. Among the techniques, phishing, ransomware attacks, and malware attacks come to the fore. The attackers betray the entities concerned with the attack by showing themselves as some trustworthy entity in a phishing attack. Ransomware is an attack that malevolent software conducts by locking data and then asking for some ransom amount to release it. Malware attacks are those attacks in which different kinds of nasty software intrude into systems to steal or even destroy data.

Insider Threats

When employees or other authorized personnel intentionally misuse their access to health information for nefarious reasons. This might include unauthorized access to patient records, data theft, or even unintentional actions that further compromise the security of the data. Insider threats are uniquely challenging to identify because they come from people who are already trusted with the information to be protected.

Physical Theft and Loss

This is a major threat to the physical theft or loss of devices holding sensitive health information—laptops, smartphones, or storage media. Unless properly protected, the potential exposure of large volumes of patient data is significant in such incidents. This risk can be controlled by the encryption of devices and their safe custody.

Human Error

Accidental disclosures or any wrong handling of data also lead to breaches. It includes sending sensitive information to the wrong recipient, failure to secure data properly, or misconfiguration on which the systems storing or transmitting health information depend [7]. Training and awareness programs for the staff can decrease human error.

Financial Consequences

Data breaches may lead to health organizations losing a lot of money. The costs include regulatory fines, legal fees, notification, and breach remediation. Indirect costs may arise because of reputational damage and loss of patient trust. It might have a long-term effect on the financial bottom line of the organization over the years.

Operational Disruption

Cyber-attacks, predominantly ransomware, can disrupt healthcare operations by making critical systems and data inaccessible. This will inevitably create delays in attending to patients, deliver a low quality of service, and fundamentally cause significant operational issues [8]. In some cases, ransomware attacks have forced hospitals to shut down entire departments or delay surgeries.

Patient Harm

Data breaches impact patients by subjecting them to identity theft, fraud, privacy violation, and psychological stress due to the compromise of sensitive health information; it causes a loss of trust in health providers. In this way, health information breaches may inflict long-term consequences on patients, such as monetary damages and vulnerability to future attacks.

Regulatory Penalties

Any healthcare organization found breaching data protection regulations faces the risk of severe penalties. Independent government agencies like the U.S. Department of Health and Human Services OCR and the European Data Protection Board are the entities charged with enforcing HIPAA, GDPR, or other laws in their respective jurisdictions by imposing fines and other sanctions for non-compliance. The non-compliance penalties may be stiff in terms of heavy fines and restrictions on the ability of the organization to practice [9].

Integrity and Accuracy

Health information must be maintained accurately and integrally for proper patient care and compliance with regulations.

DATA FRAGMENTATION ISSUES

Data quality in healthcare can be compromised by several issues, and one such issue is data fragmentation, which occurs because of:

Disparate Systems

Healthcare organizations tend to have several varied systems to manage patient data, such as EHRs (Electronic Health Records), LISs (Laboratory Information Systems), and RISs (Radiology Information Systems). Data fragmentation from these, so far as not synergized properly, creates inconsistencies and gaps within the patient records. Inconsistencies and inaccurate patient records, attributed to a dis-synergy between systems, may easily mislead the clinical decisions.

Incomplete Records

Some fragmented data may lead to incomplete patient records, where some critical information is missing or inaccessible. This impacts clinical decision-making, and the quality of care will be compromised. Incomplete records might lead to misdiagnosis, delayed treatment, and more harm to patients.

Duplication and Redundancy

If systems are not integrated, it will result in duplication and redundancy of information across multiple locations. It leads to confusion, increases storage costs, and makes data management more cumbersome. Redundant data can also make it more difficult to ensure that records are accurate and up to date.

DATA SYNCHRONIZATION ISSUES

Real-Time Updates

One of the biggest challenges is updating patient information in real-time within all the systems. Delays in data synchronization can potentially cause clinical decisions to be made based on outdated or incorrect information [10, 11]. Real time data synchronization requires the right kind of technical infrastructure and good data exchange protocols.

Interoperability Issues

Most healthcare systems have adopted different data formats and standards across them. Interoperability will become difficult in its real sense if the systems use standard protocols for interacting with each other. In the absence of standardized data exchange protocols, synchronizing data across systems becomes a complicated and error-prone issue. Hence, to make it interoperable, stakeholders must collaborate and use common data standards.

Data Consistency

Consistency in data is ensured through appropriate data governance and quality check mechanisms across several systems. Inconsistencies in entry, coding standards, and terminology lead to discrepancies and errors in patient records. The process for checking consistency in data incorporates standardized procedures of data entry and periodic audits.

BALANCING PRIVACY WITH DATA UTILIZATION

Combining the protection of patient privacy with an increasing need to utilize data in healthcare creates significant ethical as well as practical challenges.

Patient Consent and Autonomy

The regard and respect for patient autonomy, coupled with informed consent in the use of their health information, make the basis for ethical practice. The issue arises from the fact that processing activities are very complex and frequently involve the reuse of data in subsequent processing stages for research or analytics, bringing difficulties in ensuring truly informed consent. Patients should be communicated clearly regarding the purposes for which their data will be used, after which their explicit consent should be obtained for specific uses.

Data Minimization

Ethical data practices call for collecting and processing only such information, which is minimal to achieve certain defined purposes. The balance of data utility and minimization can be challenging in research and analytics; areas many times reliant on comprehensive datasets to be functional. Data minimization is the careful assessment of the necessity of the data and its collection and use only when strictly necessary.

Confidentiality and Trust

Patient confidentiality must be maintained to preserve trust in health professionals. Any compromise in this area, therefore, can lead to a loss of the doctor-patient relationship and can deter individuals from seeking medical care or engaging in research. Confidentiality entails several strict precautions that back up the element of security, coupled with building and inculcating a privacy culture in the organization.

BALANCING DATA SHARING WITH PRIVACY

Research and Innovation

Undoubtedly, the sharing of data is the basis for medical research and innovation. Large samples of data availed to researchers make it possible for them to unveil trends, develop new treatments, and improve the outcomes of patients. However, as data sharing becomes excessive, the risks of privacy breaches increase, as does unauthorized use of the information. This is a fine balance between benefiting from the notions of shared data and the necessity to observe the asylum of the patients' details by default. Governance of data should be undertaken as carefully and thoughtfully as possible.

In addition, data sharing is very critical for the management of public health and population health. Aggregated health data can identify public health threats in tracking disease outbreaks and inform policy decisions to balance these benefits against the need to protect individual privacy; hard thinking must be done when coming up with robust data governance frameworks. Public health data sharing must be done in a manner where it safeguards the privacy of the different individuals and, at the same time, maximizes the benefits for public health.

Personalized Medicine

In this way, personalized medicine will deal with big data on health and allow treatments to be fit individually according to patients' needs. While being very promising in improving health results, it raises great concerns about data privacy and the misuse of sensitive information. Ensuring that the practices of personalized medicine are conducted for the patients should be implemented through effective data protection, together with obtaining explicit permission from the patients.

Data breaches and cybersecurity risks may lead to patient information being tormentingly exposed, not just in financial ways but also operationally, regarding patient care. Delivering correct data information without its distortion is important to affect healthcare but has been complicated by issues such as data fragmentation and data synchronization. Balancing privacy and the utilization of data presents further ethical and practical dilemmas, where one must balance the greatest care one can take in patient consent, data minimization, and the trade-offs involved with sharing data [12]. Understanding and addressing these challenges will enable healthcare organizations to raise their game on privacy and compliance efforts while increasingly driving the security and data integrity of technologies like blockchain in their digital healthcare environments.

BLOCKCHAIN TECHNOLOGY: AN OVERVIEW

Blockchain technology has been rapidly gaining ground as a transformative tool in every sector, not excluding health (Fig. **2**). In simple terms, blockchain provides a secure, transparent, and consequently decentralized way of managing data. To that end, it obviates most of the problems associated with privacy and regulatory compliance challenges in the management of healthcare data. This section will thus explore the basics of blockchain technology, its types, and some features that make it very relevant in health.

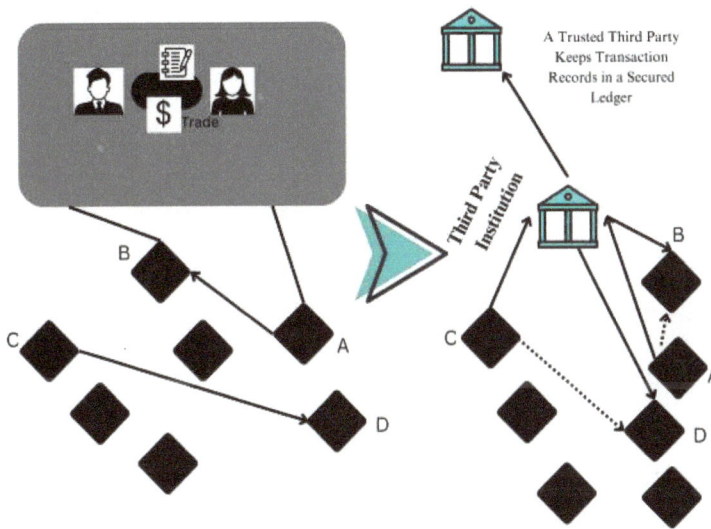

Fig. (2). Understanding blockchain technology.

Fundamentals of Blockchain

The appreciation of blockchain technology's potential applications in health should be a prerequisite.

Basic Concepts and Terminology

Blockchain

It is a ledger keeping a record of transactions across several computers in such a way that the record cannot be altered retrospectively. A blockchain is a list of transactions that are connected in blocks (Table **1**). This structure ensures that once a transaction gets recorded, it cannot be changed.

Table 1. Key blockchain terminology.

Term	Definition
Blockchain	A distributed ledger recording transactions across many computers in an immutable chain.
Distributed Ledger Technology (DLT)	A decentralized database managed by multiple participants, enhancing security and reducing single points of failure.
Cryptographic Hash Function	A function producing a fixed-size string from input, ensuring data integrity and immutability.
Consensus Mechanism	Processes like PoW and PoS that achieve agreement on data values among distributed processes.
Smart Contracts	Self-executing contracts with terms directly written into code, enforcing agreements automatically.

Distributed Ledger Technology (DLT)

It is a decentralized database managed by several participants. Unlike traditional, centralized databases, DLT spreads data across several nodes to improve security and reduce the risk of having one single point of failure.

Cryptographic Hash Function

It is a function that takes some input and returns a string of characters of a fixed size, which seems random. This assures integrity since any change in the input would create a different hash. Hash functions are core to blockchain immutability.

Consensus Mechanism

This is a process blockchain networks use to achieve a common agreement on one data value between different distributed processes. Common mechanisms would be the Proof of Work and Proof of Stake. This ensures each participant accepts the events happening in the network, securing the blockchain.

Smart Contracts

These are self-executing contracts whereby the terms of an agreement are directly written into code. They automatically enforce and execute a contract, ensuring that the terms are followed at certain conditions. Smart contracts can automate processes and eliminate much of the need for intermediaries [13].

How Blockchain Works

Blockchain operates through the secure recording of transactions in an unchangeable way. The following steps explain a very basic, simple process through which Blockchain operates (Table **2**):

Table 2. Blockchain transaction process.

Step	Description
Transaction Initiation	A user requests a transaction, which is sent to the blockchain network.
Transaction Verification	Nodes in the network verify the transaction using consensus mechanisms.
Block Creation	Verified transactions are combined into a new block of data.
Hash Generation	A unique hash is created for the block to ensure data integrity.
Chain Addition	The new block is added to the existing blockchain, making the transaction permanent and immutable.
Completion	The updated blockchain is distributed across the network, completing the transaction.

Initiation of Transaction

Whenever any user wants to be a part of a transaction, a transaction is initiated. Such a type of transaction will have one instance of sending the data to the other party or executing a smart contract with that other party. The request is sent to the blockchain network to note this.

Verification of Transactions

The transaction request is broadcast to a peer-to-peer network with several nodes, where each node's action to verify the transaction occurs independently.

Block Creation

The validated transaction is added to the data of a newly created block for the embedded ledger. This includes a hash—a cryptographic algorithm that gives a unique identity.

Hash Generation

A hash, in the form of a unique identifier for each block, is generated by a cryptographic algorithm. This is something unique to the block and is its very identification, through which the integrity of the data is maintained. When data inside the block is changed, the hash will be automatically changed, notifying that something is manipulated within the data [14].

Chain Addition

Here, the concatenation of a new block to the existing blockchain occurs. This addition is permanent and cannot be changed, therefore assuring the immutability of the blockchain. Each block contains the hash of the previous block, linking all to form a chain.

Completion

The transaction becomes complete after adding the block to the blockchain and updating the ledger across the network. In this step, the latest version of the blockchain is shared across each network participant.

Types of Blockchains

It can be classified into different types of blockchain networks concerning their access control and mechanisms of processing transactions (Table **3**). There are three types: public blockchains, private blockchains, and consortium blockchains.

Table 3. Types of blockchains.

Type	Definition	Examples	Advantages	Challenges
Public	Open, permissionless networks where anyone can participate.	Bitcoin, Ethereum	High transparency and security, decentralized.	Scalability issues, energy intensive.
Private	Restricted, permissioned networks for selected entities.	Hyperledger, Corda	Greater control and efficiency, suitable for enterprises.	Less transparency and potential for centralization risks.
Consortium	Semi-decentralized networks controlled by a group of pre-selected nodes.	Quorum, Ripple	Enhanced security and privacy, some decentralization.	Complex management and coordination.

Public Blockchains

- **Definition:** Public blockchains are open, permissionless networks that allow anyone to take part in reading, writing, or validating transactions.
- **Examples:** Popular examples of public blockchains are Bitcoin and Ethereum. These networks are decentralized and transparent, and all transactions on them are publicly available.
- **The good:** Public blockchains are highly transparent and secure. Decentralizing the blockchain means no single entity can control the network, hence being resistant to censorship and fraud. Further, this decentralization brings improved security, as it is hard to compromise the whole network by attackers.

- **Challenges:** Public blockchains can be afflicted by the problem of scalability due to the massive number of transactions and the intense energy required by the consensus algorithm being used. This will consequently result in longer transaction times and higher costs.

Private Blockchains

- **Definition:** Private blockchains are restricted, permissioned blockchain-based networks where chosen entities are participating.
- **Examples:** Hyperledger and Corda are instances of private blockchains in the Enterprise environment. This kind of network is targeted at organizations that want more control of their data and participants.
- **Advantages:** A private blockchain has more control over the network, hence being more efficient and more scalable. It is suitable for enterprise applications where more values are placed on privacy and control. One can, in organizations, fix their own rules and access permissions to make sure that only authorized users have access to sensitive data [15].
- **Challenges:** The major drawback of private blockchains is that they have a decreased level of transparency and can easily be manipulated by the central controlling entities. This centralization can undermine some of the security benefits of blockchain technology.

Consortium Blockchain

- **Definition:** A consortium blockchain is a semi-decentralized network where the consensus process is controlled by a group of pre-selected nodes.
- **Examples:** Quorum and Ripple are examples of consortium blockchains. These networks are used mainly by groups of organizations working together, which collaborate or exchange data securely.
- **Advantages:** Consortium blockchains borrow features from both public and private blockchains. They ensure better security and privacy while still being, to some extent, decentralized. Such a hybrid approach will make them more efficient and scalable than their public blockchain counterparts [16].
- **Challenges:** The management of the consortium blockchain is not an easy task as it involves coordination between the different participating entities, making it complex and time-consuming. Setting up a governance structure and the modus operandi for a decision-making process could be tricky as well.

Blockchain Features Beneficial for Healthcare

Blockchain technology has the following features (Table **4**) that can greatly enhance privacy and compliance in healthcare [17]:

Table 4. Blockchain features beneficial for healthcare.

Feature	Definition	Benefits	Applications
Immutability	Inability to alter or delete data once recorded.	Ensures data integrity, crucial for regulatory compliance.	Secure storage of EHRs, tracking the provenance of medical supplies.
Decentralization	Distribution of data across multiple nodes, eliminating central storage.	Enhances security, resilience, and availability.	Robust infrastructure for patient data management, facilitates data sharing.
Transparency	Visibility of transactions and data, allowing for auditing and verification.	Builds trust, ensures accountability, supports compliance.	Accountability in clinical trials, verification of medical credentials.

Immutability

- **Definition:** It is the inability to alter or remove data once it has been recorded on the blockchain.
- **Benefits:** This immutability ensures that health records cannot be tampered with by any unauthorized entity regarding patient data. This is very critical for maintaining correct medical histories and serving regulatory compliance. Immutable records offer dependability of truth to outcomes that are required for auditing and compliance of various natures.
- **Applications:** It can be adopted in the storing of e-Health records, hence endowing the records with immutability, making them accurate and unchanged [18]. Moreover, it can be used in the provenance of medical supplies and pharmaceuticals so that counterfeit products do not get into the supply line. This feature enriches patient safety and increases trust in health systems.

Decentralization

- **Definition:** A decentralization where data is spread over the nodes in the case of a network, not centralizing at one point.
- **Benefits:** This decentralization strengthens security through the elimination of a single point of failure, enhancing network resilience to attacks and keeping the data always available. Since a decentralized system would ensure smooth operation without much trouble, a cyber breach on one node would not necessarily mean a cyber breach on the entire system.
- **Applications**: Decentralization within healthcare can be applicable in creating a more robust and tactful infrastructure for patient data. In addition, it will be able to have easier time-sharing data between different healthcare facilities, making sure patients' information remains private. Decentralized networks provide unhindered and secure access to patient data among various healthcare facilities.

Transparency

This mainly allows every operation or transaction within a decentralized application to be visible to all the users that are part of the operation.

- **Definition:** Transparency refers to the setting where every single transaction is exposed to the blockchain for investigation by each party involved in the network.
- **Advantages:** Transparency entails trust among the stakeholders because it keeps records of all transactions that are clear and verifiable. This supports compliance with regulations by way of an audit trail on access and changes to data. Transparent systems guarantee accountability, reducing the risk of fraud and malpractice.
- **Applications:** This can be seen in ensuring accountability for clinical trials and research studies. In verifying medical credentials and certifications, transparency can aid in checking for authenticity. Transparent health records enhance the credibility of healthcare research and education.

Any successful future for healthcare privacy and compliance is trending toward the successful execution of blockchain technology, which will transform the way health information is managed and protected.

Leveraging Blockchain for Privacy and Compliance

Blockchain technology offers unique advantages for ensuring data privacy and achieving regulatory compliance in healthcare. This section delves into how blockchain can be leveraged to enhance privacy through advanced encryption and anonymization techniques, ensure regulatory compliance through automated checks and smart contracts, and explore real-world applications through various case studies.

Ensuring Data Privacy with Blockchain

Data privacy is a critical concern in healthcare, where sensitive patient information must be protected from unauthorized access and breaches. Blockchain technology provides robust mechanisms to enhance data privacy [19].

Encryption Techniques

Encryption is the process of converting data into a code to prevent unauthorized access. Blockchain employs advanced encryption techniques to secure data at rest and in transit (Table 5).

- **Public Key Infrastructure:** PKI uses a pair of cryptographic keys: a public key and a private key. The public key is used for the encryption of the data, while the private one is used for its decryption. Hence, within the blockchain, PKI would be useful to assure that the encrypted data to be studied is available only to authorized users, protecting patients' details from unwanted access.
- **Symmetric and Asymmetric Encryption**: Symmetric encryption is where the same key is employed during both encryption and encryption and, therefore, is effective when processing data at high speeds but yields less security. Asymmetric encryption is made up of public and private keys and is subsequently slower but much more secure. Blockchain relies on both in a manner used to juggle security and speed [20].
- **Advanced Encryption Standard (AES):** AES is a symmetric encryption algorithm subjected to extensive use in securely encrypting data. It ensures that patient information, when stored on the blockchain, remains confidential and is only accessed by the right personnel.

Table 5. Encryption techniques in blockchain.

Technique	Description	Use Case in Healthcare
Public Key Infrastructure (PKI)	Utilizes public and private keys for encryption and decryption.	Secure access to patient data, ensuring only authorized access.
Symmetric Encryption	Uses a single key for encryption and decryption.	Faster processing for large datasets, such as medical images.
Asymmetric Encryption	Involves public and private keys, providing higher security.	Secure communication between healthcare providers and patients.
Advanced Encryption Standard (AES)	A widely used symmetric encryption algorithm.	Ensures confidentiality of patient data stored on the blockchain.

Anonymization and Pseudonymization

- **One is anonymization, and the other is pseudonymization:** Techniques guaranteeing protection of the patient's identity by changing the data in such a way that personal identification is not possible.
- **Anonymization:** This is the process of removing or changing the PII so that the data cannot be linked to an individual. By this method, sharing and analysis of the anonymized data are possible without the possibility of leakage of patients' privacy. Blockchain can store this anonymized data so that, though it can be accessed, it cannot be traced back to the patients (Table **6**).
- **Pseudonymization:** This may be regarded as a process by which private identifiers are replaced with pseudonyms or artificial identifiers. Compared to anonymization, pseudonymized data can again be re-identified when required by another key. Blockchain will be able to hold the pseudonymized data in such a

way that it can store mapping keys safely, securing the preconditions of controlled re-identification.

Table 6. Anonymization and pseudonymization techniques.

Technique	Description	Use Case in Healthcare
Anonymization	Modifying data to remove personally identifiable information.	Data sharing for research without compromising patient privacy.
Pseudonymization	Replacing private identifiers with pseudonyms, with the possibility of re-identification.	Clinical trials where participant identity needs to be protected but re-identification is required for follow-up.

Regulatory Compliance through Blockchain

With blockchain, processes can be automated and ensure compliance with legal requirements (Table 7). Moreover, we can do the following:

Table 7. Automated compliance checks features.

Feature	Description	Use Case in Healthcare
Real-time Auditing	Continuous auditing of transactions against regulatory standards.	Ensuring HIPAA compliance for all patient data transactions.
Regulatory Updates	Automatic updates to smart contracts to reflect new regulations.	Adapting to changes in GDPR requirements for data protection.

- Real-time compliance checks.
- Compliance checking can be automated through the coding of regulatory requirements into the blockchain protocol.
- **Real-time Auditing:** The unchangeable ledger of Blockchains allows support for continuous and real-time transaction auditing. It can also code in-built blockchain compliance checks to ensure that every transaction is automatically verified to comply with the regulatory requirements [21].
- **Regulatory Changes:** The blockchain application can be programmed with features like regulatory adaptation. This means that smart contracts can be updated to reflect stipulations on obligations and be kept up to date with the latest standards in the law.

SMART CONTRACTS FOR REGULATORY ADHERENCE

Smart Contracts are self-executing contracts with the terms of the agreement directly written into code. They enforce and execute the terms when predefined conditions have been met, which are as follows:

Compliance Automation

Smart contracts can be programmed to enforce regulatory requirements. This is unlike the traditional model, which requires continuous investment in monitoring and ensuring that the actors involved adhere to the rules and regulations. For example, a smart contract can ensure that relevant data has access limited to authorized personnel, as per the set regulations of HIPAA.

Audit Trails

The use of smart contracts ensures an immutable audit trail of all transactions and access requests, therefore making the process transparent and traceable. This is critical in the light of compliance with regulations like GDPR, which provide for detailed records of data processing activities.

CASE STUDIES AND REAL-WORLD APPLICATIONS

The efficacy of blockchain in healthcare concerning better privacy and regulatory compliance has been tested successfully by various real-world applications.

Case Study 1: Blockchain for HIPAA Compliance

- **HIPAA:** The Health Insurance Portability and Accountability Act is the benchmark of protection of sensitive patient information from unauthorized parties (Table **8**).
- **Application:** A health provider in the sector implemented a blockchain-based system for patient records management. It used an encryption and smart contract-based scheme that provided access only to authorized personnel for accessing the data of the patients. Each request was logged on the blockchain, creating an immutable audit trail
- **Outcome:** Better security of the data, drastically reducing the cases of unauthorized access. Also, this immutable audit trail would provide complete transparency and accountability to make it easier to prove compliance with HIPAA regulations.

Table 8. Case study 1 summary.

Aspect	Details
Regulation	HIPAA
Blockchain Implementation	Encryption, Smart Contracts, Immutable Audit Trail
Outcome	Improved data security, reduced unauthorized access, enhanced transparency and accountability

Case Study 2: GDPR Compliance with Blockchain

- **GDPR:** The General Data Protection Regulation is a regulation about the protection of natural persons regarding the processing of personal data and the free movement of such data within the Union (Table **9**).
- **Application:** A smart consent-tracking system for data collection and usage was implemented using blockchain in a research organization. The obtained consents by the participants were put on record using smart contracts on the blockchain with the implementation of a system that ensures transparency of data processing activities and the possibility to withdraw consent at any time.
- **Outcome:** Strongly acts as a deliverable for GDPR compliance since it allows transparent and auditable consent management. This made participants feel more secure concerning their usage data. The blockchain system also made the process of consent management and answering data subject requests easy.

Table 9. Case study 2 summary.

Aspect	Details
Regulation	GDPR
Blockchain Implementation	Smart Contracts for Consent Management, Transparent and Auditable System
Outcome	GDPR compliance, enhanced participant trust, streamlined consent management

Case Study 3: Blockchain in Clinical Trials and Research

- **Clinical Trials:** Clinical trials involve collecting data for participants that helps in estimating the efficacy of a certain medical treatment (Table **10**).
- **Application:** One of the pharmaceutical companies utilized blockchain technology in their clinical trials for maintaining data integrity and complete transparency. All data that was accumulated through the process of trials was recorded on a blockchain, which could not be tampered with. Smart contracts were set in place for the digitization of consent and ensuring access to data.
- **Outcome:** The blockchain implementation establishes integrity in the clinical trial data against tampering and fraud. In addition, it improved transparency because every stakeholder would check not only the data but its provenance too. Automated consent processes enhance efficiency and support compliance with regulatory requirements.

Table 10. Case study 3 summary.

Aspect	Details
Use Case	Clinical Trials
Blockchain Implementation	Data Integrity and Transparency, Smart Contracts for Consent Management
Outcome	Improved data integrity, enhanced transparency, efficient and compliant consent management

Blockchain technology is used to advance solutions in privacy and compliance in healthcare and addresses some of the robust challenges in this particular sector. Advanced encryption techniques, anonymization, and pseudonymization secure patient data; smart contracts and automated compliance checks help drive regulatory compliance. Real-world applications and case studies prove that blockchain can enhance data security, promote transparency, and ensure regulatory compliance. As healthcare innovation continues to develop, so will blockchain technology in keeping patient information secure and creating a more secure and compliant healthcare ecosystem.

IMPLEMENTING BLOCKCHAIN IN HEALTHCARE SYSTEMS

If blockchain technology must be implemented in the healthcare systems, then structured steps need to be followed, such as assessment of readiness, design of tailored solutions, and problem-solving. The steps in integrating blockchain, common challenges of blockchain implementations, and best practices for successfully adopting blockchain are presented in this section.

Steps of Blockchain Integration

Readiness Assessment

Before making a foray into blockchain technology, a healthcare organization needs to assess its readiness. This step essentially assesses the status as it stands in terms of its IT infrastructure, identifying gaps and requirements for implementation. The critical considerations are:

Current Infrastructure

Whether the current IT system is ready for blockchain and whether some pieces would be compatible.

Data Management

Checking how data is stored, managed, and shared at this point.

Regulatory Compliance

Understanding what the regulatory landscape looks like and what compliance requirements exist.

Stakeholder Readiness

This means checking the willingness and preparedness of the various stakeholders, such as healthcare providers, patients, and regulatory bodies, in adopting blockchain technology.

Requirements Gathering

It asserts on requirements essential for blockchain implementation.

Use Cases

It clearly outlines cases where value creation from the blockchain can be seen. Examples are patient data management and clinical trials.

Security Needs

Determine the level of security needed to protect sensitive healthcare data.

Reluctancy to Scalability

Making sure that it can scale to handle large data volumes and transactions.

DESIGNING BLOCKCHAIN SOLUTIONS

Different steps in designing blockchain solutions are given in Table **11** and explained below:

Solution Design

After the requirements are clear, the next step is to design the blockchain solution. Some of the key considerations for designing include:

Blockchain Type

Selection of the appropriate type of blockchain—public, private, or consortium—based on the use case and privacy requirements.

Table 11. Steps for blockchain integration.

Step	Key Activities
Assessing Readiness	Evaluating IT infrastructure, data management, regulatory compliance, and stakeholder readiness.
Requirements Gathering	Defining use cases, security needs, and scalability requirements.
Solution Design	Choosing blockchain type, designing architecture, implementing security measures.
Prototyping	Developing and testing a prototype to identify potential issues.
Implementation Plan	Deploying the blockchain infrastructure, migrating data, integrating with existing systems.
Testing	Conducting functional, security, and performance testing.

Architecture

The architecture has to be designed to seamlessly integrate with existing systems and processes.

Data Management

It defines how data shall be stored, accessed, and managed on the Blockchain.

Security Measures

Make sure that proper security measures pertaining to encryption, authentication, and authorization protocols are implemented.

Prototyping

A prototype is developed for testing whether a designed solution is feasible and effective. It shows possible flaws and areas of improvement for its full-scale implementation.

IMPLEMENTATION AND TESTING

The implementation and testing can be achieved by following the below-mentioned steps:

Implementation Plan

The implementation plan shall be developed to indicate the steps involved in deploying the blockchain solution, including timelines and resources. The main activities involve deployment, migration, integration, and testing.

Deployment

This involves setting up and configuring blockchain infrastructures.

Migration

This means transferring already existing data to the blockchain to ensure integrity and continuity.

Integration

Ensuring that the blockchain solution will be integrated into other systems and workflows.

Testing

Thorough testing to ensure the solution achieves all functional and non-functional requirements.

- **Functional Testing:** The testing confirms that the solution works as expected for all the defined cases of use.
- **Security Testing:** It is meant to assess the level of security of the solution against potential risks and vulnerabilities.
- **Performance Testing:** This is meant to establish the scalability and performance of the solution under various loads.

OVERCOMING IMPLEMENTATION CHALLENGES

The implementation challenges can be overcome by following the points as shown in Table **12**.

Table 12. Overcoming implementation challenges.

Challenge	Mitigation Strategies
Scalability	Optimizing consensus algorithm, using sidechains and off-chain storage.
Interoperability	Developing APIs and middleware for seamless integration.
Data Privacy and Security	Implementing encryption, access control, and compliance measures.
Performance Optimization	Ensuring the solution can handle required transaction throughput without compromising security.
Regulatory Compliance	Understanding and adhering to legal requirements for data storage, sharing, and privacy.
Legal Framework	Working with regulatory bodies to develop guidelines and standards.
Smart Contract Legality	Ensuring smart contracts comply with existing contract laws.

Technical Challenges

- **Scalability:** Probably the first and foremost of the technical challenges is to ensure that the blockchain solution scales to large volumes of data and transactions. Solutions will optimize the consensus algorithm and implement sidechains or off-chain storage for large data sets.
- **Interoperability:** Ensuring seamless interaction of blockchain solutions with existing healthcare IT systems and standards is another challenge. Solutions include the development of APIs and middleware enabling data exchange.
- **Data Privacy and Security:** Ensure that strong encryption algorithms and access control mechanisms have been put in place to secure healthcare data; ensure adherence to laws regulating it, such as HIPAA and GDPR.
- **Performance Optimization:** Make sure that there is an improvement in blockchain solution performance to accommodate the throughput of transactions required, without affecting the security or integrity of data.

LEGAL AND REGULATORY CHALLENGES

- **Regulatory Compliance**: Ensuring that the blockchain solution complies with all applicable regulations and standards; for instance, clearly stipulating and understanding legal needs on storage, sharing, and privacy.
- **Legal Framework**: Lack of a clear legal framework for blockchain technology in health. The project can work in collaboration with the regulators to come up with guidelines and standards for the use of blockchain in healthcare.
- **Legal Effectiveness of Smart Contracts:** Making sure smart contracts are legally effective and compliant with existing contract laws.

BEST PRACTICES FOR SUCCESSFUL ADOPTION

As shown in Table 13, the best practices involve the following:

- **Stakeholder Engagement:** Engage all relevant stakeholders, which includes healthcare providers, patients, regulatory bodies, and technology partners. This ensures that there is buy-in and support for the blockchain solution during the entire course of its implementation.
- **Education and Training:** Education and training of stakeholders to make them aware of the Blockchain solution's benefits and functionalities. This would help them overcome their resistance to change and ensure its smooth adoption.
- **Change Management:** A change management strategy would be implemented to undertake the necessary changes culturally and organizationally to adopt blockchain successfully.

Table 13. Best practices for successful adoption.

Practice	Description
Stakeholder Involvement	Engaging healthcare providers, patients, regulatory bodies, and technology partners.
Education and Training	Providing training to stakeholders on blockchain benefits and functionalities.
Change Management	Implementing strategies to manage cultural and organizational changes.
Performance Monitoring	Tracking KPIs to ensure the solution meets standards and objectives.
Regular Audits	Conducting audits for regulatory compliance and identifying areas for improvement.
Feedback Loop	Gathering stakeholder input for continuous improvements.
Innovation and Updates	Staying updated with blockchain developments and incorporating new features.

CONTINUOUS MONITORING AND IMPROVEMENT

- **Performance Monitoring:** The developed blockchain solution will be continuously monitored to ensure that it achieves the required standards and set objectives. This can be achieved through the tracking of KPIs such as transaction throughput, data integrity, and security.
- **Regular Audits:** Regular audits ensure conformity to regulatory requirements while pinpointing areas for improvement.
- **Feedback Loop:** Create a feedback loop to get the views of stakeholders and users. Such feedback shall be used in implementing continual improvements in the blockchain solution.
- **Innovation and Refreshes:** Keeping pace with the evolution of blockchain technology, new features and improvements shall be introduced in the solution.

This approach includes blockchain in healthcare systems, from readiness assessment and solution design to overcoming technical and regulatory barriers. By following the best practices of stakeholder engagement and continuous situational monitoring, any healthcare provider can successfully integrate blockchain technology in a way that will change data privacy and regulatory compliance, bettering the efficiency of health delivery. The future of healthcare lies in the harvesting of blockchain systems for safe, transparent, and efficient use in securing patient data and realizing better outcomes.

COMPARATIVE ANALYSIS

It is critical to carry out the performance testing of blockchain technology for comparison in various scales and complexities before applying the same for diversified healthcare applications. These include throughput, latency, scalability, fault tolerance, and energy efficiency to assess its ability to process the variable loads of transactions and the volume of data that may be seen in Table **14** [13, 14]. In small-scale environments, like stand-alone clinics, the blockchain implementation focuses on low latency and moderate throughput while ensuring the secure management of data with compliance with HIPAA regulations [1]. Private blockchains, like Hyperledger, are effective in this scenario, with high integrity and privacy in data [18].

Table 14. Comparative performance observation.

Metric	Small-Scale	Large-Scale	High Complexity
Throughput	Moderate	High	Very High
Latency	Low	Moderate	Low
Scalability	Limited	High with advanced solutions	Moderate to High with IoT
Fault Tolerance	Moderate	High	Very High
Energy Usage	Low	Moderate to High	High

Large-scale networks, such as multi-hospital systems, need blockchain performance with high throughput and scalability to handle massive data exchanges while maintaining interoperability between heterogeneous systems [15]. Semi-decentralized management in consortium blockchains, such as Ripple, is effective in complying with regulatory requirements by adhering to international standards like GDPR [20]. Such configurations, however, require sophisticated resource management to counter latency and fault tolerance issues under heavy transaction loads [21]. The application of blockchain in high-complexity environments, including integrated IoT healthcare systems, involves supporting real-time data synchronization and robust fault tolerance in these systems. These health-related applications involve wearable devices and IoT components that need low latency and scalable solutions, such as off-chain storage [17].

Small-scale networks carry out well with moderate levels of throughput and low consumption of energy. However large-size networks achieve enhanced interoperability and fault tolerance but bring difficulties in scalability and also energy consumption [19]. Moreover, real-time data management is done in high complexities with robustness and security requirements and enormous resources [16].

FUTURE TRENDS AND OPPORTUNITIES

The convergence of emerging technologies, continuing evolving regulatory frameworks, and the maturation of blockchain technology will dramatically shape healthcare's future. This creates considerable opportunities to advance privacy, compliance, and healthcare delivery in general.

Blockchain Augmented with Emerging Technologies

The emerging technologies are continuously changing the future of healthcare. Some of the emerging technologies include:

Artificial Intelligence

- **Blockchain Integration:** When artificial intelligence is integrated with blockchain, data analytics, data security, and decision-making are uplifted to a very high level. AI algorithms can scrutinize vast data sets stored on the blockchain to find patterns, make predictions, and, consequently, draw out actionable insights for healthcare providers.
- **Improved Data Security:** AI will boost the data security of the blockchain network through the detection and mitigation of possible threats. Machine learning identifies abnormal activities or a security breach on real-time grounds, therefore ensuring robust protection of sensitive data in the healthcare sector.
- **Personalized Medicine:** AI-powered analytics can use blockchain-stored patient data to develop personalized treatment regimens. This process is based on not only historical health data and genetic data but also current health metrics to enable medical interventions to be targeted at individual patients to achieve the best possible treatment results with minimal side effects.

Internet of Things (IoT)

- **IoT-Blockchain Integration:** Integration of IoT devices with blockchain may reform the area of healthcare by providing secure and accurate transmission of health data. Devices, such as wearable health monitors, will be able to track the condition of a patient and record continuous data, updating it over the blockchain with its immutability and real-time access.
- **Real-Time Monitoring:** Devices within the IoT allow real-time monitoring of health conditions since any variations are signaled to healthcare providers. This data is tempered and accessible to only the relevant personnel for better care of the patient and during emergencies through the application of blockchain.
- **Supply Chain Management:** IoT devices, along with blockchain, can make the management of medical supply chains better. Sensors help in tracking the

conditions and location of medical supplies, vaccines, and drugs in a bid to ensure their integrity and timely delivery without counterfeiting and theft.

Privacy and Compliance Upcoming Developments

The upcoming developments include:

Evolution of Regulatory Frameworks

- **Adaptive Regulations:** It is expected that the regulatory framework will evolve with this uniqueness of the technology. It means that very specific guidelines need to be set concerning data privacy, security, and interoperability to make sure that any blockchain solution functions properly within the stringent specifications of healthcare regulations.
- **Global Standards:** With the escalating scopes of cross-border healthcare services, there is a need that is felt to have global standards and for regulations to be harmonized. Unified standards will ease the process of compliance, courtesy of blockchain technology that fosters healthcare services across borders and improves the protection of patient data on a global scale.
- **Smart Contracts:** The regulatory frameworks will evolve precisely in a manner that recognizes and enforces smart contracts, which can further advance compliance with the legal requirements in an automated fashion that guarantees healthcare transactions and data sharing, conducted in such a way as to conform to abreast regulations without manual surveillance.
- **Scalability Improvements:** Blockchain technology would have improved considerably to allow for the handling of larger data and transactions in healthcare systems, which are not possible now due to problems with scalability. Such innovations could be represented not only by sharding or distributing transactions into smaller groups but also by further layer-two solutions and improvements to the consensus algorithm.
- **Interoperability Solutions:** Future developments will focus on improving interoperability between different blockchain platforms and current healthcare IT systems. This would make information exchange and integration very easy for all stakeholders involved, hence leading to a more connected and productive healthcare ecosystem.
- **Quantum-Resistant Cryptography:** Since quantum computing is expected to threaten current encryption methods, quantum-resistant cryptographic algorithms would be developed to ensure the durability of security in healthcare blockchain systems.

Long-Term Impact on Healthcare

The long-term impact on healthcare includes:

Better Patient Outcome

- **Data-Driven Insights:** The integration of blockchain with AI and IoT promises to offer healthcare providers all-encompassing real-time insights into patient health. This will mean further accurate diagnosis and a personalized treatment plan, proactively managing healthcare to deliver better patient outcomes.
- **Patient Empowerment:** Blockchain hands over complete control of data associated with the health of a patient; through this, a patient can provide access to data between the users in healthcare services, providing continuity in patient care and a collaborative attempt at health management.
- **Reduced Medical Errors:** With its immutable record-keeping, blockchain has significantly reduced medical errors by ensuring healthcare providers have accurate, up-to-date patient information. Risks of misdiagnoses, wrong treatments, and adverse drug interactions are greatly minimized through this transparency.
- **Data Integrity:** Trust between the users is intrinsic to blockchain technology because of the nature of being unchangeable and transparent. The immutability and transparency of blockchain records mean that the accuracy and completeness of patient data may be relied upon by all.
- **Open Described Processes:** Blockchain-enabled transparency in processes throughout the healthcare sector—from patient consent to clinical trials—lets patients, healthcare providers, and regulatory departments and authorities trust that they support an overall more accountable and ethical environment in the practice of healthcare.
- **Patient Privacy:** The high level of encryption and data anonymization, using Blockchain technology, ensures that while data may be shared between involved parties, privacy to the client is guaranteed; it is a gain in confidence, which leads to patient participation and, in general, an improvement in the healthcare system.

The future of health care will be defined by the integration of blockchain with other emergent technology, such as AI and the Internet of Things, to foster patient outcomes, trust, and transparency while securing the healthcare ecosystem through evolution in regulatory frameworks and of the technology itself. The potential for transformative change with these innovations in the healthcare industry is enormous and holds the promise that the future of healthcare delivery will be more personalized, secure, and effective.

CONCLUSION

Privacy and regulatory compliance remain critical in ensuring the security and integrity of healthcare data. As the healthcare industry evolves, technologies like blockchain offer promising solutions to many of the challenges associated with data breaches, cybersecurity threats, and regulatory requirements. By implementing advanced encryption techniques, anonymization, and automation through smart contracts, healthcare providers can protect patient information more effectively while adhering to key regulations such as HIPAA and GDPR. The integration of blockchain with emerging technologies like AI and IoT further enhances the potential for personalized medicine, data-driven insights, and improved patient outcomes. Moving forward, healthcare organizations must embrace these innovations to safeguard patient data and meet the growing demands of privacy and compliance in a digital world.

AUTHORS' CONTRIBUTION

In Chapter 10, **Sandeep Singh, Sonal Rattan, Varinder Pabbi, and Navneet Kumar Rajpoot** collaborated to present an in-depth analysis of privacy and regulatory compliance within healthcare, with a focus on blockchain technology's potential to enhance these aspects. **Sandeep Singh** led the exploration of key regulatory frameworks, including HIPAA, GDPR, and the HITECH Act, and their impact on healthcare data privacy. **Sonal Rattan** contributed to examining blockchain fundamentals, highlighting the specific advantages of its decentralized, immutable nature for ensuring data security and compliance. **Varinder Pabbi** explored cybersecurity challenges and the application of blockchain to mitigate risks associated with data breaches and regulatory non-compliance. **Navneet Kumar Rajpoot** provided insights on future trends, discussing the convergence of blockchain with emerging technologies such as AI and IoT. Together, the authors developed a comprehensive perspective on the transformative potential of blockchain for healthcare data privacy and regulatory compliance.

REFERENCES

[1]   Oakley A. HIPAA, HIPPA, or HIPPO: What really is the heath insurance portability and accountability act?. Biotechnol Law Rep 2023; 42(6): 306-18.
[http://dx.doi.org/10.1089/blr.2023.29329.aso]

[2]   Chuma KG, Ngoepe M. Security of electronic personal health information in a public hospital in South Africa. Inf Secur J: Glob Perspect 2022; 31(2): 179-95.
[http://dx.doi.org/10.1080/19393555.2021.1893410]

[3]   Sartor G, Lagioia F, *et al.* The impact of the General Data Protection Regulation (GDPR) on artificial intelligence 2020.

[4]   Xu A, Baysari MT, Stocker SL, Leow LJ, Day RO, Carland JE. Researchers' views on, and

experiences with, the requirement to obtain informed consent in research involving human participants: a qualitative study. BMC Med Ethics 2020; 21(1): 93.
[http://dx.doi.org/10.1186/s12910-020-00538-7] [PMID: 33008387]

[5] McGraw D, Mandl KD. Privacy protections to encourage use of health-relevant digital data in a learning health system. NPJ Digit Med 2021; 4(1): 2.
[http://dx.doi.org/10.1038/s41746-020-00362-8] [PMID: 33398052]

[6] Thapa C, Camtepe S. Precision health data: Requirements, challenges and existing techniques for data security and privacy. Comput Biol Med 2021; 129: 104130.
[http://dx.doi.org/10.1016/j.compbiomed.2020.104130] [PMID: 33271399]

[7] Sharma N, Oriaku EA, Oriaku N, *et al.* Cost and effects of data breaches, precautions, and disclosure laws. Int J Emerg Trends Soc Sci 2020; 8(1): 33-41.
[http://dx.doi.org/10.20448/2001.81.33.41]

[8] Pandey AK, Khan AI, Abushark YB, *et al.* Key issues in healthcare data integrity: Analysis and recommendations. IEEE Access 2020; 8: 40612-28.
[http://dx.doi.org/10.1109/ACCESS.2020.2976687]

[9] De Sutter E, Zaçe D, Boccia S, *et al.* Implementation of electronic informed consent in biomedical research and stakeholders' perspectives: systematic review. J Med Internet Res 2020; 22(10): e19129.
[http://dx.doi.org/10.2196/19129] [PMID: 33030440]

[10] Ros F, Kush R, Friedman C, *et al.* Addressing the Covid-19 pandemic and future public health challenges through global collaboration and a data-driven systems approach. Wiley Online Libr 2021.
[http://dx.doi.org/10.1002/lrh2.10253]

[11] Bak M, Madai VI, Fritzsche MC, Mayrhofer MT, McLennan S. You can't have AI both ways: Balancing health data privacy and access fairly. Front Genet 2022; 13: 929453.
[http://dx.doi.org/10.3389/fgene.2022.929453] [PMID: 35769991]

[12] Li J, Kassem M. Applications of distributed ledger technology (DLT) and Blockchain-enabled smart contracts in construction. Autom Construct 2021; 132: 103955.
[http://dx.doi.org/10.1016/j.autcon.2021.103955]

[13] Tian H, Jian Y, Ge X. Blockchain-based AMI framework for data security and privacy protection. Sustainable Energy, Grids and Networks 2022; 32: 100807.
[http://dx.doi.org/10.1016/j.segan.2022.100807]

[14] Darwish MA, Yafi E, Al Ghamdi MA, Almasri A. Decentralizing privacy implementation at cloud storage using blockchain-based hybrid algorithm. Arab J Sci Eng 2020; 45(4): 3369-78.
[http://dx.doi.org/10.1007/s13369-020-04394-w]

[15] Attaran M. Blockchain technology in healthcare: Challenges and opportunities. Int J Healthc Manag 2022; 15(1): 70-83.
[http://dx.doi.org/10.1080/20479700.2020.1843887]

[16] Pilares ICA, Azam S, Akbulut S, Jonkman M, Shanmugam B. Addressing the challenges of electronic health records using blockchain and IPFS. Sensors (Basel) 2022; 22(11): 4032.
[http://dx.doi.org/10.3390/s22114032] [PMID: 35684652]

[17] Guha Roy D, Srirama SN. A blockchain-based cyber attack detection scheme for decentralized Internet of Things using software-defined network. Softw Pract Exper 2021; 51(7): 1540-56.
[http://dx.doi.org/10.1002/spe.2972]

[18] Chenthara S, Ahmed K, Wang H, Whittaker F, Chen Z. Healthchain: A novel framework on privacy preservation of electronic health records using blockchain technology. PLoS One 2020; 15(12): e0243043.
[http://dx.doi.org/10.1371/journal.pone.0243043] [PMID: 33296379]

[19] How HB, Heng SH. Blockchain-enabled searchable encryption in clouds: A review. J Inf Secur Appl 2022; 67: 103183.

[http://dx.doi.org/10.1016/j.jisa.2022.103183]

[20]   Barati M, Rana O, Petri I, Theodorakopoulos G. GDPR compliance verification in Internet of Things. IEEE Access 2020; 8: 119697-709.
[http://dx.doi.org/10.1109/ACCESS.2020.3005509]

[21]   Cerchione R, Centobelli P, Riccio E, Abbate S, Oropallo E. Blockchain's coming to hospital to digitalize healthcare services: Designing a distributed electronic health record ecosystem. Technovation 2023; 120: 102480.
[http://dx.doi.org/10.1016/j.technovation.2022.102480]

CHAPTER 11

The Transformative Role of Blockchain in Healthcare Privacy and Compliance

Mohit Angurala[1], Sandeep Singh[2], Navneet Kumar Rajpoot[3] and **Sonal Rattan[4,*]**

[1] *Department of Computer Science, Guru Nanak Dev University College, Pathankot, Punjab, India*

[2] *Department of Computer Science Engineering, SGT University, Gurugram, Haryana, India*

[3] *Department of Computer Science & Engineering, Graphic Era (Deemed to be University), Dehradun, India*

[4] *Department of UCRD and Apex Institute of Technology, Chandigarh University, Mohali, Punjab, India*

Abstract: Blockchain technology transforms the complicated process of verifying credentials and licensing among professionals in healthcare into an easy one, further ensuring adherence to all prerequisites of the qualification protocol and regulatory standards. Because of decentralized and immutable nature, blockchain technology holds huge potential for disrupting healthcare systems globally. It is a beacon of what blockchain can realize in creating a secure and transparent environment in the management of highly sensitive health data by using its decentralized ledger and cryptographic capabilities. This chapter explores the vital role of privacy and regulatory compliance in the healthcare sector, focusing on the protection of sensitive patient data in an increasingly digital world. As healthcare providers adopt technologies like blockchain, safeguarding data from unauthorized access and ensuring regulatory adherence become paramount. Key regulations such as HIPAA, GDPR, and the HITECH Act are examined alongside challenges posed by cybersecurity threats, data breaches, and fragmented health records. Blockchain technology is proposed as a transformative tool for enhancing privacy, security, and compliance through mechanisms like encryption, access control, and automated compliance checks. The chapter also discusses future trends, including the convergence of blockchain with artificial intelligence (AI) and the Internet of Things (IoT), offering a forward-looking perspective on how healthcare can leverage these innovations for improved data protection and regulatory compliance.

* **Corresponding author Sonal Rattan:** Department of UCRD and Apex Institute of Technology, Chandigarh University, Mohali, Punjab, India; E-mail: sonal.e15123@cumail.in

Mohit Angurala, Preet Kamal, Aryan Chaudhary, Rasmeet Singh Bali & Vijay Bhardwaj (Eds.)
All rights reserved-© 2025 Bentham Science Publishers

Keywords: Artificial intelligence, Blockchain technology, Compliance automation, Cybersecurity, Data security, Encryption, GDPR, Healthcare, HIPAA, HITECH Act, Internet of Things, Patient data, Privacy, Regulatory compliance.

INTRODUCTION

Blockchain offers some very innovative solutions to the integrity and security of the data within a sphere like healthcare through its tamper-proof and transparent ledger system. Its ability to record and track decentralized transactions securely not only enhances data integrity but also streamlines processes related to EHR, management of drug supply chains, clinical trials, patient data security, and processing of health insurance claims. This chapter reviews case studies representing the implementation of blockchain in these critical areas and their objectives, technology stacks, outcomes realized, and challenges overcome. By considering these real-life applications, blockchain's potential to disrupt healthcare delivery and improve patient outcomes comes to the fore, benchmarking new standards about integrity and privacy in health services.

Structure

The topics covered in this chapter are:

- Electronic Health Records (EHR).
- Drug Supply Chain Integrity.
- Clinical Trials Management.
- Patient Data Security and Privacy.
- Health Insurance Claims Processing.
- Comparative Analysis of Case Studies.
- Future Trends and Innovations.

Objectives

The chapter looks at several practical applications of blockchain technology in healthcare with regard to the solution of problems associated with data integrity and security. Case studies across sectors—electronic health record management, drug supply chain management, clinical trials, patient data security, and health insurance claim processing—are examined to ascertain whether they can help shed some light on how effective blockchain really is at bringing improved levels of transparency, efficiency, and trust into health systems. Case studies will underline the exact objectives pursued, the technological frameworks employed, and the outcome of the same by sending out varied signals related to successes and challenges in their implementation. What this chapter tries to do is provide examples of how blockchain can revolutionize healthcare services in terms of both integrity and privacy of sensitive healthcare data while smoothening processes for better patient care and operational efficiency.

ELECTRONIC HEALTH RECORDS (EHR)

EHR stands for Electronic Health Records as it has become imperative to maintain records electronically. Electronic Health Record systems are very vital in current healthcare through digitization and management of health information concerning patients. They promise to improve the coordination of patient care, enhance clinical decision-making, and streamline all administrative duties. Traditional EHR systems, however, face several challenges that bring about problems in their effectiveness and pose a risk to data security and integrity.

Challenges of EHR Management

Managing electronic health records means going through complex challenges, such as:

Data Security: Ensuring the confidentiality, integrity, and availability of patient information in the wake of growing cybersecurity threats and data breaches.

Interoperability: Facilitating hassle-free data exchange between heterogeneous systems and providers, helping providers offer better coordination of care to the patient.

Privacy Concerns: Safeguarding patients' privacy while ensuring adherence to the provisions laid down by the United States in the Health Insurance Portability and Accountability Act and the European Union's General Data Protection Regulation.

Data Fragmentation: Dealing with health information fragmented across a bunch of systems brings inefficiency and creates gaps in the availability of information to patients.

Role of Blockchain in EHR Security and Integrity

Blockchain technology provides a game-changing solution to such challenges by managing EHRs in a decentralized, transparent, and immutable way. Some of the key benefits include:

Immutability: Blockchain records are immutable, which means that once data has been recorded, it cannot be changed retroactively. This characteristic provides integrity to the EHRs in such a way that unauthorized modification is disallowed and maintains a transparent audit trail of changes [1].

Decentralization: Unlike traditional centralized databases, blockchain is based on a distributed network of nodes. A decentralized architecture such as this improves the security of data by avoiding single points of failure and makes it difficult for cyber-attacks or breaches in data.

Privacy and Encryption: Blockchain networks provide mechanisms for applying cryptographic algorithms on transactions, thus protecting the privacy of the patients. The encrypted data can only be accessed with the correct cryptographic keys by authorized parties to maintain its confidentiality [2].

Implementation Details

The objectives of the implementation of blockchain are as follows:

Objectives of Implementing Blockchain

The following are the primary objectives of the integration of blockchain in EHR systems:

- **Data Security:** Establish more control to safeguard patient's health information from access, breaches, and cyber threats.
- **Integrity of Data:** Verify that EHR data is accurate, dependable, and consistent with the immutable ledger technologies of blockchain.
- **Interoperability:** Allow seamless data sharing between various care providers and healthcare systems to promote better care coordination and improved results for patients.

Used Technology Stack

Integrating blockchain technology into EHR typically includes:

- **Blockchain Platform:** Choosing the appropriate blockchain platform, considering factors of scalability, security features, consensus mechanism adopted, and regulatory compliance. Some popular platforms include Ethereum, Hyperledger Fabric, and Corda.
- **Smart Contracts:** Developing smart contracts to securely automate the predefined conditions and rules about access and updating of data in the patient's EHR.
- **Encryption Protocols:** Strong encryption protocols to secure health data while residing on the blockchain network or during transit.

The use case of blockchain implementation in EHR systems serves as a representative example of how the problems with data security, integrity, and interoperability are being revolutionized in healthcare. This decentralized and immutable nature of blockchain can greatly help healthcare organizations ensure the creation of a safe, secure, and efficient ecosystem for the management and sharing of sensitive patient information [3]. In other words, the future belongs to innovation and continuous collaboration that can tap the full potential of blockchain technology in improvizing healthcare delivery and improving health outcomes globally.

Drug Supply Chain Integrity

Drug supply chain integrity is essential to ensuring that pharmaceutical products are authentic and safe for patient use, involving rigorous tracking and management from production to distribution.

Overview of Drug Supply Chain

It is a deep and worldwide network of actors, from manufacturers and distributors to pharmacies and healthcare providers. The implication is that the integrity of supply, and therefore the authenticity of pharmaceutical products across that chain, is critical in securing patient safety and public health. That said, a number of critical issues face the pharmaceutical industry at large that put these very goals in jeopardy: proliferation of counterfeit drugs, opacity within the supply chain, regulatory compliance, and inefficiencies in product tracking and tracing.

Issues Addressed by Blockchain Solutions

Blockchain technology has been becoming a solution for all the challenges through the creation of a decentralized, transparent, and immutable platform for all the traceability and verification of drug products at every point within the supply chain. Key issues resolved through blockchain solutions include:

- **Counterfeit Drugs:** With an immutable record, the blockchain ensures that the origin and journey of a drug, once registered, cannot be manipulated. This assurance offers stakeholders an easy way to detect counterfeit products with confidence.
- **Transparent Supply Chain:** Blockchain enhances transparency since, through it, one can be able to trace a product from a manufacturer up to the end customer in real time; every transaction and movement is recorded in the blockchain.
- **Regulatory Compliance:** This is made possible by blockchain, which helps in complying with regulatory needs through the maintenance of a tamper-proof and transparent record of transactions or activities carried out within the supply chain —thus making it possible for the pharmaceutical companies to prove how different standards are adhered to, and regulatory guidelines are complied with.

Implementation Details (Objectives and Goals)

The integration of blockchain in the drug supply chain can be put in place with three primary objectives:

- **Build Contextualizing Transparency:** It would give the stakeholders an open and auditable record of every transaction and the disposition of the pharmaceutical products.
- **Ensuring Traceability:** Facilitating the tracing of drugs from the manufacturer down to the consumer; as such, fake products can easily be identified and mitigated.
- **Enhanced Efficiency:** Smoothening of the supply chain process, reduction in delays, reduction of inventory discrepancy, and optimization of logistics and distribution.

Implementation of blockchain in the drug supply chain involves various technologies and tools that are leveraged (Table **1**).

Table 1. Technologies and tools deployed.

Technology/Tool	Description
Blockchain Platform	Selection of a suitable blockchain platform (*e.g.*, Ethereum, Hyperledger Fabric) based on scalability, security features, consensus mechanism, and regulatory compliance [4].
Smart Contracts	Deployment of smart contracts to automate and enforce predefined rules and conditions for data sharing, consent management, and milestone achievements.
Data Encryption	Implementation of robust encryption protocols to protect patient data and ensure confidentiality during data transmission and storage.

A case study on implementing blockchain in clinical trials management proves it as the technology to change healthcare research, solving critical challenges that evade operational efficiency, transparency, and patient safety. A secure and trustworthy environment in conducting and managing clinical trials can be facilitated using blockchain's decentralized ledger and smart contracts. Down the line, it will further need innovation coupled with collaboration and alignment of laws and regulations to really drive forward what is possible with blockchain in the progression of clinical trials and research in healthcare around the world.

Introduction to Clinical Trial Management

Clinical trials are the fulcrum of medical progress because treatments, drugs, and devices need rigorous testing for their safety and efficacy before being introduced to the public. It follows a tight protocol and methodology in the collection and analysis of data to ensure scientific validity and patient safety. However, a number of issues with conventional clinical trials include data integrity, transparency, participant recruitment, and compliance requirements from various regulatory bodies.

Blockchain Applications in Clinical Research

Blockchain technology has the potential to transform these challenges through its decentralized, secure, and transparent management of clinical trial data. The principal applications include:

- **Integrity:** The immutable ledger created by blockchain means that once it is recorded, data cannot be changed or tampered with, hence improving the reliability and authenticity of the clinical trial data.
- **Transparency:** Blockchain allows access to trial protocols, consent forms, and data management procedures in real time between researchers, participants and regulatory authorities for building trust.
- **Participant Recruitment:** Blockchain enables secure participant recruitment. Anonymized patient information is matched with relevant trials seeking qualified patients based on predefined criteria.

Implementation Details (Strategic Objectives)

The strategic goals in integrating blockchain with clinical trials management are as follows:

- **Improved Data Security:** Enhanced data security to ensure that sensitive information regarding patients and trials is safe from unauthorized access or breaches.
- **Enhanced Transparency and Trust Building:** The processes of the trial are more transparent and traceable, enhancing transparency in the conduct of the trials and accountability for protocols followed, thus gaining the trust of the stakeholders.
- **Simplification of Processes:** Accomplishing efficiencies in the conduct of trials, achieving faster administrative work, and realizing speed in collecting, managing, and analyzing data [5, 6].

Implementing a blockchain in clinical trials will definitely require technologies and tools that are highly advanced (Table **2**).

Table 2. Technical framework employed.

Technology/Tool	Description
Blockchain Platform	Selection of a suitable blockchain platform (*e.g.*, Ethereum, Hyperledger Fabric) based on scalability, security features, consensus mechanism, and regulatory compliance.
Smart Contracts	Deployment of smart contracts to automate and enforce predefined rules and conditions for data sharing, consent management, and milestone achievements.
Data Encryption	Implementation of robust encryption protocols to protect patient data and ensure confidentiality during data transmission and storage.

The case study relating to implementing blockchain in clinical trial management makes a strong point toward its potential to transform healthcare research by answering critical challenges and improving operational efficiency, transparency, and safety for patients. That is by providing a safe and trustworthy ecosystem for conducting and managing clinical trials using the blockchain decentralized ledger and smart contract features. The next frontier will be further innovation, collaboration, and alignment with regulations in a way that is powered by blockchain capabilities to advance clinical trials and healthcare research globally.

PATIENT DATA SECURITY AND PRIVACY

Data gathered through medical practice should be handled with a lot of security, given its sensitivity, which includes the medical history of such a patient, the regime they are under treatment, and their personal details [7]. Measures should be put in place to ensure data security for protecting patient privacy, meeting regulatory needs in place (such as HIPAA for America or the GDPR in Europe), and, most importantly, avoiding unauthorized access and other breaches. However, problems like the vulnerability of centralized data storage, data breaches, identity theft, and patient consent management obstruct traditional and legacy healthcare systems.

Blockchain Solutions Related to the Privacy of a Patient

Blockchain technology offers advanced solutions for both the security and the privacy of patient data using decentralization, transparency, and immutability. Some of the important applications of blockchain technology in data security for healthcare are:

- **Cryptography:** Use a highly advanced cryptographic tool to ensure secure and safe patient data at rest and in transit [8].
- **Access Control:** Smart contracts can potentially fine-tune predetermined rules of engagement with data based on patient consent and permissions.

- **Auditable Records:** Maintenance of logs of all sorts of access and change done to the data—granting transparency in all data handling.

Implementation Details (Goals and Objectives)

The key objectives of applying blockchain technology in patient data security and management of privacy involve:

- **Precedented Data Security:** Reinforce the security measures put in place to protect patients' information against unwanted access, breaches, and cyber-attacks.
- **Patient Privacy Protection:** Empowering patients with more control over health data, guaranteeing management of consent, and protecting the right to privacy.
- **Compliance and Accountability:** Support healthcare compliance with regulations such as HIPAA and GDPR and ensure the transparency and accountability of practices in handling data.

The implementation of blockchain in patient data security typically exploits the following technological infrastructure (Table **3**):

Table 3. Technological infrastructure.

Technology/Tool	Description
Blockchain Platform	Selection of a suitable blockchain platform (*e.g.*, Hyperledger Fabric, Ethereum) based on scalability, security features, consensus mechanism, and regulatory compliance.
Smart Contracts	Deployment of smart contracts to enforce data access controls, manage patient consent, and ensure compliance with privacy regulations.
Encryption Standards	Implementation of strong encryption standards (*e.g.*, AES-256) to secure patient data at rest and in transit, protecting confidentiality and integrity [9].

The architecture of the blockchain-based biomedical security system is mainly composed of four layers, as shown in Fig. (**1**): healthcare raw data, blockchain technology, healthcare applications, and stakeholders [10]. Blockchain technology is used to securely store and manage raw health data for the purpose of integrity and transparency. Secure data are used, and on top of these, healthcare applications are developed to offer services. Stakeholders like patients, doctors, and researchers benefit from easier access, leading to more secure use of information through more effective and reliable healthcare processes.

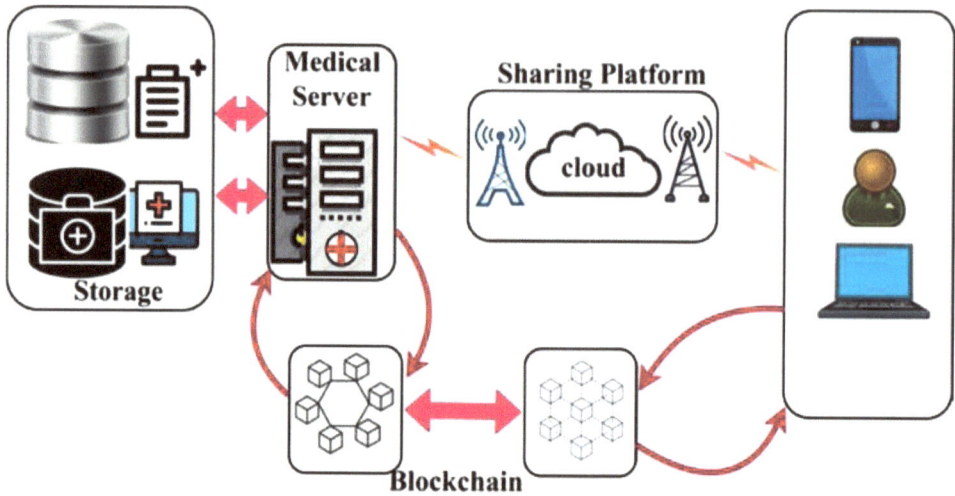

Fig. (1). Biomedical security system utilizing blockchain.

Blockchain has the potential to enable innovation, collaboration, and regulatory alignment in securing patient information and the development of healthcare data security globally [11].

HEALTH INSURANCE CLAIMS PROCESSING

Health insurance claim processing is the single most important activity within the purview of healthcare administration and in itself relates to the submission, evaluation, and subsequent settlement of claims against medical services rendered on behalf of the insured person.

Conventionally, the process has been rather inefficient, delayed, and expensive to administer due to the complex web of actors, manual checking processes, and, consequently, very high regulatory requirements. Some of the major challenges include enhanced data security, increasing transparency, and the smoother workflows required for timely and accurate adjudication of claims.

Blockchain technology decentralizes health insurance claim processing, making it safe and transparent. Some principal benefits include:

- **Automation:** In this manner, smart contracts automate the workflow of the claims process and reduce manual intervention. Acceleration in the process of adjudication and its consequent payment is achieved.
- **Real-time Data Access:** It allows access in real-time to verified and immutable data across the network and thus facilitates quicker decision-making and faster

processing times.
- **Cost-effective:** It helps in the elimination of intermediary agents and in cutting administrative costs by eliminating manual data entry errors and efforts to reconcile data due to decentralized processes.

Implementation Details (Objectives and Goals)

The main goals that can be achieved by implementing blockchain in health insurance claim processing are:

- **Quality:** Improvement of speed and effectiveness. To reduce the time taken for payment settlement of a claim from the date on which the claim is submitted. Thus, it helps to prospect the service to the policyholders [12].
- **Accuracy:** The increase in data accuracy with fewer errors in claims documentation and payment calculations helps in reduced disputes and increased trust amongst stakeholders.
- **Security:** The security measures of this data shall be enhanced to protect sensitive information, increase compliance with data privacy regulations, and mitigate risks associated with fraud and unauthorized access.

The most common technological approach to implementing Blockchain in health insurance claim processing is through the following Table **4**:

Table 4. Technological implementation approach.

Technology/Tool	Description
Blockchain Platform	Selection of a suitable blockchain platform (*e.g.*, Hyperledger Fabric, Ethereum) based on scalability, consensus mechanism, security features, and regulatory compliance.
Smart Contracts	Deployment of smart contracts to automate claims processing workflows, enforce predefined rules for claims verification and settlement, and ensure compliance with policy terms [13].
Data Integration	Integration of blockchain with existing healthcare IT systems, including electronic health records (EHRs), insurer databases, and regulatory reporting systems, ensuring data consistency and interoperability.

Implementing blockchain technology in health insurance claims processing offers several distinct benefits, as shown in Table **5**:

Over time, this case study on the implementation of blockchain in processing health insurance claims shows that, in the long run, blockchain can revolutionize a cross-section of the entire health industry concerning efficacy, transparency, and cost. The decentralized ledger properties and smart contract capabilities of blockchain can be exploited by organizations toward the automation of this workflow for the processing of claims and, in so doing, ease the administrative burden while increasing service delivery to policyholders. Indeed, future advancement, collaboration, and tuning of regulations with blockchain will be necessary to fully unleash the transformation of health insurance services across the globe.

Table 5. Benefits of blockchain in health insurance claims processing.

Benefit	Description
Enhanced Efficiency	Accelerates claims processing timelines, reduces processing delays, and improves overall operational efficiency.
Improved Transparency	Enhances transparency through real-time access to verified data, reducing disputes and enhancing trust among stakeholders.
Cost Savings	Reduces administrative costs by eliminating intermediaries, minimizing manual processes, and optimizing resource allocation.

COMPARATIVE ANALYSIS OF CASE STUDIES

Common Themes and Patterns

Analyzing different case studies of blockchain implementations in healthcare, a variety of common themes and patterns have been observed underpinning recurrent objectives and strategies across different applications.

Data Security and Integrity

One of the most frequently occurring themes across all the case studies is emphasizing enhancing data security and integrity. Blockchain technology, by nature, provides a decentralized and immutable ledger, making it a strong solution for the protection of sensitive healthcare data from unauthorized access, tampering, or breaches [14]. Note how each one of the above case studies has the underlying importance of patient privacy and the strict regulatory scenario of HIPAA in the U.S. and GDPR in Europe. Blockchain makes it possible for an organization to track the security of patient data from the point of collection to storage and sharing.

Shared Themes Across the Case Studies: Efficiency and Transparency

Blockchain seems to smoothen generally complicated processes, such as claims processing, supply chain management, and clinical trials, with automation through smart contracts [15]. Besides shared automation, it cuts off overhead administrative work, thus eliminating middlemen and transacting very first. More so, blockchain is transparent to give all stakeholders access to verified data in real-time, hence reducing disputes and increasing trust among participants. For example, in drug supply chain management, blockchain is used to establish end-to-end visibility of drug movement, thus ensuring authenticity and preventing fake products from entering the market.

Stakeholder Collaboration

This Stakeholder Collaboration occupies the center of successful blockchain implementation: healthcare providers, insurers, regulators, and technology providers [16]. Case studies underline the necessity for stakeholder involvement and consensus-building processes to first align interests so that later, their potential change resistance can be overcome in addition to ensuring the interoperability of blockchain solutions with the existing IT infrastructures. A strong partnership between countries or organizations with a clear, accurate channel of communication between them reported smoother processes of implementation with larger adoption rates of blockchain technologies.

Divergent Implementations

The functions that are common across all blockchain implementations focus on themes, but variations can be expected to develop with the organizational specificities and regional requirements for different use cases.

Varied Applications

The use of blockchain in healthcare spans from managing EHRs to improving clinical trial efficiency and drug supply chain integrity. Each such application thus manifests a different set of challenges and opportunities. For example, on the front of patient data security, blockchain can help secure sensitive health information, making it private and tamper-proof, hence reducing the risk of breach and identity theft. In clinical trial management, however, blockchain technology can ensure transparency in participant recruitment, data sharing, and adherence to regulations and protocols.

Technological Diversity

Different blockchain platforms and technologies are utilized based on the regulatory compliance needs and needs for scalability and security features. For instance, the permissioned architecture and privacy controls offered by Hyperledger Fabric make it fit for health applications in which high confidentiality of data is required. Contrarily, Ethereum's public blockchain provides transparency and decentralization but at the cost of requiring robust security layers to protect sensitive health data.

Critical Success Factors

The literature reviews conducted on the present cases assert that the effective implementation and successful adoption of blockchain in healthcare settings occur with the help of several critical success factors.

Leadership and Vision

A clear vision regarding blockchain technology and good leadership is essential. One can easily predict that most successful implementations would have been led by visionary leaders who drive innovation, create organizational buy-in, and invest resources effectively to support blockchain initiatives [17].

Regulatory Compliance

Navigating regulatory frameworks and ensuring compliance with healthcare laws (*e.g.*, HIPAA, GDPR) are important considerations in blockchain implementations. Organizations must consider the legal and ethical perspectives associated with the privacy, security, and consent of patients' data when rolling out blockchain solutions.

Scalability and interoperability issues are some of the top ones impacting the adoption of blockchain. The systems have to scale not only data volume-wise but also in terms of novel use cases at the same time, allowing them to interconnect seamlessly with existing information technologies or traditional legacy infrastructures.

RECURRING CHALLENGES AND HOW THEY HAVE BEEN ADDRESSED

Based on these very benefits, there have been several recurring challenges for blockchain implementation in healthcare, keeping the industry on its feet in terms of proactive strategy and innovative solutions (Table **6**).

Complexity of Integration

While integrating blockchain with existing IT systems and healthcare databases, considerable technical challenges are posed. Accordingly, the integration processes need to guarantee interoperability, data consistency, and reduced disruption to operational workflows [18].

Data Privacy and Security Risks

Blockchain applications in healthcare concern sensitive data about the patients; hence, one of the most critical concerns is to maintain patients' confidentiality and data security. Presented availability of encryption, access control, and compliance with use standards is a must, bearing in mind the risk of data breaches and access by malevolent forces.

The initial investments in technology, training, and maintenance for implementing blockchain are expensive. Cost-benefit analysis and securing sufficient funds are required to make an organization sustainable and scalable in the long run (Table 7).

Table 6. Summary of blockchain implementations in healthcare.

Case Study	Application Area	Blockchain Platform Used	Main Objectives and Benefits
Electronic Health Records	EHR Management	Hyperledger Fabric	Enhance data security, streamline access, improve integrity
Drug Supply Chain	Supply Chain Integrity	Ethereum	Ensure authenticity, prevent counterfeit drugs
Clinical Trials	Research and Development	Corda	Improve transparency, streamline compliance
Patient Data Security	Privacy and Security	Quorum	Protect sensitive data, comply with regulations
Health Insurance Claims	Claims Processing Efficiency	Hyperledger Fabric	Accelerate processing, reduce costs

Table 7. Key success factors in blockchain implementation.

Success Factor	Description
Leadership and Vision	Strong leadership and clear strategic vision for blockchain adoption.
Regulatory Compliance	Adherence to healthcare regulations (*e.g.*, HIPAA, GDPR) and data privacy.
Scalability	Ability to scale blockchain solutions to handle increasing data volumes.
Interoperability	Seamless integration with existing healthcare IT systems and databases.

The challenges include:

- **Integration Complexity:** Technical challenges in integrating blockchain with legacy IT systems.
- **Data Privacy Concerns:** Ensuring patient data security and compliance with regulatory standards.

- **Cost and Resource:** Initial investment costs and ongoing resource allocation for maintenance.

The comparative analysis of these cases highlights the transformation potential of blockchain technology in revolutionizing healthcare operations [19]. Through the strategic deployment of the technology, it is possible to enhance data security and operational efficiency, as well as foster greater transparency in healthcare delivery by addressing common themes, divergent implementations, critical success factors, and recurring challenges related to blockchain. Going forward, innovation, collaboration with stakeholders, and alignment of regulation will be necessary to realize the full potential of blockchain technology and drive global adoption across healthcare ecosystems.

DEPLOYMENT OF BLOCKCHAIN IN DRUG SUPPLY CHAIN MANAGEMENT

There lies a starting point for including blockchain technology in the supply chain of pharmaceuticals, as it involves the selection of a suitable platform that specifically caters to industrial needs. Most of them, such as Hyperledger Fabric, pick the permissioned architecture type so that only the participants with permission—such as manufacturers, distributors, or pharmacies—can access a blockchain network. It starts from the stage of manufacturing where a particular digital identifier is given to each batch of the drugs, usually encoded on the QR code or RFID tag. Subsequently, the identifier on the blockchain creates a permanent, tamper-proof record of each transaction. Smart contracts are executed at every node in the supply chain in order to automate the processes of verification and validation. For example, when a batch is transferred from the manufacturer to the distributor, it cross-checks the predefined conditions, such as the batch ID, quantity, and compliance certificates, to approve the transfer.

APIs are used to attach legacy systems to blockchain supply chains while ensuring that these transitions to blockchain supply chain technology ensure seamless integration. For the blockchain, this ability allows it to engage its APIs to communicate effectively by exchanging data and retrieving more information from other related places, such as logistics services or regulatory databases about particular movements. Real-time shipment monitoring is another attribute supporting improved transparency in shipments of such goods. For instance, blockchain-integrated temperature sensors can continually record environmental conditions during drug transportation. Thus, there is an assurance that storage needs are satisfied. An anomaly, such as a breach of temperature, would result in an automatic generation of alerts to take corrective actions in order to ensure that the integrity of the drug is maintained.

The final phase of the distribution phase is when the drugs reach pharmacies and healthcare providers. Here, blockchain allows for full end-to-end traceability so that the pharmacist, the patient, or, in fact, anyone holding that unique identifier of the drug can scan and find comprehensive information about the product from its origin all the way to its certification. This would also work towards combating counterfeit drugs besides creating trust among the consuming population and the regulatory agencies. By using blockchain technology, pharmaceutical companies can efficiently obtain a transparent and safe chain of supply, eliminating inefficient costs associated with fraud and improving patient safety. This will be the whole system geared toward holding stakeholders accountable to work together toward a new definition of integrity in the pharmaceutical industry.

FUTURE TRENDS AND INNOVATIONS

Emerging Technologies in Blockchain

Blockchain technology is fast evolving, and a lot of promising trends and technologies are anticipated to drive its impact and use within healthcare. Interoperability points to emerging protocols for connecting different blockchain networks, enabling seamless exchange and transactions of data across them. In healthcare, such interoperable blockchains can enable integrated health records, shape the coordination of patient care across providers, and guarantee data consistency along with privacy and security.

Scalable Consensus Mechanisms

Current blockchain platforms have a problem dealing with scalability, particularly in applications for healthcare, which will have a large number of transactions [20]. New horizons in the consensus mechanisms, like PoS and Sharding, will likely increase scalability without offering opposition to security or decentralization. These all probably empower the sharing of healthcare data, real-time analytics, and precision medicine at a massive scale.

Better Privacy Solution

Tokenization and digital assets: This, too, has also seen the light of day in privacy protection mechanisms for sensitive health-related data on public and private blockchains through techniques like ZKPs and MPCs. It allows selective disclosure of information without disclosing the data *per se*—a crucial property for meeting conformance under very restrictive data protection laws, such as GDPR or HIPAA.

In health, tokenizing assets translates to brand-new, secure, efficient, and regulated space of operating data. Blockchain tokens may be used for different purposes, such as representation of ownership rights, micropayments on different healthcare services, and data sharing for incentivized research purposes that form a decentralized economy.

Blockchain is often seen as the one technology that harbors vast potential to shift the healthcare domain from several kinds of applications. It can address systemic challenges and unlock new opportunities to innovate.

Decentralized Clinical Trials

Decentralized clinical trials, if propelled through blockchain technology, can change the R&D industry by making patient recruitment efficient, data integrity higher, and the necessary registries as desired by regulators. The use of smart contracts that automate the protocols of the trial and the verification of consents, together with secure data sharing decentralized by the researchers, patients, and regulatory authority, drives and fast-tracks drug discovery and trialing and brings down the trials' cost.

HEALTHCARE SUPPLY CHAIN MANAGEMENT

Blockchain's transparency and traceability capacities might further improve healthcare supply chain management for the authenticity and quality of drugs, medical devices, or supplies. Smart contracts embedded in procurement may bring automation and track product origin from the manufacturer up to the patient, mitigating the risks of counterfeiting and supply chain disruption [21, 22].

PERSONALIZED MEDICINE AND PRECISION HEALTH

Blockchain can be employed in genomic data and health record repositories to support personalized medicine initiatives through secure storage and the facilitation of sharing individual health information securely among the stakeholders involved. This also enables patients to take control of access to their genomic data, give consent to enter a clinical study based on genetic profile information, and receive treatment plans, bringing precision health outcomes to a new level of patient-centered care.

HEALTHCARE CREDENTIALING AND LICENSING

Digital credentials carried on blockchain networks lessen the administrative burdens and improve workforce mobility across various jurisdictions, with increased trust in the qualification of providers, thereby benefiting practitioners and patients alike.

The future of blockchain technology in healthcare holds promise for its transformative advancement in data security, interoperability, efficiency, and patient outcomes. Healthcare organizations can harness the potential of blockchain to revolutionize care delivery, research, and operational processes by embracing emerging technologies and exploring new applications beyond today's implementations. Realizing these futuristic visions and attaining sustainable healthcare innovation in the digital era will require continued collaboration with all stakeholders, regulatory support of innovation, and investment in blockchain infrastructure.

CONCLUSION

Blockchain technology offers a transformative approach to healthcare, addressing significant issues related to data security, transparency, and process efficiency. As demonstrated in various case studies, blockchain's decentralized, immutable nature facilitates the secure management of electronic health records, ensures authenticity in drug supply chains, improves transparency in clinical trials, and streamlines health insurance claims processing. While there are challenges in implementing blockchain, including integration with existing systems and compliance with regulations, its potential to revolutionize healthcare is undeniable. Future advancements in blockchain interoperability, privacy protection mechanisms, and regulatory alignment will be key to realizing its full potential in enhancing global healthcare delivery and patient outcomes.

AUTHORS' CONTRIBUTION

In Chapter 11, **Mohit Angurala, Sandeep Singh, Navneet Kumar Rajpoot, and Sonal Rattan** collaborated to provide an in-depth analysis of real-world implementations of blockchain technology within healthcare. **Mohit Angurala** led the examination of case studies on electronic health records (EHR) management and drug supply chain integrity, highlighting blockchain's transformative potential in enhancing data transparency and security. **Sandeep Singh** focused on the applications of blockchain in clinical trial management, underscoring the technology's role in improving data integrity and regulatory compliance. **Navneet Kumar Rajpoot** contributed to the exploration of patient data security, privacy, and health insurance claims processing, emphasizing the operational efficiencies and regulatory alignment enabled by blockchain. **Sonal Rattan** provided insights into the comparative analysis of case studies and identified future trends, including blockchain's integration with AI and IoT, to further enhance healthcare delivery. Collectively, the authors developed a comprehensive perspective on how blockchain can revolutionize healthcare practices and outcomes.

REFERENCES

[1]   Oakley A. HIPAA, HIPPA, or HIPPO: What really is the heath insurance portability and accountability act?. Biotechnol Law Rep 2023; 42(6): 306-18.
[http://dx.doi.org/10.1089/blr.2023.29329.aso]

[2]   Cerchione R, Centobelli P, Riccio E, Abbate S, Oropallo E. Blockchain's coming to hospital to digitalize healthcare services: Designing a distributed electronic health record ecosystem. Technovation 2023; 120: 102480.

[3]   Huang H, Zhu P, Xiao F, Sun X, Huang Q. A blockchain-based scheme for privacy-preserving and secure sharing of medical data. Comput Secur 2020; 99: 102010.
[PMID: 32895584]

[4]   Jabarulla MY, Lee H-N. A blockchain and artificial intelligence-based, patient-centric healthcare system for combating the COVID-19 pandemic: Opportunities and applications. Healthcare 2021; p. 1019.

[5]   Nanayakkara S, Rodrigo MNN, Perera S, Weerasuriya GT, Hijazi AA. A methodology for selection of a Blockchain platform to develop an enterprise system. J Ind Inf Integr 2021; 23: 100215.

[6]   Darrow JJ, Avorn J, Kesselheim AS. FDA approval and regulation of pharmaceuticals, 1983-2018. JAMA 2020; 323(2): 164-76.
[PMID: 31935033]

[7]   Sharma A, Kaur S, Singh M. A comprehensive review on blockchain and Internet of Things in healthcare. Trans Emerg Telecommun Technol 2021; 32(10): e4333.
[http://dx.doi.org/10.1002/ett.4333]

[8]   Keshta I, Odeh A. Security and privacy of electronic health records: Concerns and challenges. Egypt Inform J 2021; 22(2): 177-83.
[http://dx.doi.org/10.1016/j.eij.2020.07.003]

[9]   Dubovitskaya A, Baig F, Xu Z, *et al.* ACTION-EHR: Patient-centric blockchain-based electronic health record data management for cancer care. J Med Internet Res 2020; 22(8): e13598.
[http://dx.doi.org/10.2196/13598] [PMID: 32821064]

[10]   Parker M. Managing threats to health data and information: toward security. Health Information Exchange. Elsevier 2023; pp. 149-96.
[http://dx.doi.org/10.1016/B978-0-323-90802-3.00016-2]

[11]   Attaran M. Blockchain technology in healthcare: Challenges and opportunities. Int J Healthc Manag 2022; 15(1): 70-83.
[http://dx.doi.org/10.1080/20479700.2020.1843887]

[12]   Konrad R, Zhang W, Bjarndóttir M, Proaño R. Key considerations when using health insurance claims data in advanced data analyses: an experience report. Health Syst (Basingstoke) 2020; 9(4): 317-25.
[http://dx.doi.org/10.1080/20476965.2019.1581433] [PMID: 33354323]

[13]   Belay Y. The effect of motor insurance claim management on customer satisfaction at Ethiopian insurance corporation. St. Mary's University 2018.

[14]   Sigalov K, Ye X, König M, *et al.* Automated payment and contract management in the construction industry by integrating building information modeling and blockchain-based smart contracts. Appl Sci (Basel) 2021; 11(16): 7653.
[http://dx.doi.org/10.3390/app11167653]

[15]   Tariq N, Qamar A, Asim M, Khan FA. Blockchain and smart healthcare security: a survey. Procedia Comput Sci 2020; 175: 615-20.
[http://dx.doi.org/10.1016/j.procs.2020.07.089]

[16]   Chang SE, Chen YC, Lu MF. Supply chain re-engineering using blockchain technology: A case of smart contract based tracking process. Technol Forecast Soc Change 2019; 144: 1-11.

[http://dx.doi.org/10.1016/j.techfore.2019.03.015]

[17]   Khatib ME, Mulla AA, Ketbi WA. The role of blockchain in E-governance and decision-making in project and program management. Adv Internet Things 2022; 12(3): 88-109.
[http://dx.doi.org/10.4236/ait.2022.123006]

[18]   Dyer J, Furr N, Lefrandt C. Innovation capital: How to compete--and win--like the world's most innovative leaders. Harvard Business Press 2019.

[19]   Hussien HM, Yasin SM, Udzir SNI, Zaidan AA, Zaidan BB. A systematic review for enabling of develop a blockchain technology in healthcare application: taxonomy, substantially analysis, motivations, challenges, recommendations and future direction. J Med Syst 2019; 43(10): 320.
[http://dx.doi.org/10.1007/s10916-019-1445-8] [PMID: 31522262]

[20]   Khan D, Jung LT, Hashmani MA. Systematic literature review of challenges in blockchain scalability. Appl Sci (Basel) 2021; 11(20): 9372.
[http://dx.doi.org/10.3390/app11209372]

[21]   Jamil F, Hang L, Kim K, Kim D. A novel medical blockchain model for drug supply chain integrity management in a smart hospital. Electronics (Basel) 2019; 8(5): 505.
[http://dx.doi.org/10.3390/electronics8050505]

[22]   Pawar P, Parolia N, Shinde S, Edoh TO, Singh M. eHealthChain—a blockchain-based personal health information management system. Ann Telecommun 2022; 77(1-2): 33-45.
[http://dx.doi.org/10.1007/s12243-021-00868-6] [PMID: 34248156]

CHAPTER 12

Leveraging Blockchain Smart Contracts for Enhanced Data Integrity and Compliance in Healthcare

Sharon Christa[1,*], Raminder Kaur Khattri[2], Kamlesh Gautam[3] and Rajbir Kaur[4]

[1] *Department of Computer Science and Engineering, MIT Art Design and Technology University, Pune, Maharashtra, India*

[2] *Department of Commerce, Graphic Era Deemed to be University, Dehradun, Uttarakhand, India*

[3] *Department of Advance Computing, Poornima College of Engineering, Jaipur, India*

[4] *Department of Electronics and Communication Engineering, Punjabi University, Patiala, Punjab, India*

Abstract: As information technology underpins advances in life and healthcare sciences, there is a growing intersection of healthcare and information engineering that is opening new possibilities for remote health monitoring and the secure exchange of health information between patients and clinicians. To gain the trust of the citizens, healthcare technologies need to ensure that the information they store and process is confidential, has not been tampered with, and, in the case of large-scale processing, is conducted according to probabilistic compliance policies. Currently, the onus on data protection practices of healthcare technology providers is drawn from legislation. This paper outlines data integrity and compliance policies and shows how these can be encoded in a blockchain-based system. The study enhances this blockchain-based system to use the Ethereum blockchain for executing smart contracts, which can execute probabilistic compliance rewarding health-related workflows. These smart contracts increase transparency and data integrity by not only laying out a set of promises for citizens and public health physicians to monitor the state of a blockchain protocol to ensure there are no attempted violations, thus increasing the service's trustworthiness. While the security of the blockchain is used to ensure data privacy and security, all blockchain-located proxy healthcare data can only be accessed through patients appointing a blockchain address and the associated articulated smart contract at their own discretion, making the proposed solution particularly patient-centric.

Keywords: Blockchain, Data privacy, Data integrity, Healthcare technology, Remote health monitoring, Secure health information exchange.

* **Corresponding author Sharon Christa:** Department of Computer Science and Engineering, MIT Art Design and Technology University, Pune, Maharashtra, India;
E-mail: sharonchrista@gmail.com

Mohit Angurala, Preet Kamal, Aryan Chaudhary, Rasmeet Singh Bali & Vijay Bhardwaj (Eds.)
All rights reserved-© 2025 Bentham Science Publishers

INTRODUCTION

In a healthcare setting, managing extensive patient data, including sensitive details of medical history, treatment information, and personal identification details, securely and effectively is a core need for effective services and informed decisions [1]. At the same time, ensuring that the data collection and access processes are compliant with evolving data protection and privacy regulations is equally vital for ensuring the legal and ethical operation of healthcare organizations. Distributed ledger technology such as blockchain promises several capabilities, including the ability to provide an immutable audit trail of changes made to healthcare data and enable tracking, monitoring, and control of data access and data provenance and usage in line with applicable regulations. Additionally, as blockchain capabilities increasingly include the usage of smart contracts, which can enable new forms of extended data control, and the development of user-centric techniques for implementing compliance in a more decentralized manner, blockchain can increasingly offer new insights and solutions for ensuring effective and scalable healthcare data compliance [2]. This work examines the existing and potential role that blockchain and smart contracts may play in enabling and retaining healthcare data quality and compliance. We also argue that blockchain-based solutions require a degree of caution and user-centric design to ensure this role can provide the promised advantages. Themes taking the perspectives of healthcare compliance design, trust models, and regulatory requirements are discussed. Specifically, in the rest of the sections of this chapter, we start by providing an overview of the key challenges in ensuring the quality and compliance of healthcare data. We then describe the key blockchain and smart contract technologies and examine the role that they may currently have and the possible future roles to play a part in addressing the challenges of healthcare data quality and compliance enforcement.

Background and Significance of Data Integrity and Compliance in Healthcare

As healthcare becomes increasingly dependent on information technology, data is stored in various formats, including transcribed text files, relational databases, and machine-generated encrypted codes [3]. To achieve an interconnected healthcare ecosystem that spans care providers, medical devices, pharma companies, and insurance providers, integrated technology platforms provide the required infrastructure for multinational, multi-institutional patient data-sharing scenarios. Meeting the data integrity and compliance requirements such as data protection and security, privacy, and auditability in various national and international healthcare-related regulatory frameworks such as the Health Insurance Portability and Accountability Act (HIPAA) in the US and the General Data Protection Regulation (GDPR) in the EU has become a significant challenge [4]. Blockchain smart contracts are essentially computer programs that govern the operation of a blockchain by facilitating, verifying, enforcing, and executing credible transactions without intermediaries [5]. With these automated contracts, it is possible to address relevant health data sharing and compliance concepts, such as the ability to strictly adhere to the patient data use agreements and care continuum. This section of the paper provides the conceptual background and significance of ensuring data integrity and compliance in healthcare, especially in a national and international healthcare-related compliance framework. With the advent of and trek toward data-driven, data-powered, value-based healthcare, value-added features and services are embedded in operational healthcare processes [6]. Along with the benefits that these value-added features and services offer come challenges in how to ensure that the data generated or used is integral and compliant from individuals' perspectives (*i.e.*, patients) and from that of regulators, data consumers, industry stakeholders, and payers (referred to as data consumers collectively). In a marketplace value chain that includes medical device companies, pharmaceutical companies, care providers, and insurance providers, such healthcare data should be considered integral and inherently trusted throughout their lifecycle [7]. The technological expansion of this marketplace value chain into a country, multinational legal jurisdiction, and international trade environment requires improved or new digital data transfer models for seamless data sharing in a trusted data usage ecosystem.

Fig. (**1**) is the flowchart that details the process of data access and retrieval using blockchain technology. It begins with data collection, followed by data encryption and storage on the blockchain. Data access requests are validated through smart contracts and an access control check. Once access is approved, data retrieval takes place, ensuring a secure and compliant process from start to finish.

FOUNDATIONS OF BLOCKCHAIN TECHNOLOGY

Hyped as one of the most disruptive technologies, the blockchain is, in fact, three separate components. The first component is the "chain of blocks," linked together through the hash value (or a function), beginning with a unique block (defined as the Genesis block), with each block referencing its predecessor [8]. The second component is the actual data structure, designed to store specific information – for traditional ledgers, this data is a record of financial transactions, but in practice, it can store any data. Blocks are needed for data chaining and consistency (each new block saves the changes and any new data), and the final hash value is used to connect the new block to the previous ones. The third component, preventing "double-win" issues and, most importantly, making the blockchain effective, is the consensus algorithm [9]. The concept of consensus is closely related to cryptographic security and relates to the acceptance of the produced block in the chain by all parties. Each blockchain is divided into two main categories - the public (as exemplified by cryptocurrencies such as Bitcoin and Ethereum, a "world computer") and the private, which hosts closed, controlled environments and is not available to outsiders. This is the most important distinction since most entities are not yet willing to store personal patient information in the public environment, where it can be accessed. Although, as we shall see, there are mechanisms to protect access and reduce the risk, data is more likely to be stored in a private or consortium environment for specific stakeholder use [10]. Overall, the blockchain structure is a chain of blocks, each containing transaction data and a time reference, linked together and secured by a consensus mechanism (a record of recent transactions kept by members of a network). Its decentralized and distributed nature unfolds its manipulation resistance.

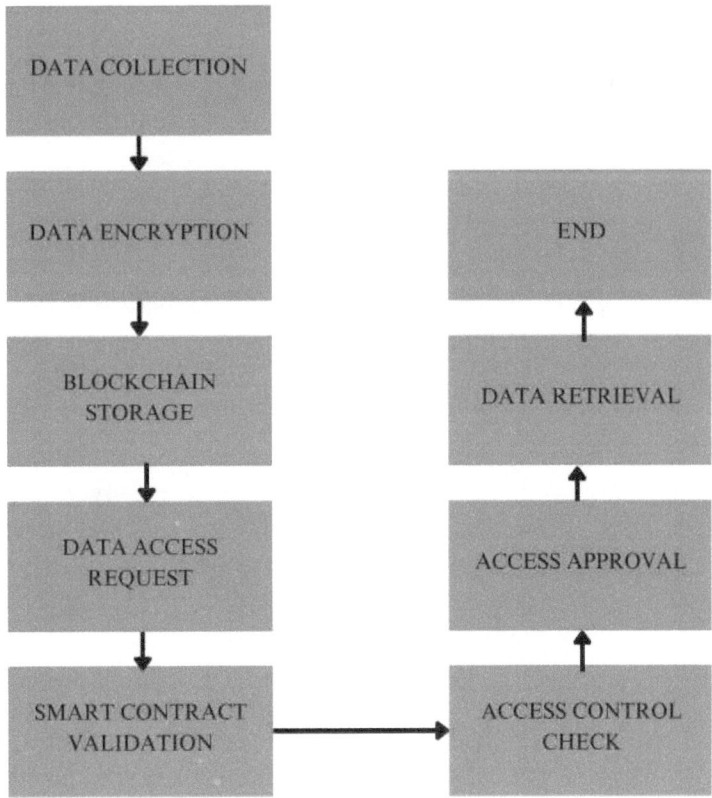

Fig. (1). Data access and retrieval process using blockchain.

Key Concepts and Components of Blockchain Technology

Blockchain can be described as a decentralized database that is updated instantaneously through a peer-to-peer network. Blockchain platforms provide a variety of consensus mechanisms to allow distributed parties to append transaction records on blockchains [11]. Transactions are encrypted using digital signature technology and can be made for a variety of purposes, such as ID verification, land or other types of asset registration and transfer, voting, oath-making, smart contracts, proof of work, tracking the supply chain, and energy trading. All transactions taking place in a blockchain can be viewed by participants within the network. The transactions that parties agree to include in a block, validated, and confirmed are added as voids to the blockchain. These transactions may hold data or encrypted code [12]. The sequence in which transactions are confirmed is preserved as blocks of transactions in a blockchain. Additionally, the blocks are linked to one another to form a chain of transactions. Such chains of blocks enable a chronological record of transactions in the blockchain and create a mechanism that securely maintains the chronological order of transactions in the blockchain. On the other hand, blockchain allows the use of smart contracts. It is important to note that, by definition, smart contracts are not related to agreements in a legal sense. Bitcoin software allows smart contracts to be written in a specific scripting language. However, Ethereum, which is a more advanced blockchain platform, allows more complex smart contracts. At their most primitive level, smart contracts can be implemented with trivial computer code or complex code that realizes the functional characteristics of a trade policy.

SMART CONTRACTS IN HEALTHCARE

Due to the complex, dynamic, and distributed nature of healthcare processes in service delivery, a number of stakeholders are often involved [13]. Services may flow through various partners, external to an HCO itself like network laboratories or hospitals with complex dependencies. A given service may be contingent upon the successful application of an external healthcare partner or even the successful outcome of a complete patient pathway. With the deemed business sensitivity and other numerous and various sources of data classifiable as sensitive, Blockchain approaches can be used to manage some of the overhead of rapid integration and verification within healthcare processes, and in some ways, suitable implementations can enforce the quality requirements and application the Institute of Electrical and Electronics Engineers (IEEE) have established [14]. Such compliance data markers, once accepted within the community, enable the generation of valuable provenance data, supporting opportunities for the delivery of innovative services over internal assets or enabling transparent partnerships, evaluating a network of entities open to collaboration based on requirements and offers for shared services.

Definition and Functionality

Smart contracts are based on the principle that transaction processing and execution are performed sequentially in consensus-based blockchain networks. This, in turn, means enforcing all parties to a contract a set of predefined conditions, and no one can alter the terms of the contract. When a condition of a contract is met under a consensus protocol, the outcome of the contract is not subject to discussions [15]. All parties are in the right to be sure that the result is foreseeable and indisputable. Executions are done automatically, and rights to access the value are transferred as a balance set. All these advantages make smart contracts computationally expensive but prevent the need for trusted third parties and intermediaries when contractual agreements are made [15]. Such environments enable the involvement of networks in contractual negotiations and agreements among different users and entities, from individuals to corporations and public organizations. Mandatory non-ability smart contracts run computer programs in response to transactions and modify a digital asset invisible to third parties.

CHALLENGES AND OPPORTUNITIES IN IMPLEMENTING BLOCKCHAIN SMART CONTRACTS IN HEALTHCARE

According to Buterin and Poon, a smart contract is a computer protocol intended to digitally facilitate, verify, or enforce the negotiation or performance of a contract. However, compared to the terms and conditions defined on paper agreements and contracts, the smart contract has an inherent feature of developing a software application usually deployed on a public network or a blockchain. One common definition was provided by a study [16], and it defines a smart contract as a computer protocol intended to digitally facilitate, verify, or enforce legally enforceable rigid bodies and performance transfer agreements without third parties. Comments on this definition may argue that the smart contract is not necessarily a legally enforceable written contract between two parties, as smart contract code executes on the blockchain itself in accordance with predetermined rules, and the blockchain can play the role of a third party [17]. The execution of all codes is transparent and traceable, and the correct execution is even given. The main idea is that the smart contract software code defines the behavior of all interacting parties. Contracts are the core tools for developing a blockchain. Since the definition of 'contract' has been used in many fields, modern blockchain technology calls the type of contract that originally appeared in Bitcoin and also commonly appeared in Ethereum smart contracts to avoid anonymity and confusion. In actuality, Bitcoin has limited programmability by consensus policy and cannot represent externally more sophisticated logic. They do a formalization of the expected rule set for a Bitcoin transaction, as well as these analogies extend to Ethereum's more complex structure, as they do with the significant increase in capabilities of its programming language. The Ethereum contract is a more mature and expressive version of the smart contract than Bitcoin. To maintain up-to-date data for the blockchain, each new update needs to append recorded transactions to the blockchain [18]. As the blockchain size increases, the cost and time required to update the database increase. To address this issue, the hash pointer in the new blocks can link to the current state of the database like the state of the account tree or hash lock box proposed by Bitcoin and Ethereum [19]. All the transactions build the account statement from the initial state of the account statement through to the latest state. However, if an outdated statement of the account is modified using 'transaction.replace (Transaction,'20180715'), creating a new output file, and adding such a statement that does not exist in the database to the transaction will also be different. In other words, it is meaningless to point a hash to an account statement since any party can make a fake statement to be attached to the transaction.

Regulatory Hurdles and Compliance Issues

Regulatory aspects are among the key factors affecting blockchain system implementation in healthcare. Hammi *et al.* have highlighted ethical and privacy challenges preventing the widespread use of blockchain in health problems. Van Heugten-Klooster *et al.* have suggested that trust and legislation are more of a hindrance in applying blockchain to the assurance of microcredits. Zimbeck mentioned the need for a combination of technical, legal, and ethical aspects. Oh, Park, and Kim were the first to discuss legislative and administrative issues when considering blockchain technology adoption in Korea [20]. Blockchain and healthcare relationship was discussed by Panch *et al.*, who reported that it is challenging to apply blockchain technology to healthcare in terms of safety and ethics and that appropriate laws and regulations would be needed. Fig. (**2**) illustrates the key components of blockchain technology as applied to healthcare. Blockchain technology encompasses smart contracts and a decentralized ledger. Smart contracts facilitate healthcare data management and compliance enforcement, ensuring security, privacy, and immutable records. The decentralized ledger provides audit trails, contributing to transparency and accountability in healthcare data management. The regulatory environment has shown that blockchain-smart contracts are a way to solve current blockchain deficiencies and make blockchain a reality for many applications [21]. The immutability of blockchains can open a lack of flexibility issue, especially when information is wrong or needs to be changed due to changes or system exceptions. This inability to adapt incorrectly has caused significant problems with data access in a broad range of fields. The introduction of a smart contract solves this problem as long as a suitable contract has been defined and implemented [22]. However, the implementation of the smart contract cannot be without some other problems, as the regulation problems are currently ongoing. In Korea, there is still no law directly related to blockchain or smart contracts, and according to the preliminary classification of Korea's Financial Services Commission (FSC), four main categories have been established.

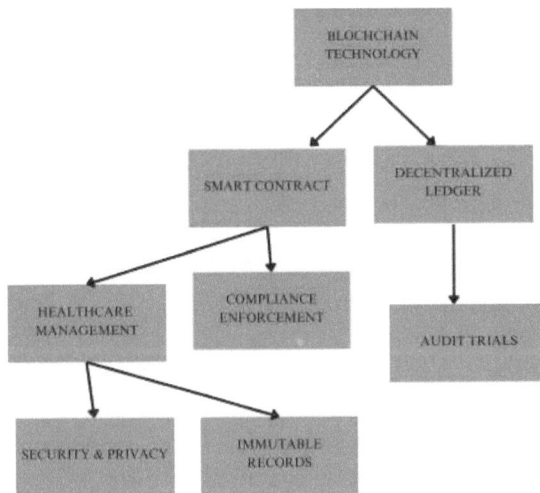

Fig. (2). Key components of blockchain technology in healthcare.

FUTURE TRENDS AND INNOVATIONS IN BLOCKCHAIN TECHNOLOGY FOR HEALTHCARE

Many blockchain platforms have been studied, designed, and proposed to achieve these properties. This paper explains the details of available blockchain studies in healthcare, their functionalities, and features, and reports on open technical questions and potential improvements based on future trends. It is expected that the use of blockchain for the integrity and security of healthcare data could be just the starting step towards a range of blockchain-derived smart eHealth applications. These applications have the potential for tracking shared administrative processes, storing and transmitting general patient data, prescriptions and their fulfillment, and electronic health records. Generally, the makers of eHealth solutions will use blockchain in the future to enjoy a number of specific, interesting advantages. This next section reports and analyzes promising directions where blockchain technology can be used to solve complex eHealth needs. Many blockchain use case proposals in healthcare are based on the idea of trust, reliability, and dynamic use of important data. Accordingly, even if the current blockchain proposals for healthcare try to solve different needs and fit the specific domain, it is necessary to concentrate and allow for common services and features for the eHealth community. From this perspective, an interesting basic aspect is to consider healthcare governance decisions as common services to external smart contracts. Principles and rules for managing the consortium blockchain itself using smart contracts are not yet fully explored.

INTEGRATION WITH IOT DEVICES AND WEARABLES

When a smart contract incorporates or interacts directly with IoT devices for function execution, it is able to respond to real-world events and adjust its behavior in a contextually appropriate manner. For example, when a cooler's temperature exceeds a certain threshold, drug smart contracts can execute the refund and return a portion of the paid amount to the buyer. Similarly, a smart contract linked with a smart refrigerator can impart wine to the buyer, provided that the buyer's age is greater than the legal drinking age. Currently, although advances in the development of IoT infrastructure are fueling various case studies that incorporate smart contracts with IoT devices, few concrete examples have been deployed and tested in practice, and even fewer involve blockchain technology. Studies claim to have designed a new scalable and efficient interoperable mechanism that employs secondary-value-based smart property contracts and IMSs. When a supplier provides certain tasks of an IoT device with a service or lease contract to a lessee, the lessee is entitled to obtain a unique virtual machine image. It is transparent to the lessee whether the service or lease was subleased from others. Once a client connects, the IVFM activates the corresponding virtual machine image. Financial transaction leaks or arbitrary changes made using the client's privileged access rights are avoided because the service contract is executed by a smart property contract with an IMS in the smart property transaction or whether a sublet is in place. The IVFM in the cloud is invoked with an MPT. After using the service, no trace of the client's data is left in the stored state by means of a data hiding function. The client pays the leasing fee to obtain service through the oracle. A hack token is used to force the IVFM to perform extra actions. In the lease instance, the hack token costs a small amount, and the lessee has control over the budget.

CONCLUSION AND RECOMMENDATIONS

We have reported on the results of our extensive study of smart contracts created to process healthcare transactions on a healthcare-specific blockchain, HSPCode, which is designed to enforce business processes by ensuring the system is compliant with privacy and security management requirements. We have found that these smart contracts go beyond just automating business processes, as they enable trust between parties by ensuring that the storage and sharing of healthcare data comply with privacy policies, which we believe is a novel approach. This is important because of the ubiquity and large scale of data breaches involving healthcare data, the lack of trust in third-party storage providers, and the need for patients to approve all the use of their own healthcare data. However, the system still lacks the ability to handle sensitive data types, such as images and videos, and scalability issues will have to be addressed before the benefits of the smart contracts in this system can be fully realized.

SUMMARY OF KEY FINDINGS

This chapter identified the key components of using smart contracts based on blockchain technologies to meet the business and ethical challenges in healthcare. This allows for the implementation of an effective, reliable, and secure health information system to meet the automatic execution of transactions, providing assurance to their patients about the integrity and privacy of their confidential data and providing high performance in compliance with national and international regulations. The future implementation of these smart contracts will protect the remarkable need for patient-centered care that has led to the growth of digital health solutions. Patients and their doctors will no longer need to question the security or integrity of their data as they work to get and keep themselves healthy. Commercial solutions based on blockchain and smart contracts would need a two-sided infrastructure: a smart contract platform and a highly robust and secure service API and database layers. The conceptual framework demonstrates how smart contracts associated with the design science research methodology can be used for compliance and data integrity purposes in healthcare and identifies the key candidate transactions together with the parties involved. The attributes that enable data integrity and privacy are discussed. One of the many challenges with blockchain technologies for smart contracts is the long-standing performance problem. This chapter identified several influential performance factors and recommended that smart contract performance be a key criterion for the healthcare industry when selecting a blockchain platform.

AUTHORS' CONTRIBUTION

In Chapter 12, **Sharon Christa, Raminder Kaur Khattri, Kamlesh Gautam,** and **Rajbir Kaur** collaboratively explored the potential of blockchain smart contracts to enhance data integrity and compliance within the healthcare sector. **Sharon Christa** led the examination of healthcare data management frameworks, focusing on smart contracts and blockchain's role in safeguarding patient information and compliance with privacy regulations. **Raminder Kaur Khattri** contributed to the discussion on the integration of blockchain with healthcare compliance models, emphasizing probabilistic compliance policies and the impact on trustworthiness in healthcare services. **Kamlesh Gautam** provided insights into the technical foundations of blockchain technology and the application of smart contracts, addressing key concepts and technological infrastructure for secure healthcare data exchanges. **Rajbir Kaur** analyzed the regulatory hurdles and future trends, examining the role of IoT devices and wearables in smart contract applications for healthcare. Together, the authors offered a comprehensive view of blockchain's transformative role in achieving secure, transparent, and patient-centric healthcare solutions.

REFERENCES

[1]   Vetrivel S. Blockchain health: Smart contracts transforming healthcare operations 2024. Available from: https://www.igi-global.com/chapter/blockchain-health/344185

[2]   Electronics AK. A blockchain-based smart contract system for healthcare management 2020. Available from: https://www.mdpi.com/2079-9292/9/1/94

[3]   Majdoubi E, El Bakkali H, Sadki S, El Majdoubi D, El Bakkali H, *et al.* SmartMedChain: A blockchain-based privacy-preserving smart healthcare framework. Wiley Online Library 2021. Available from: https://onlinelibrary.wiley.com/doi/abs/10.1155/2021/4145512

[4]   Griggs KN, Ossipova O, Kohlios P, Baccarini AN, Howson EA, *et al.* Healthcare blockchain system using smart contracts for secure automated remote patient monitoring 2018; 42(7): 130. Available from: https://link.springer.com/article/10.1007/s10916-018-0982-x [http://dx.doi.org/10.1007/s10916-018-0982-x]

[5]   El Majdoubi D, El Bakkali H, Sadki S, Baccarini AN, Howson EA. SmartMedChain: A blockchain-based privacy-preserving smart healthcare framework. J Healthc Eng 2021; 2021: 4145512. [http://dx.doi.org/10.1007/s10916-018-0982-x] [PMID: 34777733]

[6]   Omar IA, Jayaraman R, Salah K, Simsekler MCE, Yaqoob I, Ellahham S. Ensuring protocol compliance and data transparency in clinical trials using blockchain smart contracts. BMC Med Res Methodol 2020; 20(1): 224 [PMID: 32801068]

[7]   Omar IA, Jayaraman R, Salah K, Can M, Simsekler E, Yaqoob I, *et al.* Ensuring protocol compliance and data transparency in clinical trials using Blockchain smart contracts 2020. Available from: https://link.springer.com/article/10.1186/s12874-020-01109-5 [http://dx.doi.org/10.1186/s12874-020-01109-5]

[8]   Shukla R, Agarwal A. Blockchain-powered smart healthcare system 2020. Available from: https://www.sciencedirect.com/science/article/pii/B9780128198162000101 [http://dx.doi.org/10.1016/B978-0-12-819816-2.00010-1]

[9]   Griggs KN, Ossipova O, Kohlios P, Baccarini AN, Howson EA, *et al.* SmartMedChain: A blockchain-based privacy-preserving smart healthcare framework 2018; 42(7): 130. Available from: https://onlinelibrary.wiley.com/doi/abs/10.1155/2021/4145512

[10]   Optimization SDOJ. Data Integrity and Risk 2023. Available from: https://www.scirp.org/journal/paperinformation?paperid=125464

[11]   Technology SDS. Impact of controls on data integrity and information systems 2023; 2: 29-35. Available from: https://www.researchgate.net/profile/Sasidhar-Duggineni/publication/372193665_Impact_of_Controls_on_Data_Integrity_and_Information_Systems/links/64a8d256b9ed6874a5046bc3

/Impact-of-Controls-on-Data-Integrity-and-Information-Systems.pdf

[12]   Available from: https://scholar.google.com/scholar?hl=en&as_sdt=0%2C5&q=Data+Integrity+and+Compliance+in+Healthcare&btnG=

[13]   Sookhak M, Jabbarpour M, Safa N. Blockchain and smart contract for access control in healthcare: A survey, issues and challenges, and open issues 2021. Available from: https://www.sciencedirect.com/science/article/pii/S1084804520304045
[http://dx.doi.org/10.1016/j.jnca.2020.102950]

[14]   Vacca A, Sorbo A, Vissagio C, Canfora G. A systematic literature review of blockchain and smart contract development: Techniques, tools, and open challenges. J Syst Softw 2020; 174: 110891.
[http://dx.doi.org/10.1016/j.jss.2020.110891]

[15]   Programming XGS. Smart payment contract mechanism based on blockchain smart contract mechanism. Wiley Online Library 2021. Available from: https://onlinelibrary.wiley.com/doi/abs/10.1155/2021/3988070

[16]   Khan SN, Loukil F, Ghedira-Guegan C. Blockchain smart contracts: Applications, challenges, and future trends. Peer-to-Peer Netw. Appl 2023; 14(5): 2901-5. Available from: https://link.springer.com/article/10.1007/s12083-021-01127-0

[17]   Yaqoob I, Salah K. Blockchain for healthcare data management: opportunities, challenges, and future recommendations. Springer 2022. Available from: https://link.springer.com/article/10.1007/s00521-020-05519-w
[http://dx.doi.org/10.1007/s00521-020-05519-w]

[18]   Yaqoob I, Salah K, Jayaraman R, Al-Hammadi Y. Blockchain for healthcare data management: opportunities, challenges, and future recommendations. Neural Comput Appl 2022; 34(14): 11475-90.
[http://dx.doi.org/10.1007/s00521-020-05519-w]

[19]   Deshpande A, Stewart K. Distributed ledger technologies/blockchain: challenges, opportunities and the prospects for standards 2017. Available from: https://www.bsigroup.com/LocalFiles/zh-tw/InfoSec-newsletter/No201706/download/BSI_Blockchain_DLT_Web.pdf

[20]   Choudhury O, Sarker H, Rudolph N, Foreman M, Fay N, Dhuliawala M. Enforcing human subject regulations using blockchain and smart contracts. BHTY [Internet] 2018. Available from: https://www.blockchainhealthcaretoday.com/index.php/journal/article/view/10

[21]   Kushwaha SS, Joshi S, Singh D, Kaur M, Lee HN. Ethereum smart contract analysis tools: A systematic review. IEEE Access 2022; 10: 57037–62.
[http://dx.doi.org/10.1109/ACCESS.2022.3169902]

[22]   Yeoh, P. Regulatory issues in blockchain technology, J. Financ. Regul. Compliance 2017, 25 No. 2, 196-208. Available from: https://www.emerald.com/insight/content/doi/10.1108/JFRC-08-2016-0068/full/html

CHAPTER 13

Facilitating Patient Consent and Data Sharing with Blockchain Smart Contracts

Kiran Deep Singh[1], Prabh Deep Singh[2,*], Ankita Gupta[3] and Rohan Verma[2]

[1] Department of Computer Science and Engineering, Chitkara University Institute of Engineering and Technology, Rajpura, Punjab, India

[2] Department of Computer Science and Engineering, Graphic Era Deemed to be University, Dehradun, Uttarakhand, India

[3] Department of Computer Science and Engineering, C.T. Institute of Engineering, Management and Technology, Lambri, Punjab, India

Abstract: The healthcare sector has vast untapped potential in data management in biotech, pharmaceutical companies, research centers, and other clinical institutions. Health research that involves access and analysis of individuals' health information can lead to a much-improved understanding, prevention, and treatment of health conditions. Blockchain's potential has been identified in various applications, including managing personal health data. There are extensive data sets that can advance patient care protocols and deepen the understanding of patient pathology, fostering the development of new treatments. However, there has always been a privacy concern, and the financial value of these datasets deters stakeholders from sharing their data. The regulatory body has provided protection in promoting patent rights and data sharing through initiatives like common health research data spaces and fair data principles. Trust in the healthcare industry is paramount, where the protection of patient information is critical. While patients can withdraw consent for data use in research, blockchain technology offers a solution for managing patient consent and facilitating the securing of the data. This research implements a smart contract system for patient consent management and data sharing amongst state holders, which includes patients, researchers, data controllers, and supercomputer owners. Unlike traditional healthcare data management models, this mechanism shifts power from data controllers to a consortium of stakeholders. This chapter proposes a permission blockchain and smart contract mechanism that can enhance data sharing and consent management in healthcare, offering a more flexible and secure approach to handling sensitive health data.

Keywords: Consent management, Data governance, Electronic health records (EHR), Healthcare industry, Permissioned blockchain.

---

* **Corresponding author Prabh Deep Singh:** Department of Computer Science and Engineering, Graphic Era Deemed to be University, Dehradun, Uttarakhand, India; E-mail: ssingh.prabhdeep@gmail.com

Mohit Angurala, Preet Kamal, Aryan Chaudhary, Rasmeet Singh Bali & Vijay Bhardwaj (Eds.)
All rights reserved-© 2025 Bentham Science Publishers

INTRODUCTION

Distributed Ledger Technologies (DLTs) in the healthcare domain concerns the use of smart contracts to manage consent and associated settings that regulate the sharing of electronic health records across industry and geographical boundaries. Several DLT implementations attempt to take control of Personal Health Records (PHRs) and consent a step further by leveraging permissioned and semi-permissioned ledgers in conjunction with identity mechanisms. Moreover, advanced signature schemes can rely on DLT protocols and tools to enable differential privacy in record sharing. Today, however, breaking silos and embracing interoperable solutions are paramount to reaching the meaningful and widespread success of DLT use in the healthcare domain, and little to nothing has been briefly discussed or addressed about the smart contract logic that would be needed to rely on a public, un-permissioned ledger infrastructure for such goals [1].

This chapter will argue that thanks to such logic, it is indeed possible to embrace public, un-permissioned ledgers in the healthcare domain to cater to data sharing (and hence consent management) needs without relinquishing the trust assumptions that firms have agreed upon and embraced when deciding to use distributed ledgers in the first place. Blockchain technologies permit the creation of smart contracts and computer protocols used to facilitate, verify, or enforce a contract's performance or negotiation. This allows automatic consent by the contracting parties, immutability of the agreement, and semi-automated contract execution [2]. This chapter explores the feasibility of using blockchain smart contracts for patient consent and data sharing across systems. It describes the design of several smart contracts covering a wide variety of patient consent types. Support for consent delegation, bilateral agreements, informational self-determination, and safeguards to prevent erosion of patient consent are described.

Background and Rationale

Prior research related to blockchain has attempted a decentralized blockchain solution to eliminate an intermediary who brokers patient consent and mitigates the possible risk of data breach [3]. Implementing a blockchain zero-knowledge proof to validate the authenticity of the patient consent and preserve patient privacy, more security and privacy compliance on the blockchain can be enhanced. However, no existing research further assesses the integrity of the patient consent in the blockchain once it is formed and verified.

Research Objectives

Blockchain-related research offers strengths and includes a stream customized to healthcare, identifying emerging principal drivers of patient (age, gender, education) and health data trust (financial status, requiring interoperability, perception concerning use cases and industries). Further, a particular blockchain tool (smart contracts) in the form of database triggers and stored procedures the innovations offer is critically evaluated. Fifty one experts' insights are operationalized and used to understand why currently smart contracts see limited practice and to suggest a possible way to overcome these barriers. Moreover, it is argued that tools can deliver direct advantages for patients by enabling a more transparent and comprehensive assessment of the informed consent and data-sharing process. In doing so, a five-level maturity model is used to point out the likely factors that will affect the progression from non-disclosure to total transparency levels of Smart Contract Governance over health data [4].

The objective of the chapter is to demonstrate how the smart contract minimizes human error in facilitating patient consent records while increasing trust and transparency among all stakeholders using a private blockchain. The numerical example depicts the intensity of the interaction among each stakeholder and finally presents the exchange done by all stakeholders. The research questions about how electronic patient consent can be promoted and validated in blockchain have been partially answered in a recent study. With a focus not only on breaking the information silos and enabling patients to share more data with different stakeholders for various purposes but also supporting the full operation of a collaboration agreement, as well as informing or enforcing healthcare policies, this chapter goes beyond e-patient consent and is an extension to the work by implementing blockchain smart contract.

This research aims to examine the practical use of blockchain technology, in particular the developer tools where self-enforced procedures are stated, outlined, and translated in a language easily understood by both healthcare professionals and patients, *i.e.*, smart contracts. No insight is linked to encrypted data on the blockchain or requires regulatory support as a patient is still struggling with personal data protection.

BLOCKCHAIN TECHNOLOGY IN HEALTHCARE

Blockchain technology supports the NHIN Detailed Participant Directory (which is a part of the NwHIN Directory), for it supports the secure and private exchange of electronic health information. It is used for the authentication of the providers for the purpose of public health reporting using the NwHIN Direct, as there is a report that states that data integrity and signature are needed, apart from the secure and private exchange of electronic health information. NwHIN Direct does not specify any specific accountable parties regarding this. Blockchain technology forms a nexus across scalable technologies that form a poly-concentrated market across the functionality of Bitcoin blockchain edges, efficiently supporting complex functionalities [5].

Blockchain allows patients to retain encrypted control over their patient health records. Blockchain in healthcare has the attributes to revolutionize various healthcare processes due to its characteristics like security, transparency, immutability, and reliability [6]. Blockchain records the sequence of events and ensures the integrity of the algorithms, enabling data analytics to give results that are reliable and trustable. Blockchain technology has an essential role in governance, regulation, and law because it can determine the agreement about the timing and outcome of the transferred information. Blockchain greatly facilitates and sustains various high-quality shared services, but network effects related to digital infrastructure provisioning often result in a heavily concentrated market with a detrimental effect on societal convenience and social justice [7].

A smart financial market can counteract these negative externalities and encourage investment in financial infrastructure. Blockchain can handle digital documents, integrating multiple components of an electronic health record and ensuring that its users always possess valid and authentic data. With blockchain in healthcare, there are clear insights about the data and the data integrity of the data owner. The rest of this section reviews the potential benefits of blockchain use in healthcare, possible limitations, and current use cases of blockchain in healthcare. The advent of blockchain technology has disrupted many sectors of the global economy [8].

The architecture diagram depicted in Fig. (1) is a blockchain-based healthcare system where the patient portal interacts with the blockchain network. The blockchain network includes a smart contract layer and a data storage layer. The system facilitates interactions with multiple stakeholders, including healthcare providers, research institutions, and analytics platforms, ensuring secure and compliant data exchange and management. In healthcare, blockchain is transforming how patient data is stored and managed. Blockchain is a decentralized distributed ledger that may increase the security, privacy, and interoperability of medical information, allowing patients to take control of their data and decide who has access. Smart contracts and automated cryptographic scripts on blockchain facilitate agreements between patients and healthcare systems about how these data are used. To the best of our knowledge, this study is the first to take advantage of blockchain technology to legally enforce patient consent, ensuring patients understand how their data is used. Patients' consent as the basis for sharing data will be used and consented for its specific purpose, allowing and encouraging data sharing and enhancing patient privacy [9]. The work is centered on a hospital-based cohort of patients with available dose-response data, as granularity of data sharing is essential in showing potential benefits and risks. The study augments existing smart contracts code used to enforce context and purpose.

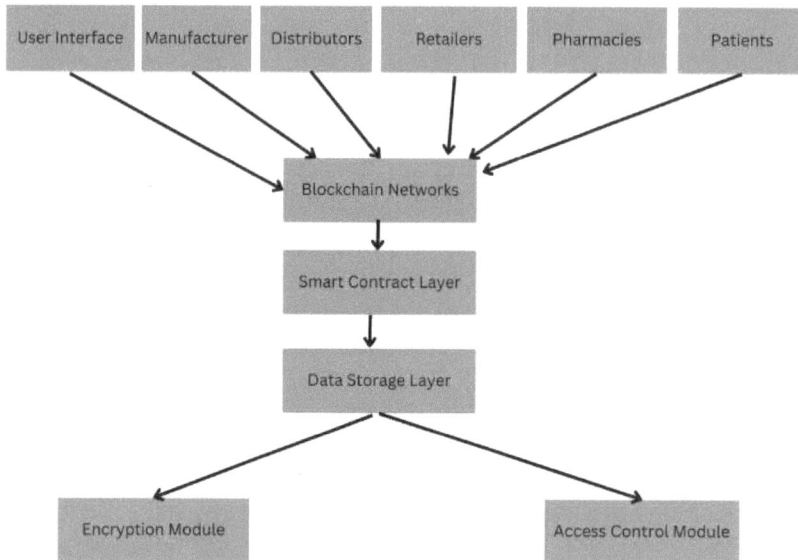

Fig. (1). Smart contract-based consent management architecture.

Overview of Blockchain Technology

Blockchain's features lie in the technology's three core characteristics: transparency, immutability, and security using cryptographic processes. The transparency of data in a blockchain reflects the fact that it is visible to all members of the network, defining the distributed ledger [7]. Second, immutability means that once a set of transactions has been confirmed and added to the blockchain, their history is recorded in a cryptographically protected manner, tampered through consensus, and therefore cannot be altered, recalling that tampered personal data is often the root cause of fraud [10]. Finally, to provide security that uses cryptographic techniques, cryptography has been widely used to protect digital data and transactions in multiple domains. Importantly, the security provided by a distributed system is dependent upon a trust model developed that combines the properties of transparency, immutability, and cryptography.

"Crypto economics" operates as a decentralized network. Blockchain technology is a decentralized digital ledger that allows logically related data to be distributed and shared across a large network. In this ledger, units of information are combined into blocks, which are then cryptographically linked to produce a chain [11]. Created in 2008, blockchain was originally developed to underpin cryptocurrency, but numerous applications in various industries are now conceivable. Blockchain decentralization, the central feature of this technology, suggests that no central authority is needed to intermediate or validate transactions between interested parties, such as peer-to-peer interactions [12]. Indeed, blockchain is being used for an increasing number of data-related management tasks across different industries. This includes stakeholder identification, consent management, provenance, validation, auditing, and other uses for ensuring and validating the creation, handling, and sharing of personal data.

Fig. (2) depicts how patient consent is managed and data is securely shared in a healthcare system using blockchain and smart contracts. The process involves the patient providing consent, which is stored on the blockchain and managed by smart contracts, authorizing access for healthcare providers, research institutions, and analytics platforms to request and receive data securely.

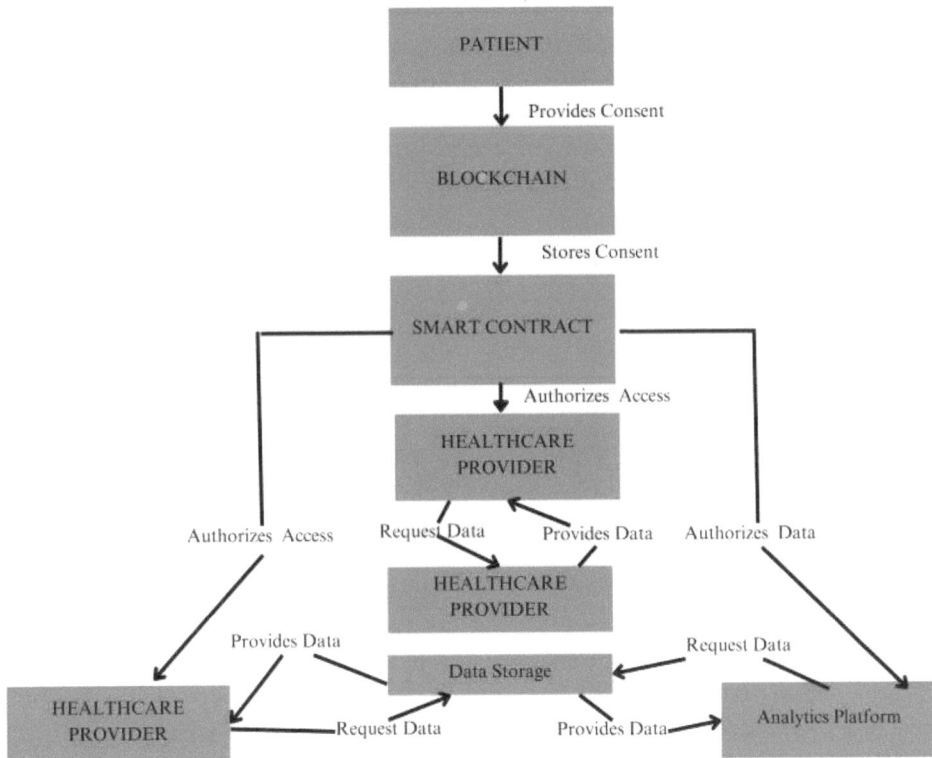

Fig. (2). Blockchain-based patient consent and data-sharing workflow.

Applications in Healthcare

Building on mechanisms for consent management and data sharing, the development of blockchain-based systems improves prescription drug monitoring, provides medication support by ensuring trustable and transparent provenance data for drug development, packaging, and logistics, contributes to trustworthy medical document certification services (providing a decentralized, secure, immutable, transparent point for medical records verification), and offers granular consent service infrastructures that focus on complete, correct management, and provision of healthcare consumers' consent information to relevant parties [13].

Although blockchain-based technology solutions for healthcare have the potential to improve healthcare services in various ways, the improved sharing, security, and trust components raise privacy and data protection concerns in the presence of GDPR regulations, which impact the development and deployment of the solutions [14]. Blockchain technology has the potential to enable many advances in the healthcare domain, including the improved access, management, and sharing of health data, and the provision of data infrastructures for value-based healthcare and wellness innovative services. Researchers in certain domains that generate large amounts of health or healthcare-related data have experienced recent significant advances in data acquisition and analysis, with the development of the capability to generate immense amounts of structured data (both clinical and "real-world settings") and massive unstructured data from deep learning applications [15].

SMART CONTRACTS

The system of smart contracts has its origins in the early 1990s when cryptographer Nick Szabo began exploring the idea of self-enforcing contracts. Szabo himself did not introduce the term, using instead the phrase "a set of promises, specified in digital form, including protocols within which the parties perform on the other promises" to explain what we now recognize as smart contracts [16]. More recently, it has been the focus of attention in the insurance sector. These smart contracts rely on the creation of a distributed Turing machine (DTM), a concept that underwent additional development in the intervening period immediately following Szabo's initial observations and did not begin to see greater attention and discussion until recently. It was the rise of interest in Bitcoin in 2013 when it exploded into the public consciousness that appears to have triggered a flurry of interest in what had, up to that point, been relatively niche and academic considerations.

Since then, follow-on developments have occurred at an unbelievable pace in innovative new applications, and increasingly, they are moving in from the protection of purely computer-based contractual clauses to a much wider variety of real-world uses [17]. Smart contracts are neither "smart" nor "contracts" in the traditional sense; they are actually pieces of computer code. However, they can be used to verify, facilitate, or enforce contractual clauses. Smart contracts can automatically verify arbitrary conditions and cause an action to take place if certain conditions are fulfilled. Indeed, in this sense, they are "smart". But they are not "contracts" as we normally understand them. Rather, they are typically used as contract "clauses" that rely on self-enforcing code, potentially encapsulating, automating, and "trustlessly" executing certain contractual commitments [18].

Fig. (3) illustrates the lifecycle of patient consent management using blockchain technology. It begins with the submission and storage of the consent form on the blockchain, followed by smart contract initiation, consent verification, data access request and authorization, data sharing, and potential consent revocation.

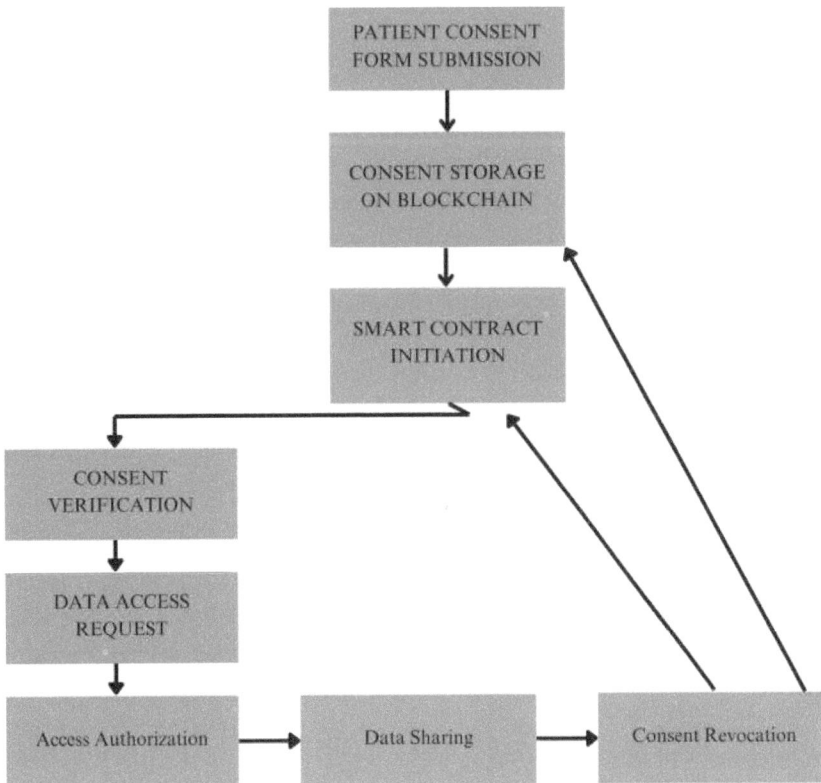

Fig. (3). Patient consent lifecycle using blockchain.

Definition and Functionality

Any blockchain-enabled device may read the smart contract code, the constant values, the balance, and any other discrete information. Smart contracts generate outputs *via* transactions, and transactions are issued, signed, and broadcast to the network. Properties of a smart contract include state, owner, balance, visibility, address, and code. The data state is comprised of variables that represent the agreed-upon constraints that define the behavior of the system and the transition between system states [19].

The owner refers to the Ethereum account that initiated the contract, while the balance pertains to the amount of ether stored in the smart contract. Functions are the operations that the contract carries and are defined in the source code. The former is a regular account, whereas the latter forms the rules that govern a decentralized application or the DAO. The decentralized autonomous organization contract comprises the overall rule, which allows users to vote on collective outcomes. This study will concern itself with the more prevalent form of smart contracts that are invoked from an external account and are used for specific tasks. In this study, the execution emanates from recording the agreement in a blockchain instead of storage, contract law, and performance monitoring. Smart contracts are rules governing the participants' behaviors, which are recorded in a smart contract language such as the Ethereum Foundation's Solidity and Serpent, and execute when certain rules or conditions are met [20]. There are two types of smart contracts: one is initiated from an external account, and the other is from the account of another contract. The goal of this study is to explore the utility of blockchain contract features for deploying patient-consented AI models and scripts at hospital facilities. In this section, we will explore the functionality of the blockchain smart contract. Facilitating this access control management is the automatic effectuation of blockchain code when certain code conditions (or transactions) are met. Smart contracts work in a similar way to regular contracts by locking these agreement assets until certain conditions are met by the different parties [21].

A specific open challenge in the design of the system that will prove my work will regard data treated in the case of inalienable partial or forced guardianship. The key point in the model is the guarantees offered by the smart contract address and the stored data. The owner declares and agrees to share and access the data. A potential extension state is to guarantee that the data owner has always shared the information with all the smart contracts through auditing procedures implemented in the smart contracts. One of the most famous applications aims to potentially use blockchains for personal health records (PHR) [22]. In this system, patients create an electronic medical record distributed to third-party authorized individuals. It can be freely shared with other physicians, improving the care the patient receives. This ensures a higher degree of integration, coherence, and tamper resistance and finally generates an aggregate analysis of all internal data.

In particular, the rapid progress of machine learning and data analysis sets a steep path for the use of data provided in the form of a stock. The trainees' willingness to share data in open databases is influenced by privacy concerns [23]. This will foster seamless remote care of intelligent devices based only on pragmatism. Blockchain technology supports this trend by increasing the level of confidence, maintaining guarantees, and reinforcing agreement in the collective exchange and collaborative use of intimate data. Despite the ethical and legal constraints that currently bound proprietary and commercial behaviors and strategies in healthcare, the general paradigm shifts in personalization, remote care, and wearables, as well as the increasing desire of patients for more control over their own data, are expected to break these barriers into new paths and indexes. These paths can be "trained" and analyzed to create insights that today cannot be disclosed without excessive effort [24].

PATIENT CONSENT IN HEALTHCARE

The study implements the OmniLayer in a web interface that overlays medical data held in digital repositories such as FHIR. The OmniLayer is a sort of wrapper to the conventional layers. It has prescribed resources, metadata, and services. We believe that the CHIRON clinical trial and research ecosystem is the first to link patient consent and research access directly to clinical trial metadata and protocol [25]. We curate the layer by initiating the launch of each trial. Launching a trial against the layer is only possible after ethical review, regulatory approvals, and data access agreements are in place. Future work will implement secure wallet technology, allowing hospitals to charge patients as an allocation for the complexity and storage costs of storing their consent forms. Before discussing smart contract usage, it is important to grasp the nature of patient consent. At a high level, patient consent is required in most countries for their data to be used in research studies [3]. Obtaining patient consent is fraught with challenges. Patients need to be provided with adequate time and information to make an informed decision about giving consent. While electronic and cloud storage of consent forms has improved the situation, several problems remain. Consent forms are hard to access and link to patient data. Once consent is obtained for a research project, ensuring adherence is problematic [26]. Typically, a global narrative directs the ethical considerations for a research project with researchers confined by these constraints. Ethical considerations become both disassociated from the protocol and susceptible to funder and researcher pressure. To the best of our knowledge, there are no other smart health contracts to manage patient consent and research access. Our approach is unique and a part of our CHIRON architecture. We believe that patient consent is a two-way social contract with standards set by international treaties such as the Nuremberg Code, the Belmont Report, and the Helsinki Declaration [27].

Importance and Legal Frameworks

It is a fundamental tenet of GDPR that consent must be freely given. However, there are difficulties faced by many dApps when introducing a new system that uses individuals' personal data in accordance with the GDPR. Their worry is that they will put off potential early adopters who have shown particularly strong concerns about their data and will become clients of a new dApp. The goal of the dApp chain is to capture and then share these educational tips with other dApps as part of their customer outreach programs [28]. Currently, it is easy because developers do not have access to a testing database and, therefore, have no actual data to use to build their dApps. Thus, to get access to data, a formal consent flow must first be implemented. Using the dApp chain allows the developers to see some examples of educational tips and offers opinions on them that help the other interested dApps understand the features they look at to implement within their own system design. This then alleviates the challenge of data privacy in the development of dApps.

Consent data alone is stored in a manner that builds trust between data subjects and controllers. The most important reason for centralizing consent data under GDPR is that 'data subjects should have various means available to them to manage, control, and oppose the processing of personal data'. This explanation means that the data subjects need to be able to trust those who require their consent. Therefore, the focus should be on improving the quality of all consent mechanisms and the trust that the data subject has in those who require consent. In other words, data subject consent is vital, based on open consent rather than an artificial short-term agreement that may rapidly become out of sync with actual uses of data. The dApp chain's single goal is to 'facilitate the capture and use of the patients' own health data and applications of the patients'. The dApp will not operate directly on the health data but will instead use the patients' own copies of the data, as stored on IPFS.

Challenges and Limitations

In the meantime, technical solutions will be created, as cloud use proliferates for blockchain, to curtail the rawness of shared data and eventually create the potential for population scale transparency around shared data results, provided the throughput and cost issues. Related points can be made about the current blockchain unbiased pattern of treatment in value-based care incentives [29]. Over time, purity demand will help shift from data sharing to a commitment to health and care value planning. This intention will manifest through the transition of value-based care to blockchain. Right now, any potential technical solution to this problem is speculative in the context of the research data network representative enough to evaluate the viability of the approach. Data sharing, like EHR use, can be thought of as a multi-party transaction, with all parties concerned with semantically sensitive data. Conclusions that are unfair, low interpretability of findings, opportunities lost from lack of shared data, poor quality of life for individuals, and a waste of time for professionals as well as policymakers arise from missed opportunities for data sharing but do not diminish the value of data itself. This study is primarily qualitative in nature, and the quantitative component does not compare this solution to other existing solutions, as there are none. We expect success to be predicated on achieving scale, which we have addressed [30]. The primary goals of this study are to test the regulatory feasibility of deploying a participant-centered approach at scale in a research setting and to create a test bed for further technical development by building a community around patient data sharing. This work demonstrates the use of a blockchain-based approach to give more control to research participants, enabling dynamic control over how data is used. However, we recognize some limitations and technical challenges.

DATA SHARING IN HEALTHCARE

Healthcare data is critically important. There have been advances in techniques and tools for data storage, analysis, and sharing, as well as in medicine - diagnostics, bioinformatics, therapeutics, and interventions. The increasing capabilities of technology, the corresponding problems of the cost of healthcare, and the fragmentation of patient records down to small details proliferate in proprietary applications [30]. Furthermore, security and access to the data are increasingly critical issues. Patient data must be shared ever more widely as more specialist roles develop in healthcare every year. Patient data is consumable and reusable in applications for chronic care management and AI/analytics applications. The need for distributed patient data in healthcare is increasing, whether it is for research purposes or to reduce duplication of patient examinations across multiple providers [31]. Consent-based access control has, therefore, become increasingly important as data needs to be shared widely with different parties, under different regulations or compliance restrictions, and in different use cases. In this chapter, we look at how blockchain-based smart contracts are developed to facilitate data sharing in healthcare and the challenge of setting the granularity of consent [32].

Current Practices

In the absence of immediately beneficial treatment, most patients can cope with the responsibility that comes from participating in their healthcare, provided they are guided by an experienced and qualified healthcare professional. When considering taking part in medical research, patients often harbor far more altruistic motives than the quest for increased financial status from business. Informed patient consent is, however, a big hurdle and can be cumbersome and time-consuming to administer, with opt-outs or blanket consents often leading to different issues with the accuracy or validity of the research results. Blocking is an attractive solution, but in contrast to medical treatment, where patients accept the transfer of decision-making authorities by transferring personal data to a data collector, patients do not have adequate control of their data and suffer varying degrees of recourse and loss of privacy and confidentiality. In return, the big data market is extraterritorial and reports annually growing revenue generated by academic research. Secondary data use is an important public research capacity. For healthcare research, anonymized datasets are most often used, but it takes time and effort to assemble them, and the researchers only see what they need for their specific research question. A growing number of projects are using blockchain technology in a patient-led model that would unlock medical data at the point of care without the need for a data-sharing agreement. The current chapter outlines some of the legal and technical implementation difficulties in moving from traditional data-sharing models to permission-on-blockchains (POB). In conclusion, the administration of informed patient consent is facilitated by more sophisticated Dapps, with E-biobanks being preferable because they retain the work-in-progress of traditional biobanks and are less legally and technically complex. Although discussions on using blockchain technology for alternative consent models are now becoming too loud to be ignored, they do not consider viable ways of distinguishing consent from consent from multiple overlapping projects in any usable way.

Benefits and Risks

Programs have been extensively discussed, and awareness is growing, yet tangible measures are still scarce. The incorporation of smart health contracts can bring them closer to a degree of automation that satisfies all stakeholders. Additionally, it will economize the costly process of establishing and enforcing contracts between entities. If the latter had to be done manually by each participant, the proposed distributed and peer-to-peer model ceases to be scalable. Using such an approach also avoids the establishment of trusted intermediaries. Current models and regulations and existing data access procedures do not yet address the vast opportunities given that markets and regulatory models are expanding [33]. In contrast with our approach, although proposed sharing networks secure user-determined control and permission mechanisms, the mechanisms mostly depend on participating organizations and do not always ensure that the data source (the patient) and beneficiary (the organization) profit from the exchange. In other cases, trust must be established first between the parties involved. Our approach addresses the limitation by incorporating enriching value into the permissions, thereby encouraging no-data policy establishments to participate and avoiding the building of ad-hoc negotiation processes and, therefore, decisions, which often lead to inconsistencies in the treatment of the various contractual arrangements.

The use of blockchain for health data sharing to support consent can deliver several benefits for stakeholders. The need for and challenges with patient consent to health data usage are well documented. We present a novel approach for delivering health data solutions to address patient needs. The approach smartly aligns that all the stakeholders have their perspectives fulfilled and, at the same time, all the privacy and security requirements accomplished. By ensuring that users have power over their health data permissions and that sharing health data economically benefits each patient, our approach should contribute to increased willingness by individuals to participate in studies and in the long-term sharing of their health data, resulting in a level of distrust among potential users. Our approach can help reduce this challenge by increasing user confidence in what data sharing will entail and also securing compliant and responsible data sharing throughout the research process, *i.e.*, not only by data owners but also by the eventual data consumer as well.

INTEGRATION OF BLOCKCHAIN AND SMART CONTRACTS

More generally, these transaction management function business models circumvent traditional oligopolies and potentially increase the efficiency of local small enterprises in providing locally relevant and real-time informational and transactional services that can possibly increase customer satisfaction and reduce the economic barriers to healthcare, including access to information. By aligning the interests and resources of patients, research, and healthcare providers, blockchain technology can contribute to democratizing healthcare and addressing concerns. Regular patient condition updates will be key in preventing avoidable health issues, measuring effectiveness, gaining insight from many treatments, and experiencing paneled results optimal for an individual treatment path.

The blockchain stores a series of records and links by appending a secure hash at the end of the record. A blockchain, after being accepted, is a shared digital file that keeps track of transactions, confirmed sequentially through a process of network consensus [34]. The blockchain enables recording and validating transactions and maintaining the latest state of information through real-time sharing of these records across a network of participants. However, the matching of medical records and scheduling appointments may not require the extensive collaboration protocols and trust-assuring mechanisms used when exchanging the value of bitcoins.

A major issue with blockchain is the viable bridging of different data sources to provide decision-support for an individual patient while appropriately limiting the potential abuses of these data. Blockchain is useful for cryptocurrencies such as Bitcoin, an encapsulating data structure that exchanges value, but the broader question is whether more limiting personal healthcare is an urgent need.

One potential solution to this problem is a blockchain, which is a distributed ledger that provides secure and transparent records of data sharing. Blockchain policy levels can be created, and data management and access can be carried out according to rules specified in smart contracts, which are self-executing and decentralized policy enforcement. Given the need for cryptographic enforcement of access control, this approach may be practical only for public health records, and in these cases, the extra privacy protections offered by sophisticated cryptographic techniques may not be beneficial. Nonetheless, blockchain approaches hold promise as a practical means of incorruptible patient consent, which has been an ongoing issue; numerous studies have been focusing on patient authorization and the security of patients' data.

Blockchain technology can alleviate the challenges of patients' consent and authorization associated with health information sharing across multiple partners, a key problem in integrating various sources of data to create patient profiles. Patients digitize their personal health data on different websites and must visit these sites to authorize the sharing of this data with other providers. However, there is no technology to facilitate the integration of the information and the extension of the permission for each self-owned data piece.

Use Cases

Informed consent in healthcare is a pillar of ethics; meaningful and informed consent by patients for the use of a variety of medical and clinical data is a foundational principle. The current trend by technology companies around the world is collecting and using the data for medical and clinical research without hospitals or any other type of partnership. Blockchain smart contracts enable patients to be in control of their medical data by allowing them to register from first use. Consent preferences can easily be expressed and stored by patients, and the data use becomes much more legitimate for companies or hospitals. Hence, this technology is the next generation of data sharing between hospitals and technology companies to discover and develop future health applications. It is proven to be successful against fraud, non-compliance, and ambiguity. Hence, better hospital operation and trust will result in larger and more diverse databases through security, privacy, and transparency enhancement. Also, when required, automatic remuneration of people can be done by smart contracts. In our review of the literature on blockchain smart contracts for healthcare and life sciences, several key use cases emerged. We discuss the use cases of consent and data sharing, prescriptions, regulatory reporting, device tracking and provenance, clinical trials, supply chain, and credentialing. We highlight a few of the noteworthy aspects of these use cases: patient control of personal data, data immutability, high availability and security of smart contracts, high-level security against tampering with results of clinical trials, reduction of counterfeit drugs through achieving small markets by distribution channels digitization, the reduction of resume fraud of healthcare professionals, and traceability of medical devices achieved with the help of blockchain smart contracts.

Technical Considerations

Blockchain-based systems, through smart contracts, can provide a secure, shared, and decentralized infrastructure that facilitates novel patient consent processes. These systems can durably record patient consent, manage and authorize access to patient data, and enable transparent distribution of data revenues directly to the patients. Prior work in the blockchain community in data sharing has demonstrated mechanisms based on the use of Ethereum smart contracts to provide compensation to patients renting their data to researchers, enabling the fair redistribution of the data renting fee to patients instead of arbitrary third parties such as the clinical data network platform owners. The work demonstrated how the rental mechanism could comply with the European Union General Data Protection Regulation (GDPR) and that it was effective in enabling patients to autonomously control their data, increasing data rental revenue for patients by removing the intermediaries from the data renting process.

Smart contracts provide a means for patients, researchers, and providers to establish clear consent and data-use agreements that are securely and durably recorded within a virtually incorruptible distributed ledger. Smart contracts are programs executed on a blockchain and are a key enabler of blockchain technology. These self-executing, self-enforcing contracts can automatically implement, manage, and digitally enforce agreement terms between multiple consenting parties. Smart contracts provide a unique opportunity to automate the consent process and directly link the consent record to the control of the data. This can significantly enhance the scalability, reliability, and trustworthiness of consent and data-sharing mechanisms. Providing clear and transparent consent processes, as well as enabling both patients and providers to have a clear understanding of who accesses patient data and for what purposes, is essential in the process of securing increasingly larger amounts of data from participating institutions.

ETHICAL AND PRIVACY CONSIDERATIONS

Public attitudes toward data use and preferences for patient control should, therefore, be empirically informed. Patients, radiologists, and NLP specialists are used to crowdsource a crucial medical text for informed radiologic imaging consent. The term "smart contracts" might be inappropriate as they are not smart and not necessarily contracts, but they can be used in medical research to automate patient engagement, including any processes that arise from a consent form, consent documents, and consent preferences. While future uncertainty gets translated into broad consent language in some jurisdictions and economies, in others, it is simply not feasible to seek out information about future uses.

Informed Consent and Autonomy

Ultimately, shortcomings may serve to contribute to the problem of patient data siloing, as a lack of perceived patient ownership or control over their health records inhibits their ability or willingness to share these data resources when possible beneficial use cases emerge. Their lack of control operates as a significant barrier to the person-centered precision medicine delivery model that promotes patient data ownership and control. We, therefore, feel it opportune to lend direction and coherence to the principles above – given a learned interest in promoting person-centered precision medicine strategies – by facilitating more effective clinical consent processes. Informed consent is a guiding ethical principle for the domain of clinical care, designed to preserve patient autonomy and self-determination. Patients are believed to have the right to decide what happens to their bodies and up to what point other individuals or entities may access their bodies. This concept has prompted a commitment to facilitate informed consent through the delivery of clear information to all patients regarding their states, treatment options, benefits, and risks. However, the reality of standard informed consent practices today does not always live up to these principled aspirations. Patients are often provided with and requested to sign lengthy, jargon-filled, opaque consent forms within a matter of minutes and, in some cases, seconds prior to suffering a medical procedure. The problem here is that traditional and electronic consent form paradigms remain rare in their use and effective means of conveying relevant information such that informed consent can be initiated.

Data Security and Anonymity

When more advanced payment techniques or personal charitable grants are employed, many concerns regarding who pays turn into confidentiality interests where the patient should not learn the source of funds. When treatments need to be pursued for genuine compassion, knowledge about the source of funding may skew proper medical dialogue. Deliverable on-ramps have the power to quickly entice participants into a long-term insurance plan for their families. Autonomous platforms that use externally instantiated risk pools would want property rights for their learning intelligence, according to fair social dosage. An all-encompassing advocate might be a good fit for a medical appointment that involves assisting in the negotiation of the right to become aware.

Genealogy research is possible in crowdfunding applications for pursuing family ancestry goals. It would require highly secure access with a limited duration, with safeguards against parallel construction attacks. Salary information and tax withholding for workers are use cases that would require extremely secure and careful implementation. The idea of a firewalled blockchain is also appealing when physical restrictions need to be added to a legalized contractual agreement. If the person is not capable of attestation and parenthetical updates, then a temporary legal affiliation can be established to offer protection, such as a maintenance person can file tax withholding with the IRS on behalf of all household emergency contacts. As the blockchain update transactions need to be created, ones for inferior partial delegation agreements can be crafted that might positively persist as partial permanent agreements. Marriages and expected children are good examples where both parties might prefer ongoing use of secured automation. After permanent filing, changes to partial delegation clauses might be sporadic and harsh, such as marriage dissolution through parental estrangement.

REGULATORY LANDSCAPE

In healthcare, it is well-known that there are different data privacy concerns associated with different types of data. The regulatory landscape for health data is complex, particularly since different countries have different laws and requirements. Globally, health researchers and developers must work within the constraints of regulations that are trying to ensure the privacy and appropriate use of health data. This can make it more difficult for health developers to work with real patient data to evaluate and improve their applications. Blockchain solutions have been put forward as a way for patients to control how their data are used and protected without exposing health researchers and companies to liability. This requires smart contracts that capture patients' privacy requirements and account for the possibility that they may change their minds. This chapter reviews the regulatory landscape for patient data in the healthcare sector and identifies the different types of data to which alternative regulations and smart contracts might apply.

HIPAA Compliance

We think that the use of tokens to represent data is a powerful concept that can help patients own more of the health infrastructure that supports their care. In fact, we modeled the Health Data and Health Token contracts—our specific blockchain implementations—using healthcare organizations as tenants and investors who lease to own. Patients are given just the level of control that they are willing to take on fully in the BTC case and act as rent-collecting investors in the ETH case [35]. These models are just our first considerations; we expect future work to further integrate token models in healthcare settings. Our primary contribution is to introduce an architecture that allows for this additional level of patient control to meet and exceed existing requirements for security, trust, and scalability [36].

This first step to providing patients with the ability to share their health data in a manner compliant with HIPAA is for a patient, a healthcare professional, and any participating organizations to first agree that the patient has the authority to share the data. Smart contracting agencies provide the means for medical professionals to be involved in and make decisions about the patient's health data and thus help define whether the patient's health data is for the purpose of any health data sharing contract. These contracting agencies also allowed parties to agree to sanctions for contract breaches. We recognize that health data sharing remains a complex issue, but we believe that patients should have more of a role in the decision-making process; patient consent is required to enable that.

GDPR and Other Regulations

The General Data Protection Regulation (GDPR) has been in effect in the EU since 2018. It applies to data controllers and processors of all sectors and mandates compliance with several principles regarding data processing, security, and consent. Personal data cannot be transferred out of the EU without confidentiality and integrity guarantees. Blockchain properties, like confidentiality of sensitive data in public blockchains or the impossibility of modifying personal data, along with the removal of personal data, stress compliance efforts. Since the penalties for non-compliance are substantial, any system processing or storing personal data must be thoroughly designed with data protection in mind. Looking at this challenge in the healthcare sector, where every entity faces strict regulations, it is important to also protect the patient's right to choice when it comes to sharing personal data and reusing medical history through blockchain [37]. Blockchain implies data protection, security, integrity, and traceability properties. It is no surprise that the values of these properties are sometimes taken for granted. Moreover, the consensus needed for changes to the system makes it an attractive solution for storing large volumes of data and ensures it is trusted by the parties involved and can pass through different regulation frameworks. In the context of smart contracts, after they are triggered, they result in changes to a system that is maintained by all players (in the case of public blockchains, for solutions targeting a restricted number of users, smart contract-based solutions may require having a specific consensus mechanism). However, not all the information stored in blockchains should be available to everybody, and not all players should be able to make changes to contracts they were involved in. Anonymous transactions and design requirements that shield personal information in healthcare blockchains, introduced in this chapter, are instruments to meet this demand and make this kind of technology practical.

FUTURE DIRECTIONS AND OPPORTUNITIES

The vision of consent smart contracts we presented in this chapter is only a partial solution to the practicality and other limitations in the design, collection, interpretation, and use of patient consent and opt-out data presented in the introduction of this series of chapters. Impeccably designed blockchain smart consent mechanisms, which may incorporate consent voting or even the use of external expert assessors in addition to or instead of the use of computable consent settings, are not capable of expunging or preventing data from non-computable metadata (for example, medical humanities, social vulnerability or resistance behavior in the individual, cultural/historical differences, societal estimations beyond the traditional health data that need to be respected and followed by the clinical researcher). Neither can they solve privacy, data quality, and control issues in this scenario. The evaluation of the Consortium system is an important first step toward realizing the previously hypothetical potential for blockchain smart contracts to support patients' informed decision-making and improved exchange and refinement of consent data. Although we are encouraged by our own evaluation findings, we suggest further developmental work as an urgent priority and that consent smart contract developers must address the practical, sociotechnical, and legal limitations we set out in this chapter.

Research and Innovation

Health data is obvious data, and increasingly, queries about, for example, how a nation should prepare and react to challenges like the recently emerged COVID-19 disease should sooner rather than later lead to further useful insights into which health data to assemble and how other stakeholders should be combined pragmatically. Every year, three or four organized groups of types of organisms contribute to global human disease. Disease problems are not only confined to rich nations' hospitals; we need nationally grounded perspectives to give a comprehensive understanding of the patient-in-mutual-ecosystem context. What are the mutations, and are they enabling host jumps or cross-species infections of a current or future health problem, or just following convoluted and complex viral crossover pathways for a one-time event occurring about every 10 years? A corollary of the patient's right to access biobanking information is that health economic injunctions requiring all health data and associated party interactions *via* expensive yet inefficient central intermediaries must be treated as only one of an increasing number of difficult yet prime-node multi-agent authorities available to direct and manage the permissions patients have authorized; hard-coding of internal and external identities must be rejected.

Earlier sections of this chapter provided examples of how some patients managed their data privacy and combined decentralized data to enable important patient-led research. The "Who Owns My Medical Data" project demonstrates one of a number of paths to shared ownership of health data among stakeholders and the use of data technologies such as blockchain and smart contracts to transparently orchestrate operations between patients and other stakeholders *via* symbols of meaning like medical record pointers and patient consent bits held in blockchain data structures. The objective of many other studies, which have been included in this chapter, is to systematically devise and evaluate strategies that can be used in situations in which individual data empowerment is currently difficult.

Potential Impact on Healthcare

The potential for reduced administrative workload is a factor that can attract providers as a means of freeing them up for patient care. However, the fact that smart contracts are self-executing can lead to a lack of restraint by patients on demand and an increase in costs to healthcare providers. Smart contracts, when used in business services to provide more visibility and transparency, as well as better control of business transactions between parties, have been argued by several authors to have considerable potential to disrupt traditional relationships. Scalable platforms have been developed for productive chain integration. A recent review of the blockchain literature by Tavares and Pinho found that stakeholder benefits for public entities and private organizations have been the main subject of discussion.

Key Findings and Recommendations

Smart contract technology has great promise, and in particular, it can facilitate greater respect shown to patient participants by treating those who do not want to share their data at all or who want to participate differently. However, to date and based on the legal issues, it seems that many of the lawyers are applying traditional analog contract law to digital assets, which might lead to an underestimation of digital capabilities. Since a smart contract is merely a set of pre-written codes, smart contracts cannot, of course, be drafted as traditional contracts. So, they need to reflect the reality of form to avoid this mismatch and potential disharmony. This requires a basic understanding of the new form.

Smart contract technology can be a powerful way to facilitate the many different potential arrangements for data sharing and treat patient preferences in a comprehensive fashion. This level of nuance probably needs to be captured in how smart contracts are offered to patients. Rather than many different contract templates, the options need to be organized so that patients can easily understand the arrangements for which they are selecting. There should probably be a few of these common contract configurations that are understood and appreciated by the patient and to which healthcare enclaves and scientists also agree. In fact, if a multitude of different contract options are proposed by different enclaves, many would be at a disadvantage, and many more would not be able to discern meaningful differences. Furthermore, too little critical mass around preferences or the absence of transparency and clarity would probably slow contract adoption, lead to impatience, and cloud the use of data.

CONCLUSION

Due to infrequent patient consent, data donations, or data sharing events, the EDM patient data management ecosystem has been in a potential transition from a narrow ocean of a few pharmaceutical and genomic research companies. Fully public blockchain solutions may also suffer from decreased utility due to publicly available patient records and donors having no further control or more application advantages than just having done the "right" thing. Faced with these and other similar concerns, a group of like-minded companies and their hundreds of patient participants have or are transitioning toward a permissioned, consortium, and a non-profit blockchain with an emphasis on patient privacy preservation. The "open pharma" approach has identified, contemplated, and mitigated various consent and blockchain impacts of potential patient data-sharing programs. Such programs allow donors to help control research directionality and share in the economic benefits of data commercialization. Finally, the CODA platform breaks down the smart contract administration barrier and empowers the common patient through automated blockchain contract generation, permissioned rule set adherence, and marketplace participation *via* Ethereum ERC20. The timely progress of research activities and the financial phase of those activities depend largely on the facilitation of patient participation and the ability to share patient data in support of those activities. Not possessing these precious assets not only delays innovation but might also prevent breakthroughs in changing the course of disease. Decentralized blockchain technologies, featuring consensus-based trust in transaction transparency, are positioned to reduce infrastructure and human-based barriers to sharing patient health data. Simpler interfaces for patients have been proposed. New aerospace-enabled blockchain solutions have further minimized the entry and educational burden of blockchain on patients. EDMs can certainly benefit from the addition of blockchain for scalable privacy, integrated security, and simplified smart contract administration. This study reviewed a broad-cased patient data management platform, emphasizing consent and patient benefit, undergirded by blockchain infrastructure. Future work can be done with industry or academic leaders in patient activity, patient data exchange, patient data storage, and patient data interaction to ascertain entry barriers to public or private blockchain infrastructure. Further open pharma, CODA, and other like-minded patient activities will take patients and other contributors to the healthcare ecosystem to the promised blockchain land: a land where research synergies are untapped, innovation-based treatments flourish, business-driven treatment binaries are rare, and patients more fully reap the economic rewards of their participation.

AUTHORS' CONTRIBUTIONS

In Chapter 13, **Kiran Deep Singh, Prabh Deep Singh, Ankita Gupta,** and **Rohan Verma** worked collaboratively to investigate blockchain's potential in patient consent and data sharing within healthcare. **Kiran Deep Singh** contributed to the literature review, focusing on blockchain's role in enhancing data governance, privacy, and consent management. **Prabh Deep Singh** led the design of blockchain-based consent management models and reviewed their practical applications in healthcare data sharing. **Ankita Gupta** analyzed the legal and ethical frameworks surrounding patient consent, highlighting compliance requirements under regulations like GDPR and HIPAA. **Rohan Verma** provided insights into the technical challenges and future trends in using permissioned blockchain systems, focusing on security and interoperability. Together, the authors provided a comprehensive view of blockchain's transformative impact on patient-centric data management in healthcare.

REFERENCES

[1] Deshpande A, Stewart K. Distributed ledger technologies/blockchain: Challenges, opportunities and the prospects for standards. 2017. Available from: https://www.bsigroup.com/LocalFiles/zh-tw/InfoSec-newsletter/No201706/download/BSI_Blockchain_DLT_Web.pdf

[2] Bacon J, Michels J, Millard C. Blockchain demystified: A technical and legal introduction to distributed and centralized ledgers. HeinOnline 2018. Available from: https://heinonline.org/hol-cgi-bin/get_pdf.cgi?handle=hein.journals/jolt25&section=4

[3]   Porsdam Mann S, Savulescu J, Ravaud P, Benchoufi M. Blockchain, consent and prosent for medical research. J Med Ethics 2021; 47(4): 244-50.
[http://dx.doi.org/10.1136/medethics-2019-105963] [PMID: 32366703]

[4]   Omar IA, Jayaraman R, Salah K, *et al.* Ensuring protocol compliance and data transparency in clinical trials using Blockchain smart contracts. Springer 2020; 20: 1. Available from: https://link.springer.com/article/10.1186/s12874-020-01109-5
[http://dx.doi.org/10.1186/s12874-020-01109-5]

[5]   Just KB. Healthtech: How blockchain can simplify healthcare compliance. Wash & Lee J Civ Rts & Soc Just 2018. Available from: https://heinonline.org/hol-cgi-bin/get_pdf.cgi?handle=hein.journals/walee25&section=10

[6]   Vetrivel S. Blockchain health: Smart contracts transforming healthcare operations. 2024. Available from: https://www.igi-global.com/chapter/blockchain-health/344185

[7]   Kumar V, Ali R, Sharma PK. A secure blockchain-assisted authentication framework for electronic health records. Int J Inf Technol 2024; 1-13. Available from: https://link.springer.com/article/10.1007/s41870-023-01705-w
[http://dx.doi.org/10.1007/s41870-023-01705-w]

[8]   Narikimilli N, Kumar A, Antu A. Blockchain applications in healthcare–a review and future perspective. Springer 2020. Available from: https://link.springer.com/chapter/10.1007/978-3-0-0-59638-5_14
[http://dx.doi.org/10.1007/978-3-030-59638-5_14]

[9]   Reegu FA, Abas H, Gulzar Y, *et al.* Blockchain-based framework for interoperable electronic health records for an improved healthcare system. Sustainability 2023. Available from: https://www.mdpi.com/2071-1050/15/8/6337
[http://dx.doi.org/10.3390/su15086337]

[10]   Muhammad U.T. Revolutionizing health data management with blockchain technology: Enhancing security and efficiency in a digital era. 2024; 1-23. Available from: https://www.igi-global.com/chapter/revolutionizing-health-data-management-with-blockchain-technology/339350

[11]   Angraal S, Krumholz HM, Schulz WL. Blockchain technology. Circ Cardiovasc Qual Outcomes 2017; 10(9): e003800.
[http://dx.doi.org/10.1161/CIRCOUTCOMES.117.003800] [PMID: 28912202]

[12]   Narikimilli NRS, Kumar A, Antu AD, Xie B. Blockchain applications in healthcare – A review and future perspective. Lect Notes Comput Sci 2020; 12404: 198-218.
[http://dx.doi.org/10.1007/978-3-030-59638-5_14]

[13]   Liang X, Zhao J, Shetty S. Integrating blockchain for data sharing and collaboration in mobile healthcare applications. Proc IEEE Annu Int Symp Pers Indoor Mobile Radio Commun 2017. Available from: https://ieeexplore.ieee.org/abstract/document/8292361/
[http://dx.doi.org/10.1109/PIMRC.2017.8292361]

[14]   Alromaihi S. Cyber security challenges of deploying IoT in smart cities for healthcare applications. Proc IEEE Int Conf Commun 2018. Available from: https://ieeexplore.ieee.org/abstract/document/8488188/
[http://dx.doi.org/10.1109/W-FiCloud.2018.00028]

[15]   Shah M, Li C, Sheng M, Zhang Y. Smarter smart contracts: Efficient consent management in health data sharing. Lect Notes Comput Sci 2020; 11924: 345-56.
[http://dx.doi.org/10.1007/978-3-030-34482-5_31]

[16]   Sookhak M, Jabbarpour M, Safa N. Blockchain and smart contract for access control in healthcare: A survey, issues and challenges, and open issues. Elsevier 2021. Available from: https://www.sciencedirect.com/science/article/pii/S1084804520304045
[http://dx.doi.org/10.1016/j.jnca.2020.102950]

[17] Staples M, Chen S, Falamaki S. Risks and opportunities for systems using blockchain and smart contracts 2017. Available from: https://www.academia.edu/download/102517822/Blockchains_20and_20Smart_20Contracts.pdf

[18] Griggs KN, Ossipova O, Kohlios P, *et al.* A blockchain-based smart contract system for healthcare management. mdpicom 2018; 42(7): 130. Available from: https://www.mdpi.com/2079-9292/9/1/94

[19] Ribeiro Mda F. MedBlock: Using blockchain in health healthcare application based on blockchain and smart contracts 2020. Available from: https://cointhinktank.com/upload/crypto/Healthcare%20 Application%20based%20on%20Blockchain%20and%20Smart%20ContractS.pdf

[20] Liu K, Desai H, Kagal L. Enforceable data sharing agreements using smart contracts. arXiv preprint arXiv:180410645 2018. Available from: https://arxiv.org/abs/1804.10645

[21] Haque A, Muniat A. An automated approach towards smart healthcare with blockchain and smart contracts. Proc IEEE Int Conf Intell Comput Control 2021. Available from: https://ieeexplore.ieee.org/abstract/document/9397158/
[http://dx.doi.org/10.1109/ICCCIS51004.2021.9397158]

[22] Hasan H, Salah K, Jayaraman R. Blockchain-enabled telehealth services using smart contracts. Proc IEEE Int Conf Telemed eHealth 2021. Available from: https://ieeexplore.ieee.org/abstract/document/9605640/
[http://dx.doi.org/10.1109/ACCESS.2021.3126025]

[23] Choudhury O, Sarker H, Rudolph N, *et al.* Enforcing human subject regulations using blockchain and smart contracts Available from: https://www.blockchainhealthcaretoday.com/index.php/journal/article/view/10

[24] Chapter S, Rupasinghe T, Burstein F, Rudolph C. Blockchain-based dynamic patient consent: A privacy-preserving data acquisition architecture for clinical data analytics 2019. Available from: https://research.monash.edu/en/publications/blockchain-based-dynamic-patient-consent-a-privacy-preserving-dat

[25] Available from: https://scholar.google.com/scholar?hl=en&as_sdt=0%2C5&q=Facilitating+Patient+Consent+and+Data+Sharing+with+Blockchain+Smart+Contracts+&btnG=

[26] Jaiman V. A consent model for blockchain-based health data sharing platforms. IEEE Access 2020. Available from: https://ieeexplore.ieee.org/abstract/document/9159120/
[http://dx.doi.org/10.1109/ACCESS.2020.3014565]

[27] Kiseleva A, Kotzinos D, De Hert P. Transparency of AI in healthcare as a multilayered system of accountabilities: Between legal requirements and technical limitations. Front Artif Intell 2022; 5. 879603.
[http://dx.doi.org/10.3389/frai.2022.879603] [PMID: 35707765]

[28] Azaria A, Ekblaw A, *et al.* Medrec: Using blockchain for medical data access and permission management. IEEE Trans Open Big Data 2016. Available from: https://ieeexplore.ieee.org/abstract/document/7573685/

[29] Liu K, Desai H, Kagal L, Kantarcioglu M. Enforceable data sharing agreements using smart contracts 2018. Available from: https://arxiv.org/abs/1804.10645

[30] Shah M, Li C, Sheng M, Zhang Y, Xing C. CrowdMed: A blockchain-based approach to consent management for health data sharing. Lect Notes Comput Sci. 2019; 11924: pp. (LNCS)345-56.

[31] Albalwy F, Brass A, Davies A. informatics AD. A blockchain-based dynamic consent architecture to support clinical genomic data sharing (ConsentChain): Proof-of-concept study. JMIR Med Inform 2021; 9(11): e27816.
[http://dx.doi.org/10.2196/27816] [PMID: 34730538]

[32] Vardhini B, Dass S. A blockchain-based electronic medical health records framework using smart contracts. Proc Int Conf Commun Comput Netw 2021. Available from:

https://ieeexplore.ieee.org/abstract/document/9402689/

[33] Sneha S, Panjwani A, Lade B. Alleviating challenges related to FDA-approved medical wearables using blockchain technology. Proc IEEE Int Conf Real-Time Comput Robot 2021. Available from: https://ieeexplore.ieee.org/abstract/document/9520233/

[34] Elkourdi F, Wei C, Xiao L. Exploring current practices and challenges of HIPAA compliance in software engineering: Scoping review. JMIR Med Inform 2024; 12(3).

[35] J. Clavin and K. P. Joshi. Policy integrated blockchain to automate HIPAA Part 2 compliance. IEEE International Conference on Digital Health (ICDH), Chicago, IL, USA, 2023; 307-14. Available from: https://ieeexplore.ieee.org/abstract/document/10224728/

[36] Ettaloui N, Arezki S, Gadi T. An overview of blockchain-based electronic health record and compliance with GDPR and HIPAA. Lect Notes Netw Syst 2024; 838: 405-12. [http://dx.doi.org/10.1007/978-3-031-48573-2_58]

[37] Ettaloui N, Arezki S, Gadi T. An Overview of Blockchain-Based Electronic Health Record and Compliance with GDPR and HIPAA. Lect Notes Netw Syst 2024; 838: 405-12. [http://dx.doi.org/10.1007/978-3-031-48573-2_58]

CHAPTER 14

Startup Innovations: Blockchain Solutions for Integrity and Transparency in Pharmaceutical Supply Chains

Riya Sharma[1,*], **Kiran Deep Singh**[2], **Prabh Deep Singh**[3] and **Ambika Prakash Mani**[1]

[1] *Department of Commerce, Graphic Era Deemed to be University, Dehradun, Uttarakhand, India*

[2] *Department of Computer Science and Engineering, Chitkara University Institute of Engineering and Technology, Rajpura, Punjab, India*

[3] *Department of Computer Science and Engineering, Graphic Era Deemed to be University, Dehradun, Uttarakhand, India*

Abstract: The pharmaceutical supply chain plays a critical role in infrastructure that ensures the delivery of safe and effective drugs to consumers. However, the prevalence of counterfeit drugs poses a significant risk to public health, intellectual property, and industry development. Blockchain technology, with its decentralized and immutable ledger, offers a robust solution to these challenges. This chapter is an attempt to explore the role of blockchain technology in ensuring the integrity and transparency of the pharmaceutical supply chain. The study presents a comprehensive overview of research studies and patents on the use of blockchain technology in diverse industries. Essentially, a blockchain is a string of transactional blocks linked by a hashing algorithm to the previous block. This chapter proposes blockchain-based processes designed to ensure the integrity and transparency of the supply chain in the pharmaceutical industry. With a detailed case study and examples, this chapter illustrates how startups and pioneering blockchain-based solutions create a secure, transparent supply chain. Additionally, this chapter also examines the integration of smart contracts in transactions, emphasizing their role in automating compliance and streamlining processes. The study discusses regulatory compliance in deploying blockchain solutions. Analyzing the potential of blockchain to enhance the supply chain's integrity and transparency, this chapter offers valuable insights for entrepreneurs, industry professionals, and policymakers. The study demonstrates how blockchain technology can be leveraged to combat counterfeit drugs and ensure a more sustainable and resilient pharmaceutical industry.

Keywords: Automation, Blockchain solutions, Drug safety, Intellectual property protection, Industry development, Public health.

---

* **Corresponding author Riya Sharma:** Department of Commerce, Graphic Era Deemed to be University, Dehradun, Uttarakhand, India; E-mail: riyasharma6568@gmail.com

Mohit Angurala, Preet Kamal, Aryan Chaudhary, Rasmeet Singh Bali & Vijay Bhardwaj (Eds.)
All rights reserved-© 2025 Bentham Science Publishers

INTRODUCTION TO THE PHARMACEUTICAL SUPPLY CHAIN

The role of the pharmaceutical industry has evolved in developing chemical and biological compounds capable of curing diseases and health problems. While the development stage of a drug is particularly complex and involves numerous elements, the elements usually highlighted are of a scientific nature [1]. However, the development of new drugs and medications is not only based on chemical and pharmaceutical elements but also involves economic and business considerations that are key during the production, distribution, and sales stages. It is in these stages that the collaboration and cooperation of all actors involved are key to ensuring the correct functioning of the pharmaceutical supply chain. The pharmaceutical industry involves the production and selling of pharmaceutical products and services. Thus, the industry is complex and needs a comprehensive approach to incorporate all players in the supply chain [2]. There are different key stakeholders associated with the production and selling of pharmaceutical products that interact with each other to ensure that patients receive medicines at the right time. One of these is the manufacturers who undertake research and development, manufacture pharmaceuticals, and finally extract the pharmaceutical products. They ensure that pharmaceutical products are made available to the retailers or the wholesalers. The transportation companies are responsible for moving the products from one player to the other [3]. The task needs to be completed in a timely manner so that the drug order arrives in good condition. Although each of these players is significant, this study focuses on wholesalers in the pharmaceutical supply chain, and more specifically counterfeit drugs, to find out how blockchain technology can be used to ensure integrity and transparency in the pharmaceutical supply chain. In the evolutionary landscape of the pharmaceutical industry, where product integrity and patient safety are paramount, startups are pioneering innovative solutions that are powered by blockchain technology. Blockchain's immutable leisure system helps startups to reshape the traditional supply chain paradigm, which ensures transparency and traceability of the pharmaceutical journey at every stage [4]. From research and development to distribution and consuming engagement, blockchain offers a robust structure for verifying product origins, validating the manufacturing process, and safeguarding against counterfeit products. With groundbreaking initiatives, startups are not only revolutionizing the supply chain but also building trust and confidence among consumers, ultimately leading to the advancement of the industry toward a more secure and sustainable future. An illustration of how different stakeholders in the pharmaceutical supply chain interact with the blockchain network is presented in Fig. (1). The system includes a user interface and involves manufacturers, distributors, retailers, pharmacies, and patients. The blockchain network integrates a smart contract layer and a data storage layer, which further utilizes an encryption module and an access control module to ensure secure and transparent transactions. Firstly, this chapter defines the pharmaceutical supply chain in order to refer to the main problems and risks in this area. The study also addresses the legislative and regulatory measures that have been implemented to control and regulate the activities of companies in this sector. Finally, we will also explore the solutions, especially blockchain technology, that can be implemented in the supply chain, allowing greater visibility and integrity, eliminating intermediaries, and increasing cooperation between the different actors involved. The chapter ends with a brief reflection on public policies that can be established in this area and identifies future opportunities for analysis and research in this area.

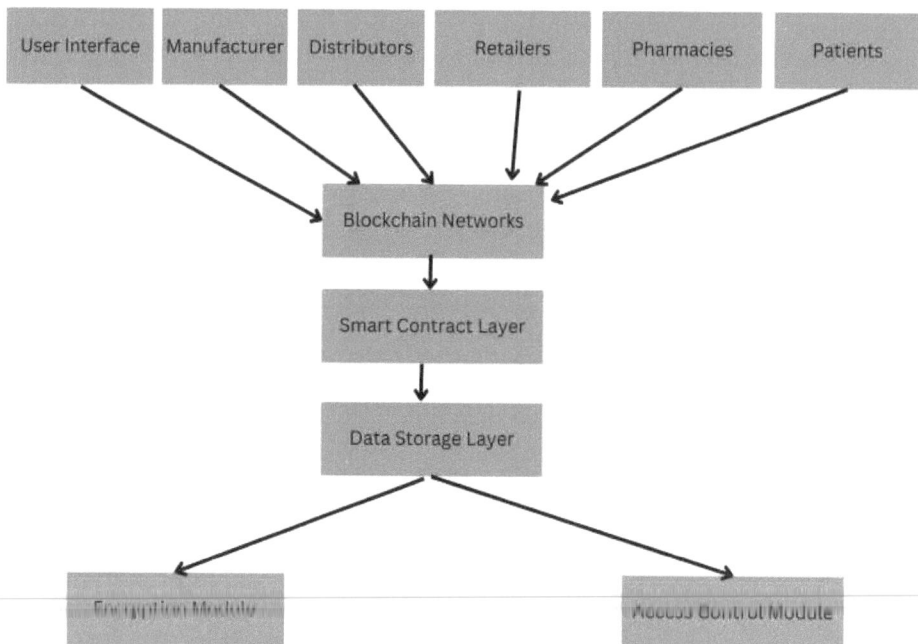

Fig. (1). Blockchain-based pharmaceutical supply chain architecture.

Challenges in the Current Pharmaceutical Supply Chain

In the case of detection of counterfeit drugs available for consumers, the company appears in the press and headlines negatively. This is because the population fears that the product that they have bought is fake and does not meet the necessary standards and sanitary standards, which increases the possibility of harming health, making complaints, and demanding compensation [5]. For this reason, the use of blockchain technology appears as a technology that provides several solutions to minimize these threats and risks, thus creating a transparent, efficient, and reliable link, making it possible to distribute high-quality medicines to patients with more agility and efficiency in their care [6]. The supply chain used in the pharmaceutical industry is complex and demands a high level of control and surveillance, as well as engagement on the part of all the links involved, in order to guarantee the integrity, safety, quality, and efficacy of the medicines that are traded [7]. The supply chain of the pharmaceutical industry is extensive and involves a vast pyramid with several links; for this reason, it encompasses various agents, such as manufacturers, distributors, suppliers, patients, hospitals, pharmacies, and health service providers [8]. The fact that the supply chain is very broad results in various potential risks that may lead to the possibility of distributing counterfeit [9], fraudulent, deteriorated, or expired drugs to patients, which is detrimental to the pharmaceutical chain and, above all, to the final consumer [10]. These are risks of loss of credibility, increasing insecurity in the production chain, and damage to the current company or investor and various societies caused by these threats to the health and integrity of individual consumers [11].

Counterfeit Drugs and Substandard Medications

Counterfeit drugs are those intended to deceive and contain misleading information about their contents, origin, or history. Counterfeiting is commonly associated with drugs that are produced without legal authorization or using false information [12]. Such drugs often do not contain or are contaminated with other substances, *i.e.*, external substances may not be effective, but more often, they have dangerous side effects and are poisonous. Counterfeit drugs, corruption, and organized crime are generally interconnected issues. Such drugs are usually sold at prices similar to their original counterparts. In fact, all mislabeled drugs are substandard, but not all substandard drugs are counterfeit [13]. Counterfeit drugs are usually a subject of intentional wrongdoing, and their effects may result both in immediate and long-term health as well as economic consequences. In recent years, there has been considerable interest in this issue both by governments and the pharmaceutical industry. According to the World Health Organization (WHO), substandard drugs are those with active ingredients whose content is not within the acceptable range or drugs that fail to meet established standards for their qualities, as well as description, packaging, and labeling of such drugs that do not meet the specification or labeling [14]. Substandard medications may be a result of negligence, fraud, accidental contamination, tampering, low quality of production, storage and handling, or intentional misinformation. Substandard drugs are a common issue in less developed countries where only a fraction of the drugs in markets are registered with health authorities, and law enforcement of drug manufacturers is unreliable to a great extent. Substandard drugs are frequently a result of negligence, usually on the part of manufacturers, which is associated with the companies' pursuit of profits and negligence in the process of producing drugs, including the ambiguous race to drive down prices and reduce costs [3]. Fig. (**2**) illustrates the track and trace process of pharmaceuticals in a blockchain-enabled supply chain. Manufacturers provide pharmaceuticals, which are then stored on the blockchain network. Smart contracts are executed to validate the data, after which distributors handle the distribution of pharmaceuticals to retailers. Retailers supply the pharmaceuticals to pharmacies, which then dispense them to patients. Feedback from patients is collected and provided back to the blockchain network to ensure continuous monitoring and improvement.

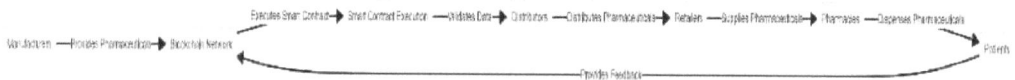

Fig. (2). Track and trace of pharmaceuticals using blockchain.

UNDERSTANDING BLOCKCHAIN TECHNOLOGY

There are four critical components of a blockchain that allow it to function effectively. Identity verification, such as digital keys, ensures the accuracy and integrity of the data. A decentralized peer-to-peer network, referred to as a distributed ledger, allows all participants to communicate and update transaction details [15]. A consensus method is implemented to ensure that once a transaction has been verified, it can only be written to the blockchain once and cannot be tampered with. Finally, once a transaction is verified and added to the block, it becomes tamper-proof, achievable through cryptography and distributed consensus to securely add new transactions to the tamper-proof blockchain. Due to these characteristics, a well-implemented blockchain has strong security, data integrity, and trustworthiness features, making it well-suited for applications requiring the tracking of information, including pharmaceutical molecules, in the supply chain. Blockchain technology is a decentralized and distributed digital ledger that records and maintains a history of transactions [16]. Blockchain technology operates on a peer-to-peer network architecture where every member in this network has access to the entire ledger, and all members execute the functions of a central authority serving the need to track, authenticate, and verify transactions [17]. To ensure the ever-increasing number of transactions are processed and added to the ledger, the technology incorporates a consensus algorithm that ensures consensus among network members is reached. Once verified, the transactional blocks are added to the chain and effectively become an unalterable record [18].

Definition and Basics of Blockchain

The process of creating a chain of blocks is an ongoing activity known as mining. It involves nodes continually solving computational problems. Anyone who first solves a given problem can add the next created block to their copy of the blockchain and distribute their new copy. Blockchain technology is the underlying technology of the Bitcoin cryptocurrency. A blockchain is a chain of data blocks. In this case, the data blocks can contain Bitcoin data. In general, however, they can contain any kind of data. A blockchain is decentralized and distributed. All participants, which are called nodes, have their own copy of it. More simply, the blockchain is a linked chain of blocks. A block is a collection of data. Essentially, it is a form of immortal timestamp and is maintained by multiple parties. When a transaction happens, a digital signature is created. All transactions are broadcast to all nodes. Each node gets the data and creates a new block, which is then added to their local copy of the blockchain. We can think of the blockchain as a shared ledger, but it works in a different way from the above classical way. The shared ledger is maintained by nodes (although each node may not have the entire ledger) and not by a central trusted authority. The integrity of the blockchain relies on the cryptographic strength of the data in each block of the chain, as well as the linking to the previous block back to the original block.

Applications of Blockchain in the Pharmaceutical Supply Chain

Besides the blockchain-based pharmaceutical market authorization system, the authentication of market authorization documents, delivery notes, invoices, transport bills, *etc.*, that confirm the correct origin of the pharmaceutical can be done. As the blockchain is a list distributed among network participants, any change in the token, digital document base, or its snapshot leads to the desynchronization of the chain participant [19]. Then, synchronization among the chain participants can be recovered only by mutual consent and an adequate level of trust in the system. Finally, a platform with anti-forgery, which is based on blockchain technology, can provide pharmaceutical consumers with guarantees of high-quality and safe products that have undergone all stages of controlled production [20]. When manufacturers of full-cycle drugs and intermediates use domestically produced excipients and API, then the guarantee of the origin of the pharmaceutical starts from R&D. It is then possible to talk about different types of printing materials at the level of API production, labeling, and packaging, which must be in the process of obtaining a QR code with information about the origin of the pharmaceuticals. The main point of using blockchain technology in the pharmaceutical supply chain is to ensure the integrity of the products [21]. This can be realized through a comprehensive approach that includes verification of manufacturers and product origin, verification of pharmaceutical manufacturing processes and accompanying documentation, protection of product visual characteristics, and patient identification and validation. Fig. (3) illustrates which blockchain features can be used at which stage of the pharmaceutical product supply chain.

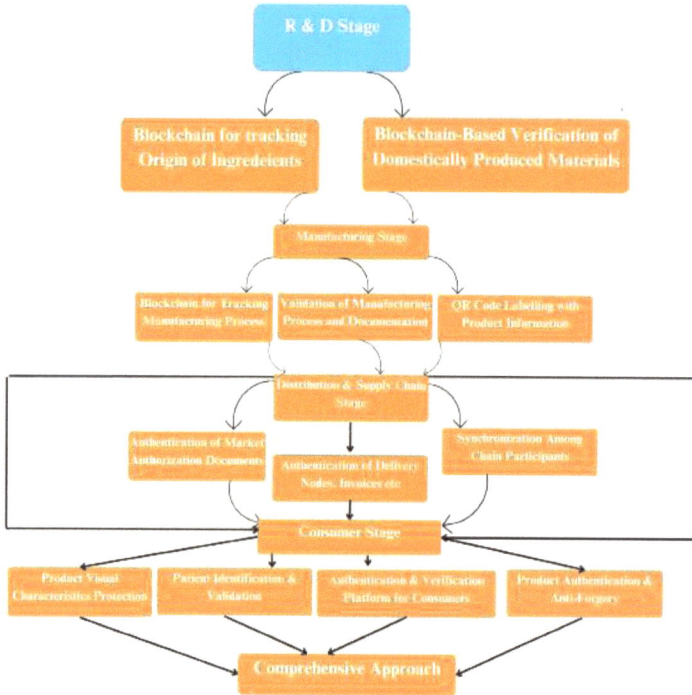

Fig. (3). Blockchain-based framework for ensuring integrity in the pharmaceutical supply chain.

TRACKING AND TRACING PHARMACEUTICAL PRODUCTS

Blockchain technology links as a chain of blocks involving cryptographic techniques and algorithms. The theoretical aspects include earlier time or transaction-dependable entries linked as blocks-balancing hash values, including current time stamped and transaction data elements [22]. Hash computations further yield the previous block's content and thereby cement the sequence of time impending to the present blocks. The graphical methodology, such as fan-in or fan-out, is included for ease of understanding. The procedural path is used to validate each transaction that occurs by the consensus-building investigating procedure [23]. Arrested blocks yield cryptographic accuracy and trustworthiness when the maximum number of participants are online. This trait enables the decentralized network to use board consensus system functionality runtime facilitated once the privately maintained data is imposed on the users, entities, and parties with pre-defined trust issuing and resolution authorities such as commercial regulations, laws, and policies. Productive generic data are included in a block to enable multi-faceted attributes of real sectoral business dealings.

The pharmaceutical landscape relies largely on integrity, transparency, and assurance, as depicted in Fig. (**4**). Public trust largely backs the pharmaceutical environment. In this perspective, the pharmaceutical landscape fades under various shadows, such as counterfeiting, terrorism, infiltration, money-laundering, fraud, and glitches. The integrity and security of the pharmaceutical landscape are addressed by deploying cryptographic protocols, digitization, and documentation. It failed considerably to improve the pharmaceutical landscape's integrity and natural eco-friendly policies, offering social and policy benefits and consequences. This is due to diligent improvement and mainly attributed to blockchain yielding operational ability, transparency, consensus-building effectiveness, decentralization, and non-compromising, facilitating continuous integrity and enabling tech.

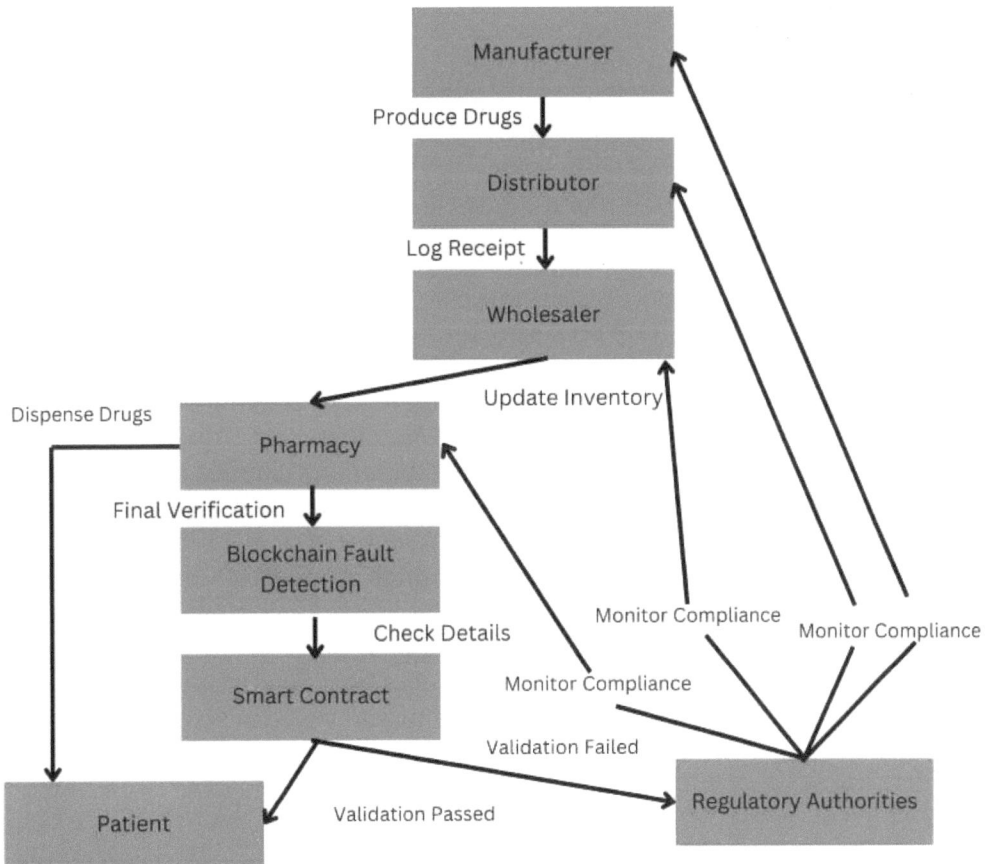

Fig. (4). Blockchain-integrated supply chain mechanism using smart contracts.

BENEFITS OF IMPLEMENTING BLOCKCHAIN TECHNOLOGY

Companies implementing blockchain solutions also notice a significant reduction in inventory costs. With real-time data about the location and journey of a medicine, companies can more accurately anticipate demand. This helps to reduce the large amount of working capital needed to secure the availability of necessary drugs. Another benefit is that the prices for the medicines can be reduced. The tendency of counterfeit goods to dodge tariffs and taxes creates costs that companies are forced to pass on to consumers. People end up paying more for products than they would if no additional costs had to be considered due to a lack of visibility. Another significant benefit of pharmaceutical blockchain technology is that it improves patient safety by giving clinicians the resources they need to ensure the effectiveness of the treatment they provide patients. They will be able to prevent potentially dangerous interactions and also ensure that the medication is appropriately prescribed. Companies and organizations that are part of the pharmaceutical supply chain can also benefit from the data that blockchain technology provides. This becomes especially true when recalls need to be made from the market, as the available data will be critical to identify the patients who need to change the medicines they take. Companies that implement pharmaceutical blockchain technology realize several key benefits. One of the most critical benefits is that blockchain significantly reduces the chances of counterfeit drugs entering the pharmaceutical supply chain. There is a guarantee that the drugs arriving are of the best quality and that they are not from questionable sources.

Enhanced Transparency and Traceability

Enhanced transparency and traceability can be the key for supply chain efficiency, positively impacting patient safety. As discussed earlier, one instance where blockchain has been deployed in healthcare is to support pharmaceutical companies in their compliance endeavors. Pharmaceutical companies often deal with different countries' regulations. In addition, the raw materials necessary for producing a certain pharmaceutical drug are often sourced by these countries. In this case, counterfeiting activity often occurs during these movements. By using blockchain as a platform, pharmaceutical companies can easily prove and verify their compliance with regulatory guidelines at every stage of the production and shipment process. This would increase the integrity and, hence, the trust of the public towards the pharmaceutical companies.

The implementation of blockchain-enabled technologies in pharmaceutical supply chains materializes as pharmaceutical companies increasingly recognize its value, revolutionizing the core functions of the pharmaceutical sector. The first main benefit of adopting blockchain for stakeholders in the pharmaceutical supply chain is found in the improvement of transparency and traceability. Such a feature can increase the trust of the patient in the medication that they are consuming by being more transparent about the information available. With integrity granted in the data, all stakeholders in the supply chain have confidence in the data, hence being able to make the best decisions when it comes to medical purchases or the prescription of medicine.

REGULATORY CONSIDERATIONS AND COMPLIANCE IN THE PHARMACEUTICAL INDUSTRY

So far, regulatory approaches have mainly evolved towards controlling market access and actions after illicit products have been detected. Although increased granularity of product information exists today, such as unique identification numbers and data matrix codes, significant data integrity challenges still persist. The intersection of life sciences companies, governments, manufacturing, wholesale, and retail locations is complex and influences all four attributes of supply chain interactions, namely provenance, consensus, immutability, and finality. The counterbalance to ensure information integrity, transparency, and the immutability of data originating within pharmaceutical supply chain networks could well be provided by decentralized ledger technologies, such as the blockchain. However, legal provisions for the use of blockchain solutions within heavily regulated industries may or may not be met based on current regulations. Large pharmaceutical companies are, therefore, faced with challenging questions of regulatory compliance. These questions are addressed in the following section through analysis and potential channels for legal compliance. The development of new medical treatments over generations has resulted in continued advancements in public health and increased human lifespan. The pharmaceutical industry plays a foundational role in the delivery of these treatments at a global-enabled scale. In order to support large-scale manufacturing, the pharmaceutical supply chain network has grown in size and complexity through the involvement of multiple stakeholders who are interconnected in order to deliver raw materials and components to the final products. Supply chains within the pharmaceutical and food industries share common characteristics in how they are managed. Strong regulatory requirements aim to protect consumers by overseeing distribution activities. However, within the pharmaceutical contrast to food supply chains, the integrity of medical products has been challenged by unauthorized trade channels. Counterfeit and falsified medicines do not only threaten human health but also the long-standing reputation and business continuity of the involved manufacturers.

Current Regulations and Guidelines

According to current GTFA regulations and guidelines, proprietary data, which may include all patient information other than certain limited data and data submitted with a drug application, should remain confidential and limited to those who need to know [4]. It will only be provided to parties with the consent of the patient or under certain legal conditions. All member companies of GTFA have adopted or are in the process of adopting GTFA security agreement standards and evaluation standards for handling proprietary data in the chronic phase of the clinical trial lifecycle. In addition to proprietary data security agreements and evaluations, all member companies of GTFA are also taking careful and deliberate steps to ensure that GTFA's mission and the security practices and procedures they follow in the field of clinical research are consistent with the relevant requirements of the data privacy and protection regulatory framework in each region. Only in this way can proprietary data be best assured. To ensure drug supply integrity and protect drug safety, many countries have formulated and promulgated laws, regulations, and guidelines according to their own national conditions to regulate the pharmaceutical supply chain.

CASE STUDIES OF SUCCESSFUL BLOCKCHAIN IMPLEMENTATIONS IN THE PHARMACEUTICAL SUPPLY CHAIN

The chapter highlights blockchain through successful case studies that provide transparency and authenticity in pharmaceutical product delivery, tamper-proof their integrity, and steadfastly reinforce the secure pharmaceutical supply chain. Most importantly, the case studies tell us how the pharmaceutical sector can sustain its profitability, its primary objective of safeguarding people's health, and the bigger picture of sustaining the life and existence of humanity [24]. Hurdles, possible action plans, and suggestions are tabulated and summarized at the end of the paper, and the unanswered blockchain debate posed by critics remains unresolved. In this section, a case study of successful blockchain implementations in the pharmaceutical supply chain-based startup is presented to illustrate how the technology can bring not only transparency but also authenticity within the supply chain, safeguard the integrity of products at risk of tampering, and improve the delivery and storage practices of medical treasures [25]. Various hurdles faced are summarized, too. There is no perfect solution to implementing blockchain technology, and - more importantly - emerging dilemmas and unresolved problems continue to saturate discussions. Appropriate countermeasures are suggested. Careful scrutiny of these blockchain healthcare projects would provide pertinent insights to those who plan to venture into the pharmaceutical horizon.

Project MediLedger

In the private sector, different solutions have been developed for several use cases, for blockchains to aid in securing the supply chain for the end customer. These implementations are mainly privately initiated and serve, for example, the purpose of ensuring assurance in the trading of responsibly manufactured methanol, allowing stakeholders to share transport data of fresh produce, ensuring that cobalt in Li-ion batteries comes from ethical sourcing, ensuring responsible gold trading, and the secure trading of diamonds. They all demonstrate the capability of blockchain-based systems to ensure the integrity and transparency of their respective supply chain and, in this case, show their relevance for ensuring integrity and transparency in the PDO supply chain as well. Project MediLedger aims to create a blockchain-based system for the United States Drug Supply Chain Security Act. This act requires that all parties trading prescription drugs should not just provide a paper-based chain of custody but also a digital one. The act sets out that the blockchain-based system should allow for permission-based exchange of ownership, support interoperability with the different systems of the stakeholders in the pharmaceutical supply chain, and enable a report from the Secretary of the U.S. Health and Human Services that confirm the quality of the trading transaction information that can be documented and proven by a blockchain-based solution. Thereby, the transparency and integrity of prescription drugs can be ensured. With this requirement, the U.S. requires all parties to implement and maintain systems that are secure and able to support the proper management of serialized data and exchange of information, as well as a secure electronic system that enables verification and investigation at a later point in time.

The Medrec Case

The Medrec case - a medical smart contract: Medrec was developed at the MIT Media Lab with the aim of implementing a decentralized record management system for globally distributed medical data. The fundamental concept was to replace a single organization with a smart contract, essentially creating a virtual database managed by the Ethereum platform. Smart contracts are not meant for managing large databases. As it is made to execute specific functions, creating a large virtual file and allowing access do not require a giant copy to be placed in each Ethereum wallet in the world. A logical solution to this scaling issue might be to logically make the file itself virtual, managing the way each server within the network can access a piece of the file. The fact that everybody within a network has a full copy of that network can create scalability issues. Imagine having all Bitcoin transactions saved in every single wallet. This would happen if each wallet was part of a transparent "ledger-like" network. It is natural that some wallet developers would try to scale to accommodate a very small percentage of that network, as not everyone could fit in every wallet. The logical way to slice the network would be around the number of transactions within some timeframe. This is one of the blockchain's unfinished tasks [26]. Bitcoin is made to distribute transactions with a need to be "signed" by the hash of the previous one (almost like a series of passwords), which keeps the network secure. However, there are several areas of non-voting documents where a complete copy of the network is not necessary.

CHALLENGES AND LIMITATIONS OF BLOCKCHAIN TECHNOLOGY IN THE PHARMACEUTICAL SUPPLY CHAIN

Regulatory issues state that blockchain technologies can sometimes be in breach of possible inconsistencies in the transfer of the organization. While regulations typically specify how current technologies should be implemented, emerging legislation is frequently cited as a barrier to the implementation of the platform. A certain number of legislation suggested that in January 2019, in the pharmaceutical supply chain, blockchain can be used. Such laws also aim to prevent and monitor illegal supply chain operations by utilizing the technology. The CAL. State. Sec. 116365 codicil, proposed in 2017, extended this guideline in express wording. For example, the US Food and Drug Administration (FDA) and the European Parliament have made efforts to delegate those who develop and enforce blockchain restrictions to facilitate and oversee the specific drug traceability dynamics [27]. Tech organizations have made credential or pharmaceutical serialization services accessible that utilize blockchain technology to further reduce distribution inconsistency. Full party-wise control and clearance will exist in a blockchain-based closed-loop facility. Designed to be computer intensive and work in authentic vast network settings, blockchain network capacity solutions are still restricted. The low capacity of the blockchain network can easily have major implications for widespread transaction usage and is also present in the pharmaceutical supply chain. With only two to ten drugs available from the manufacturer to the wholesaler and pharmacy, constraints in the number of transactions per second in Bitcoin make the technology a small solution. As for public Ethereum, the number of operations per second is much lower [20], and a huge trading volume in large-scale pharmaceutical supply chains will surpass this. It can have extremely high environmental costs as a result of the significant amount of energy used to mitigate network congestion by raising miner fees. With a small percentage of economic transactions in Europe or the US, blockchain consumes proportionately up to 1% and 2%. With massive transaction amounts, minimal consumer fees will be high. Such drop-out transactions in the pharmaceutical field will be denied access or induced for unauthorized sales.

FUTURE TRENDS AND INNOVATIONS IN BLOCKCHAIN FOR PHARMACEUTICAL SUPPLY CHAIN INTEGRITY

Numerous limitations and concerns surround current electronic healthcare record systems related to privacy, security, and patient control. Blockchain technology can address these limitations because its unique characteristics ensure the integrity of electronic healthcare records. An in-depth analysis of the specific aspects of blockchain integration in the healthcare sector is provided, such as reducing healthcare costs, decreasing user error and fraud, privacy, data security, reducing paperwork, providing access to critical information, establishing transparency, and providing the complete track and trace of records without any intervention of a third party. The adoption of blockchain technology in the healthcare system is, however, at a preliminary stage; therefore, it is important to identify future research themes and forecast future development trends. Emerging blockchain technology presents numerous potential benefits for securing electronic healthcare records. The unique characteristics of blockchain technology address some of the limitations and concerns of current electronic healthcare record systems related to privacy, security, and patient control. They consider innovative platforms that integrate secondary technologies for more effective implementation.

Integration with the Internet of Things (IoT)

The primary aim of the research is to address how to achieve a good integration of blockchain technology at interfaces with IoT devices, which play a significant role within the supply chain. This research uses a multiple case study qualitative approach in a specific supply chain case. By integrating findings from literature review and case studies, new procedural guidelines are presented. Five factors are identified that are needed to integrate the two technologies: how the case company sees the potential of the technology and contextual differences, aspects of understanding, understanding the implementation (technology-specific issues), the life cycle of the technology, and lastly, regulatory issues from various points of enforcement. These factors will benefit both management and researchers and act as a basis for further technology integration development within the supply chain.

Over 40% of pharmaceuticals in the world are counterfeit, with the highest proportion affecting developing countries. The pharmaceutical supply chain, especially in developing countries, is very fragmented as a result of outrageous numbers of intermediaries in the distribution chain. Other problems identified also include counterfeiting, poor-quality drugs, inefficient recalls, *etc.* The application of blockchain technology is promising and can help address the issues of integrity and transparency throughout the supply chain. However, the technology is still in its infancy in actual practical implementation. Specifically, how the technology acts within the supply chain is unknown, as there are currently very few existing solutions at this level.

CONCLUSION

Integrity and transparency in the pharmaceutical supply chain are pressing policy challenges today. Aggregation of transaction records, which removes any information related to the underlying set of lines of data linked with the transaction record, creates a permanent silent record of every transaction event for the passive participant. The aggregation of DSCSA transactions would have to evolve in the current US and global supply chains before such information can be included in the T3 system from embedded blocks involving product data sharing. Organization of the supply chain transactions for these states will need to have a more detailed level of information included in addition to the DSCSA information. The organization of these aggregated systems would need to be organized. Blockchain, as we saw, can be an alternative approach to the organization of these systems. A unique view, for example, uses currently produced data to follow step-by-step events in which a separate product changes.

What are the software's major testing characteristics? Although some testing procedures are now more complex, the already-known methods and practices can be used. However, because of the mandatory requirement for at least one "system" test by 1 July 2019, acting agents may need to perform phased experiments in the early phases. Developed for a known company, the third-party logistic provider currently offers logistics of product transport, storage, and supply chain processes and also provides other value-added services, such as procurement support, healthcare, *etc.* It specifies the timing through which they will become the third-party logistics

The biggest challenge of implementing the DSCSA is predictable, safe, and reliable access to new learners by means of a data exchange system. Because the acting agent market has very high market barriers (legal authorization, competence, *etc.*), an alternative regulatory model is needed to alleviate or weed out these barriers. A combination of technical, economic, and legal regulations can alleviate the foreseeable challenges that cloud-based FWDs will bring forth. The sponsors will also ensure that methods are in place for sufficient monitoring of the FWD logistic activities.

AUTHORS' CONTRIBUTION

In Chapter 14, **Riya Sharma, Kiran Deep Singh, Prabh Deep Singh,** and **Ambika Prakash Mani** collaborated to analyze blockchain applications in pharmaceutical supply chains, focusing on integrity and transparency. **Riya Sharma** led the exploration of blockchain's potential in enhancing supply chain efficiency and traceability, with emphasis on its role in mitigating counterfeit risks. **Kiran Deep Singh** contributed to reviewing the technical aspects of blockchain, including its decentralized framework and implications for regulatory compliance in the pharmaceutical industry. **Prabh Deep Singh** conducted a case study analysis of startups using blockchain solutions to improve drug safety and traceability. **Ambika Prakash Mani** focused on smart contract automation in supply chains, identifying blockchain-based solutions for transparency and compliance. Together, the authors provided insights into blockchain's transformative impact on pharmaceutical supply chains and offered a roadmap for startups and industry stakeholders.

REFERENCES

[1] Journal SSI. Digital traceability of pharmaceutical drugs in the supply chain 2022. Available from: https://www.researchgate.net/profile/ShambhuSarkar/publication/361119086_Digital_Traceability_of_ pharmaceutical_drugs_in_supply_chain/links/629e7f27a3fe3e3df8637eda/Digital-Traceability-of-pharmaceutical-drugs-in-supply-chain.pdf

[2] Tseng J, Liao Y, Chong B. Governance on the drug supply chain *via* gcoin blockchain. 2018. Available from: https://www.mdpi.com/1660-4601/15/6/1055

[3] Singh D, Chaddah JK. A study on application of blockchain technology to control counterfeit drugs, enhance data privacy and improve distribution in online pharmacy. Asia Pac J Health Manag 2021; 16(3): 59-66.
[http://dx.doi.org/10.24083/apjhm.v16i3.1013]

[4] Institute KD. Case studies on the regulatory challenges raised by innovation and the regulatory responses 2021. Available from: https://books.google.com/books?hl=en&lr=&id=XpJUEAAAQBAJ &oi=fnd&pg=PA3&dq=Decentralized+ledger+Smart+contracts+Compliance+automation+Regulatory +compliance+Startup+innovations+Case+studies&ots=IBSSLpGSX5&sig=HNA304c0TZxeF3BsSUT hQsYGB0s

[5] Safety MTC. Medicines counterfeiting is a complex problem: a review of key challenges across the supply chain 2013. Available from: https://www.ingentaconnect.com/content/ben/cds/2013/00000008/ 00000001/art00007

[6] Kumar V, Ya K. Mapping the key challenges and managing the opportunities in supply chain distribution during COVID-19: a case of Myanmar pharmaceutical company. J Glob Oper Strateg Sourcing 2022. Available from: https://www.emerald.com/insight/content/doi/10.1108/JGOSS-01-2022-0002/full/html

[7] Alkhouri M. Pharmaceutical supply chain–new obstacles and challenges 2024. Available from: https://dspace.lib.uom.gr/handle/2159/30186

[8] Singh RK, Kumar R, Kumar P. Strategic issues in pharmaceutical supply chains: a review. Int J Pharm Healthc Mark 2016; 10(3): 234-57.
[http://dx.doi.org/10.1108/IJPHM-10-2015-0050]

[9] Available from: https://scholar.google.com/scholar?hl=en&as_sdt=0%2C5&q=Challenges+in+the+ Current+Pharmaceutical+Supply+Chain&btnG=

[10] Engineering NSC. Engineering NSC, chemical Pharmaceutical supply chains: key issues and strategies for optimisation 2004; 28: 929-41. Available from: https://www.sciencedirect.com/science/article/ pii/S0098135403002333

[11]   Srai JS, Badman C, Krumme M, Futran M, Johnston C. Future supply chains enabled by continuous processing—Opportunities and challenges. May 20–21, 2014 Continuous Manufacturing Symposium. J Pharm Sci 2015; 104(3): 840-9.
[http://dx.doi.org/10.1002/jps.24343]

[12]   Samanta Singhar S, Snigdha Sahoo S, Sahoo M, Sahoo M, Singhar SS, Sahoo SS. A blockchain-based model to eliminate drug counterfeiting 2020; 1101: 213-2. Available from: https://link.springer.com/chapter/10.1007/978-981-15-1884-3_20

[13]   Alam N, Tanvir M, Shanto S. Blockchain-based counterfeit medicine authentication system. Proc IEEE Int Conf Intell Sci Eng (ICISE) 2021.
[http://dx.doi.org/10.1109/ISCAIE51753.2021.9431789]

[14]   Uddin M. Blockchain Medledger: Hyperledger fabric enabled drug traceability system for counterfeit drugs in pharmaceutical industry. Int. J. Pharm. 2021; 597: 120235. Available from: https://www.sciencedirect.com/science/article/pii/S0378517321000399

[15]   Quzmar A. Reducing counterfeit drugs with blockchains: A survey. Proc IEEE Int Conf Ind Electron Syst (ICIES) 2021. Available from: https://ieeexplore.ieee.org/abstract/document/9491695/
[http://dx.doi.org/10.1109/ICIT52682.2021.9491695]

[16]   Yu Y, Li Q, Zhang Q, Hu W. Blockchain-based multi-role healthcare data sharing system 2021. Available from: https://ieeexplore.ieee.org/abstract/document/9399028
[http://dx.doi.org/10.1109/HEALTHCOM49281.2021.9399028]

[17]   Available from: https://scholar.google.com/scholar?start=10&q=Pharmaceutical+supply+chain+Counterfeit+drugs+Blockchain+technology&hl=en&as_sdt=0,5

[18]   Dangi S, Sharma R, Tomar R, Mani AP. Blockchain-based framework for Indian retail market in SMEs 2023. Available from: https://link.springer.com/chapter/10.1007/978-981-99-1620-7_22
[http://dx.doi.org/10.1007/978-981-99-1620-7_22]

[19]   Yu X, Li C, Shi Y, Huang MY. Pharmaceutical supply chain in China: current issues and implications for health system reform. Elsevier [Internet] 2010; 97: 8-15. Available from: https://www.sciencedirect.com/science/article/pii/S0168851010000564
[http://dx.doi.org/10.1016/j.healthpol.2010.02.010]

[20]   Moosivand A, Agheli GR, *et al.* Supply chain challenges in pharmaceutical manufacturing companies: using qualitative system dynamics methodology. J Pharm Policy Pract 2019. Available from: https://www.ncbi.nlm.nih.gov/pmc/articles/PMC6706717

[21]   Wen-Jie Z, Jian-Wen L. Supply chain option contract model with random yield and stochastic demand. J Ind Eng Eng Manag 2016; 20(3): 121-128.

[22]   Tamayo S, Quantumblack G, Nguyen A, Lamouri S, Pellerin R, Lekens B. Data analytics in pharmaceutical supply chains: state of the art, opportunities, and challenges. Taylor & Francis 2021; 60(22): 6888-907. Available from: https://www.tandfonline.com/doi/abs/10.1080/00207543.2021.1950937

[23]   Kumar V, Ya KZ, Lai KK. Mapping the key challenges and managing the opportunities in supply chain distribution during COVID-19: a case of Myanmar pharmaceutical company. J Glob Oper Strateg Sourc 2023; 16(2): 187-223.
[http://dx.doi.org/10.1108/JGOSS-01-2022-0002]

[24]   Dal Mas F, Dicuonzo G, Massaro M, Dell'Atti V. Smart contracts to enable sustainable business models. A case study. Manage Decis 2020; 58(8): 1601-19.
[http://dx.doi.org/10.1108/MD-09-2019-1266]

[25]   Cole R, Stevenson M, Aitken J. Blockchain technology: Implications for operations and supply chain management. Supply Chain Manag 2019; 24(4): 469–83.
[http://dx.doi.org/10.1108/SCM-09-2018-0309]

[26]　Fraga-Lamas P, Fernandez-Carames TM, Blanco-Novoa O, Vilar-Montesinos MA. Next generation auto-identification and traceability technologies for Industry 5.0: A methodology and practical use case for the shipbuilding industry. IEEE 2021. Available from: https://ieeexplore.ieee.org/abstract/document/9568924

[27]　Eggers J, Hein A, Weking J, Böhm M, Krcmar H. Process automation on the blockchain: an exploratory case study on smart contracts 2021. Available from: https://scholarspace.manoa.hawaii.edu/handle/10125/71301
[http://dx.doi.org/10.24251/HICSS.2021.681]

CHAPTER 15

The Future of Blockchain in Healthcare: Trends, Opportunities, and Challenges

Mohit Angurala[1], Rajeev Kumar Bedi[2,*], Gurpreet Singh Panesar[3] and **Navneet Kumar Rajpoot[4]**

[1] *Department of Computer Science, Guru Nanak Dev University College, Pathankot, Punjab, India*

[2] *Department of Computer Science and Engineering, I. K. Gujral Punjab Technical University, Jalandhar, Punjab, India*

[3] *Department of Computer Science and Engineering, Chandigarh University, Mohali, Punjab, India*

[4] *Department of Computer Science & Engineering, Graphic Era (Deemed to be University), Dehradun, India*

Abstract: Blockchain technology is revolutionizing the healthcare industry by enhancing data integrity, security, and interoperability. Healthcare data are principally fragmented by different systems and formats, making smooth data sharing difficult. Blockchain has the ability to standardize data exchange in health by putting up any similar protocol of data storage and sharing. These standardizations guarantee the consistency of data and its accurate, easy accessiblity and availablity across different healthcare providers and systems. For any implementation of blockchain solutions, the regulatory, technical, ethical, and social considerations must be taken into account. From safe management of patient data and transparent supply chains of pharmaceuticals to frictionless claim processing, the current applications of blockchain can only demonstrate the potential for solving some of the perennial problems of the healthcare sector. This chapter delves into the future trends and opportunities of blockchain in healthcare, focusing on areas like decentralized clinical trials, patient data control, and supply chain transparency. The adoption of blockchain can transform patient care, streamline clinical trials, and improve pharmaceutical supply chains by reducing fraud and ensuring data authenticity. In addition to providing insights into emerging technologies like quantum-resistant cryptography and blockchain-AI integration, the chapter explores regulatory challenges, technical considerations, and the ethical implications of deploying blockchain in healthcare. By examining case studies and identifying key success factors, this chapter offers a roadmap for healthcare professionals, researchers, and policymakers to leverage blockchain for a more secure, efficient, and patient-centered healthcare ecosystem.

* Corresponding author Rajeev Kumar Bedi: Department of Computer Science and Engineering, I. K. Gujral Punjab Technical University, Jalandhar, India; E-mail: drrajeevbedi@ptu.ac.in

Mohit Angurala, Preet Kamal, Aryan Chaudhary, Rasmeet Singh Bali & Vijay Bhardwaj (Eds.)
All rights reserved-© 2025 Bentham Science Publishers

Keywords: Blockchain, Data integrity, Decentralized clinical trials, Healthcare, Patient data security, Smart contracts.

INTRODUCTION

Blockchain technology is already creating a revolution in the healthcare space by enhancing the level of data integrity, security, and interoperability. The real power of blockchain is in the future applications. It becomes even more important to explore the emerging trends and opportunities that blockchain opens as we stand on the threshold of its mass adoption. The better prepared and adept stakeholders are carving out the future with this technology, the more they can understand potential improvements from these emerging trends. This chapter will investigate the upcoming promising trends of blockchain in healthcare and the opportunities lying in the patient, provider, researcher, and insurer domains.

Structure

The topics covered in this chapter are:

- Emerging Trends in Blockchain for Healthcare.
- Opportunities for Healthcare Stakeholders.
- Challenges and Considerations.
- Case Studies and Pilot Projects.
- The Future Outlook.

Objectives

This chapter, "Future Trends and Opportunities," presents a discussion on the future potential developments and disruptive effects of blockchain technology in healthcare. The chapter attempts to go in depth into the analysis of blockchain's emerging trends, such as decentralized clinical trials, advanced interoperability, and security features, together with its integration using AI and patient-centered care solutions. The chapter will identify trends to underline the opportunities that exist for the different stakeholders—patients, healthcare providers, researchers, and payers—while drawing attention to the challenges and considerations from a regulatory, technical, and ethical point of view. It will attempt to provide readers with insights into how blockchain can change healthcare by proposing case studies or future outlooks on how this technology can revolutionize healthcare by improving data integrity and, hence, spur innovation in this industry.

Emerging Trends in Blockchain for Healthcare

Blockchain technology is most likely to make a significant difference in healthcare regarding data integrity, security, and interoperability. We shall now discuss some of the emerging trends that have the potential to transform this sector and also provide insight into each domain in detail.

Decentralized Clinical Trials

Decentralized clinical trials leverage the power of blockchain to redesign a traditional model of clinical trials by making the process more efficient, ensuring better data integrity, and guaranteeing more engagement amongst patients.

Improved Data Integrity

In typical clinical trials, the available data is subject to loss of integrity, particularly due to errors, manipulation, and reporting when conducted manually at the conversational-data-entry level, among other issues; the blockchain provides an immutable ledger with which entries are timestamped and cryptographically sealed. Each exchange is also authenticated by the participants of the network, thus ensuring the integrity and irrefutability of data. This transparency not only serves to improve the validity of clinical trial data but also eases regulatory compliance with a view to the full and tamper-proof history of all entered data [1]. Decentralization guarantees that data cannot be manipulated by a single entity, making the clinical trial process more trusted and accountable.

Patients can dole out and lease their health data if there is a need for it, with privacy ensured by data protection legislation [2]. Smart contracts further automate the process of taking and maintaining permission from the patients. Trust and participation can be encouraged by the increased transparency and control of data, leading to more robust and representative patient populations within clinical trials. Researchers will be able to capitalize on patient engagement potential even more by utilizing token-based incentives to drive and sustain long-term patient interest during the clinical trial process.

Interoperability and Data Sharing

Data sharing and interoperability have been the backbones of improved healthcare and collaborative research. Blockchain technology can equally play a very important role by providing a standardized exchange of data in a secure platform.

Standardizing Data in Health

The use of blockchain will help healthcare organizations circumvent the problems of interoperability, which often act as barriers to sharing and coordinating health data [3]. Moreover, standardized data can build interoperable applications and systems for use by different healthcare providers in their attempts to provide more coordinated and efficient care.

Cross-Institutional Collaboration

In this regard, blockchain allows the secure and efficient collaboration of researchers with other similar parties through a shared yet transparent platform for their data exchange. Such a shared environment ensures the security of sharing, while respect for patient anonymity maintains the integrity of the data. With seamless exchange enabled through blockchain, collaboration among medical researchers can help speed up research and further improve patients' treatment while decreasing the duplication of medical tests and procedures. One of the most outstanding features of blockchain is its decentralization, which ensures data is out of the control of a single individual, thus building trust and cooperation among various institutions [4]. Besides, blockchain can easily facilitate collaborative efforts in real-time in the manner through which it offers the capacity for several stakeholders to have simultaneous access to the same data set; hence, it encourages a more dynamic and integrated research environment.

Advanced Security Features

With the sophistication of cyber threats, advanced security in healthcare is necessary. Blockchain possesses several innovative ways to strengthen data security and protect sensitive health information.

One way in which security in healthcare may be improved with blockchain is:

Multi-signature Transactions

Multi-signature, or multi-sig, transactions are those that require more than one party's approval for a transaction to take place. Applicably, in a health context, this can be used to give added security in data access and sharing. For instance, access to a personal health record may require the agreement of a patient, their primary care physician, and a healthcare administrator. This ensures that sensitive information is proceeding in the path of authorized individuals and, at the same time, minimizes any breach and illegal access. In addition, multi-sig transactions can be set to require different levels of authorization depending on the sensitivity of the data, concerning setting up a very flexible and strong security boundary regarding healthcare information.

Quantum Resistant Cryptography

Following the advancement and progress in the field of quantum computing, the most widely used cryptographic functions have become vulnerable to new cyber threats. Blockchain can use quantum-resistant cryptographic functions to ensure the security of data in both the long and short terms. These are more advanced encodings, ensuring that health data is kept safe with the new advancements in technology, including those from quantum computers. This will embed the assurance for the future of healthcare data in the time of new cyber threats by embedding the quantum-resistant cryptography in blockchain networks. Being proactive in adapting these cutting-edge security measures ensures that any kind of healthcare institution protects sensitive information and maintains it within data systems into the future.

Care-Centered Care for Patients

Blockchain technology empowers patients to control their health data and enhances the way personalized care will be administered.

Personal Health Records

PHR will offer a patient control over his health information. PHR applications can be further expanded with these features, considering the blockchain ensures a completely secure and decentralized environment. This enables patients to make their PHR accessible to healthcare providers when the need arises, and therefore, their medical history is always up to date and available. This not only improves the continuity of care but also empowers patients to take an active role in managing their health [5]. On a different note, blockchain ensures patients have portable health data in the sense that the data are transferable through different health providers without the risk of seepage or distortion.

Management of patient consent comes in here; compliance with various data protection regulations may be affected, hence respecting the patient's wishes and will. It uses smart contracts to record and enforce patient permissions. Patients can easily edit their consent preferences, and healthcare providers can easily verify consent records in real time. This transparent and efficient consent management system fosters trust among the patient and ensures their data is used in accordance with their demands [6]. This would enable them to make granular decisions about what parts of their health data can be accessed by whom, thus extending control over personal data.

Integration with Artificial Intelligence

The combination of blockchain with artificial intelligence might provide new ways for data analysis in support of prognostics and be helpful for decision-making in healthcare.

Data Analysis and Predictive Analytics

Artificial intelligence is one discipline that works on big datasets for perfect prediction. Blockchain can provide a means of securely and efficiently sharing health-related data, thus feeding AI systems with high-quality datasets. The reliability of AI-driven analysis improves since blockchain will give proof of the data's integrity. This will further lead to diagnostic tools and treatment plans that are even more precisely designed for each patient, ensuring improved outcomes. In addition, blockchain makes sure that the data on which such AI analyses are grounded becomes dependable and does not create a problem of biased or flawed analyses, thus boosting the overall quality of the final AI-driven healthcare solutions.

Enhancement of Decision-Making Processes

It aids healthcare providers in making informed decisions, typically based on analyses carried out over huge volumes of complex data. Blockchain ensures the reliability and integrity of the data used for such analyses [7]. In addition, the blockchain can provide an auditable trace of transparent activities for any decisions taken by AI, adding to the reasons for healthcare providers to be able to know and trust the decisions that are made by AI. This integration of blockchain with AI has the potential to improve clinical judgment, patient care, and healthcare operations. With blockchain validation and verification for AI systems, health organizations are assured of building trustworthy and high-performing AI-driven tools for clinical support.

Opportunities for Healthcare Stakeholders

Blockchain technology has a diverse array of opportunities for various stakeholders in the healthcare sector. The application of blockchain, in concert with the enhancement of data integrity, security, and interoperability, is transformative, changing the dynamics in which patients, care providers, researchers, and insurers engage and transact with each other in the healthcare industry. The following part of this section is a discussion detailing the type of value perceived by each type of stakeholder.

The four layers of a blockchain-based healthcare application (Fig. **1**) workflow are healthcare raw data, blockchain technology, healthcare application, and stakeholders [8, 9]. Blockchain, in this respect, is a decentralized technology, therefore supporting numerous stakeholders with secured and effective access and enhancing the benefits of healthcare applications with better data integrity in a healthcare system.

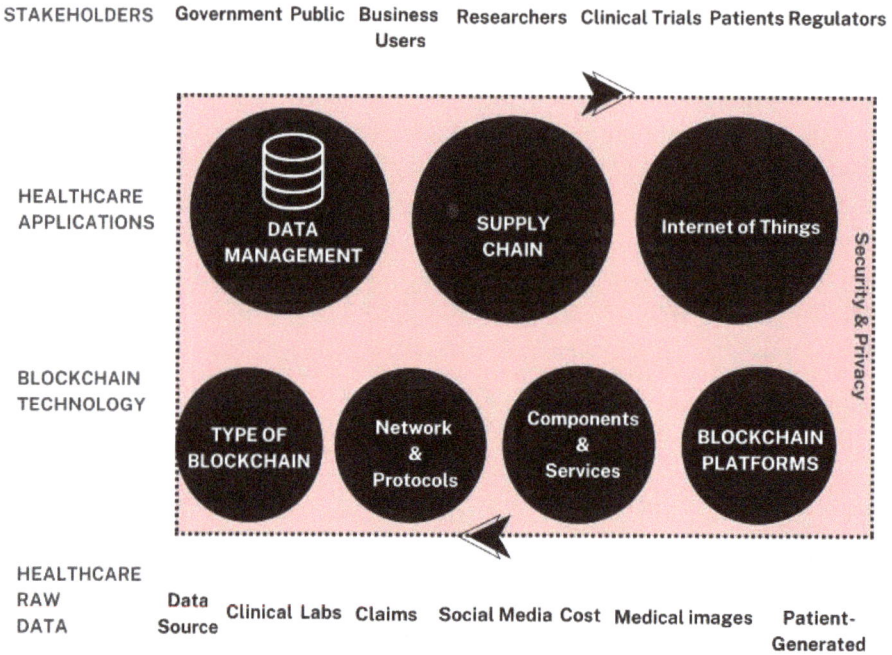

STAKEHOLDERS   Government Public Business   Researchers Clinical Trials Patients Regulators
                                   Users

HEALTHCARE
APPLICATIONS   DATA   SUPPLY   Internet of Things
                    MANAGEMENT   CHAIN

BLOCKCHAIN
TECHNOLOGY
                   TYPE OF   Network   Components   BLOCKCHAIN
                  BLOCKCHAIN   &   &   PLATFORMS
                                Protocols   Services

HEALTHCARE
RAW   Data   Clinical Labs Claims   Social Media Cost Medical images   Patient-
DATA   Source   Generated

Fig. (1). Blockchain-based healthcare application workflow.

For Patients

Blockchain technology can, therefore, empower patients by granting them more control over their health data, hence resulting in better privacy and security.

Empowerment through Authentication of Ownership of Data

The first reason patients can gain from blockchain is pertaining to the fact that the technology allows for the authentic ownership of healthcare data. Conventionally, healthcare providers store and manage healthcare data; it is quite hard for any patient to have access, manage, or share their health information. Blockchain achieves this by decentralizing data storage and putting it under patients' PHR. It gives the patient the right to choose who to give access and for how long, which can create feelings of autonomy, participation, and active responsibility in decisions about healthcare. This ownership also means that patients can carry their health-associated data with them from one healthcare provider to another, hence ensuring continuity of care and reducing redundancy in tests and procedures. Moreover, the patient can witness, through the transparency mechanisms of blockchain, how their data is used and by whom. This helps to build trust in the system.

Privacy and security of health information takes this issue head-on by providing a secure state and an unalterable environment in which data can be stored and shared. Each transaction that occurs in the blockchain is encrypted and time-stamped, which makes it impossible to alter or erase data without being detected. Additionally, the decentralized nature of blockchain eliminates this single point of failure, which makes it considerably more cyber-attack resistant [10]. In this way, the patients feel more assured of the fact that their sensitive health information is not accessed by any entity unauthorizedly, nor allowed to suffer from any breach. Blockchain can be used to provide fine-grained access control in such a way that patients can precisely assign information. In addition to the protection of patient data through the described tight security structure, a safe and credible healthcare environment is also contributed.

Healthcare providers can use blockchain to ensure operation efficiency and provide improved patient outcomes through better data management and collaboration.

Operation Efficiency

Blockchain can smoothen healthcare operations through the automation of administrative processes, therefore reducing inefficiencies. For instance, blockchain-based smart contracts will help automate some administrative tasks, like billing and claims processing, and reduce paperwork and administrative overhead. These contracts can ensure the fulfillment of each condition and clause of the agreement before the release of payment, therefore minimizing the chances of errors and disputes. In addition, blockchain technology can provide secure sharing and exchange of information between different departments and institutions without requiring any physical entry, hence reducing the chance of error. In this way, this streamlined approach can save humungous money and allow healthcare providers to focus more on the care of patients [11, 12]. This transparency that blockchain offers can further enhance operational efficiency by reducing the time taken by reconciliation and audits.

Better Patient Care

Better data integrity and interoperability for better patient care are made possible by blockchain. With access to accurate and recent patient data, a healthcare provider can make more informed decisions and give personalized care. It can also offer excellent coordination among healthcare stakeholders, thereby providing them with the same information for formulating treatment plans. In addition, blockchain can facilitate remote monitoring and telemedicine, which can provide health providers with real-time data about patients' conditions and allow them to take measures in time. Such innovations can provide an opportunity for earlier diagnosis, more efficient forms of treatment, and consequently, better outcomes for patients. Moreover, an integration of several sources of data, such as wearables and health applications, can offer a holistic view of the health status of each patient, thus bettering tailored care plans and defining more effective ones.

For Researchers

With blockchain technology, researchers can access high-quality data to foster collaboration and innovation in medical research.

Access to High-Quality Data

One of the challenges in medical research is access to high-quality data that can be relied on. It is this transparency and immutability in health information, which is assured through blockchain technology, that would solve the problem. Informed trust in the accuracy and provenance of data will increase confidence in study results and make them more reliable. Blockchain can also enable secure data sharing between different institutions and offer researchers access to larger and more diverse pools of data. This would mean more nuanced studies and accelerated medical research. Secondly, blockchain can help in maintaining the provenance of data—that is, it provides a record of the origin and history of the data in use to a particular researcher, which is a critical component of both the validation of study results and the reproduction of experiments.

Facilitating Collaboration and Innovation

Blockchain can provide an impetus to collaboration and innovation through the provision of a secure platform for data sharing and coordination among researchers. This way, different research institutions can easily share data and resources. This would increase the pace of discovery further by reducing duplication of effort. It is possible to support a blockchain-decentralized research network in which researchers from around the world can work on their projects without the need for any central coordinating body. This decentralized approach will democratize research and permit more researchers to contribute and innovate. In addition, it would enable token-based incentives to compensate researchers for their results, thereby making the research community more cooperative and driven. The same tokens might be reimbursed for additional research, purchasing data access, or rewarding important discoveries, hence creating a self-sustaining innovation ecosystem [13].

For the Insurers

Direct benefits can be reaped by the insurers through blockchain technology *via* fraud prevention and streamlining the handling of claims, both of which provide cost savings and efficiencies.

Fraud Prevention

Fraud is perhaps one of the most serious issues in the insurance industry and has always been very costly. Blockchain helps to prevent fraud by giving a clear and unchangeable record of each transaction. Insurers confirm the authenticity of a claimant and any discrepancy or foul play in a claim by using blockchain. Smart contracts can also automate the process of determination of claims in such a way that all the pre-set terms and conditions are found in order before payments are made [14]. It reduces the occurrence of human error and fraud, thus offering more accurate and fair claim processing. More precisely, the implementation of blockchain can enhance communication and further promote coordination among the involved parties. Through blockchain, insurers can also establish a shared database of fraudulent activities and flagged claims in order to track and prevent fraud across the industry more efficiently.

Efficient Claims Processing

It enables a more operative and cheaper flow of work in the processing of these claims. Smart contracts allow every activity in making a claim, including the processed amount of making a repayment, to occur automatically, in turn reducing the delay and the number of cases in which a human intervenes for paperwork. Such contracts can ensure that prior documents and requisites have been filed before a claim is entirely processed, therefore improving accuracy and reducing loss. Insurers can also track in real time the status of those claims through blockchain solutions, which increases observation and control in the process. Such a streamlined approach can result in faster claims processing, improved customer experience, and significant cost savings for insurers [15]. With the use of blockchain, disputes can be resolved faster due to the transparency and immutability of each transaction and communication in relation to the filings, which will lessen the time and cost spent on investigations and legal activities that will result from such disputes.

There are numerous potentials of blockchain technology from different end-users in the healthcare industry. Hereby, blockchain will revolutionize patient, healthcare provider, researcher, and insurer interaction and operation in the healthcare ecosystem through increased data integrity, security, and interoperability. Elaborating on these opportunities creates the ground for a more efficient, transparent, and patient-oriented healthcare system, which can help improve outcomes of care for all stakeholders involved. The future of blockchain in healthcare is great since it solves problems of one of the hardest-hit industries, which lacks possible solutions to make ways for innovative answers and improvements.

CHALLENGES AND CONSIDERATIONS

While blockchain holds immense potential to create a revolutionary change in healthcare, it comes with several challenges and considerations that need to be addressed to carry it out correctly. The latter spans the range of problems in regulatory, technical, ethical, to social domains—all needing attentive analysis with strategic solutions certain to be developed.

Regulatory and Legal Concerns

Blockchain's decentralized and immutable nature creates unique regulatory and legal challenges that need to be outsmarted in the bid to guarantee compliance and the safeguarding of stakeholders.

Healthcare Regulation Compliance

One of the most regulated industries is healthcare, as it contains laws and standards that have to be followed with regard to the quality of care patients receive and their privacy. In the case of the United States, the Health Insurance Portability and Accountability Act creates the baseline for protecting sensitive data for patients. Correspondingly, the General Data Protection Regulation sets out strict data protection and privacy rules within the European Union. For instance, weaknesses that are hard to overcome and must be met are in the way the blockchain solutions are to be structured to comply with the above-stated directives on storing, processing, and sharing of patient data in a legally appropriate manner, while it is the transparent and immutable nature of the blockchain that is said to possibly conflict with the Right to be Forgotten in the GDPR.

For example, it mandates under GDPR that any person should be able to obtain erasure of personal data pertaining to them—an assurance that is difficult to make with blockchain's non-removal features. One way of doing this may be by use of off-chain storages where sensitive data is stored off-chain, whereas only references or hashes are stored on-chain. This might, therefore, help in realizing such a request without affecting the chain's integrity of information. Second, with the advancement of blockchain solutions supported by privacy-preserving technologies, such as zero-knowledge proofs, it will be possible to implement requirements more easily by regulators while reaping the transparency and security benefits that come with blockchain.

Cross-Border Data Transfers

Health data is often shared across borders, mainly emerging from global research collaborations and patient care. These are currently subject to a mass of national and international regulations. Basically, it is quite difficult to execute blockchain solutions. Compliance with different data protection laws and standards across different countries is a huge challenge. Blockchain should be able to accommodate these regulatory variations for secure and lawful transfers of data [16]. Managing this problem requires an interoperable blockchain system that takes into consideration jurisdictional boundaries and data sovereignty.

For instance, the different laws on data protection by the European Union, the United States, and other regions require blockchain solutions that come out with flexible compliance mechanisms. In the same way, geofencing techniques can be applied on blockchain networks, where the same are stored and processed across specific geographies in adherence to respective local regulations. On the other hand, international agreements and frameworks for data protection can make cross-border data transfers easier by uniforming an approach to compliance. These healthcare blockchain solutions can ensure worldwide use and compliance with relevant legislation if regulatory bodies, technology developers, and healthcare organizations come together to implement standards globally.

Technical Challenges

The technical challenges with the adoption of blockchain in healthcare are among the most significant ones that are faced in wider diffusion [16]. They relate to the scalability of blockchain networks and their integration with previous healthcare systems.

Scalability of Blockchain Networks

Scalability is one of the biggest technical issues that blockchain technology is facing today. The contemporary blockchain networks, such as Bitcoin and Ethereum, have quite a lot of problems in trying to process an increased level of transaction volume effectively. In healthcare, where huge amounts of data are generated every time, blockchain networks have to see to it that high transaction throughput can be accommodated without a decrease in performance. Solutions such as sharding, off-chain transactions, and consensus algorithm improvement are considered to enhance the scalability of blockchain [17]. This calls for ensuring that blockchain networks can indeed support data-driven healthcare applications.

Sharding

Sharding is dividing the blockchain into smaller, easily manageable parts known as shards. Each of the shards can then handle and process the transactions independently, parallelizing processing across multiple shards and thus enhancing transaction throughput tremendously [18]. This can also be realized with off-chain transactions, whereby transactions are processed outside the main blockchain network and registered on-chain at the second moment. Improvements in consensus algorithms, for instance in moving from energy-consuming PoW to efficient PoS algorithms, further enhance scalability and reduce the environmental impact of blockchain operations.

Most healthcare providers and entities have significant sunk investments in existing information technology systems for supporting EHRs, billing systems, and supply chain management platforms. Replacing or integrating blockchain into such legacy systems is not an easy task and requires huge investments in technical skills and resources. Running standards and protocols for the interoperability between pre-existing healthcare systems and blockchain networks need to be established so that data exchange can be easily facilitated. This needs to be carried out without any disruption to current activities and with great regard for the integrity and security of data. The development of middleware solutions and APIs may even provide ease of integration between blockchain and legacy systems.

For example, middleware would have to act as some kind of intermediary that will serve as a translator and router between blockchain networks and traditional information systems. These solutions can support data formatting, protocol conversion, and other interoperability tasks, making integration seamless without much change to the legacy systems. APIs provide the standardized interface for communication between blockchain networks and legacy systems, and, therefore, the process of integration is simplified with continuous data interchange [19, 20].

Second, the implementation of open interoperability standards, such as FHIR, allows better integration of systems and platforms through a common structure for the exchange of healthcare data.

Ethical and Social Implications

The implementation of blockchain in the healthcare industry raises several ethical and social considerations that have to be mapped out to ensure fairness and responsible implementation.

Data Privacy Concerns

While blockchain offers better data security through its immutable and decentralized nature, it also raises concerns over data privacy. Such transparency within blockchain—where each transaction is recorded and visible to every participant in the blockchain network—may come at odds with the need to protect sensitive health information. Mechanisms include zero-knowledge proofs, encryption, and permissioned blockchains to make sure that only the parties with a need and authorization access the data, hence tackling privacy concerns [21]. Any blockchain solutions for healthcare must still respect the confidentiality and consent of patients.

Zero-knowledge proofs allow for the verification of claims without the claims being disclosed themselves, thus providing privacy-preserved transactions upon blockchain. Encrypted data storage ensures that sensitive information is kept confidential and accessed by only authorized individuals. This can be further improved by using permissioned blockchains, where access is ensured only to trusted entities. Blockchain solutions must also be designed with the implementation of strict consent management mechanisms that will give patients fine-grained control over access to their health data, ensuring that their choices regarding privacy are respected.

Equity in Access to Technology

The digital divide comes into play, where some people do not have access to technology, and there is a variation in digital literacy levels among different population segments. Thus, in the implementation of blockchain in healthcare, these discrepancies become a concern in ensuring that the current gaps are not further expanded. Blockchain solutions (Table **1**) should be made accessible to all patients, whether they are tech-savvy or belong to a high or low socioeconomic class. It can be done through educational programs, friendly user interfaces, and following inclusive design practices.

Table 1. Comparison of blockchain scalability solutions.

Solution	Description	Advantages	Disadvantages
Sharding	Divides the blockchain into smaller partitions (shards)	Increases transaction throughput	Complexity in implementation and security concerns
Off-chain Transactions	Processes transactions off the main blockchain network	Reduces load on the main chain, faster processing	Potential security and trust issues
Consensus Algorithm Improvements	Enhances the efficiency of the consensus process (*e.g.*, Proof of Stake)	Reduces energy consumption, increases scalability	May require significant changes to the blockchain architecture

For instance, making user-friendly interfaces that simplify the way one would interact with a blockchain system might make this technology accessible to the community at large, which is non-technical. Education initiatives can also raise awareness and understanding of blockchain technology, allowing users to use these solutions effectively. Inclusive design practices can pay attention to the needs and preferences of diverse user groups to make sure that blockchain solutions are designed, accessible, and useable by everyone [22]. Moreover, community-based organizations and local healthcare provider partnerships can help reach out to the less privileged, creating higher adoption rates for blockchain healthcare services.

Addressing the strategies (Table **2**) needed to overcome these challenges, the healthcare industry can improve data integrity, security, and interoperability, leading to better outcomes among all stakeholders. In the long term, blockchain holds great promise for healthcare since it can potentially solve some of the most important challenges in the industry and pave the way for innovative solutions and improvements [23 - 25].

Table 2. Strategies for integrating blockchain with existing systems.

Strategy	Description	Benefits	Challenges
Middleware Solutions	Acts as a bridge between blockchain and legacy systems	Facilitates seamless data exchange	Complexity in development and maintenance
APIs	Provides standardized interfaces for communication between systems	Simplifies integration processes	Security concerns and potential for API mismanagement
Interoperability Standards	Establishes common protocols for data exchange	Ensures compatibility across different systems	Requires industry-wide adoption and collaboration

CASE STUDIES AND PILOT PROJECTS

Blockchain technology has been receiving increased interest and implementation in several different areas within healthcare, a fact that bodes well through successful cases of implementation and lessons learned from pilot projects.

Successful Implementations

Case Study 1: Blockchain for Medical Records

Its application in managing electronic medical records helps introduce transformative changes in health operations, with a focus on data security, interoperability, and patient-centered care. MedRec is one of the pioneering examples of the use of blockchain's decentralized ledger for enhancements in integrity and privacy. MedRec uses cryptographic techniques, combined with decentralized storage, to ensure that all patient data is tamper-proof and can only be accessed by encrypted keys under the control of the patients themselves. This not only provides security for sensitive information against possible unauthorized access but also paves the way for easy sharing of medical histories among healthcare providers for better care coordination and, hence, better patient outcomes. MedRec implementation diminishes the administrative burden of conventional EMR systems, allowing for seamless management of data with an innate feature that empowers patients, offering them more control over their health data.

Case Study 2: Blockchain in Pharmaceutical Supply Chains

The supply chain of the pharmaceutical industry has undergone a notable change in technology. The introduction of blockchain technology in the pharmaceutical supply chain has incorporated transparency, traceability, and security. An evident case of such technological advancements is the Medi Ledger Network, which uses blockchain to track and trace the origin of pharmaceutical products from production facilities to the final consumer or end-users. The sale of counterfeit drugs will, therefore, significantly decrease with blockchain, ensuring the truthfulness and integrity of the medicines by embedding each transaction into an indelible ledger. This visibility would offer supply chain efficiency, time, reduced discrepancies, and optimization of inventory management. Additionally, compliance with regulatory requirements such as those by the FDA is increased through traceable records of drug distribution; hence, patient safety is enhanced, and stakeholder's trust is built.

Key Success Factors

Several critical factors contribute to the very basis of efficacy and scalability in terms of blockchain implementations across healthcare. These include:

Collaborative Ecosystem: Engaging a diverse array of stakeholders — healthcare providers, patients, regulators, and technology developers — forms the collaborative framework that assures blockchain solutions meet the needs and standards of the industry.

Interoperability Standards: Adherence to interoperable standards, such as HL7 FHIR, enables a seamless flow of data across blockchain networks and existing healthcare IT systems. This increases the ease of integration, enhances scalability, and maximizes the full utility of healthcare data toward quality patient care.

Privacy-preserving Technologies: Building in privacy-enhancing technologies, such as zero-knowledge proofs and encryption, guards the confidentiality of the patient while being firmly compliant with data protection laws and acts like HIPAA and GDPR. The technologies will protect the integrity of data and enable transparency within blockchain networks without violating individual privacy rights.

Common Pitfalls and How to Avoid Them

While blockchain in healthcare can be promising and provide a great many benefits, its path of adoption is riddled with pitfalls that an organization needs to effectively navigate:

Scalability: This necessitates the innovating of an approach to solving the scalability issues; some problems with these networks involve the throughput in transactions and capacity in running the stored data. Ways in which the network performance can be optimized in a manner that will fit both the volume and complexity of health data transactions include sharding, off-chain processing, and consensus algorithm enhancements.

Regulatory Compliance: To ensure compliance with the numerous, detailed, and burdensome healthcare regulations and data privacy laws, the regulatory requirements need to be built into the very design and implementation strategies employed in the use of blockchain. This involves the coordination and collaboration with legal and regulatory experts and entities to ensure that compliance is met with the existing frameworks, all in adherence to best practices in data governance and the management of patient consent.

Complexity in Integration: Overcoming existing IT infrastructures and legacy systems with robust middleware solutions and APIs seamlessly integrates these blockchain platforms with traditional healthcare IT systems. This creates a clear means for interaction between blockchain platforms and traditional healthcare IT systems, ensuring seamless data exchange and continuity in operation alike.

Using successful case studies as a guide and proactively considering the common challenges, stakeholders in healthcare have the ability to reap the transformational benefits in operational efficiencies, quality of care for patients, and the creation of innovation in the delivery of healthcare. All these factors make it incredibly important that moving forward, blockchain technology be used to its fullest potential in healthcare with a focus on continued collaboration, diligence in relation to regulations, and technological innovation.

THE FUTURE OUTLOOK

Blockchain is, however, undoubtedly a game-changer in the healthcare industry on the brink of the new era that creates transparent, efficient, and patient-centric characteristics. As blockchain technologies develop, the potential for reshaping different dimensions of healthcare becomes apparent. The major areas range from data management and interoperability to fostering the integration of rising technologies and enhancing innovative business models.

Predicting how blockchain will reshape healthcare:

Short-Term Predictions

In the short run, the impact of blockchain on healthcare is likely to be felt in the following areas:

Data Security and Integrity Improvement

The decentralized and immutable ledger established by blockchain ensures that all healthcare data, whether records for patients or for transactions, is secure and tamper-proof. This has thus enhanced worries associated with data breaches and unauthorized access, thereby staying true to the very meaning of information traffic among various healthcare networks.

Interoperability can improve substantially *via* standardized blockchain platforms and interoperability protocols, such as HL7 FHIR, which can enable seamless information sharing across disparate healthcare systems and stakeholders. A common framework for sharing data, blockchain enhances care coordination to diminish administrative burden and improve outcomes for patients.

Optimization of Supply Chain Management

In pharmaceutical supply chains, blockchain technologies will be a backbone. Blockchain tends to mitigate the risks related to counterfeit drugs by recording every transaction, from manufacturer to the end user, over some immutable ledger, which ensures the authenticity of a product and enhances efficiency along the supply chain.

In the longer run, blockchain can be the impetus for radical changes in healthcare:

- **Patient Ownership of Data:** Blockchain-based systems restore the patient's control over access to their health records. The decentralized nature of blockchain also secures patient health records while paving the way for data portability and continuity of care with different providers, finally empowering the patient with up-to-date decisions on their health.
- **Integration of Advanced Technologies**: It will endow health delivery with genuinely life-altering improvements as blockchain synergizes with AI and IoMT. AI algorithms integrated with blockchain data can analyze massive datasets to improve diagnostics and predict the progression of disease; it can also provide personalized treatment plans. Secure connection of IoMT devices to blockchain networks will enable monitoring real-time patient vitals, therefore remotely managing patients for proactive healthcare interventions.
- **Healthcare economics transformation**: The power of blockchain-based smart contracts and tokenized ecosystems is defining healthcare financing and payment. Smart contracts allow for automatic and safe performance of transactions, eventually making billing linear with less use of administrative costs and increasingly used financial transparency. This feature of tokenization can be used to incentivize features that will provide for more quality care outcomes for the health provider, patient involvement in clinical trials, and more research collaboration.

Future Possible Inventions

Integration with Other Emerging Technologies

Integration of this technology with other emerging technologies in healthcare is going to unlock lots of new synergies and possibilities.

Integration with emerging technologies will be the integration of blockchain technology with an array of other emerging technologies relating to healthcare, efficiency, security, and outcomes for patients, as shown in Table **3** below:

Table 3. Integration of emerging technologies with blockchain.

Emerging Technology	Potential Integration with Blockchain
Artificial Intelligence	AI-driven insights from blockchain-secured data can optimize treatment strategies, predict patient outcomes, and automate administrative tasks such as claims processing and billing reconciliation.
Internet of Medical Things (IoMT)	IoMT devices integrated with blockchain networks ensure data integrity, patient privacy, and interoperability, enabling secure transmission of real-time health data for remote monitoring and personalized healthcare delivery.
Edge Computing	Edge devices processing healthcare data can interface with blockchain for decentralized storage, enhancing data security and reducing latency in critical healthcare applications such as telemedicine and surgical robotics.

New Business Models in Healthcare

The disruptive potential of Blockchain extends to the creation of new business models, challenging the traditional paradigms in healthcare:

- **Tokenized Healthcare Ecosystems:** Blockchain-based tokens incentivize patients' engagement in their health, reward healthcare providers for quality delivered care, and facilitate open and auditable transactions between payers and providers.
- **Decentralized Clinical Trials**: Automating and securing trial protocols by smart contracts on the blockchain will ensure data integrity, management of patient consent, and compliance with regulatory requirements. This approach will speed up drug discovery and development through reduced administrative burdens and increased participant recruitment and retention.
- **Healthcare Data Marketplaces**: Blockchain-powered platforms for sharing healthcare data in an ethical and consent-driven manner among researchers, pharma companies, and healthcare providers. Through secure aggregation and anonymization of healthcare data, these marketplaces further collaborative research, accelerate medical breakthroughs, and drive better population health outcomes.

A good number of studies have explored the transformative potential of blockchain technology by integrating it into various industries. For example, in the agri-food sector, blockchain has proven its potential in value chain management, including improved traceability, transparency, and trust among stakeholders, though there are implementation challenges [26]. Analogous applications of blockchain technology for improving additive manufacturing processes are implemented within the manufacturing industry for developing digital twins in that domain. For example, its use in the aircraft industry provides evidence for its effective adoption and has been effectively developed within the manufacturing lifecycle of data management [27]. Blockchain technology within healthcare is a revolutionizing innovation; it opens the doors for new, game-changing solutions to age-old issues while ushering a pathway toward a new, smarter, patient-focused healthcare system. This will happen only if stakeholders keep working together, if regulatory frameworks become more proactive in finding balances between innovation and patients' privacy, and if the necessary technological evolutions continue to mitigate scalability and interoperability issues. Integrating blockchain with other emerging technologies will enable health organizations to leverage what blockchain can offer and, in the end, unlock their potential for innovation in care delivery to help people around the globe live healthier lives.

CONCLUSION

Blockchain technology holds the potential to transform the healthcare sector by addressing some of its most pressing challenges, including data security, supply chain transparency, and patient consent management. The future of healthcare will see blockchain integrated with emerging technologies such as artificial intelligence and quantum-resistant cryptography, offering a more secure and efficient system. However, successful implementation requires overcoming regulatory, technical, and ethical challenges. By focusing on collaboration, regulatory alignment, and technological advancements, blockchain can pave the way for a healthcare ecosystem that is transparent, efficient, and truly patient-centric. The continued exploration of blockchain's capabilities promises to revolutionize healthcare delivery, research, and operations, unlocking new opportunities for innovation and improvement across the industry.

AUTHORS' CONTRIBUTION

In Chapter 15, **Mohit Angurala, Rajeev Kumar Bedi, Gurpreet Singh Panesar, and Navneet Kumar Rajpoot** collaborated to examine the future trends and potential of blockchain technology in healthcare. **Mohit Angurala** led the analysis of blockchain's transformative impact on healthcare data integrity, security, and interoperability, particularly focusing on applications in clinical trials and patient data control. **Rajeev Kumar Bedi** provided insights into advanced blockchain integration with emerging technologies such as AI and quantum-resistant cryptography. **Gurpreet Singh Panesar** focused on the exploration of case studies and success factors for blockchain implementations in healthcare, detailing regulatory and ethical considerations. **Navneet Kumar Rajpoot** contributed to the discussion on blockchain's role in enhancing healthcare supply chain transparency and the development of innovative business models. Collectively, the authors presented a comprehensive roadmap for leveraging blockchain in healthcare for researchers, policymakers, and industry professionals.

REFERENCES

[1]   Oakley A. HIPAA, HIPPA, or HIPPO: What really is the heath insurance portability and accountability act? Biotechnol Law Rep 2023; 42(6): 306-18.
[http://dx.doi.org/10.1089/blr.2023.29329.aso]

[2]   Kalkman S, Van Delden J, Banerjee A, Tyl B, Mostert M, Van Thiel G. Patients' and public views and attitudes towards the sharing of health data for research: a narrative review of the empirical evidence. J Med Ethics 2022; 48(1): 3-13.
[http://dx.doi.org/10.1136/medethics-2019-105651] [PMID: 31719155]

[3]   Yaqoob I, Salah K, Jayaraman R, Al-Hammadi Y. Blockchain for healthcare data management: opportunities, challenges, and future recommendations. Neural Comput Appl 2022; 34(14): 11475-90.
[http://dx.doi.org/10.1007/s00521-020-05519-w]

[4]   Li W, Wu J, Cao J, Chen N, Zhang Q, Buyya R. Blockchain-based trust management in cloud computing systems: a taxonomy, review and future directions. J Cloud Comput (Heidelb) 2021; 10(1): 35.
[http://dx.doi.org/10.1186/s13677-021-00247-5]

[5]   Damen DJ, Schoonman GG, Maat B, Habibović M, Krahmer E, Pauws S. Patients managing their medical data in personal electronic health records: scoping review. J Med Internet Res 2022; 24(12): e37783.
[http://dx.doi.org/10.2196/37783] [PMID: 36574275]

[6]   Pickering B. Trust, but verify: informed consent, AI technologies, and public health emergencies. Future Internet 2021; 13(5): 132.
[http://dx.doi.org/10.3390/fi13050132]

[7]   Krittanawong C, Aydar M, Hassan Virk HU, *et al.* Artificial intelligence-powered blockchains for cardiovascular medicine. Can J Cardiol 2022; 38(2): 185-95.
[http://dx.doi.org/10.1016/j.cjca.2021.11.011] [PMID: 34856332]

[8]   Zaabar B, Cheikhrouhou O, Jamil F, Ammi M, Abid M. HealthBlock: A secure blockchain-based healthcare data management system. Comput Netw 2021; 200: 108500.
[http://dx.doi.org/10.1016/j.comnet.2021.108500]

[9]   Chen PT, Lin CL, Wu WN. Big data management in healthcare: Adoption challenges and implications. Int J Inf Manage 2020; 53: 102078.
[http://dx.doi.org/10.1016/j.ijinfomgt.2020.102078]

[10]   Singh S, Hosen ASMS, Yoon B. Blockchain security attacks, challenges, and solutions for the future distributed IoT network. IEEE Access 2021; 9: 13938-59.
[http://dx.doi.org/10.1109/ACCESS.2021.3051602]

[11]   Zayas-Cabán T, Haque SN, Kemper N. Identifying opportunities for workflow automation in health care: lessons learned from other industries. Appl Clin Inform 2021; 12(3): 686-97.
[http://dx.doi.org/10.1055/s-0041-1731744] [PMID: 34320683]

[12]   O'Connor C, Joffe H. Intercoder reliability in qualitative research: debates and practical guidelines. Int J Qual Methods 2020; 19: 1609406919899220.
[http://dx.doi.org/10.1177/1609406919899220]

[13]   Sobe D. Token economy--towards building a sustainable blockchain token ecosystem framework [master's thesis]. Universidade Nova de Lisboa; 2022.

[14] Chen CL, Deng YY, Tsaur WJ, Li CT, Lee CC, Wu CM. A traceable online insurance claims system based on blockchain and smart contract technology. Sustainability (Basel) 2021; 13(16): 9386.
[http://dx.doi.org/10.3390/su13169386]

[15] Miyachi K, Mackey TK. hOCBS: A privacy-preserving blockchain framework for healthcare data leveraging an on-chain and off-chain system design. Inf Process Manage 2021; 58(3): 102535.
[http://dx.doi.org/10.1016/j.ipm.2021.102535]

[16] Renwick R, Gleasure R. Those who control the code control the rules: How different perspectives of privacy are being written into the code of blockchain systems. J Inf Technol 2021; 36(1): 16-38.
[http://dx.doi.org/10.1177/0268396220944406]

[17] Attaran M. Blockchain technology in healthcare: Challenges and opportunities. Int J Healthc Manag 2022; 15(1): 70-83.
[http://dx.doi.org/10.1080/20479700.2020.1843887]

[18] Guruprakash J, Koppu S. EC-ElGamal and Genetic algorithm-based enhancement for lightweight scalable blockchain in IoT domain. IEEE Access 2020; 8: 141269-81.
[http://dx.doi.org/10.1109/ACCESS.2020.3013282]

[19] Maaroufi S, Pierre S. BCOOL: A novel blockchain congestion control architecture using dynamic service function chaining and machine learning for next generation vehicular networks. IEEE Access 2021; 9: 53096-122.
[http://dx.doi.org/10.1109/ACCESS.2021.3070023]

[20] Moritz P. Johannes S. Daniel P. *et al.* The energy footprint of blockchain consensus mechanisms beyond proof-of-work. In: 2021 IEEE 21st International Conference on Software Quality, Reliability and Security Companion (QRS-C) 2021; 1135-44.
[http://dx.doi.org/10.1109/QRS-C55045.2021.00168]

[21] Belchior R, Vasconcelos A, Guerreiro S, Correia M. A survey on blockchain interoperability: Past, present, and future trends. ACM Comput Surv 2022; 54(8): 1-41.
[http://dx.doi.org/10.1145/3471140]

[22] Pop CD, Antal M, Cioara T, Anghel I, Salomie I. Blockchain and demand response: Zero-knowledge proofs for energy transactions privacy. Sensors (Basel) 2020; 20(19): 5678.
[http://dx.doi.org/10.3390/s20195678] [PMID: 33027996]

[23] Sin J, Franz RL, Munteanu C, Barbosa Neves B. Digital design marginalization: New perspectives on designing inclusive interfaces. Proceedings of the 2021 CHI Conference on Human Factors in Computing Systems 2021; 1 11.
[http://dx.doi.org/10.1145/3411764.3445180]

[24] Madine MM, Battah AA, Yaqoob I, *et al.* Blockchain for giving patients control over their medical records. IEEE Access 2020; 8: 193102-15.
[http://dx.doi.org/10.1109/ACCESS.2020.3032553]

[25] Reegu FA, Abas H, Gulzar Y, *et al.* Blockchain-based framework for interoperable electronic health records for an improved healthcare system. Sustainability (Basel) 2023; 15(8): 6337.
[http://dx.doi.org/10.3390/su15086337]

[26] Zhao G, Liu S, Lopez C, *et al.* Blockchain technology in agri-food value chain management: A synthesis of applications, challenges and future research directions. Comput Ind 2019; 109: 83-99.
[http://dx.doi.org/10.1016/j.compind.2019.04.002]

[27] Mandolla C, Petruzzelli AM, Percoco G, Urbinati A. Building a digital twin for additive manufacturing through the exploitation of blockchain: A case analysis of the aircraft industry. Comput Ind 2019; 109: 134-52.
[http://dx.doi.org/10.1016/j.compind.2019.04.011]

SUBJECT INDEX

A

Advanced encryption standard (AES) 194
Advancements, transformative 229
Aggregated health data 186
Aggregation, secure 307
Algorithms 53, 75, 98, 189, 201, 205, 206, 247, 270, 276, 306
  cryptographic 75, 189
  hashing 270
  quantum-resistant cryptographic 206
Alignment, regulatory 220, 229, 308
Anonymization 193, 195
  and pseudonymization techniques 195
  techniques 193
Anti-cryptographic tools 165
Anti-money laundering (AML) 95
API 275, 302
  mismanagement 302
  production 275
Attribute-based encryption (ABE) 57
Auditing tools 108
Authentication, transparent 168
Automated 26, 27, 125, 197, 247
  adherence 125
  consent processes 197
  cryptographic scripts 247
  policy management 26
  service delivery 27
Automation, fintech 96

B

Billing 24, 26, 41, 86, 87, 98, 104, 107, 111, 121, 122, 123, 161, 295
  double 111
  management processes 87
  medical 161
  transparent 123
Billing processes 86, 87, 88, 98
  automated 88
Biobanking information 264

Biobanks, traditional 256
Biomedical security system 220
Bitcoin 71, 74, 75, 89, 162, 170, 190, 235, 236, 238, 247, 250, 258, 275, 281, 282
  blockchain edges 247
  cryptocurrency 275
  data 275
  network 89
  software 236
  transactions 238, 281
  wallets 89
Blockchain 2, 12, 13, 14, 22, 26, 59, 60, 88, 106, 107, 120, 130, 133, 137, 139, 140, 142, 148, 149, 154, 155, 166, 196, 197, 198, 199, 200, 203, 204, 214, 222, 224, 225, 229, 239, 246, 266, 277, 279, 303
  adopting 198, 279
  cryptographic hash transition 88
  -derived smart eHealth applications 239
  for HIPAA compliance 196
  for medical records 303
  for telehealth and telemedicine 26
  -fueled healthcare systems 133
  implementations 12, 13, 14, 197, 198, 199, 204, 214, 222, 224, 225
  in pharmaceutical supply chains 303
  industries 149
  infrastructure 106, 107, 120, 200, 229, 266
  -integrated supply chain mechanism 277
  IoT and wearable devices 2
  -powered EHR system 22
  security measures 166
  systems 59, 60, 130, 137, 139, 140, 142, 154, 155, 197, 203
  tool 246
  transformations 148
Blockchain-based 6, 46, 59, 78, 79, 133, 138, 141, 145, 196, 232, 247, 250, 259, 281, 306
  applications 46
  EHR management architecture 78
  healthcare systems 133, 247

Mohit Angurala, Preet Kamal, Aryan Chaudhary, Rasmeet Singh Bali & Vijay Bhardwaj (Eds.)
All rights reserved-© 2025 Bentham Science Publishers

www.ingramcontent.com/pod-product-compliance
Lightning Source LLC
Chambersburg PA
CBHW050808220326
41598CB00006B/148